Spencer W. Kimball

Spencer W. Kimball

Twelfth President
of
The Church of Jesus Christ
of Latter-day Saints

Edward L. Kimball
Andrew E. Kimball, Jr.

Bookcraft
Salt Lake City, Utah

Library of Congress Catalog Card Number: 77-14714
ISBN 0-88494-330-5

16th Printing, 1980

Lithographed in the United States of America
PUBLISHERS PRESS
Salt Lake City, Utah

To Camilla Eyring Kimball, equal partner

Contents

Preface

In 1951, at a time when Spencer Woolley Kimball had heart trouble and thought he might die, he wrote: "I might hope that my children will take from my many journals and write a simple little story or biography for me. I would like for my posterity to remember me and to know that I have tried so very hard to measure up and to live worthy."

When Spencer Kimball's own father died in 1924 he left behind journals, letters, carbon copies of business correspondence, newspaper clippings, old photographs — enough to fill a dozen cardboard boxes. Nothing was in order; much was inconsequential. Of the six surviving children Spencer, then twenty-nine years old, felt the greatest interest in the boxes and the history they contained. So he kept them for the family. Over the next fifty years he would spend hundreds of hours culling the materials, filing them, and drafting the first chapters of a biography of his beloved father.

In 1943 when he was called to the Quorum of the Twelve, Spencer began keeping faithfully a detailed journal of his own, typed and stored in large black ring-binders which year by year spread along the wall shelves in his study. Beside them stood Whitney's biography of Heber C. Kimball, his father's journals, some small diaries kept by his mother, and fragmentary diaries and daybooks he had himself kept in Arizona. There were more binders of notes and draft chapters of autobiography covering his youth.

These journals and writings, the diaries and personal history of his wife, Camilla Eyring Kimball, and interviews with dozens of people who have known Spencer Kimball as an apostle and in his younger years, are the primary sources for this biography.

We have tried to be candid, neither omitting weaknesses and problems nor exaggerating strengths. Happily we were faced with no real test of our integrity as biographers, since our burrowing into the past only confirmed our personal impressions that this was a man of rare consistency, exemplifying in his private life the same virtues ascribed to the public man.

Spencer and Camilla Kimball read through the manuscript for this book in rough draft stage and made factual corrections and a few suggestions, but neither had a hand in writing or editing the book beyond that. They would not have written the same book, but they were trusting and generous enough to allow us our own perspective on their lives. The responsibility for selecting the events which would paint a fair picture and for the resulting emphases is wholly ours, though the whole undertaking was possible only because of their willingness to talk and write openly about themselves.

Although a full biography of a living person constitutes a radical assault on his privacy and that of his family, Spencer and Camilla Kimball graciously consented to the publication of this book during their lives because of the legitimate interest of members of the Church in the life story of their President.

After some prior beginnings, serious work on the biography began early in 1973, and in the years from then to publication a great many people helped by providing information and insights. In addition, George Bickerstaff, Richard Cracroft, Arthur Henry King, and several Kimball family members spent a great deal of time reading the manuscript at various stages of development and offering valuable suggestions. Marie Jensen carefully retyped the final draft of the manuscript. Our wives, Evelyn Bee Madsen Kimball and Kathryn Bush Kimball, were deeply involved in the project from the outset and not only gave useful advice on the manuscript but provided unfailing encouragement and support. For all these we are deeply grateful.

1

Succession in the Presidency

— "a giant redwood has fallen"

Spencer W. Kimball, tired but composed, spoke deliberately. "President Lee has gone. I never thought it could happen. I sincerely wanted it *not* to ever happen. I doubt if anyone in the Church has prayed harder and more consistently for a long life for President Lee than my Camilla and myself. I have not been ambitious. I am four years older than President Lee, to the exact day. I have expected that I would go long before he did."

With the sudden passing of President Harold B. Lee, who had been President of The Church of Jesus Christ of Latter-day Saints for only eighteen months, the weight of responsibility to lead more than three million Church members as God's spokesman to them bore heavily on Spencer Woolley Kimball. Age seventy-eight, he had had no formal training for this new position. Yet his life had been a continual preparation, from his boyhood on a small Arizona farm to his missionary service as a young man, his years as a local businessman and Church leader, and his thirty years as a member of the Quorum of the Twelve Apostles.

Just a few days earlier, on Christmas Day, 1973, Camilla Kimball had bustled about, putting a turkey in the oven and setting an extra table in the living room for a crowd. Elder Kimball had helped with the table and offered a hand in the kitchen, knowing he was in no danger of having the offer accepted.

He spent most of the morning at his desk in the study, working through a never-finished stack of correspondence. He sat surrounded by books and papers which cluttered two tables as well as the desk, with piles under the tables and on the filing cabinets which crowded the room. On his desk was a pile of scratch paper used on only one side; posted by the desk and under its glass were pictures of family members and Church leaders; in front of him stood silent the pendulum clock his parents had received as a wedding gift; on the wall hung a painting of an Indian scene; two walls of the study were lined from floor to ceiling with books, mostly about religion, with thirty-three black binders containing his journals and with other binders of sermons and sermon ideas; file drawers bulged with family genealogy and correspondence. As he typed he occasionally stopped to turn the records of Christmas music playing on the phonograph.

About noon the family began arriving. The table was set for twenty-six people — children, grandchildren, great-grandchildren; Camilla's sister Mary; Arlene, a Zuni foster-granddaughter living with their daughter under the Church Indian Student Placement Program; and a man Elder Kimball had baptized in a river in India thirteen years earlier, Mangal Dan Dipty. As always, they knelt in prayer, then ate of Camilla's cooking enthusiastically. Through the afternoon the family chatted and sang songs together and nibbled on leftovers and candy until evening, and then went their separate ways. Elder Kimball returned to his desk.

On the twenty-sixth he worked at his office in the Church Office Building. It was quiet; most offices in the building remained closed. The stores in the city across the street hummed with thousands of after-Christmas shoppers. Elder Kimball returned home for dinner and settled again at his desk for an evening's work.

That day in the LDS Hospital, on the hillside above Salt Lake City, Harold B. Lee, eleventh President of the Church in succession from Joseph Smith and Brigham Young, had come for a medical checkup. At seventy-four he had worn himself to exhaustion during the preceding eighteen months. There was nothing definably wrong, but he had found himself still weary despite a long night's sleep. After having dinner with him in the hospital, his wife, Joan, had returned home, leaving Arthur Haycock, his secretary and aide, to watch.

About eight o'clock, as Arthur sat reading the newspaper, President Lee suddenly woke, rose to a sitting position on the edge of his bed, and pulled off the oxygen mask he wore to make breathing easier. He spoke a sentence or two, looking beyond Arthur vaguely, and did not respond to questions. He was white; beads of perspiration started on his face. Arthur laid him down and ran for a nurse, then for a doctor. In moments the room filled with medical people responding to the alarm "Cardiac arrest!"

While they worked frantically over the President, Arthur called Sister Lee and the counselors in the First Presidency, Marion G. Romney and N. Eldon Tanner (who was out of town), to tell them the frightening news. Then he called Elder Kimball, feeling that unless the Lord intervened President Lee might die, and that therefore his probable successor should be present.

Elder Kimball answered the telephone cheerfully. "Hello, Arthur, how are you tonight?"

"Not very well, Brother Kimball. President Lee is very ill. I think you ought to come." His voice strained with tension.

Elder Kimball left on the run.

In about ten minutes he reached the hospital, arriving moments before the others. The doctors would not allow anyone in the room where they worked, trying almost brutally to resuscitate the President, so Elder Kimball and Arthur prayed together. When Elder Romney came, Elder Kimball asked him, since he was the presiding officer, "What would you like me to do?"

He answered, "There is not much to do right now. About all we can do is pray and wait."

They retired to a room and prayed again, fervently. When they approached the room where President Lee lay, the doctor came out and said, "We have given up." President Lee was dead.

With the First Presidency now dissolved, Elder Romney turned to Elder Kimball and said, "President Kimball, what would you like me to do?" The mantle had fallen on Spencer W. Kimball, as President of the Quorum of the Twelve, to lead the Church.

Weeping, President Kimball called Camilla to tell her that their friend of thirty years had gone. "Pray for me," he pleaded.

Distraught, she in turn called their children. When her son answered the telephone and heard her anguished cry, "Oh, Ed!" he assumed his father had died. She had some idea of the additional strain

*President Harold B. Lee and Spencer W. Kimball at
general conference, 1973*

the new responsibility would place on her husband and she knew his
inability to give less than 100 percent of his energy to the task. She
feared for him. In the thirty years he served as an apostle President
Kimball had suffered a major heart attack and recurring cancer of the
throat. He had survived open-heart surgery less than two years before.
President Lee, four years younger and apparently healthier, had
seemed sure to outlive her husband, and Camilla had relaxed, thinking
the Church presidency one burden he would not be called upon to
carry. Now a new door had opened on fearsome responsibility.

When President Kimball had moved with his family from Arizona
to Salt Lake City in 1943 to serve in the Quorum of the Twelve
Apostles, the Church, after 113 years of persecution, colonization and
growth, had numbered not quite a million members. Now it numbered
3-1/3 million and was swelling fast. The number of stakes had grown
from 146 to 633 in those three decades, and the missions from 40 to
107. The missionaries, mostly young men between nineteen and
twenty-one, numbered 17,500. When President Kimball was born the
Church was regional, with only a relative handful of members scattered beyond the Great Basin. When he became a general Church

leader, the Church was essentially an American organization. But by the time he became President of the Church, it had become truly a worldwide organization.

President Kimball authorized the announcement of President Lee's death to the press, and almost immediately the information was on radio and television and the telephone began to ring for further information. He arranged for the Quorum of the Twelve and various others to be called immediately. Dr. Russell Nelson, who had performed his heart operation, came of his own accord to be on hand in case he should be needed.

Throughout the evening President Kimball, Elder Romney and Arthur Haycock were at the telephone, calling, planning, organizing. They arranged a meeting of the Council of the Twelve for the next morning. President Kimball finally got home about midnight to a restless, largely sleepless night, until exhaustion claimed him for a while. He felt as though the world had fallen in on his shoulders. He knew, under the pattern of succession which had been followed in the Church from its beginning and four times during his service as an apostle, the near certainty of his becoming President of the Church. He had foreseen he might eventually serve as President of the Quorum of the Twelve, but he had expected by virtue of his age to die in that harness. The next morning, early, he wept as he prayed, overwhelmed with the magnitude of his new responsibility.

He felt numbed, personally inadequate, but assured that God would not have left him this responsibility without being willing to give His support. He recalled one occasion when he had mentioned to President Lee how he wished he could speak with the power of Elder Albert E. Bowen, and another time when he had wished for the eloquence of Stephen L Richards. Elder Lee had said, with a tone of disappointment: "Spencer, be yourself. Use the talents the Lord has given you." He determined simply to do his best.

The telephone rang constantly, friends calling with messages of reassurance.

President Kimball visited Sister Lee to offer comfort and appointed a committee of the Council to consider with the family the funeral arrangements. The funeral was scheduled for Saturday. President Lee's body lay in state on Friday and on Saturday morning, and thousands waited through the rain and snow to file by.

Spencer W. Kimball speaking at the funeral of
President Harold B. Lee

At noon on Saturday the cortege moved from the Church Office
Building to the Tabernacle. The Brethren lined up, and the eight
grandsons of President Lee who carried the bier passed between the
two lines into the building. The counselors in the former First Presidency sat in their accustomed seats, an empty chair between them,
and President Kimball sat on their immediate left. In his position as
President of the Quorum, which now as a body presided over the
Church, he conducted the service.

After the opening, he spoke briefly to the people who filled the
Tabernacle, gathered to express their love and respect for President
Lee, and to the tens of thousands who watched on television:

> President Harold B. Lee was a mighty prince among us. He
> was a dynamic leader, easy to follow. Everybody knew that Presi-
> dent Lee was a prophet, as did Israel concerning Samuel.
>
> . . . with the mantle of authority upon him, he came to be
> another man with a new heart and the revelations continued to
> illuminate him and the people through him.
>
> . . . A giant redwood has fallen and left a great space in the
> forest.

In eulogy, President Kimball listed some of the traits he had come
to appreciate in his valued colleague:

> A man endowed with a rare native intelligence, quickened by a
> capacity to discard extraneous information, thus freeing the mind
> for decisive action. A giant whose shadow fell across the world,
> bringing under the influence of the gospel millions of members
> and friends of the Church. A giant, who, while carrying the chal-
> lenges of the apostleship and First Presidency under divine influ-
> ence, anxiously still took time to share his thoughts and counsel
> with countless thousands on an individual basis.

When the service ended, the cortege passed through the cold
drizzle to the cemetery.

The next day the fourteen apostles met in the temple, as they had
done on similar occasions before, and after their partaking of the
sacrament and participating in their prayer circle President Kimball
posed the question whether there should be immediate reorganization.
After the deaths of Joseph Smith and Brigham Young there had been
periods of more than three years before the Quorum of the Twelve

reorganized the First Presidency. But from the death of John Taylor onward, the longest period had been eleven days.

After each apostle had had opportunity to speak, Ezra Taft Benson, the second in seniority, nominated Spencer W. Kimball to be President of the Church and the group unanimously approved.

President Kimball reiterated his shocked surprise at the turn of events and acknowledged his limitations, but expressed his wish now to be a fit person to receive the messages the Lord had to give to his people. He announced his wish that Elders Tanner and Romney serve with him as counselors, as they had with President Lee. They accepted graciously. Mark E. Petersen, as third in seniority, nominated Ezra Taft Benson to be the President of the Quorum of the Twelve, and that received unanimous approval.

With the ordination and settings apart, the Church stood again fully organized.

That night Dr. Russell Nelson, who also served as president of the Church Sunday Schools, brought to President Kimball a letter concerning his health, knowing the President would be faced with questions about it. The letter commented on the fact that President Kimball had recently undergone a careful physical study which indicated that his body functioned superbly. "Your surgeon wants you to know that your body is strong; that your heart is better than it has been for years; and that by all of our finite ability to predict, you may consider this new assignment without undue anxiety about your health." This information President Kimball passed on at the press conference held the next day.

He did not, however, read to the public another passage of the letter relating to his open-heart surgery: " . . . in the performance of that critical operation done April 12, 1972, . . . I was keenly aware of your apostolic calling, and of my own human frailties, in anticipating one of the most risky and complex operations ever done. This operation turned out to be technically perfect in every detail, and I acknowledge gratefully the help of the Lord, for rarely does a surgeon have this unique experience. Most special of all was the fact that, as the operation was nearly completed, it was made known to me that one day you would become the President of the Church."

2

Lineage and Legacy

— "a father far greater than I am"

I n 1634 Richard Kimball, a Puritan wheelwright, stood on the deck of the ship *Elizabeth,* a fugitive from the religious oppression of Charles I of England. He looked across the Atlantic toward Massachusetts Bay Colony, where he and his family could settle in peace and worship God as they pleased. After a long voyage across a stormy ocean they landed in the New World.

Richard established himself as town wheelwright in Ipswich and reared his family there.

Successive generations of Kimballs were born and lived as artisans and farmers in New England — Richard, Benjamin, David, Jeremiah, James, Solomon. In 1801, to Solomon Farnham Kimball of Vermont was born Heber Chase Kimball. This child would in his middle years cross the great prairie of North America, an ocean of grass rolling ahead of the wagons of the Mormon pioneers, seeking again a haven from religious persecution, this time in the Great Basin.

In 1811 President James Madison's embargo against commerce with England wiped out the value of Solomon's Vermont investments in salts, potash and pearlash, and the family, with nine-year-old Heber, migrated to western New York. Four years later Joseph Smith, Sr., also left Vermont for New York, stalked by debts and hunger after successive years of crop failures, and settled on a farm outside Palmyra, fourteen miles northeast of the Kimballs. And in 1829 another native Vermonter, Brigham Young, moved into Heber's village of Mendon.

One of the items of great interest in the area was the rise of young Joseph Smith as the prophet and founder of a religion which claimed to be a restoration of the pure gospel of Jesus Christ. Though both Brigham and Heber must have heard of this event, taking place as it did just a few miles from their home, they had no direct contact with Mormonism until 1831, when five elders of The Church of Jesus Christ of Latter-day Saints passed through. Their message impressed the two men, and when the elders returned the next spring Brigham and Heber accepted baptism within two days of one another. In another three years they were called as apostles in the first Quorum of the Twelve, and thenceforth their lives stood intimately linked with the history of the Church.

Six feet tall and weighing two hundred pounds, with big sloping shoulders, Heber looked the part of blacksmith and potter. Blunt in manner, he was handier with an anvil than with a book. Grammar mystified him, but a meeker man never lived. Tenacious in his loyalty to the Church, he bowed again and again under the rod of anti-Mormon oppression without a whimper. By the time he was fifty-three, he could tell a congregation of Latter-day Saints in the old tabernacle in Great Salt Lake City: "I was taught in my youth that after death I had to go directly into the bowels of hell, and go down, down, down, because there is no bottom to it. I am not troubled about any such thing as that, for I never expect to see any worse hell than I have seen in this world."

He joined the Mormon Church at thirty. Before a year passed he had seen "death, hell, and the devil." In Kirtland he slept weeks in his clothes, armed, expecting to be murdered by venomous apostates who were trying to split the Church into fragments. When there were few men left in the Church who would declare Joseph Smith a prophet, when to say that he was was to risk death, Heber testified without flinching that he knew Joseph Smith was a prophet.

Anti-Mormon persecution in Missouri became intense in 1833 and continually increased in brutality. In 1838 at Haun's Mill 250 mounted Missouri militiamen rode into the tiny Mormon community, guns blazing. They left seventeen dead, houses smoldering, dogs howling, cattle maddened, and women and children sobbing with fear.

At the same time a mob militia of three thousand Missourians was gathering at Far West, screeching, wrote Heber, "like Satan in Hell." Their intent was to exterminate the Mormons or drive them from the state. "Hell couldn't match such an army," he wrote.

The Mormons fled into Illinois, where they built a city on the marshland and hill overlooking the Mississippi River. But in 1844 Joseph Smith and his brother were murdered at Carthage Jail. And by February 1846 the Saints were fleeing Illinois mobs, deserting their warm homes, some crossing the frozen Mississippi in dead of winter on wagons or foot into temporary camps in Iowa. "We travelled," Heber remembered, "through sorrow, misery, and death."

In the summer of 1847 Heber was one of an advance company which scouted a trail to the Salt Lake Valley, a trail followed in subsequent years by tens of thousands of other refugees and converts. There the Saints settled, to build up Zion.

In December of 1847 the First Presidency was reorganized, with Heber appointed Brigham Young's first counselor, a position he held the rest of his life.

Heber left Nauvoo with about twenty of his wives. Two decades later at the funeral of his first, Vilate, he would point at her coffin and say, "There lies a woman who has given me forty-four wives." She had consented after a personal manifestation persuaded her that the principle of plural marriage had divine sanction. The pressure of this great family bore down on him so heavily that he would often say that plural marriage, with its multiplied cares and perplexities, had cost him "bushels of tears."

Two of his wives were sisters he married in Nauvoo. Their father, William Gheen, a Pennsylvania Quaker farmer, had joined the Church, sold his farm, and moved to Nauvoo. Two months after Joseph's assassination in 1844 the older sister, Ann Alice, a delicate, intensely spiritual woman, became Heber's seventeenth wife. "This I did," she wrote, "for the sake of salvation and exaltation in the Celestial Kingdom of God with a man I thought the best in the world." Fifteen months later Heber married Ann's younger sister, Amanda. With Heber's other wives, the two sisters crossed the plains to Salt Lake. There in 1858 Ann Alice bore twins.

One of them was a boy, Heber's thirty-fifth son. When Heber called his sons to prayers he could start at Enoch and go on down the list of patriarchs and prophets: Abraham, Isaac, Jacob, Joshua, David, Solomon, Jeremiah, Daniel. Most of the names came from the Old Testament. For this thirty-fifth son Heber chose the name Andrew from the Gospels.

When Andrew was eight, he and a crowd of brothers, some of them as old as eleven, were baptized en masse. Heber rounded them up, along with any stray neighbor boys who yet lacked the ordinance, and led them down to a pool opposite his gristmill on City Creek. Baptizing one boy himself to start things off, Heber turned the rest over to his older sons, just home from missions.

Schooling was accomplished by the same mass process. Heber built what was reputedly the first schoolhouse in the Great Basin, put one of his wives in charge, and invited any children in the neighborhood to attend without fee along with his own. One day Heber strode into the school. In his right hand was a long carriage whip. He asked the teacher, "Who is the worst boy here?" She named him, tearfully. It was her own son. The husky boy was ordered to the center of the floor and whipped. "Next," demanded Heber. The next worst was named, ordered forward, and whipped. By the time a good sampling of the school's bottoms had felt the light touch of his whip, Heber was satisfied that he had put across his point. He meant school to be taken seriously.

In 1868, when Andrew was nine, his father died, leaving a great many widows and fatherless children. The day he was buried eight thousand people crowded the Tabernacle, flags flew at half-mast, and a large procession, including Brigham Young, nine apostles, most of Heber's living wives, a large crowd of his children, and Captain Croxall's brass band, marched through drenching rain down Main Street behind the coffin. As the first clods fell on the lowered coffin at the family burying spot, a block from Temple Square, the sun burst through the clouds and a brilliant rainbow glowed in the sky.

For Andrew, the death of his father meant an early end to his schooling. His older brothers, Sam and Dan, soon struck out on their own, leaving Andrew to help support his mother, who was weak from acute bronchitis, and his twin sister Alice and younger sister Sarah. His mother was a faithful woman, Quakerish in dress, shy in society, tall and plain-faced, with a soft heart for the weak and sick. Her gentleness and the slow patience of her suffering through her last years eased her

Heber Chase Kimball (1801-1868)   Ann Alice Gheen Kimball (1827-1879)

Edwin Dilworth Woolley (1807-1881)   Mary Ann Olpin Woolley (1824-1894)

Andrew Kimball (1858-1924)   Olive Woolley Kimball (1860-1906)

son back into Church activity in his teenage years. He was ordained a deacon at twenty, just a year before his mother died.

By 1880 Andrew was working as a fireman on the Utah Central Railroad, making good money, and in love with one of Bishop Woolley's daughters. The Woolleys were Pennsylvania Quakers dating back to William Penn, and before that to Wales. Edwin Woolley, an obstinate man, had resisted the Mormon elders who proselyted his town in 1837. A family tradition has it that when his wife, Mary, joined he needled her, saying, "Mary, I will give thee a new silk dress if thou wilt say that Joseph is not a prophet." But the story of the gold plates and the Mormon Prophet worked on him till he could not rest without seeing Joseph Smith for himself. His mind made up, he impulsively made the trip to Kirtland on horseback, a distance of eighty miles, between sunrise and sunset. His astonished neighbors noted the event as "Ed Woolley's wild ride to see the Prophet Joseph Smith." He was baptized within the month.

Edwin set up a mercantile business in Nauvoo and later joined the exodus to the Rocky Mountains. By 1854 he had become one of Salt Lake City's twenty bishops. Brigham Young hired the shrewd trader to manage his private businesses. Edwin's stubbornness was proverbial. Friends said of him that if he were to drown, the searchers should look for his body upstream.

In 1850, on his way home from a business trip in the East, Edwin met a young English convert in St. Louis, hired her as a cook for the trek between there and Salt Lake City, and two weeks after they arrived made her his fourth wife. Mary Ann Olpin bore Edwin eleven of his twenty-six children. It was Mary Ann's sixth, Olive, whom Andrew Kimball married in the Salt Lake Endowment House on February 2, 1882.

Olive was brought up to hate idleness and all of "the devil's wiles." She was a staunch "Saint," and would suffer what had to be without complaint. Twenty when she married, Olive was just five feet high, pretty, blue-eyed, and had mild red hair and such clear skin that Selena Phillips declared "she must never have touched coffee or tobacco." She was not forward as a woman, and as a girl had been so timidly fearful in public that she had shied away from Young Ladies MIA lest she be asked to pray or speak.

When Olive married him, Andrew was working in the machine shops at the railyards. Six feet tall, slender, rigidly straight, immaculate in dress, he was the perfect gentleman. Strictly honest, he had piercing black eyes which seemed to strip one's private soul bare.

In December, Olive bore a daughter, Maude. The baby died at ten months, but Olive bore other children, eleven in all. She felt close to her own family and was especially close to her mother. When Andrew was away she often walked the mile and a half to her mother's house. Andrew was gone a great deal in his work and in Church service.

In 1884, after three years of married life, Andrew was called to the Indian Territory as a missionary. The territory held twenty Indian nations — almost eighty thousand people, most of them deported from eastern states to make room for white settlers. In January 1885, with James West of Salt Lake, Andrew bought a ticket for thirty-three dollars to Vinita in Indian Territory. From there the two men traveled south to the Verdigris River, which boasted a mild fame for water so brackish the stock wouldn't drink it. Bridges were a luxury in that country, and the swollen Verdigris, a three-hundred-yard-wide mass of roaring ice and uprooted trees, held them back for over a month. At the end of February they forded the river and slogged nine miles through mud and snow, wading streams.

They stayed with friends where they could, earning their keep with their hands. At the Hendricks farm near Muskogee, Andrew whittled a churn dasher, filed and set two saws, fixed a gate catch, helped a blacksmith repair a mowing machine. Planting corn or hauling wood, he wrote, was as good a time as any to tell a farmer of the gospel. Five weeks out, the first letter from Olive caught up with him. He broke into tears as he read it.

By May, summer had come. The mosquitoes from the swamps set the elders wild. Their legs were bitten raw by chiggers, fleas, and ticks. By August, Andrew had malaria, the disease which had scourged elders in that mission for thirty years. Back in 1855 Orson Spence had died of malaria contracted in the territory. Washington Cook was buried near Dog Creek and Robert Petty on Grand River the following year. In 1877 John Hubbard was buried just five months after leaving Salt Lake City. Robert Lake in the same year deserted his mission after five days in the territory. The last missionaries out, Israel Ball and Frank Teasdale, had returned to Utah early, sick and discouraged, just two months before Andrew was called. Each day at noon, chills would shake Andrew's body, then give way by 2:00 P.M. to terrible fever and headache. After a profuse sweat, the fever would die out and leave him feeling well until the paroxysm at noon the next day.

By September, Andrew's companion, James West, had suffered enough, and when the pair received a wire from Salt Lake instructing them to consider themselves released and free to go home due to illness, he left. But Andrew determined to stick it out the whole two years. He answered the wire: "I have the Priesthood with me. I will get well and prefer to stay." He stayed another year and a half, walking long miles, sometimes in wet clothes, wading swamps, sleeping in the woods, missing a good many meals, sweating, cramped and chilled day after day. But he preached the gospel.

His time completed, Andrew was released as a missionary in April 1887 and was called instead to serve as president of that mission. He was free to return home and find work, but he was to remain in charge of the mission. Olive wept as she held him in her arms again after two and a half years.

Restless, looking for a better income, Andrew clerked for a succession of firms, selling groceries, farm machinery, fruit and produce, eventually drifting into selling out on the road. His territory extended from Idaho down into southern Utah. He drummed Grant soap in 1894, adding baking powder, Utah chewing gum, King candy, then, in 1895, vinegar, paper, patent medicines, and, in 1896, Mt. Nebo salt. Drumming was a hard life and took him from his family for long weeks, bouncing over bad roads in an open wagon. He almost froze in an Idaho blizzard, the temperature at thirty-two below, the horses unsteady, the road icy. In the summer he baked in the desert heat on his southern route. It was harder to leave home each trip. But it seemed to Andrew the best way to earn a living, to feed his growing family.

Wherever he travelled through Utah and Idaho Andrew was pointed out as president of the Indian Territory Mission. He was said to be one of the few to last a full mission in that territory since it had opened in 1855. People found he had a strict sense of duty, firm ideas, and a straightforward manner.

Andrew ran the Indian Territory Mission with strict thoroughness. He expected his missionaries to be gentlemen and to dress accordingly. They were instructed to enter the mission field with white celluloid bosoms, collars and cuffs and wide necktie, and full-weight, black Prince Albert suit. One new missionary arrived in Indian Territory with a cutaway coat on, explaining that he had asked Elder

B. H. Roberts of the First Council of the Seventy if a Prince Albert suit was necessary and that Elder Roberts had thought not. "Elder Roberts," replied the mission secretary, "is not running this mission. President Kimball wants all to dress becoming to their profession." The missionary ordered a Prince Albert.

In 1897, a rough element in Pollard, Arkansas, hurled rocks through the schoolhouse window during a Sunday meeting that was under Andrew's direction, causing cuts and bruises. The meeting ended and Andrew walked outside, where he was immediately surrounded by the mob. "President Kimball tried to reason with them," wrote John Farley, "while all the time the mob was yelling at a large fellow next to him to 'Hit him. Hit him.' President Kimball finally could stand it no longer and told them they were cowardly curs." The mob left, then ambushed them part-way home, throwing rocks from the brush. They hit Andrew six times in the back. "One rock," recalled Farley, "hit by the foot of President Andrew Kimball and he exclaimed, 'Oh, if I could just lay this Priesthood down for a minute.' There was no one injured further."

There had been a time when he was the only missionary in the Indian Territory. When his presidency of the mission ended in 1897, the missionary corps numbered sixty-one.

Through the 1880s the Church practice of plural marriage brought mounting federal persecution. The issue became critical during Andrew's mission in Indian Territory. President John Taylor wrote him that the country was "quickly becoming what the prophets of modern times have declared it would become, a nation ruled by mobs." He regarded those attacking the Church's plural marriage system as warring against God. In 1885 nearly all of the Church leaders went "underground" to escape federal prosecution. President Taylor died in 1887. Shortly thereafter the Edmunds-Tucker Act was used to seize all the Church's property in a direct effort to destroy the temporal power of the Church. Without property, enmeshed in litigation, bereft of much of its leadership, the Church wallowed in heavy seas.

With Mormon polygamists disenfranchised by court order, the anti-Mormon element was close to ruling Utah government. In this chaos Andrew saw his duty in political work. He won the post of election judge in 1889, signing a certificate that he did not aid or abet polygamy, nor associate with "polygamously acting persons." As mission president he had continual contact with polygamous Church leaders, but he did not have close personal associations with them. He did not himself have plural wives, but he did with Olive's consent seriously consider taking other wives. The subject was an open matter between them. One woman came to their home for dinner with the family. Another he sent to the theater in company with Olive, while he stayed home with the children. For various reasons none of these prospective marriages were entered into.

At October Conference 1890 President Woodruff's Manifesto received approval. The Manifesto marked the end of open plural marriage in the United States, but "the Principle" was considered by many to be no less binding than before. Mexico and Canada offered haven for men and women willing to make such sacrifice. Many prominent Church leaders had families outside the United States. Andrew consulted his brother-in-law, Joseph F. Smith, and received the advice that he should give up the idea of plural marriage, for its time had passed. For both Andrew and Olive the willingness to obey the Principle would have to serve for the deed.

With the Church's changed stand on plural marriage, national political leaders withdrew their opposition to statehood for Utah. The Mormons desperately wanted statehood as a partial escape from federal control. In anticipation of statehood a convention met in 1895 to draft a constitution for Utah. Andrew, a Democrat, was elected a delegate.

The constitutional provisions forbidding plural marriage raised no controversy. The most contentious issue proved to be the vote for women. Andrew stood committed, as did most of the Church leaders, in favor of woman suffrage; B. H. Roberts led the opposition.

Olive was pregnant with her sixth child. On March 28, 1895, a cool cloudy day but warm for the time of year, Andrew returned home from the convention at five o'clock and found Olive ready to deliver her child. He went for her sister, Rachel Simmons, who had delivered four of the others, and at 7:50 P.M. a nine-pound baby boy was born. When the baby had been washed, Andrew recorded in his journal: "I took the children in to see him. Clare [ten years old] had made up her mind for a girl, was badly disappointed, had a crying spell."

The effort to find a suitable name began. Despite his taking the opposite position on the vote for women, Andrew had the highest regard for B. H. Roberts. That day Roberts had delivered in a losing cause what Andrew called "the greatest oration I have ever heard."

Andrew decided to call his baby Roberts Kimball. "The only thing that stands in the way," reported a newspaper item, "is Mrs. Kimball. As she is an enthusiastic woman suffragist and fully understands the meaning of equal rights he has not yet carried the day." They named the baby Spencer Woolley Kimball.

By 1897 people were talking about Arizona — cheap land, a new start, plenty of room. As far back as 1884 Andrew had frightened Olive with rumors that he would be called by the Church to settle there. William Kimball, a half-brother, had already gone and other brothers were to follow, but Olive was terrified of that forbidding land. Mormon colonists as far back as the 1870s had settled on the Little Colorado River and on the San Pedro, near the Mexican border, and in 1879 on the Gila, a valley forty-five miles long bordered by an Apache reservation. ·Those that gave up and came home to Utah carried with them tales of misery and disgust. One settler in the Gila Valley said of the flora and fauna: "If you touch it, it stings you; if you pet it, it bites you; and if you eat it, it kills you."

It had not been many years since news reached Salt Lake periodically of renegade Apaches on the Gila. The Wright brothers, Seth and Lorenzo, had been killed from ambush, and Jacob Ferrin, the Merrills, and Frank Thurston had been murdered. As late as 1892 Indians killed Lot Smith farther north. Back in 1854 General Sherman reputedly gave his blunt opinion of the territory: "We have had one war with Mexico and took Arizona. We should have another and compel them to take it back."

Sometimes what one fears becomes one's cross. In Pocatello in 1896 Andrew was approached by Matthias Cowley, who said to him: "You will be called to labor among the stakes of Zion. I prophesy it in the name of the Lord." Andrew remembered of the words, "It went through me like electricity." A year later, drumming on the southern route, he was told by the apostle Owen Woodruff in Sevier that Christopher Layton, president of the stake in Arizona, had been released, and that Andrew Kimball was to replace him. Andrew returned to Salt Lake City, stunned. He met with Church leaders in President Wilford Woodruff's office. Among other things, they asked about his financial circumstances. Andrew was paying off a home and rental house and was $1500 in debt. Olive had hoped their financial situation would disqualify them, but the leaders showed little concern for this situation.

Andrew left the office "under a gloomy cloud, dark and heavy," he wrote in his journal. "I had been called on a mission and to me there was but one answer and that was to go." Andrew carried home his news and with Ollie prayed for strength. Andrew wrote of "that couple bowed before God trying to pray while their hearts were so swollen with grief. They bubbled over with scalding tears and after a long and hard struggle a petition was made to the throne of Grace while a flood of tears gushed forth. This over, nothing remained but to go to work."

As word of Andrew's call got out, family and friends dropped in to weep tears of consolation. Arizona was a life sentence, a prison, hot and dry, infested with savages and spiders and flies. A death in the home would have brought fewer mourners, less sorrow. To send a man to Arizona was to bury him alive, they thought. The quickest route back to Salt Lake City was two thousand miles by train through California or Colorado. Arizona was another world.

Andrew made a trip to Arizona to be sustained as stake president, then returned to make preparations for the move. During this time the city and nation grew excited over the crisis with Spain, the *Maine* incident, and Admiral Dewey's conquest of Manila, but the Kimballs had other concerns. Andrew obtained a large loan on their property and used the cash to pay off a bundle of little debts. At a farewell party Andrew's half-brother, J. Golden Kimball, thinking of Heber C. Kimball's fifty-two sons, said he "considered Andrew the best boy in the family," after which Andrew spoke and "caused many to become melted to tears." Olive paid a last tearful visit to the grave of little Maude, who had died of pneumonia in their second year of marriage.

Spencer was three years old when the family of eight left Salt Lake City on May 3, 1898. "With heavy hearts we boarded the train," wrote Olive. It was a sad parting. A persistent rain drenched the air. A little group of well-wishers, many in tears, stood on the platform beneath dripping umbrellas. The train left at 8:40 A.M. A hundred miles out of Salt Lake, wrote Andrew in his journal: "a large golden rock rolled onto the track. Delayed us."

Smoke, cinders, heat poured through the open windows. All the family except Andrew and the baby grew seasick. The train's wheels klop-klop-klopped over rail joints as the days dragged on in the wearisome travel over desert and mountains. To Colorado, then south and west to Arizona.

They reached Bowie — a dry, colorless, barren junction — on the third day. Riding the diamond-stack, wood-burning "Gila Monster" from Bowie down the dry San Simon valley, they found the land "a formation of lava rock and sand, with here and there a poor unfortunate cactus or desert weed." But the Gila Valley itself proved less of a desert and more of an oasis, a strip of fertile, irrigable farmland two miles wide along the river bottom.

On the fourth day the train pulled into Thatcher. The town was too small to boast a depot. Crated furniture was simply pushed off the train. Some broke. A crowd of adults and children met them, intending to sing. But the wind began blowing so hard that the singing was postponed. Instead they showered the Kimballs with armfuls of roses in welcome from the 3400 scattered members of the stake.

Fifteen years before, in Salt Lake City, Andrew's predecessor Christopher Layton had been set apart to preside over a new stake to be named St. Joseph in honor of the martyred Prophet, then sent south to colonize a desert whose occasional Mexican and white villages were isolated by Apaches and desolation. Leaving six wives behind in Utah, Layton moved south with his youngest, Elizabeth, and with $21,000 set to work building an empire in southeastern Arizona. He bought two thousand acres, called the place Thatcher, divided it into lots, and sold them to Mormon settlers. He bought a gristmill, built roads, canals, homes. By 1898 he was seventy-six, ill, and close to death. New leadership was needed there, and the General Authorities had seen in the long-time president of the Indian Territory Mission the man to call.

While the Kimball family was getting settled they first housed with Layton's son Charles, then took a room at Hyrum Claridge's, and finally moved into a three-room adobe house, with no bath, no sink, no running water. Andrew expanded the living quarters by pitching a big, six-room white tent just outside the house. It was dubbed "the white house." When Spencer was five he woke the family one night by falling out of the tent. A big wind had come up and shaken loose the tent hook by his bed, letting him drop outside onto the ground. "We were awakened by his pitiful cry," wrote Olive, "as it frightened him to fall onto the ground in the night. He came walking around to the tent door. We had a good laugh over it next morning but he did not think it funny while he was passing through the tent."

Andrew and Olive Kimball and their children, 1897: Clare (13), Gordon (9), Delbert (7), Ruth (5), Spencer (2), and Alice

The stake had bought Andrew ten acres of land, and the members turned out on a Saturday to help him grub 450 mesquite stumps. Del and Gordon, seven and ten, were set to work helping their father farm. But Spencer was younger. Gordon remembered him as a "busy-body around the place all the time." He would tie a stick like a broom handle to a little makeshift wagon and ride it round and round on trails in the cornfield back of the house.

Andrew hadn't moved to Arizona for riches. Just feeding his six children taxed his resources for a time. "You will yet be rich," his half-brother J. Golden Kimball joked, "— in wisdom." By October of that first year Andrew had to let his life insurance policy lapse. He was finding it hard to make a living out on the frontier, with Church work taking a good share of his time. He began picking up income anywhere he could. He sold Bible scrolls ordered from a Colorado Springs firm. The manager wrote to Andrew, "Don't miss a Catholic priest, for we hardly fail to sell to them." He sold insurance and Prince Albert suits, opened a farm machinery business which developed into a general store, made collections for loan companies, worked as an agent for a Tucson bank, did some farming, sold his peaches to purchase school books, served a term in the legislature, took a contract to lay a stretch of railroad up toward Morenci. But he never did get rich.

It never bothered Spencer that the family had little cash. "We didn't know we were poor," he recalled. "We thought we were living pretty well." Hand-me-down sweaters and coats were normal for a small farming community. Homemade shirts were common. So were pants patched together out of the worn ones bequeathed by older brothers. And when the meat platter and serving dishes were empty on the table, Andrew would joke about his father's hired man who used to comfort himself with the saying, "the nearer the bone, the sweeter the meat." "We laughed," Spencer would recall, "and picked the bones a little cleaner." When Ma bought fancy foods it was usually to feed conference visitors. Spencer would patiently wait while the guests ate, hoping something special would be left for him. A basket of plums and apples from Sister Jones was, wrote Olive, a "very acceptable" gift.

Spencer envied Clarence Naylor, whose father ran a confectionary. A nickel dish of ice cream cost Clarence nothing. For Clarence, stick candy was free. And since Tom Naylor was also a barber, Clarence's hair was always smooth and slick. Every summer Clarence had a new straw hat, every winter a felt hat, while Spencer wore the same worn hat every season as long as it stayed on his head. Some boys Spencer knew didn't have to work weekends and summers, but he did. And his family had to make every penny count. On the Kimballs' farm there was never a new staple or a new strand of wire. Always they must fix the fence with what there was, put it together again somehow so that it would hold.

The stake over which Andrew presided, one of thirty-seven in the Church, included ten wards. Eight were in the Gila Valley, the other two in St. David, ninety miles south, and Duncan, forty miles east. When Andrew took over the stake, parts had fallen into disorder. In one ward he found the bishop chewing tobacco. The chapel was dirty, the fence down, everything out of joint. At Matthews there were two factions. Neither side could stand the other. In Layton fathers were letting their daughters work away from home in the rough mining camps. Andrew did what he could. Wards were reorganized, new officers chosen, resolutions passed.

Spencer grew up with a lively notion of his father's dignity and importance. He often stated in later years that his father had been well liked by the leaders of the Church, had entertained Arizona's governors and senators in his home, had spoken in general conference. There could be no question that for a generation Andrew Kimball was the most important man in his community.

Since the Gila Valley was several days' travel from Church headquarters in Salt Lake City, as stake president Andrew personified the Church for his people. Joseph F. Smith had blessed him that his people might "seek unto him as children to a parent." Andrew worked for his people, ordered books for them through George Q. Cannon and Sons of Salt Lake City, arranged excursion fare for them on the railroad at conference time, counseled them on their marital troubles, blessed their sick. Politicians besieged him for his endorsement, businessmen for the use of his name to bolster their schemes.

People came to him at all hours of the day and evening with their business and Church and family troubles. "They came in the field while we loaded hay," remembered Spencer. "They came in the corral while we milked the cows, they came before breakfast while we worked in the garden and among the flowers and always went away blessed." Many a Kimball meal was delayed until Andrew could get free. To service the miserable, Andrew started keeping two handkerchiefs in the tail of his Prince Albert coat, one for himself, one for others.

When word reached him that the Walkers, six years married, could not have children, he stopped them on the street and asked them about it. Suddenly, taking hold of Mary Walker's hand and looking her straight in the eye, he said, "I promise you in the name of the living God that you will have a baby." Turning to Arthur, he said, "You will be a father." Then he said goodbye and left abruptly, astonished at his own words. Thirteen months later Mary bore a baby boy. "Impossible," responded a medical specialist in Los Angeles who had examined her. "You have never had a child, and you never will. It is impossible."

One unusually dry spring, when the Gila River had shrunk to just a trickle, and with no snow on the mountains, Andrew advised the farmers at church to go ahead and plant. If they were faithful in their Church assignments, he promised, there would be moisture enough to grow their crops. His promise seemed ridiculous, impossible. Rupert Wixom asked him after the meeting if he didn't regard that as a pretty risky statement he had made. "Yes," Andrew answered, "and it scares me to think about it. But it will come true." That year unprecedented night dews watered the valley, giving normal harvests.

Andrew was determined that Gila Valley should be no backwater. He took the floundering Church academy in Thatcher (students paid tuition in molasses, hay, squash, honey), trumpeted it up and down the valley, begged the people to support it, and ultimately resurrected it. His son Spencer would graduate there in 1914. Andrew was one of the first in the valley to purchase a piano, to install running water, to buy a bathtub. In Salt Lake City at conference, year after year, Andrew met barbers, choristers, schoolteachers on the streets. Gila Valley needed men. "Why not try Arizona?" he urged. He enticed Utahns with enthusiastic tales of an Arizona sweet potato that weighed in at thirty-six pounds, corn stalks ten feet high, peaches as big as a double fist, red root weeds so large they had to be hacked down with an ax. Arizona sunflowers, he reported, would almost make good fence poles; a limb of a certain tree grew nine feet in one year; a graft in a poor tree grew six feet in its first season and bore fruit. There was no rheumatism, no lung trouble, no gnats, no fleas, no mosquitoes. "We guarantee you'll be happy," he told people.

Spencer adored his father and tried to imitate him. Plagued with stomach trouble, Andrew would soak his toast in pure olive oil bought by the gallon. Spencer copied him, dipping his toast in the oil. For the rest of his life, over and over he would insist that his father had been the greatest of all the Kimballs. As a boy he thought his father was near perfect, able and worthy to be an apostle. In his nightgown at night, Spencer would join in as Andrew led the family in exercises taken from physical culture magazines. Even chores he almost didn't mind, "if I could be helping my father." My father "was an expert swimmer," he wrote later. "My father could ride horses or operate train engines. His hands were those of a near-artist. His grammar was near perfect." Governors, lawyers, educators, though sometimes his peers, were "never his superiors." He was a carpenter, farmer, salesman, administrator.

"My father was the most important man in Arizona," Spencer insisted years later to his son. "In that part of Arizona," qualified his wife, Camilla. Spencer echoed her, not quite convinced: "Especially in that part of Arizona." When an apostle, he would still insist that his father had been "far greater than I am."

Spencer inherited his father's nervous energy. Andrew was quick and vigorous, with not an ounce of deadness in him; a live wire. He would hammer the podium when he grew excited in a meeting. Vera Berryhill, then a girl, remembered that he "used to frighten me to death. Whenever he stood up to speak I felt the tremblings, as the scriptures say. He spoke with a voice that was mighty and strong."

Much of his father stuck to Spencer permanently — even details. In 1971 he mentioned that his father had wished his own nose were not quite so red. "I've got it myself, you see," he added, pointing to his nose. When it was suggested to him that he was unlike his father behind the podium, he disputed it, pointing out that he had the same habit of pounding the pulpit, the same tone of voice.

In Andrew's zeal that things be run right and that everyone do his duty, the Church grow, and the people prosper, he was sometimes severe and pointed in his rebukes from the pulpit. One of his high councilors still spoke thirty years later of a stake conference session in which Andrew rose to take charge and, spotting the high councilor's wife seated alone, asked her before the entire congregation, "Ella, where's your husband?" To which she answered, "He's home tending the children so I could come." "He should be here," said Andrew. One of Andrew's daughters-in-law half a century later would remember feeling "like he could tell every thought inside me. I would just want to shrink from him." "He was a sharp-spoken man," Francis Hancock said. "When he had any advice to give, he always gave it very plain and straight. His eyes would just snap."

He was called in to bless the Nash baby and give her a name. Brother Nash was on a mission in Australia. Andrew took the baby girl in his arms, ready to begin the blessing, then asked what her name was to be. An argument sprang up, the mother urging one name, the Nash girls another. An impatient man, accustomed to command, Andrew began the blessing and simply named the baby Olive, a name no one had suggested. The Nashes decided that Olive was better than either of their suggestions anyway.

In this one aspect Spencer departed from his father, having a softer temperament. Andrew was a formal man, without the gift for easy geniality his son developed. His social life largely occurred in a Church context.

Spencer never knew his grandfather, yet his grandfather stood as a major influence in his life. Spencer had a consciousness as he grew up and as he received responsible callings in the Church that his grandfather watched and approved, that in some measure the callings could be attributed to the merit and influence of Heber C. Kimball. The sacrifice and dedication of his grandparents to their religious belief served as an inspiration; the leadership positions of his grandfathers and father gave him a sense of potential within himself, however weak he might feel at the time he assumed responsibilities.

But of all the influences, the influence of his father, Andrew, counted most. The son followed his father closely in many things — in willingness to respond to Church callings, sense of loyalty, unquestioning faith, thrift, love of work, enthusiasm for a cause, vigor and indefatigability, firm insistence on doing right, love of people and deep concern for others in trouble.

3

A Small Boy in a Small Town

— "I could outwrestle almost any boy"

Spencer quickly fitted into the small desert farming community of Thatcher, population about eight hundred. He learned its characters and quirks like a map. There was Sim Drollinger, the mailman, with one ear missing. There was Edgar Sessions, a notary, who lived two doors east; his hair so long and bushy that Del and Gordon would joke "each time we lost a pair of scissors, or a tool, or our shoes, or a mowing machine, or one of the cows, 'Maybe it is lost in Brother Sessions' hair.'" There was "Deef Davey," who was hard of hearing, and "Monkey Bill," who capered about at ball games. The children called Ernest Jones' horse Napoleon Bonaparte because he had such "bony parts." North of Thatcher was a shantytown of poor Mexicans from which came stories of drunken brawls. There were spots of fear in the town, places where one never ventured. Up on the hill near the cemetery an eccentric squatter lived in a small shack. "The mere mention of his name," remembered Spencer, "made my backbone tingle with excitement and fear." In 1898 this squatter and another had fought with shovels over water rights. He suffered such shovel cuts on head and face that for a while the doctor thought him lost. Then up at Frank Tyler's ranch was a Yaqui Indian who, it was whispered, was fearsome when drunk.

So isolated was the town in some ways that new experiences counted for a lot. When a Miss Freeland came from the East to teach school she brought along a black cook. "This was a novel thing for us," commented Spencer, "a colored lady in our town." And when a new boy moved in, he paid for a while with fist fights and bloody noses. New acquaintances would ask whether Spencer had a middle name. "Woolley," he would say. They would snicker, "Woolley? Woolley? What a funny name!" Sometimes they misheard it as "Willie," and then Spencer would just keep quiet. He began introducing himself simply as Spencer Kimball. But he bristled if they shortened it to Spence.

Life in a small town could have its shocking aspects. When Spencer was five a spectacular fire burned the Collier house to ashes. The mother, a widow, had gone to a dance at Robinson Hall, locking her five children in the house for safe keeping. When her house burst into flames someone saw it from the dance hall two blocks south. Men rushed over with buckets of water, but nothing could quench the blaze. All the townspeople gathered. The mother was frantic with grief. Her locking the doors had kept the children from escaping the holocaust. Bits of their bodies were later found in the ashes. "I remember her screaming," wrote Spencer. The men had to hold her back from leaping into the flames and burning with her children.

Thatcher was a Mormon town. On July 24 there was always a Pioneer Day celebration, remembering the day the first Saints had reached Salt Lake Valley in 1847. Every year there was a parade, with Indians and firecrackers and handcarts, bunting and bonnets. Then at the commemoration in the Thatcher meetinghouse, all those who had seen the Prophet Joseph were seated on a raised platform. There were still seven the year Spencer was eleven, and he watched as year by year their number dwindled.

The Church had advice on practically everything in Thatcher. In 1898 it was voted that ladies at church meetings be obliged to remove their hats so everyone could see. When a shortage of trained midwives plagued the town, Andrew, as stake president, simply called Sisters Talley and Maxham on a "mission" to learn obstetrics in Los Angeles. The eye of the Church was especially diligent in watching over the morals of the youth. When John W. Taylor the apostle visited the stake in 1898 he solemnly warned the young people against the danger of kissing. Round dances — an "abominable" innovation to Christopher Layton — were limited to a maximum of three a night for fear passions might rise beyond control. Joseph Foster asked in priesthood meeting whether waltzing should be permitted at all.

There were some non-Mormons living in Thatcher, but just a handful. Most preferred Safford, a "gentile" town three miles away. A good Thatcher Mormon didn't normally trade with Safford merchants. In 1907 Andrew complained about the "people going wild over a cheap-john outfit at Safford, turning their cash into the laps of transient gentiles." Christopher Layton a decade before had complained that, instead of hiring Mormon schoolteachers, "we employ infidels in our district schools to teach our children." A Mormon might have his teeth fixed in Safford, might buy at Welker's store (Welker was a Mormon), but to socialize in Safford was frowned on. To be seen at a dance at Safford's Brier Hall was as much as a girl's reputation was worth. Andrew forbade his sons and daughters to dance there.

The year Spencer was five, the stake fasted and prayed for rain. "No breakfast," wrote Olive in her journal. "We were fasting." The same the next Sunday. Finally a week later it rained hard. "That," she wrote, "was in answer to the prayers of the saints in this stake."

Rain was life for a small agricultural town. That year there had been enough water for planting, but in the summer the ditches ran little water. "The water in the town ditch failed last turn to enter Pima at all," Olive wrote. "Many people are endeavoring to save their trees by hauling water in barrels from the river." The problem recurred every few years; fierce sun, no rain for months, the river sandy, the upper canals dry, just a trickle in the Union canal a block away. With a horse and lizard (a sledge made of a tree limb) Spencer hauled barrels of water from the canal up to the trees. He welcomed it when the water sloshed on him. The cracks around the trees, Spencer remembered, "were like open thirsty mouths. Did they think we had oceans of water?" When even the Union went dry, the family watched the clouds, hoped, and in the family prayers "mentioned the dryness to the Lord."

At the other end of the scale a cloudburst could wash out gardens. In September 1904 the Big Hail Storm battered crops, broke seventy-four windows in the Academy and all but two on the west side of the chapel. Spencer marvelled at the dents the hailstones put in the woodwork at home.

Living so at the mercy of the elements, people could feel a real dependence on God.

Church and gospel had central importance in Spencer's earliest memories. Always, it seemed to him, Ma had sat with her children on the fourth row of the Thatcher meetinghouse for Sunday School and sacrament meeting. Always the family knelt before meals to pray, their chairs turned back from the table, dinner plates upside down. Always there were night prayers at Ma's knee. Always there was fasting. Always tithing. "I feel sorry for children who must learn these important lessons after they are grown, when it is so much harder." For Spencer the lessons were a basic part of childhood.

Again and again Spencer watched his parents take their problems to the Lord. One day when Spencer was five and out doing his chores, little one-year-old Fannie wandered from the house and was lost. No one could find her. Clare, sixteen, said, "Ma, if we pray, the Lord will direct us to Fannie." So the mother and children prayed. Immediately after the prayer Gordon walked to the very spot where Fannie was fast asleep in a large box behind the chicken coop. "We thanked our Heavenly Father over and over," Olive recorded in her journal. "We could think of nothing else all evening." When her horses bolted on the road to Safford, Olive was terrified that someone would be hurt and the buggy broken. "We were frightened awfully. But the Lord heard my silent prayers and we got the horse stopped. Praise be to our Heavenly Father for His goodness to us."

One afternoon that same year Spencer walked with his mother up the dusty road to Bishop Zundel's house. "Why are we going?" he asked. She told him it was to take the tithing eggs. "Are tithing eggs different than other eggs?" Then Olive reminded her boy how he separated one egg from ten when he gathered them. She told him why he did so, that one belonged to Heavenly Father, nine to them. From that time gathering eggs had another dimension to it. During breakfast at haying time Andrew would tell his boys: "The best hay is on the west side of the field. Get your load for the tithing barn from that side. And load it full and high."

Tithing was an important issue in those years. For the previous decade receipts had been going down at a startling rate. The Church debt by 1899 had skyrocketed to between one and two million dollars, undermining the entire financial structure of the Church. Lorenzo Snow was pleading with bishops to collect tithing to save the Church from financial embarrassment. The entire Church membership was being reeducated on the Lord's law requiring a return of one-tenth on all income.

In a letter to the First Presidency in January 1902 Andrew reported that in his stake of 3634 members there were 1099 tithepayers and 117 non-tithepayers. "We find our bishops carrying on their records a great many 'dead-heads' who are in truth not Latter-day Saints at all. We have passed a resolution to give this class until Dec. 1902, and if they do not round to, their names will not diminish our percentage as [they do] now. Of course, you understand, this will follow a year's hard work to reclaim them."

In the summer when Spencer was five, his father gave to him and Alice a patch of planted potatoes. When Spencer had dug them with a garden fork and Alice had cleaned them, Spencer put on clean overalls, Alice a dress, and off they went with a box of potatoes in Spencer's red wagon. The potatoes sold. Spencer and Alice returned home jubilant. Andrew listened to them count their money, then said: "That's capital! Now what will you do with the money?" The children answered: ice cream, candy, Christmas presents. Andrew gently said: "Now, you haven't forgotten the bishop have you? The Lord has been kind to us. We planted and cultivated and harvested, but the earth is the Lord's. He sent the moisture and the sunshine. One-tenth we always give back to the Lord for his part." "Pa made no requirement," remembered Spencer, "he merely explained it so convincingly that we felt it an honor and privilege to pay tithing."

Spencer had a record of near-perfect attendance at church. But his mother's lap was an inviting pillow, and few sacrament meetings passed that Spencer did not drowse partway through. "I was unconsciously absorbing the sermons," he joked years later. He was also absorbing the habit of being in church. When testimony meeting lagged, he would watch for old Samuel Claridge, the short, white-haired stake patriarch, to burst spontaneously into "Redeemer of Israel" or "We Thank Thee, O God, for a Prophet" from the stand.

In 1902, when Spencer was just six, Andrew was asked to come out to the Cluff ranch and bless three-year-old Leo, who had been gored in the side by a cow. Dr. Platt washed the intestines hanging out, poked them back in with a finger, and sewed up the gash. As Leo changed color, he gave him up for dead. He told the Cluffs their boy's body was so filled with infection he would soon turn black. Leo's parents got in touch with President Kimball. Andrew laid his hands on the boy's head and blessed him by the power of the priesthood that he would be healed. The next day Dr. Platt waited in town for the Cluffs to come in and make funeral arrangements. When they did not show up, he took his buggy out to the farm and was dumbfounded to find the boy awake and healing. In amazement he admitted, "There has been a greater power than mine at work here." This was the first miracle Spencer was ever aware of.

At home at special times the Kimball family knelt around the revolving piano stool to pray. Andrew put a hand on the seat, Olive covered it with hers, and so on till each hand in the family was touching. "We felt very close together on those occasions," wrote Spencer.

On his eighth birthday Spencer was baptized. Although the canal was just a block away, someone suggested the hog-scalding tub, used by the Kimballs as a bathtub. That seemed a novel idea, so on March 28 Andrew filled it to the brim with water from the well, then baptized Spencer, immersing him in the tub. On Sunday he received his confirmation blessing at church. Proud of his new status, he told his family of overhearing someone remark: "What a big boy. He looks more than eight years old. He is a chubby little bishop." Gordon and Del teased "the bishop" with high glee. Four years later the propriety of baptism in a tub was questioned, since the baptizer had not gone down into the water too, as John the Baptist did. The ordinance was redone in the Union Canal, just to be sure.

In Thatcher, most children started school at six. But Olive had a fixed idea no child should start school till he was seven; so Spencer began a year late. He took school seriously and won certificates for perfect attendance, having been neither absent nor tardy. One day when in the second grade he raced the three blocks home to pump water in the trough for the cows and horses, feed the pigs, snatch lunch, and make it back to the schoolyard in the hour allotted. Olive saw him coming and met him at the door to ask what was wrong. "It's not noon. What are you doing home at recess?" Panicky at his mistake, Spencer fled back to the schoolyard only to find it empty. He walked into the classroom, his face red, his schoolmates laughing. Embarrassed, Spencer broke into tears. Finding him inconsolable, the teacher announced to the class that Spencer was ahead of them all and that it had been decided he would move up a grade with the others his age.

Recess, just fifteen minutes long, was precious. The schoolyard was peppered with marble rings and "perg" holes. Chalkies and peewees were common marbles. But to own an agate or a glassie or a steelie was a distinction. Spencer didn't play for keeps much. "Maybe it was because there were often those who could shoot better than I could." Pop-the-whip, kick-the-can, pom-pom-pull-away, stink-base, all were a part of recess. Sometimes ordinary leapfrog gave way to a wilder version, spats and spurs, where the one who was jumped over might be either spurred in the side or spatted on the rump. When girls joined the game, the boys switched back to the tamer version.

A prize giggler, Spencer was set on the dunce seat occasionally to quell his overflow of energy. One time in fourth grade he started giggling with Agnes Chlarson across the room. Agnes "was a pretty girl and a happy soul and giggled like I did and seemingly couldn't stop." In stern rebuke the teacher ordered Spencer to walk over and sit beside Agnes, a terrible thing for the condemned, a great delight to the rest of the class. But Spencer and Agnes only tittered the more. So the teacher exiled Spencer to the seat by her desk. "I got serious finally."

"Everybody liked Spencer," remembered his older brother Gordon. "He was a boy's boy." After school he jumped in the hay pile, though this was frowned upon. Sometimes at night he and his friends swam naked in the Union Canal, where a curve shielded them from notice.

Good-natured and friendly, he seldom quarreled. For the most part he avoided the bloody noses, fist fights, and bullies. He remembered being in only one fight at school, and that was a draw. Both he and Benoni Coleman had had enough of the sport after a couple of blows.

Spencer remembered another fight, too. When Spencer was seven, Arizona Governor Alexander Brodie visited the Kimballs in Thatcher. Sandy, his boy, fought with Spencer, was beaten, and came crying into the house, mussed up, his nose bloodied. Mrs. Brodie was upset. Andrew and Olive lectured Spencer, until Governor Brodie interrupted, saying that Sandy was as big as Spencer and should learn to defend himself. Spencer was pleased when his father named a bay colt Brodie in honor of the Governor.

"I could outwrestle almost any boy that was near my size," said Spencer seventy years later, "I was tough and strong. . . . I was pretty husky." He remembered the scoldings he got from his sisters and his mother when he came home from play with his overalls worn out at the knees, sometimes with the patches on the knees of his overalls worn through, toes stubbed, knees scabbed, knuckles so grimed with dirt they cracked and chapped when scrubbed clean. "It seemed my long underwear was always poking out of my stockings," Spencer wrote. "My knee pants often had a bulge at the knee."

But he was not really tough of heart. A thrashing of a boy in school unsettled him. "My blood seemed to curdle and my breath stopped as the tall man came in with a leather strap, pulled the surly youth from his seat, and laid it on with vengeance."

At about age seven Spencer went on a community picnic under the cottonwoods out at Cluff's ranch. After lunch everyone went in swimming, wearing long dresses and stockings, or overalls. Spencer later wrote down his memory of what followed:

> Father is such a good swimmer. How I wish I could swim like he does. All over the great pond he moves easily and seemingly without effort. Now he comes for me, his little boy. I am on his back with my arms around his neck so tightly that he must constantly warn me. The water is deep and I am scared and I plead with him to take me back to the shallow water. At last we feel ground and I say: "I'm all right now, Pa," and I see him turn and swim off toward deep water. I take a step toward shore and fall into a deep hole. Down, down, down! Water is filling my lungs. . . . I cannot scream! Why doesn't someone get help? Will they never rescue me? Someone has now seen my predicament. Pa has heard their screams and is after me. I am full of water and coughing, spitting, crying for a long time. I thought I was drowned.

Though he later learned to swim, Spencer would never again feel brave in deep water. He often wondered why he had been saved from death this time and repeatedly later — whether there was not some providence in it.

When Spencer was very young, his brothers learned he could cock hay, small though he was. So Andrew bought him a four-tined fork with a short handle and set him to work. He proudly became "one of the sweating, tired men who came hungry and weary to the supper table at eventide," though he soon found to his dismay that the extra chores left him too little playtime.

Andrew was strict with his sons. Through summers and on Saturdays and holidays Spencer trimmed trees, raked leaves, mixed paint,

beat the carpets, rode the plow horse, herded cows. There was no
loafing. Sometimes he fell asleep at the supper table. The shade offered by a hay load tempted him. He could dig post holes nearly asleep.
At night he hit the bed and fell asleep at the same time.

Evans Coleman, the town wit, remarked that he could tell stake
conference was coming when he saw Spencer out cleaning up President Kimball's yard. This rankled Spencer. The yard was always kept
neat, though perhaps Andrew required extra care at conference time.

The work never ended. Johnson grass, cockleburs, sunflowers and
pig weeds tried to spread across the yard; all had to be hoed out. He
pumped well water into a trough for horses and cows which seemed
never to fill up. In the summer the iron pump-handle was blistering, in
the winter frigid, and his hands would hop in and out of his pockets.

To kill boredom as he pumped water, Spencer counted strokes,
estimated gallons, watched the bellies tighten, and wondered if the
horses would empty the well. "I said the ABC's forward and backward,
I said the times tables, I repeated the Articles of Faith." And then, to
make things worse, the horses would slosh water from the trough with
their noses, spilling the hard-pumped water.

Andrew exacted precision from his sons. Pointing to a piece of
carpentry such as a cedar tool-chest or a corner cupboard, he would say
to his second son, "Del, people won't ask how long it required to make
the chest or build the cupboard, but how well it was done." A meticulous dresser, Andrew expected the same neatness about the farm.
Spencer was taught to soap and oil the harness, hang the collar and
bridle and blinds just in place on pegs in the harness shop. The surrey
had to be washed, greased, painted. "Too frequently to suit me,"
remembered Spencer. "Why wash the buggy?" he would moan. "It will
just get dusty the first mile out anyhow." But for Father it had to be
clean. For Father the hairline of trim paint on the buggy had to be
flawless. The fences had to be whitewashed, the trellis painted green,
the barn, the granary, the harness shed, all painted. "Sometimes I did
not mind work," Spencer recalled. "But looking back, I am sure my
folks must have felt that I was always tired or lazy."

Andrew Kimball loved his animals. He would wash and curry his
horses, pick their tails free of burs, sometimes braid ribbons in their
manes. When the Maltese cat was poisoned the family gathered in
earnest prayer for its recovery. It raised Andrew's anger when one of

the boys failed to feed or water the animals. To strike one was almost unpardonable. It was Spencer's job to feed the pigs. When his father heard them squealing he would angrily scold Spencer, "Haven't you fed your pigs yet?" It seemed to Spencer they never filled up. Years later he joked that it was lugging an endless succession of five-gallon cans of slop to the pigs which stunted his growth.

No fence could hold the pigs. No matter how many holes Spencer plugged in the pig wire, the pigs located new ones. When he found a pig missing, Spencer would run to the neighbor's lot, sure the creature would be rooting in their garden or their garbage. And when he got it home, the beast never seemed able to squeeze back through the hole where it got out.

At age twenty-three, Spencer, watching the place while his folks were away, wrote:

> Those blamed hogs are enough to worry one bald-headed. One gets out and then they manage it so they keep me chasing pigs all the time. You might be interested in the fact that Nora has had her confinement, bringing a litter of ten. One was ruptured and died in spite of all I could do. A second she deliberately or accidentally laid on. Anyway, it was mashed like a pancake the third morning. A third died last night from some cause that I could not understand unless it too was crippled in the back from being stepped on or knocked about. A fourth is limping on three legs; the old elephant stepped on its front leg. So taking them all together it is not very encouraging.

The young Spencer watched with mixed emotions as his father slammed the beasts on the forehead with a sledge hammer and slit them open with a knife in hog butchering season. The killing and blood at once shocked and fascinated him. But the butchering meant one less pig to feed and something good to eat. He always asked for the bladder. Washed, the fat cleaned off, and blown up, it became a ball.

When Gordon and Del put up hay they would take Spencer along. They would pitch it up on the wagon and Spencer would tromp it down. The older boys liked to reach the wagon at the same time, both with huge forks of hay. One would pitch his hay on top of Spencer, knocking him down, then the other would add his load. They would laugh while Spencer picked himself out, infuriated, threatening terrible punishments when he grew up, sometimes bawling in exasperation.

Occasionally he would enjoy a minor revenge. One hot Monday afternoon, hearing the half-hour Primary bell a mile across the fields, Spencer said, "I've got to go to Primary." As Spencer told the story years later: "They said, 'You're not going to Primary.' I said, 'If Pa were here he'd let me go to Primary.' And they said, 'Well, Pa is not here, and this is one time you're not going to Primary.' Gordon was seven years older than I was and Del was five. They were much larger. I was just a little boy. They kept throwing the hay up and it all piled in the center of the wagon. They said, 'What's the matter with you up there?' There was no sound. They looked off across the field and I was halfway to the meetinghouse. I've always gotten lots of credit from people for being a very good Primary boy." Gordon, remembering the incident, commented, "He was a great kid for Primary." Spencer corrected him: "You mean I was a great kid to get out of work."

Later remembering himself as "the laziest boy that ever lived, especially in that generation," Spencer used his wit to avoid drudgery. When he discovered that his father was eager to have his children learn to play the Kimballs' new piano and that he would let a boy stop work in the fields on a hot Arizona day to sit in the cool parlor and practice, Spencer lost no time. While Gordon and Del sweated through the heat of the day, Spencer took the opportunity to run over his finger exercises and practice his pieces. "Where there was work to do," he later joked, "I could always find a shady place to sit down and dream." Some jobs Spencer missed because he was too small. Gordon had to clean the irrigation canal as part of the family assessment. Spencer could not dump the scraper.

Gordon and Del found fun in working Spencer. When he tromped hay they scolded him for sticking to the center of the pile, leaving the edges — dangerously high above the ground — unpacked. When there were hoes, mowing knives, axes, scythes to be sharpened at the grindstone, Spencer was not smart enough, said his brothers, to sit on the seat and hold the blade. So they assigned him instead to turn the huge wheel stone with his small arms. It seemed to him as he turned that his arms would never again get rested. Gordon and Del were most ingenious in coming up with chores little brother could do. If it was an errand, "they generally wanted me to 'Run!' and strangely I was in those days 'allergic' to running except in play." Later Spencer would joke that Gordon and Del took off with the girls and left him to do all the chores.

Already at nine he milked the cows, from two to nine of them. He found ways to break the dullness. He practiced squirting the stream of milk into the mouths of the cats that gathered around at milking time. Spencer memorized the Articles of Faith and the Ten Commandments word perfect to the beat of milk squirts into the pail. He sang to the cows. On a one-legged stool, his head burrowed in the cow's flank, he memorized most of the songs in the hymnal from sheets of paper onto which he had copied them.

Cows tried his patience. Their tails, swishing at the swarms of flies, inevitably slapped Spencer's eyes as he milked. A cow's tail with a solid mat of cockleburs had the wallop of a billy club. Spencer's harshest cuss word, *Darn,* was reserved for such moments. Sometimes, as he herded the cows to the hayfield to graze, they would get excited and stampede, and then nothing could stop them. Spencer might chase them all over town and get so mad he could kick them.

More than once he forgot and left the cows too long in the pasture. Their stomachs would over-fill, then their insides begin to bloat with gas, until the pressure would drive the beasts crazy with agony. One Sunday Spencer came home from meeting and found five cows bellowing. He had forgotten to put them up. He yelled for help. Gordon and Del ran up and all three set to work in their Sunday clothes, propping the cows over the manure pile, then punching their flanks desperately with elbows to loosen the gas. Three began to belch their way to safety. The other two fell and stretched out on their sides, near death. Gordon took a butcher knife and plunged it into the first cow's side, then the second's. The gas exploded out with a sickening odor. Spencer was set to work digging the alfalfa out through the wound with his fingers. Days of deep repentance followed. "In those many weeks," concluded Spencer, "while the hole was healing and partly digested food was spilling and the gases continued to escape, I was reminded constantly of my forgetfulness in leaving the cows in the new alfalfa too long when I had been instructed to watch them."

When the hay crop was cut, Spencer would herd the cows to the ten-acre field about a mile from home, racing with bare feet across the hot dirt from shade to shade. If the distance between shade was too great he plopped down on his bottom and gave his feet relief. Sometimes he bounced his rubber ball the whole distance or shot marbles as he walked. Ma and Pa, he later conjectured, "must have been exasperated many times." Sometimes he took his hoop and rolled it against the slower cows. Or he tossed stones or words at them, though stones were generally the more effective. In the early morning, trailing the cows, his feet luxuriated in the cool dirt as the soft pulverized dust oozed up between his toes.

One morning at the breakfast table Gordon and Del broke into laughter. "Look at Spunk," they called. (Spunk, remembered Spencer, was a "nickname which made me bristle every time.") Spencer was astonished to discover a tight feeling in his face — no pain, just a deadness. His lips wouldn't pucker to whistle, his left eye wouldn't wink, his speech was a little muddled. Half his face was paralyzed. When he smiled or laughed "it was a one-sided affair." The family worried that the condition might be permanent and called old Dr. Platt, the community physician. Dr. Platt looked at the paralysis and prescribed some liniment, which Spencer dutifully rubbed on his face for some time without effect.

The paralysis got worse. His aunt Alice wrote from Salt Lake that "to have that beautiful face of his disfigured through life would certainly be a calamity." His friends at school felt sorry for him. The family prayed for his face. Andrew administered to him. Gradually, over months, the deadness left. "Pa intended to send me to Salt Lake City to be treated," Spencer wryly complained several years later, "but unfortunately my face got well and I could not go to Utah." He recovered completely from what presumably was Bell's palsy, a puzzling ailment of the facial nerves which sometimes leaves residual paralysis.

In 1905, though, when Spencer was ten, Andrew did take him to Salt Lake City, to general conference. It was the boy's first trip out of the Gila Valley since he arrived. It was the first time he could remember seeing country without mesquite, sage and chaparral covering spiny ranges of hills. But Jack Tyler, another Thatcher boy, had told him what a big city was like. Jack said, enthusiastically, that Los Angeles, with its crowds of people, was "just like stake conference letting out."

Andrew and his son took the train north by way of Los Angeles and San Francisco and then across Nevada. Once in Salt Lake, they stayed with Aunt Alice, Andrew's twin sister, fifth wife of Joseph F. Smith, President of the Church. Spencer watched the President. He was surprised to see the old man, in a full patriarchal beard, stoop down and kiss each child as he came home at night. That was not the custom at the Kimballs', but Spencer liked it.

In Salt Lake City, Spencer felt at the center of things. This was the heart of the Church. Many Woolleys and Kimballs had homes there. His grandfathers had both been close to Brigham Young. Uncle Golden was a General Authority. Uncle Dan Kimball kept the gate at Temple Square. Aunt Alice was married to the prophet. His father was received respectfully. "Salt Lake was to me a mecca," he wrote. The Tabernacle and organ, the temple, the broad shady streets, the blocks and blocks of buildings, and cool streams of water running in the gutters, all awed him. He had seen no other life but that in a small farming community. "I knew there was a bigger world," he remembered, "but didn't get to have very much to do with it."

On the way back Andrew showed him around old San Francisco. The city was just a year away from the great earthquake and fire of 1906. Spencer rode the shoot-the-chutes and giant racers, saw the seals down at the cliffs, rode the cable cars, toured Chinatown. They visited Andrew's friend Joseph Robinson, who kidded Andrew, wrote Spencer, "saying it was quite evident from my dirty neck and ears that Pa was taking care of me. I was embarrassed and incensed."

But whatever Spencer thought of the world, home still seemed good. After five weeks away, as the train chugged the last forty miles toward Thatcher, "I was dancing and weeping for joy to be home again."

Life was hard for Olive. Year after year, as Andrew drove the horse and buggy to visit outlying Church wards or as he worked at a variety of jobs, Olive carried much of the family responsibility. She was a "Church widow." With Andrew gone, she would call the children for morning and night prayers and read to them from the Bible. She supervised their baths in a number two iron tub, heating buckets of water on the wood stove. ("Saturday night bath," wrote Spencer, "was my private enemy No. 1 in those years.") She kept her griefs to herself, confiding them to her journal. In 1901, she wrote: "I was sick with a pain in my bowels all night. It just poured down with rain. . . . All the beds and bedding got wet. Our house leaked in every room. I felt discouraged as every place but our front room was so wet but we got through the day alright and lived." Andrew understood her trials. When he first arrived he begged the people, "Be kind to my dear little wife, no matter what you do to me."

There was a stubborn strength about her. Following Andrew so far from her home and family had been a hard trial. But it was her "duty" and she went. As with Andrew, a fierce loyalty soon attached Olive to her new home. When Bishop Zundel advised the young people to save up and move to green Oregon, she resented it. Why leave, she asked when we "are already in a good country"? Her quietness was not weakness. People who met her quickly forgot she was just five feet high. "Your mother," J. Golden wrote to Spencer, "is a queen." Spencer in those days had no idea his mother had made any sacrifice in living in Arizona. He had never known another life, and to him the little isolated community was at the center of the world.

Sickness and death plagued Olive's children. Yet she was no worse off than others. In those years there were few Thatcher homes not invaded by sickness. Dysentery, pneumonia, and whooping cough stole children from nearly every family. Months of health would be followed by an epidemic of infection, taking a dozen children from the town in a single month. In late winter 1899, Tom Kimball, Andrew's nephew, was on a mission. His wife, Fannie, was alone, frantic, with four sick children. She sent for Andrew, begging him to hurry and administer to her boy Murray, who was in a bad way. But the child died before Andrew could get there. In a week Fannie lost a second boy. At the same time Annie Layton, whose husband also was on a mission, lay sick in bed, four of her children with her; she lost a boy to measles and whooping cough. The Merrills lost a boy, the Claridges a girl, the Thompsons a girl. The next year typhoid fever laid whole families low, occasioning double and even triple funerals.

The year after, Olive tried to find two ladies to sit up during the night with the Zingers, who were sick with typhoid. It was almost impossible. No one wanted to get that close to the disease. The fear of death was everywhere. Christian Zinger died and the corpse began bloating, so Olive helped sew together burial clothes that same night. The doctors seemed helpless in the matter. The sick lived or they died.

A few years later Spencer spent seven weeks in bed with what he characterized in his journal as a "light case" of typhoid.

Much ignorance prevailed about elementary sanitation. People often let drainage from outhouses and corrals seep into the open wells and ditches from which they drew their drinking water. Milk was left out and soured. Flies bred in swarms. The water bucket and dipper at public places serviced tobacco chewers, diseased people, and babies. Appendicitis was passed off as "inflammation of the bowels" and left undoctored. Disease was a dark secret. No one understood it well.

Andrew had spent twelve years in malaria country boiling his drinking water, totally unsuspicious of the bites of the annoying mosquitoes.

The mountains were a refuge. With a child near death from dysentery, parents would rush him into the cool mountains, hoping for his life. But sometimes the parents too were sick. In July 1902, while Sister Coles lay ill with typhoid fever, Olive had to tell her that her baby was dead. And two weeks later Sister Coles lost a second child.

None of this could condition Olive to the death of her own little ones. She waded with pain "through the deep river of sorrow," wrote Spencer. Years before, she had lost her first child, Maude, in infancy. In 1903 her tenth child, Mary, was born. Andrew had hoped it would have red hair and blue eyes like "Olive, my precious jewel of a wife." But this child, wrote Spencer, "stayed only long enough to get her body and her name and hurried away." Her upper jaw on the left side was crushed in. Olive's heart nearly broke. She could hardly keep up courage. The ward choir sang at the funeral, "They are treasures you've laid up in heaven." But heaven seemed so far away. As the tenth child, Mary had been the Lord's, said Andrew, and he had taken her back to himself as a tithe. Andrew spoke of Mary as his tithing child.

A month later five-year-old Fannie was taken sick. The illness dragged on, so Dr. Platt was called in. He said her heart had been damaged by inflammatory rheumatism. Painfully ill, her legs swollen, her heart fearfully weak, her breath almost smothered, Fannie suffered for weeks. On March 28 Andrew had her in a baby buggy in the front yard. She asked for a lump of dirt. He gave it to her. She ate some of it till Olive took it away. In the afternoon Fannie grew so sick she could barely breathe. She screamed and quivered with pain for hours, then died at 9:30 P.M. Spencer remembered that "on my ninth birthday Fannie died in Mother's arms. All of us children were awakened in the early night to be present. I seem to remember the scene in our living room . . . , my beloved mother weeping with her little dying five-year-old child in her arms and all of us crowding around." The horror stamped itself on his mind. "I shall never forget the anguish and pain which she was suffering. We laid her away in the cemetery on the hill in the dry gravel all alone," the third child they had buried.

Olive "broke down and mourned for her child and couldn't be comforted," wrote Andrew. He worried that it might kill her. "Death is a blessing," counseled J. Golden from Salt Lake, referring to the Church's teaching that a child who dies under eight is saved by God's

Thatcher Ariz.
Sept. 28, 1906

Dear Mamma—
Papa says for us all to write to you. How did you feel when you got to Bowie? Papa says that the ticket agent had a hard time marking a hard time marking your feet and taking the complexion of your hair. Well how does Helen feel riding on the train? When will you get in

Salt Lake? Maud asked Rachel where mama was and she said "Mama toot toot." this afternoon I got my chores done safely and went over to Curtis's they made some candy, ate so much of it it gave me the cramps but I am alright now.
    My school got the half-day-holiday for having the least tardy marks.
    We all feel sorry to have you leave

but are glad to see you have a good time give our relatives and friends my love well I guess I will go to bed good-bye your loving son
                Spencer
                        Kimball

Letter written by Spencer to his mother three weeks before her death

grace. "At least you have one child that is saved." Her friends criticized, saying she grieved more than was right, that there were things worse than death. Olive listened to such counsel in meekness. "I do not wish to grieve too much and displease my Heavenly Father," she wrote. But the despair took months to subside.

In 1906 Olive was pregnant for the twelfth time, having averaged a birth every two years for the previous twenty-four years. This time she became ill and got steadily worse. The family knew she was worn out and miserable but had no idea she was deathly ill. It was decided to send her up to Salt Lake where she could be with her own people, and then come back well and happy. It was to be like a holiday.

There were signs that Olive's sickness was dangerous. Andrew had gone with her as far as Bowie and had watched her grow sicker by the hour. Reports drifted back of her suffering on the train. Olive wrote from Salt Lake that she could not seem to gather strength, that she felt weak and faint. The letter, dated October 3, was never signed, but just trailed off down the page. George Woolley wrote to Andrew that Ollie was sick to the stomach, nauseous, discouraged. The doctor couldn't determine the cause. (The family would later learn of her utter misery at LDS Hospital in Salt Lake, far from Andrew and her family.) Andrew began talking about an operation. He wrote to Olive, "We all feel now we will take better care of Mama if she comes home soon." The dark undercurrent of death was still invisible to the family.

Spencer and his brothers and sisters fasted and prayed in the hope that their mother might recover more rapidly. Andrew went north to be with her. Spencer wrote again on October 17:

> As Clare told me to write a few lines to you, I will try. . . . Clare and Ruth are doing the house work. They have the house all cleaned but the kitchen. We are all well now. We are very lon[e]ly without you. Gordon has hauled all the corn fodder from Bro Branham's. We are very busy around here. We received the telegram and were very glad to know that mama was out of danger. . . . I think I will close for it is getting bed time. Sister Allen told us in Religion Class that we should go to bed at eight o'clock so we could have enough sleep. Now it is nearly half past eight. Good bye. Your loving Son. Spencer Kimball.

A day later Olive was dead; the baby had miscarried and infection had killed the mother.

The next morning the Kimball children, still unsuspecting, were called out of school. "We ran home, all reaching there about the same time," recalled Spencer. Dear Bishop Moody gathered them around and told them, "Your Ma is dead." "It came as a thunderbolt. I ran from the house out in the backyard to be alone in my deluge of tears. Out of sight and sound, away from everybody, I sobbed and sobbed. Each time I said the word 'Ma' fresh floods of tears gushed forth until I was drained dry. Ma — dead! But she couldn't be! Life couldn't go on for us. . . . My eleven-year-old heart seemed to burst." Fifty years later in a hospital room, unable to sleep, his mind wandered back to that day. The old pain was still there. "I feel like sobbing again now in my room in New York as my memory takes me over those sad paths."

The house was empty to Spencer. Just bricks and lumber. Five interminable days passed, all the children waiting for the train that would bring their father and their mother's body from Salt Lake. "I cried at my milking; tears blinded me at my cattle feeding; my pillow was wet at night." He missed church meeting, missed school. He was lost and empty. "How could we continue on?" he wondered. "But I found then, as I have found out many times since, that one can endure almost anything."

Joseph Robinson wrote from California: "My children wept with Minnie and I as we heard of the prayers of little Spencer and how the loss of his mother weighed so heavily upon his little heart and yet how bravely he battled with his grief and sought comfort from the only source."

The train from Salt Lake finally reached Thatcher. It was on the same double track with no station where the family had arrived eight years back. Again there was a welcome, with many people and baskets of flowers.

Olive Woolley Kimball's body lay in the parlor until the funeral. "To play was unthinkable." The house grew still as death. The children tiptoed as if afraid of waking their dead mother. ("Oh, that we might!") Spencer would slip into the parlor to gaze at her. She was so quiet. He kissed her forehead. Cold. Her mild red hair looked as always. But the blue eyes were closed.

Spencer's eleven-year world had circled around this small woman. Just home from school, "I would hang my cap on the hook by the door over the wash dish and holler, 'Ma! Ma! Ma!' But when I found her in the house and she asked what I wanted, I just said, 'Nothing.' " Nothing

Spencer Kimball (left) and Clarence Naylor

Children of Olive Kimball at the time of her death, 1906: Alice, Ruth, Rachel, Gordon, Helen, Clare, Delbert, Spencer

but to know she was home. Even a long church meeting was bearable if Mother was there. "I just liked being with Ma." Riding the buggy with her over the chuckholes up the dusty road to Layton was a holiday.

Eleanor Peterson remembered visiting Olive one Sunday afternoon. Spencer, nine or ten years old, quietly walked in and asked his mother "if he could go hayrack riding with a crowd of boys and girls. His mother put her arms around him and calmly said: 'Spencer, you know we don't allow our children to go hayrack riding on Sunday, as that is not the right thing to do. On some other day you may go.' He took it just as calmly as she had given it to him, and quietly walked away without any outward demonstration of his disappointment."

"My mother was faultless," Spencer wrote. "She was a saint . . . , the epitome of perfection." Who, he asked, "could even mention one virtue that she had not possessed?" She seemed holy "when the light would shine through her light red hair and make a halo." Young when she died, Spencer grew up remembering her as he had seen her at eleven years of age.

After lying in the parlor four days the body was taken to the chapel, where a thousand people crammed the building. Spencer remembered hundreds of them hugging him for solace and kindly patting his head. The Relief Society sisters, dressed in white, filed by the casket, each leaving a handful of white chrysanthemums on the box. There were eight speakers. They said such beautiful things about her, remembered Spencer. "Why shouldn't they!" One remark, he continued, "impressed itself upon me profoundly." It was said of her that "when others spoke in condemnation, her lips were always silent."

Sixty-five carriages followed her coffin to the cemetery, where it was lowered into the ground. Olive had often said she could not stand the thought of having rocks and gravel dumped on her casket; the sound had been painful as she had watched the dirt cover Maude and Mary and Fannie. So Andrew had Brother Fuller build a vault of bricks over the box; then the friends who had remained gently shoveled the gravel onto the bricks until the hole was filled.

Though his mother was gone, Spencer kept a place for her in his heart. His father was conscious of this. Nine years after Olive's passing, Andrew inscribed a gift copy of the Pearl of Great Price, "Andrew Kimball and Olive Woolley Kimball to Spencer Woolley Kimball, January 25, 1915." Inside the book cover Spencer attached a picture of his dear mother.

Older people who had known her would sometimes tell him he was like his mother. No compliment ever pleased him more.

4

An End to Boyhood

— "I am going to be serviceable"

When Olive died in Salt Lake City, Andrew's twin sister, Alice, comforted him. She came back with him to Arizona, tended the children, fixed their clothes, shampooed their hair on Saturday night. When she took the train back to Salt Lake three days after the funeral Andrew was left to himself. "Was terribly broken up in my feeling," he wrote. "More lonesome than ever." He plunged into his work, trying to keep the pain in control. When he broke down in the parlor a month after Olive's death, he sobbed until he was sick. Apologetically he explained in his journal, "somehow at some times I can't help it." His health sank and his stomach ulcers grew worse. "The loss by Death of my sweet wife and companion undermined my health considerable."

Four months after Olive's death he was still upset, couldn't sleep most nights. He wrote to his brothers and sisters in 1908: "I would be ashamed to complain at my lot, the Lord has been very merciful to me and notwithstanding the many trying experiences and the sorrows that have come into my life, I am able to praise His holy name and acknowledge His hand in all things, though at times I have to bring to bear upon my mind all the experiences and testimonies that I have to enable me to become so reconciled." Spencer would never forget his father walking the floor with baby Rachel in his arms, night after night. He sang to her "Come, Come Ye Flowers," over and over in his loneliness, long after she dropped asleep. When the children were in their nightgowns, Spencer remembered, his father would lead them all in exercises, to build strong bodies, he said. "But he seemed to be lonely and want us near him till the last minute when we must go to bed and leave him alone with his thoughts and memories — and loneliness."

The bottom dropped out of the household. After Aunt Alice returned to Salt Lake, Spencer's oldest sister, Clare, brought her two children and tended house for a couple of months. But finally she had to go home to her husband fifteen miles south in Artesia. So Ruth, who was two years older than Spencer, dropped out of eighth grade and tried to fill the emptiness. She cooked meals, bandaged sores, did the laundry on the washboard in a metal tub, heated the Saturday night bath water in buckets and kettles. To Spencer she was less a sister than "an angel-mother." "I idolized her."

But the family needed a mother. Clare, twenty-two, was gone; and Gordon, eighteen, and Del, sixteen, were fairly independent; but that left Ruth, thirteen, Spencer, eleven, Alice, nine, Helen, five, and Rachel, one, still too young for Andrew to take care of alone. Andrew looked about for a new wife, a woman who would take care of his children.

Josephine Cluff had long been a close friend to the family. Before she died, Olive had told Andrew that Josie was a good woman and would love his children. Heartsick with Olive's death, Andrew went through the motions of courting Josie within weeks of his wife's funeral. His heart was still so much with his dead wife that Josie wrote her sister even after she had married Andrew: "He and his wife were as one and it will take years to wear off the sting of her death. Everything about the house reminds us of her, her picture is in every room. All this only time can heal." But, she reasoned, Andrew's attachment to his first wife promised the same treatment for herself. "He was good to her — he will be good to me."

Spencer remembered his father's courting Aunt Josie. After his father had brought her home several times, he took each child aside and asked, "What would you think of my getting married again?" Spencer remembered answering, "That would be fine." Andrew went on, "You need a mother, don't you?" "Yes," said Spencer. Finally his father asked, "What would you think about Aunt Josie?" Andrew got the consent of each child before he remarried.

Josie was a unique woman for a small town like Thatcher. A divorcee with an annulment of her temple marriage, she had taken back her maiden name, packed her things, and moved herself and two children out to frontier Arizona to teach school. After twenty-two years as a schoolteacher she had served a mission from 1904 to 1906 and now worked in the stake Young Ladies MIA. A fancy dresser, a good talker, high-strung and nervous, quick at repartee, a clever and experienced actress, she was soon a favorite of many. Quieter women were quelled by her quick tongue. Jessie Killian told of attending a popular play, "East Lynn," as a little girl, with her mother and Josie. As the play became sadder and sadder, the tears began to trickle down the mother's face. Josie looked over at her and in a brisk, professional tone reminded her: "Why, Sister Ellsworth, this is only a play. Look how well they're doing." Jessie's mother dried her tears in a hurry.

A woman of such aristocratic tastes and sharp opinions would not be easy to get used to after a gentle and soft-spoken mother. To change his mother for another woman was hard, but any criticisms Spencer had, he carefully suppressed out of a characteristic refusal to speak badly of others. And to a mother, even a stepmother, special loyalty was due. On his mission some years later, Spencer would be quizzed about his stepmother. Wasn't she unkind to him, wasn't she a "typical" stepmother? "I always said, No," he explained, because "it would be unfair to her" to emphasize the hard things and forget the good. "She was a wonderful woman, a wonderful mother, and she took good care of us. A good Latter-day Saint." At forty-seven, Josie was the same age as Olive, but it was not easy to take over a family of seven children at home. No woman would lightly take on such a task; it was a Christian service she could render. She did not expect or ask that it be easy, and it was not. It helped somewhat that the man she married was highly respected in the community.

What to call her posed a problem. Spencer and the younger girls used "Mother," since Olive had always been "Ma" and no one could ever be that to them again. So the adjustment was made. Spencer made the best of his situation. He found there were things about this new mother he could prefer even to his real one. She kept an immaculate house, made excellent head cheese, and cooked a delicious pot of beans.

Andrew Kimball home in Thatcher, Arizona, 1907: Andrew and Josephine Kimball seated center, Spencer (12) on the right

In June 1907 after Andrew and Josephine, with a party of friends
going to MIA conference, took the train for Salt Lake City to be
married in the temple, two-year-old Rachel grew violently sick of
diphtheria. "I want to sob again," wrote Spencer, years later, "as I see
little Rachel struggling for breath." Nothing helped the suffering
child. The doctor's care was useless. While Gordon held his dying
sister, Spencer and the others stood looking on in awe and terror.
Gordon's teenage diary laconically noted: "I got up at 3 o'clock and
took the water. Rachel got worse. I had to run around for the Dr. and
etc. She died at twenty minutes to twelve. I didn't do much in the
afternoon."

A telegram brought Andrew and Josephine hurrying back to
Arizona. It was a sad beginning to a marriage. The body of the little
child lay in the Kimball home. It was not even taken to the funeral
service at the chapel for fear of spreading what the local paper called a
"Mysterious and Dreaded Disease." Andrew, who had nicknamed her
"Ray," buried his little sunshine in the gravel hill with her sisters and
her mother.

This sorrow, too, passed. Spencer grew into adolescence. He was
proud when he began to do a man's work, when his father and brothers
trusted him to mow the hay, when he was kept home from school
occasionally to irrigate or harvest. Just tromping hay and running
errands wasn't dignified any more.

Because of Spencer's size and age, Andrew often kept him in when
the other boys worked the farm. Andrew maintained a huge volume of
correspondence — replies to men who wrote from Kentucky or Maine
or Idaho asking what Arizona was like and whether they should move
there, letters to Salt Lake City on Church business, reminders to
insurance clients, exchanges of letters with relatives, messages for
politicians in Phoenix or Washington. He averaged half a dozen letters
a day. By the time Spencer turned ten Andrew had set him to taking
dictation longhand, then copying it over on the typewriter to be mailed.
Spencer enjoyed working with his father. He devised symbols for
common phrases, a homespun shorthand good enough to let him keep
up with the rapid dictation. He did the typing with two fingers. With
practice he developed good speed. Andrew paid for a few lessons from

Miss Freestone in Safford, but Spencer's two-finger habit stuck. He learned a good deal about his father's varied affairs. He took pride in efficiency, in doing the job his father entrusted to him.

As Gordon left on his mission and Del left home to be on his own, Spencer took over their chores. He now had full charge of the cows and horses and pigs and tended the crops and fruit trees with his father. But it all took some learning. Once Andrew asked him to dam off with a nearby pile of pulverized manure an irrigation ditch running into the orchard. After his father left, Spencer went to work shoveling the manure dust into the water. But the faster he shoveled, the faster the manure floated downstream toward the orchard. Spencer ran and found some boards and stakes, pounded them into the muddy ditch for a dam, then piled the manure dust on top. About then Andrew walked over, saw the dam, and complained at Spencer's literal-mindedness. Damming the ditch had been a figurative request. What he wanted was to fertilize the orchard by letting the manure float down the channel and around the tree roots.

One day the sheriff stopped by the house with news that one of Spencer's schoolmates had been discovered with a cache of stolen buggy robes and whips under his front porch. Spencer was aghast. They called the boy a kleptomaniac. But seventy years later Spencer called it "a pitiable weakness to steal."

Spencer watched other boys steal watermelons from neighbors' patches, or — just out of sheer orneriness — take knives and slash fifty melons open to rot, and then run. Spencer kept clear of that sort of "fun." It wasn't fair, he thought. Any farmer in Thatcher, if you asked him, would give you all the melon your belly could hold. On Halloween night some of the boys turned privies upside down or hoisted them on top of sheds, lifted buggies onto roofs, carried away gates, marked windows. But Spencer did not join in. He saw it done, but he wouldn't lift a hand to help.

At twelve — the year he was baptized a second time — Spencer was ordained a deacon. Later he became president of his quorum. He and the other deacons sat on the front pew at meetings waiting to pass the sacrament, slightly unruly and inconveniently noisy. They passed the sacrament with a brand new ninety-dollar set of silver plates and goblets. Because the entire congregation drank from the common goblets, the more fastidious members would twist the cup so their lips touched the rim by one of the two handles. But this supposedly un-touched spot quickly became the most used part of the cup's rim, or so it seemed to the amused deacons.

One time at Monday night deacons meeting Spencer playfully put his hand in Charlie McDonald's shirt collar, pulling it tight. Charlie, playing tough, refused to rise to the bait. He blacked out and slumped down, frightening Spencer half out of his wits.

In spite of the fidgeting, Spencer took his priesthood seriously. He did the work assigned him and, except in real emergencies, never missed a meeting. Deacons quorum minutes show entries in 1909 in Spencer's neat, clear, strong hand, signed as assistant secretary. On June 20 attendance was thirteen, an increase of one; "The Priesthood Meetings were discontinued during the Summer." The next entry was on October 3: "There were 12 Deacons present, a decrease of 1 as compared to the previous meeting." His minutes are more informative than most.

As part of their job, the deacons hitched up horse and buggy each month before fast day and went house-to-house collecting offerings for the poor of the Church. Afterwards they took their gatherings to the bishop — bottles of fruit, flour, squash, honey, occasionally a half-dollar or so in loose change. So eager was Andrew to teach his boy his duty that nothing else interfered with Spencer's collection on that day. The Kimball horse and buggy was never too busy to be used for deacons quorum work. If the other boy assigned to collect with him didn't show up, Spencer went out alone and got the job done.

When Spencer was fourteen, as he left Sunday School class one Sunday he was stopped by the superintendent. He expected a scolding for teasing the girls and pulling their hair in class. Much to his surprise, the man asked him to teach a Sunday School class. Of course he agreed to do it. At fifteen Spencer was called as stake chorister.

About this time, Spencer heard Brigham Young's daughter, Susa Gates, speak at stake conference. She asked how many in the congregation of a thousand had ever read the Holy Bible, cover to cover. Spencer, with everyone else in the hall, craned about to see who had. Only five or six hands went up. So Susa Gates urged the people to go home and begin. The meeting over, Spencer walked the block home, took down the family Bible, climbed the stairs to his attic room, lit the coal-oil lamp with a match, and began at Genesis. Night after night, by the flickering light of a kerosene lamp in the unfinished attic where he slept, and which his imagination sometimes peopled with ghosts and robbers, he plowed through the pages. At some points Spencer had only half an idea what he was reading, but he had made up his mind. It did not matter if long stretches were boring; he plodded on. He was sure it was a worthwhile project. At least he would have some idea what the Bible contained. He kept at it for about a year until he could shut the book with great pride, finished. The experience built his confidence. He had learned he could count on his own resolution.

Spencer grew self-conscious about his plain clothes. It seemed to him he was the only boy still in overalls, instead of trousers. He still wore stogies, a coarse heavy clodhopper which, his parents assured him, would outwear the more modish styles. "Sitting in class, I would often push my feet far back under the seat, as I did not want my stogies contrasting with the fancy shoes of others." When he became old enough to date, he would tidy up his clothes and black his shoes with soot from under the lid on the wood stove. He borrowed his father's old felt hat lined with red silk and wore that. "I knew it was too large. I was sensitive about it, but it was that or nothing. I wore it just the same."

Spencer had some skills other boys did not. He played the piano.

Spencer's history as a pianist dates back to about two dozen lessons as a child. Even though Andrew made do with old wire and used staples on the farm in order to economize, he had bought a piano, one of the first in the valley, announcing that the children were to learn to play. Spencer, with great enthusiasm, went to Miss Ella Heywood for his first lesson. "My fingers were short and chubby," he remembered, "and chappy with marble playing, but my father still had high hopes." Piano playing didn't look so good after a couple of weeks, however, and Spencer's career at the keyboard might have ended except for his father's persistence. He excused Spencer from hotter, "more onerous" jobs to practice music in the cool parlor. With that incentive Spencer plugged away at it. "My brothers," he admitted, "accused me of always wanting to practice when it was hottest and when there was ditch-digging, plowing or weed-pulling to do. They were not far wrong." Del and Gordon teased their younger brother that his memory was perfect: every time he went through a piece he remembered the same mistakes he had made the time before. But despite his father's urging, Spencer soon stopped lessons, starting and stopping again several times in the years to follow.

At fourteen Spencer had only a few formal lessons behind him, but he learned to chord the music and picked up the popular songs quickly off sheet music he bought for ten cents a sheet in the drugstore. His friend Charlie McDonald played the cornet, Joe McDonald played the violin, and Leslie Clawson the bass fiddle. They formed an orchestra and asked Spencer to join them as pianist. "I did not do it well, but they kept me," he recalled. Generally they had a job every weekend. Their take was ten dollars, which they split between them. Sometimes they were hired at Brier Hall in Safford, a strictly gentile dance-place, where Spencer would not have gone to dance.

As Andrew travelled about the St. Joseph Stake, with five thousand members and a growing number of branches scattered over two hundred miles of Arizona and New Mexico desert, he often took one or two of his children with him in the buggy. On one occasion, when Spencer was thirteen, he rode to Lebanon with his father and his older sister Ruth and her friend. On the way home Spencer and the girls discussed "a crazy woman" in the Lebanon Ward. "Don't call her that," said Andrew. "Speak of her as that unfortunate woman." So they did. And when they were caught in a flash flood and had to wait for the washes to subside, that was also "unfortunate" to Spencer and the two girls. Everything that day was "unfortunate" to the three of them. They giggled all the way home.

Spencer took another trip with Andrew, this time to St. David, ninety miles south. They stayed with Spencer's cousin Crozier Kimball. Crozier's boy Edwin (Eddie) remembered the visit many years later. His mother set seven or eight tables for the many guests who attended the conference in St. David. Only Spencer, aside from her own children, helped her with the dishes. When one of the children was cut in playing "duck on the rock" or "run sheep run," Spencer was the first to run in the house for peroxide or iodine. On Monday morning before Andrew and his nephew went to call on one of the other members of the bishopric, Andrew told Spencer to pack the suitcases and be ready to leave by the time he returned. Respectful of his instructions, Spencer told his aunt and cousins that he must pack right away and could visit more when that was done. His aunt helped him pack and they carried the bags to the front gate, then visited. After Andrew had returned and left with Spencer in the buggy, Edwin's mother put her arm around Edwin's shoulder and said: "Spencer is certainly a wonderful young

*Spencer, graduating from
eighth grade in 1910*

man. Someday he will be one of the apostles." Because Edwin believed
his mother had the gift of prophecy, he remembered the incident.

In 1910, as Spencer finished eighth grade, he began thinking
about the LDS Academy in Thatcher. It was a big building, two stories
high, and a bit frightening. As grade-school graduation neared,
everyone asked everyone else, "Are you going on to the Academy?"
Most were not. Some of them intended to marry, some to work, some
hadn't the money to go on. But Spencer and a few others "bravely
determined to continue our training into high school."

The school had seen some rough times. Operated on a shoestring,
it had stumbled on from year to year; no one was ever quite sure if it
would reopen the next fall. William Johnson, in stake conference in
1890, had complained that more saloons were operating among the
Saints than schools. Five years later, with the Academy still on the verge
of collapse, Johnson had wished the bishops would kick every man out
of the Church who fought against the school. At stake conference,

George Cluff tried to shame the members into active support, speaking of widows who slaved all day for four bits and then gave it to the Academy to educate their children. But sermons did not turn up hard cash or students, and two years before Andrew took over as stake president the school had closed its doors.

As soon as he assumed responsibility for the Academy, Andrew hired a Utah man as principal for nine hundred dollars a year, sent out the school board members to scour the valley and all of "Mormon" Arizona for recruits, then reopened the school. In 1902 he established a procedure that each congregation send either 3 percent of its members as students or else pay the equivalent tuition anyway. Classes were patched together and the school was kept running for thirty weeks a year, so that by 1910, with the valley growing and interest in schooling picking up, the Academy was healthy once more.

The Academy was a bigger "pond" than grade school. "I was very much frightened at first," remembered Spencer, "in this sophisticated place." He was close to being the youngest student in the building. And then there were many strangers from all over the valley, even from other parts of the state. It seemed strange to have a different teacher for each subject. Even German was taught here.

Two weeks after school started, the fifty-six members of the freshman class held a meeting to elect a president. As a chairman called the meeting to order, one flustered Thatcher girl began, "Mr. Chairman, I make an emotion that we elect Spencer Kimball as our class president." Than Urilda Moody shouted, "Mr. Chairman, I close the ballot." Since no one else was sure what to do, Spencer became president. Thirty years later Ella Lee, a classmate, joked about how he got himself reelected each of the three remaining years. "At the beginning of each school year, he would tell us how unwise it would be to change horses in the middle of the stream and how he had everything under control, and each year he was reelected president."

Spencer's post as class president was mostly honorary. But when the Academy sponsored a "Nationality Ball" Spencer wrote in his journal, "Being a President of Class, I had a great responsibility." His class dressed for the ball as Indians. Class meetings he conducted according to Roberts' Rules of Order. When Addie Bryce, a class member, died, Spencer was asked to speak at her funeral for the class. "I was a frightened boy," he recalled, "and about all I could say was that

Addie was a fine girl and I repeated it over and over with variations and was much embarrassed."

Spencer found the Academy teachers "most lenient in their grading for I received but one B in the four years, all the other marks were A's." In chemistry, "our first escapade was to make H_2S or 'rotten eggs.' The fumes were so strong on the upper floor that school had to be dismissed. We were not in good favor just then." He earned his lone B in chemistry.

When his physical geography class went to the mountains on a field trip, Spencer and some of the boys borrowed an old surrey. On the rough road a spring broke. At a meeting of the class the next day, Spencer, as class president, said that the spring had to be paid for. When no one volunteered, he said, "That spring's going to be paid for if I have to do it myself." Finally two other boys offered to help, and the three paid for the broken spring.

There were lots of parties in Thatcher, usually given by the girls. The parties almost always included a few kissing games. "I never was at home with them," complained Spencer. They made him feel awkward, and he wished the girls would pick "more dignified games." But he still played them.

Spencer showed a neighbor boy, Walter Harms, how to milk, then paid him a nickel to milk the Kimballs' cows on Sunday evenings so Spencer could stay with his friends. He was a universal favorite. At class parties, remembers Laura Blake, "he always kept us laughing." "I don't believe I've ever heard a laugh that was so musical."

After the group had played "the silly games," someone would usually suggest, "Let's sing." So someone would say, "Priscilla, play the piano for us." Priscilla would answer, "Oh, I haven't my music with me." Then someone would say, "Bessie, you play." "Oh, I can't play without my music." "Well, Ella, you play." "Oh, I can't play. I haven't practiced for so long." So the crowd would end up singing a cappella. Finally Spencer, out of patience, made up his mind that he "was going to be serviceable," even though the girls "could play a hundred times better than I." He began memorizing bass chords in different keys, then practiced picking out the melody line with his right hand, until he could play tolerably well by ear. "When we'd come to the parties after I got a little bit proficient," he recalled, "they wouldn't even ask the girls anymore. They said, 'Spencer, you play.' So I'd play and they'd all sing. I sang as lustily as any of them."

Spencer's father sometimes insisted he take Alice, who was two years younger, to his parties. "That was a great trial to me those sensitive years when a young person is so anxious to conform to what others think is proper." But he did as asked. To disobey Father was unthought of.

That year, when two of Spencer's crowd were married, they invited all their Gila Valley friends to the wedding. After it was over, Spencer joined the other boys in a shivaree. The point was to dump the groom in the canal or to provide the newlyweds with unwanted company for their entire wedding night. But the bride and groom escaped together. The boys tracked them down and found them huddled in the corner of a shed. Spencer was startled by the bride's frightened look. "I made up my mind that that kind of business was not for me. Marriage was too sacred."

On holidays the group rode into the desert for a corn roast or a watermelon bust, or up a canyon on hayracks for a swim or picnic. There was one cold dip in an icy pond high in the mountains with some other boys, just to prove to each other that they had the nerve to do it.

The lumber flume was the most popular thrill. Constructed of two-by-twelve boards, shaped like a watering trough, it snaked eight miles down the side of Mount Graham on trestles, bringing lumber into the valley from sawmills high in the mountains. To ride it a person sat on a board in the icy water that streamed down the flume; then, when the water dammed up against his back, he shot down the steep mountain like a bullet until the grade levelled enough so he could get off.

Sometimes Spencer would spend an afternoon with just Iretta and Grace Layton and Ella Tyler. Spencer and the three girls would walk from one house to another's, talking, laughing, and eating whatever they could find. When he dated, it was with any one of these girls. "I went out with him some," recalled Ella. "He tried us all." One Friday at midnight, the dance just over, Spencer took Ella home and the two of them stood outside her house, leaning against the warm chimney bricks. It seemed they had only been there a short while when the clock struck two. Spencer, astonished, scurried home and Ella sneaked inside, upstairs and into bed. Next morning Ella suspiciously asked what was wrong with the clock. "Nothing," said Mrs. Tyler. "I just put it ahead so you kids wouldn't stand outside any longer." Spencer thought that a good joke.

At a dance after Christmas vacation, in Spencer's senior year, he met Lucille, a petite girl from Utah, who had lots of big-city charm. For three months Spencer courted her avidly. But at the end of the term she went home to Utah. Sixty years later, in Salt Lake City, someone pointed Lucille out to Spencer. He asked the old lady whether she remembered him. The memories of so long ago were hard to resurrect. She replied, "Yes, vaguely." When he got home he told Camilla teasingly of the meeting, patted her on the knee and said, "Well, Mama, I'm glad I married you, after all."

In athletics Spencer discovered that he could do as many muscle grinders as anyone, could hold his own in tennis and baseball with his quickness and grit, and could star in basketball. In 1912 the St. Joseph Stake boys rode the train into Mesa to compete against the LDS boys of Maricopa Stake. On the first day in town the Thatcher team was beaten at basketball by Tempe. On the second day they lost to Mesa. On the fourth day Tempe High School defeated them. On their sixth day they were crushed at baseball and placed last in a track meet.

At the track meet in Mesa Spencer earned himself a mild fame. After most of the other events had been lost by the Thatcher team, the mile run came up. Dudley Jones, their coach, looked the boys over and, to his dismay, found them exhausted. Spencer, not a fast enough runner to compete in the sprints, was the only one still chipper. "Spencer," announced Jones, "I guess we'll let you run the mile."

Naively confident, Spencer pranced forward and took his place on the line, outfitted in overalls and tennis shoes.

> The signal was given and away I went. I tried to keep up with those who had trained, and I did fairly well until my wind began to be lost and they sprinted on ahead of me. My loyalty would have taken me to my death, I think, if the mile hadn't finally terminated. I'd rather die than quit or fail my stake. I ran on and on — would it never end? Finally all seemed to blur and on the home stretch all I could see was a large crowd of people with waving arms and a melee of noise and shouting. I fell across the line. My good friends patted me on the back anyway. One person commiserating with me said: "Well, Spencer, you came in third anyway." Of course, I knew that there were only three of us running.

At the time, he recorded the event in his journal: "Mr. Jones had no one to enter to run so he put me in. I ran mile race and did the best I could. Came out 3rd close behind 2nd man but there were only 3 of us running. Ha!! It nearly did me up as I was not used to running so far."

By 1913 their basketball team had improved. They bought their own basketballs and their own dollar rubber shoes and moved off their outdoor gravel court into the chapel basement, where they learned to shoot the ball low enough to miss the overhanging support timbers. They dubbed their tiny gymnasium "the cracker-box." Spencer played forward. Though he was the smallest, youngest-looking boy in his class, he was quick, a good shot, and enthusiastic. His own memory was that "I played basketball always as a star."

One of their first games was with "some little high school spindlings" from Globe. Cocky with assurance, Spencer and the rest of the team crushed their visitors. Noting the game in his journal, eighteen-year-old Spencer wrote: "After we got the score to about 40 to 10 we began playing with them. We would miss the basket purposely, throw it to them accidentally, etc." They also "skunked" the Safford team, which "couldn't figure out what was going on."

When the Thatcher team lost, remembered Spencer, "like most teams we had a good alibi." The game against Mesa, he claimed in his journal, "would have been tied at 28-28 but Mr. Jones accidentally blew the whistle just as I threw the last basket and consequently it did not count." Then a 42-14 loss in 1913 to the Clifton team was "not so much because of their superiority in playing BB but because of their being used to the floor and had suction soles. They could stop where we would slide."

Away games demanded an expedition. One boy would borrow one horse, another the second; then they would hire a hack from the livery stable, and set off together. When they reached the town where they were to play, the rival team would put them up until after the game.

For a while everything else took second place to basketball. Even Aunt Josie's hot beans after school. Even his chores. Spencer would practice with the team in the afternoon, on and on, as the time approached for him to milk the cows. "I seemed to forget time when I was playing." It always seemed he could shoot just one more basket and still make it home in time. Finally, when his conscience had gotten the better of him, he would run home to face a bench of neighbor boys waiting for the milk he would sell them. He could also expect a scolding from "a justifiably aggravated mother. It happened so many times."

That winter Dudley Jones, the Academy's basketball coach, challenged the University of Arizona to play them in Thatcher. The boys advertised the game all across town. The university team arrived in Thatcher with their noses in the air, certain it was a great condescension to play a mere high school team. Spencer wrote his memory of the game years later:

> It is a great occasion. Many people came tonight who have never been before. Some of the townsmen say basketball is a girl's game but they came in large numbers tonight. Our court is not quite regulation. We are used to it, our opponents not. I have special luck with my shots tonight and the ball goes through the hoop again and again and the game ends with our High School team the victors against the college team. I am the smallest one and the youngest on the team. I have piled up the most points through the efforts of the whole team protecting me and feeding the ball to me. I am on the shoulders of the big fellows of the Academy. They are parading me around the hall to my consternation and embarrassment. I like basketball. I would rather play this game than eat.

The college team would not play a second time in the crackerbox, and the next night won against the Academy on the larger floor at Pima, but nothing could take away the thrill of that first victory.

On the last day of March in 1914, Spencer's senior year, A.C. Peterson, principal of the Academy, stood before the students in assembly and pugnaciously warned them: "We have had some pretty raw things pulled off here in the school on April Fool's Day, but I want to tell you that's passed. We've outgrown such nonsense and it will not be tolerated. We hold school tomorrow as usual." Peterson's sternness almost made his announcement a challenge. At the conclusion of the assembly Spencer and a few other boys decided to take the dare. They huddled just outside the door of the study hall and "winked the boys out one by one, told them of the plans, pledged them to secrecy."

The next morning hardly a boy showed up for school. "The assembly looked like a girls' school," remembered one of the girls. The boys had gone up the mountain in hayracks with lunches to ride the flume all day. Andrew Peterson took the podium, looked down at his assembly of girls, and burned red hot. He expelled the boys, cancelled their sports trip to Tucson, ruled out graduation that year for senior boys, and demanded an apology if any of them expected ever to set foot

*LDS Academy basketball team (1912-1913): Oscar Jesperson,
Howard Blazzard, Leo Mortensen, Frank Martineau,
Ernest Haws, Spencer Kimball; (seated) coach Dudley Jones
and James Smith*

*High School boys expelled for April Fool's prank, 1914,
Spencer standing second from left*

in school again. Then he dismissed school and allowed the girls to picnic on condition they not go to the canyon where the boys were.

The next day, when the boys showed up for class, they were ordered off the grounds, expelled pending a hearing before the faculty in the afternoon. They left in a bunch, wandered around, finally ended up down by the old livery stable, where thirty-two of them posed for a group photograph in front of a huge Bull Durham tobacco sign. "That Bull Durham background was evidence of bedlam and revolution," joked Spencer, later.

The boys drifted down to the weeping mulberry tree by the Kimballs' front gate. They sat on the front lawn and argued their case. "Sometimes we were about ready to 'take the rap' and return and apologize," Spencer remembered, but "then our haughty pride negated that." The senior girls reinforced their stubbornness, vowing that unless the boys graduated, the girls would not either. Finally John Nash, a teacher, walked up. He took Spencer, the student body president and ringleader, aside and said: "Spencer, you've had your fun. Now go and beg forgiveness. Take your medicine and come back to school." The boys talked it over and finally agreed to give in. They went to the school building, apologized in a faculty hearing, and were admitted back to school on condition that they all publicly apologize next day in assembly and sign a paper promising never to repeat the offense.

Spencer was left with mixed feelings. Though he had good-naturedly put an end to the squabble by giving in to the faculty, still he wasn't happy with all the fuss they had made over what seemed a harmless prank. In his journal he commented a bit sarcastically, "We were *good* children for a while." Though he would later write of his part in the prank as being "to my shame, I suppose," he would take pleasure in telling the story to his children and grandchildren.

A graduating class often makes a gift to the school. In Spencer's class, twenty-one remained of the fifty-six who began high school. The survivors, full of self-confidence, decided to erect a pillar in front of the building on which they would mount a plaque containing their names. Ralph Bilby, a prominent Arizona attorney, recalled at the class's sixty-first reunion: "I remember when we graduated we were so cocksure some of us were going to become famous we built our own monument and erected it out front. It took us a long while, but we made it." Jesse Udall, Arizona Supreme Court justice, added, "I doubted the advisability then of us having a monument put up here and our names inscribed in granite, but after I've seen how important we are I've kind of concluded it was the right thing to do." Spencer's name, as class and school president, headed the list.

In 1914 Spencer went to graduation exercises, thinking that fall would find him at the University of Arizona along with a few others of his class. As part of the graduation exercises he gave a speech as class president, sang in a quartet, and sang a baritone solo, "The Plains of Peace." Andrew Kimball, president of the board, delivered an address. In the course of it he announced that Spencer would not be in college next fall; he would be on a mission. Lela Udall, a classmate, remembered: "I thought Spencer was going to pass out." Spencer, in his journal, expressed the shock more mildly: "Father informed me in these exercises before all the people that I was to be called on a mission. This took me by surprise for I had been planning to go to college." But he would do it. He had no objection to the idea of a mission; it had just come unexpectedly.

Four days after graduation he was at work in Globe, eighty miles west. His job had already been arranged. Two summers back his father, hard-pressed financially, had helped him find a job with the Anderson-Blake Dairy at $47.50 a month plus meals and a bunk. The second and third summers he earned $62.50 a month at a different Globe dairy. Except for tithing and an occasional five-cent ice cream or chocolate bar — "once in a while I would indulge myself" — Spencer had saved his whole wage to pay for books, clothes, and pocket money at Gila Academy through the winter. Now the money would go for his mission.

Spencer described life at the dairy:

> June 22. Nothing extraordinary happened. Same work each day. Arise at 8 a.m. Eat breakfast. String from 30-40 bales of hay around the mangers and remove wires therefrom. Help wash about 300 bottles. 10 a.m. help yoke up the cows. 10:30 milk till 12 m. when I turn separator and feed calves. Clean the refuse hay out of the mangers. Dinner at 12:45. Sweep up boards in barn and clean up waste hay. Rest. 5 p.m. Help wash bottles again. Saw wood, put separator and strainers together. Milk again from 11 p.-2 a.m.

*Spencer butchering hog,
Thatcher, Arizona*

*Spencer (front center) as
dairy hand, Globe, Arizona, 1914*

It was tough work. The scalding water he and the other boys used to wash the milk cans made their fingers tender. As soon as he would start to milk his two dozen cows, morning or night, the pressure on his tender fingers would split the flesh. They swelled and cracked until the blood would ooze out. "I could have cried many a time," he remembered. Some of the boys' fingers got so sore their fingernails fell off and their forearms swelled. Some of the cows' udders seemed so hard, Spencer remembered, that "it was almost like getting milk out of iron bars." When he would walk into town for Sunday School with some of the other boys, their fingers would throb so badly they would hold them over their heads to help the blood drain out. "I always made the joke," said Spencer, "that we supposed people who saw us thought we were giving up, surrendering. But of course, we put our cracked and bleeding hands in our pockets if we passed anyone."

Globe gave Spencer a first major exposure to the gentile world. He reacted to it with characteristic adaptability but lack of interest in its lures. There were also a few Mormons in Globe. He got acquainted with Paul Talmage, son of the apostle James E. Talmage. There were a number of Gila Valley girls in Globe, married to nonmembers and inactive in the Church. Week after week Spencer and Ben Blake were about the only young men available to administer and pass the sacrament.

Spencer's non-Mormon boss this summer always had a cigar in his mouth. One of his buddies at work, Clell Haynie, smoked and stayed away from church. But George Lee was a returned missionary. Two tough boys also worked there. One of them cracked George over the head with a metal nut slung in a handkerchief. Spencer found George bleeding badly. The other boys were fired, remembered Spencer with satisfaction, and "we then had total peace."

Occasionally Spencer went along with George to help him deliver milk. Globe was a wide-open mining town. Its red-light district, one of the dairy's best areas, made Spencer uneasy; he followed George there no oftener than he had to.

Through the summer Spencer's prospective mission occupied him. When he could, he studied. His father ordained him a priest on a visit to Globe. Spencer and George took long walks in the hills. George told stories from his own mission and sometimes "suggested that we pray and we knelt down in the sand and poured out our heart to our Maker in thanks."

Spencer's mission was on his father's mind as well. The four older children had all left home and Andrew had come to depend on Spencer. Andrew had shed more than a few tears. He wrote: "Well, dear boy, I am lonesome without you and to think of being without my boy for a long time yet makes me feel very peculiar at times. Our letting Alice go to Utah and you away is too much at one time in the face of unfavorable conditions that exist at times, as you know. But I work it off. All I can do is just keep pitching in and drowning my feelings. Work, work, is the greatest thing in the world."

The summer ended. Before Spencer left the dairy, his boss, Louis Walliman, a cigar-smoking non-Mormon, put on a farewell party for him at which they gave him an engraved gold watch worth a month's pay. Though most were not Mormons, all the dairy boys attended. Spencer was touched that "these strangers, non-members, would do so much for me."

When Spencer's train pulled into Thatcher from Globe, he found a crowd of friends to greet him. They had scheduled picnics and parties for the time until he left for his mission. At a dance in the Snow's barn he was introduced to a pretty blonde girl, new in the valley, Camilla Eyring. "But the dance was over," he recalled, "before I even got around to dancing with all the old girl friends, and she disappeared from view."

In October, when Spencer left for his mission, with a large crowd waving goodbye at the train stop, his boyhood ended. On his return from his mission, many of that crowd would be married and gone. His life in Thatcher would never be the same as before.

5

A Mission and Camilla

— "Popular Young Couple Married"

While milking cows back in May 1914, a week after the surprise announcement at graduation, Spencer had received his letter from Box B, Salt Lake City, calling him to proselyte in the Swiss-German Mission. The letter, signed by Joseph F. Smith, sixth President of the Church, stated he should leave in October. Europe was an exotic, exciting prospect. The German that Spencer had studied at the Academy would give him a head start on learning the language.

Then in July the situation in Europe changed drastically. A Serbian student assassinated Archduke Francis Ferdinand, heir to the throne of Austria-Hungary. On July 28 Austria-Hungary declared war on Serbia. The conflict quickly spread to Germany, Russia, France, Belgium and Britain.

Because of the European war Spencer's missionary assignment was switched to the Central States Mission, whose headquarters were in Independence, Missouri. He felt disappointed. But he reconciled himself to the change; this had been his father's mission area and his stepmother's and his brother Gordon's. As the train crossed the Arizona and California deserts into Nevada and Utah, Spencer, a newly ordained elder, looked ahead with apprehension at the pending changes in his life, but with curiosity and excitement as well.

Since missionaries or their families paid their mission expenses, Spencer had sold his spirited young black horse for $175, enough money to keep him for six months. To that he added his wages at the dairy. What money he still lacked, his father added. But these arrangements didn't make for luxurious living. He and Lawrence Holladay packed along a two-day lunch for the long, cold train trip to Salt Lake. All Spencer had to keep him warm through his mission was an old overcoat.

In Salt Lake City he stayed with relatives while he received his endowments at the Temple, was ordained a seventy by Uncle J. Golden Kimball of the First Council of the Seventy, and sat in general conference at the Tabernacle where his uncle, Joseph F. Smith, President of the Church, presided. He was welcome wherever he stayed. To little four-year-old Thelma Woolley, Spencer was a favorite cousin, not too old to play hide-and-seek in the big poplars bordering the house or to play the piano at request. She asked for one song over and over:

> And the little ol' Ford, it rambles right along,
> Now cut that out, you naughty tease!
> It's a left-hand turn and a right-hand squeeze.

She asked for the song again the day he came back, set apart as a missionary. Spencer refused. "Oh, no. Not that song, Thelma. I have to put things like that out of my mind. I'm a missionary now."

Spencer boarded the train and made his way to Independence. There he cut sod, installed seats and scraped windows for the new chapel, soon to be dedicated by President Smith. A month later he was assigned a companion; the two missionaries were put on the eastbound train and told to eat and sleep in the homes they tracted. They sat up that night on the train and got off early Thanksgiving morning in Jefferson City, Missouri, tired and hungry.

Spencer's companion, a red-faced, red-haired Canadian, ten years his senior, seemed to Spencer to be stubborn. The two didn't even look as if they went together: the companion, angular and lanky, towered over Spencer, who wore an oversized, family hand-me-down overcoat and a derby.

Spencer at time of high school graduation, 1914

Departure for Central States Mission, 1914

They set off down the road out of Jefferson City, knocking on every door, hauling their suitcases crammed with tracts and books, having no breakfast, no dinner, and just store crackers for lunch. At dark, exhausted and feeling starved, they began to ask for a place to stay. "Sorry," was the usual answer, "we can't fit you in." They marched on till about midnight, when they caught sight of a light back through the trees. Not even an "ominous pack" of "huge vicious dogs" guarding the house, Spencer later remembered, could frighten the tired missionaries from knocking at the door. A gruff, unfriendly man answered the door, finally let them in, showed them to an attic bed, and left them. Despite the bedbugs, Spencer and his lanky companion sank into sleep on the lumpy bed, the heavy quilt stiff as a board. They woke in the morning covered with bug bites, the bed spotted with blood. Their host, as if to restore their loss, served breakfast of blood pudding.

Fifty years later, an encounter with mosquitoes or fleas or bedbugs would still send Spencer's mind traveling back to the small, frame shacks in those dark woods in the Missouri Ozarks. He would recall also the night when they preached in a schoolhouse in a clearing in the woods. As the proselyting meeting closed, Elder Kimball timidly asked for a place to stay. They got an offer and in silence followed the man with his wife and six children down an endless trail between black, overhanging trees, shadows looming on either side from the man's lantern, as they stumbled darkly through puddles. Finally, after miles and miles, it seemed, they were shown into a one-room shack. The children disappeared one by one into a dark attic hole in the ceiling; then the mother went up. The father, pointing at the one bed, said to the elders, "That is yours." The man and his son shared a narrow cot.

In daylight the next morning the two missionaries could joke about their hard night. To young Elder Kimball it had seemed like a battle in the Great European War against a whole army of bedbugs foraging for new blood, missionary blood. But he remained awed by the impoverished backwoods family which had treated him "like a Prince."

His early letters home sounded a note of discouragement. He was enthusiastic about proselyting, but as a junior companion he was subject to his partner, who "tried my soul," he remembered later, "because I wanted to work, and found it difficult to work without him, and was unable to stimulate him, he being the senior companion."

There was another source of dissatisfaction at first.

I wanted to be very honest with myself and with the program and with the Lord. For a time I couched my words carefully to try to build up others without actually committing myself to a positive, unequivocal statement that *I knew.* When I approached a positive declaration it frightened me, and yet when I was wholly in tune and spiritually inspired, I wanted to so testify. I thought I was being honest, very honest, but finally decided that I was fooling myself to be reticent when the spirit moved me.

Additionally there was the discouragement of too little success in proselyting. Andrew wrote with encouragement and some practical advice:

Thatcher, Arizona
12/5/14

Elder Spencer W. Kimball
My Dear Spencer,

I read your letter to the family with considerable interest. After you get into your work more fully you will only write achievements. Many of those hard knocks will fade away as you get the sweeter experiences. . . . family news . . . I have just ordered the Guardian for you with our conference news in it. A very interesting issue. I have Bro. Brown here from Globe, the Book of Mormon man from Roosevelt. He is waiting for his call for a mission, is helping me work. The girls are busy at school and well. Mother is working hard as you may imagine. I have rented the 10 acres to Lee and will hire him to do irrigating and help about here. We killed a pig and put him away. You would enjoy some of Mother's good sausage, I am sure. I traded one little pig for a Christmas turkey and sold another two. I will keep four. Dry stock in 10 acres, two cows doing well. We had heavy rain and a cold spell, settled now. . . . I am pleased with your game spirit. You will make good, Spencer. You are small in stature — so was your sweet mother — but big natured and whole souled. You will make good, my boy. Your hard experiences will enable you to know just a little of what it costs to be a Latter-day Saint and something of what your father and grandfather waded through. Keep up a good courageous spirit, but don't get to think it is too much for you to bear. It will all come out well and you will have something to tell your posterity. Your girls are O.K. so far as I know. I am doing my best to keep at least one for you. Chester is doing chores, but can't seem to get time for much else. I am getting considerable done while Bro. Brown is helping me. Personal: Be careful about bed clothes and towels. You may get the itch and sore eyes or something worse. . . . Don't go in wet feet and clothes longer than necessary. God bless my sweet boy.

> Affectionately,
> your father,
> Andrew Kimball

His mission did not shield Spencer from personal tragedy. His father wired the shocking, incredible news from Los Angeles May 28, 1915: "Your sister Ruth died here last night. I go with H. and remains to St. Johns for burial. Father." Just that. Death had taken his beloved sister, just twenty-one, leaving behind her baby, Nicholas, with her stricken husband, John H. Udall. Ruth, with whom he had pooled his money to buy Christmas presents, who had mothered him after Olive's death, who had softened life for a little brother faced with a concerned but strict stepmother — gone! Grief washed over him; he wept and brooded and moped around for a time before his sense of responsibility to his missionary work reasserted itself.

He developed as a dutiful, energetic missionary. After about a year the mission president, Samuel O. Bennion, called Spencer into St. Louis, where he soon designated the twenty-year-old Spencer president over the East Missouri Conference. Put in charge of twenty-five missionaries, all older than he, Spencer worried that he was not good enough, not impressive enough to preside effectively.

President Bennion frightened him at first. At a conference he would peer at Spencer, his glasses down on his nose, and sternly command, "Elder Kimball, come up and speak."

Spencer worried about his responsibilities. He worked hard. During the first half of 1916, during most of which he served also as conference president, he personally contacted 3844 nonmembers, about 150 a week. He participated in an average of fourteen meetings a week.

Spencer still found ways to mix fun with missionary life in the big city. He liked to joke about the night Elder Hawkes took charge of a street-corner meeting. After the elders had sung a hymn, prayed, and sung again, still no one had stopped to listen, not even the usual drunks hanging onto lamp-posts. Undaunted, Elder Hawkes stepped forward, waved his arms, and repeated his regular line, "If you will all give me

Missionary in Central States Mission, 1915

Washing feet, Pea Ridge, Missouri

your attention, we'll begin our meeting." Apart from the missionaries themselves, there was no one on the street within a block of him.

Spencer, with five of his missionaries and four lady missionaries, spent one Christmas with the Strauser family at Pea Ridge, ten miles out in the hills. The missionaries mixed testimony meetings with pranks and games. One evening the elders burst out singing: "Ere you left your room this morning, did you think to pray?" aiming the words in good fun at the lady missionaries. The women quipped back with "Hark, Listen to the Trumpeters." The two sides fired back and forth in a hymn duel. Later the lady missionaries dressed in white and posed for comic photos as nurses in the act of cutting off Spencer's legs with a carpenter's saw.

Missionary rules were different then from what they would become. On a day off, Spencer and five others bought special six-dollar one-day round-trip excursion tickets for the train to Chicago. What collective guilt they felt at taking a holiday was augmented when they visited the Northern States mission home and were confronted by President German Ellsworth, who said with disgust, "Tell President Bennion, if he can't keep his people busy down in St. Louis, transfer them up to me."

While in St. Louis during the summer of 1916 Spencer attended all four days of the Democratic National Convention. He found the political process fascinating and viewed this as a once-in-a-lifetime chance to observe a convention. (Though he was never himself to be very active in politics, his father had served as a legislator and as a member of the Utah Constitutional Convention, and continued to be interested in Arizona politics.) At the convention, renomination of Woodrow Wilson for a second term was a foregone conclusion, and "He kept us out of war" proved his strongest campaign slogan.

Spencer worked hard at being a missionary. He baptized five people in his two years, though disclaiming any personal credit. "They were probably more the fruits of the work of other missionaries who preceded me," he explained. "But I tried to do my part," planting seeds for others to harvest.

He would tell missionaries a story years later about using ingenuity in making contacts. While tracting in St. Louis he noticed a piano through the partly opened door, and he said to the woman, who was in the act of shutting the door in his face, "You have a nice-looking piano."

"We just bought it," said the woman, hesitating.

"It's a Kimball, isn't it? That's my name, too. I could play a song on it for you that you might like to hear."

Surprised, she answered, "Surely, come in."

Sitting on the bench, Spencer played and sang, "O, My Father."

So far as Spencer knew, she never joined the Church, but it was not because he had not tried.

At one time on his mission, Spencer and his companion had just sunk their last quarter into a metered gas stove, praying to the Lord that something would turn up, when a letter arrived from one of the boys at the dairy who smoked and stayed clear of the Church. It contained two dollars, "the most welcome two dollars I have ever seen in my life."

Spencer's mission did not provide him with a flash of spiritual development; he had always had a testimony of the gospel, it seemed. The rigorous missionary life — studying, preaching, tracting, visiting members, teaching, trudging miles over rutted back roads and city pavements — simply solidified his commitment. Sacrifice made the cause dearer and the conviction deeper. He returned home much as he had left, but matured.

Spencer arrived back in Thatcher on the first day of January 1917. Many things had changed.

His oldest sister Clare had been abandoned by her husband and was trying to make ends meet in Los Angeles with her four children. Gordon, married to Clara Curtis, lived in Tucson. Del lived away, working and still single. Ruth had died of pneumonia. His younger sister Alice had married George Nelson while he was gone. Helen, the youngest living sister, was in high school.

Spencer found many of his close friends scattered to college or marriage. Those still left were gracious and friendly, Spencer remembered, but it wasn't the same — "There was emptiness." Ella Tyler thought he looked lonely that June when he watched six couples board the train for Salt Lake to be married in the Temple. He knew all twelve. Four had graduated with him two years back. "Everybody is getting married but me," he joked with them as they waited in their seats on the train.

At the end of January he had registered as one of five hundred students at the University of Arizona. He stayed with Gordon and Clara, which helped with expenses. Between classes and on Saturdays he picked up twenty-five cents an hour working for Miss Jones, who was partly paralyzed. When Spencer arrived at her house, he would lift her out of bed into a wheelchair, then wheel her outside where she could supervise his work in her garden.

One day in Binghampton, where a number of Mormon refugees from the Mexican revolution lived in poverty, Spencer saw a pregnant woman of twenty-nine standing on the sidewalk waiting for a chance to cross the dirt street between buggies and horses. He went to her assistance and helped her across. Her family remembered the little act of courtesy sixty years later.

At the university Spencer received college credit for some of his high-school work. In class he found things much as he had at Gila Academy. He worried at first that he wouldn't be smart enough to compete, but he soon found he did better than most of the other students. His grades were A's and B's on seventeen credits. The history professor told Spencer his themes set the standard by which he graded the other papers. His term paper, "A Treatment of 'The Great and Glorious Revolution of 1688,' " was marked "A, Especially good."

It was 1917, the year America would enter the war in Europe, and all male students were required to register for a military training class. They were expected to dress in their khaki uniforms and show up for target practice. Though his father kept no guns and Spencer had never hunted, he was delighted to find himself about as good a shot as anyone on the line. "We had planted a big orchard on Father's farm," he jokingly explained, "and all those trees had to be sighted perfectly in straight rows."

After one volley had been fired, a couple of men were sent out to readjust the targets. A shot went off. The sergeant exploded, yelling down along the line of green trainees "What __ __ idiot did that?" No one seemed to know. Relieved that he had killed no one, Spencer kept quiet.

The friends from Thatcher who had enrolled the year Spencer left for his mission were gone. Some of his enthusiasm began to seep away. He found it hard to get out of bed Sunday mornings for priesthood meetings. After missing a few, he argued with himself: "What are you doing, Spencer Kimball? You know that is the way to eventual apostasy. What are you doing?" With that he faced about, "and made new resolutions which I carried out precisely through the balance of the school year and largely through my life."

Throughout the semester at Arizona, political news was tense. Germany, banking on a quick end to the war which had dragged on for more than two years, had on January 31 notified the United States that German submarines would sink any ships trying to supply the Allies. President Wilson immediately severed diplomatic relations with Germany. National sentiment supported him. When in March the Czarist government held temporary power, the Allies could claim that the war was to make the world safe for democracy. Congress declared war on Germany on April 6.

What the war might bring him Spencer did not know, but by summer he was restless. He itched to be out of the classroom and doing something new. The sound of the whistle, drifting across the desert from the Southern Pacific trains beyond Tucson, "set my feet tingling." When he arrived home his father suggested he stay with Clare in Los Angeles and find a summer job. He jumped at the chance.

In Los Angeles he found a job at the Southern Pacific freight yards, pushing two-wheel trucks loaded with up to a thousand pounds. "My strong body and muscles of iron, developed on the farm, came in handy." To save the nickel streetcar fare for his college fund, Spencer normally hiked the long miles to Clare's home after work. He often carried a book with him and read it as he walked. He had found an arcade between Main and Spring streets where he could buy paperback "pocket classics" for ten cents.

Spencer never complained about the fourteen-hour days "of heavy slave-labor" or the low pay or the tons of freight he had to haul. That was the job. But he lost patience over the men he worked with. Most were uneducated, burly immigrants, their conversation so crude that Spencer soon found their curses and low expressions sticking in his mind. When he caught himself rethinking some of their dirty jokes, he decided to quit his job. But his boss, sorry to see him go, rehired him into another section as a freight checker, with better work and better pay.

After the declaration of war in April, the government mobilization of manpower began. In May a Selective Service System was created. In June men registered. Men engaged in essential occupations, which included farming, could obtain deferral, but the war was a popular one and deferral for anything less than compelling reason made one liable to being called a slacker.

Spencer had registered before he went to California. While he was there his father wrote him concerning the draft. Since he was a community leader, Andrew gave a copy to the newspaper for publication:

> I advise you, Spencer, to volunteer, and if accepted be enrolled with the regiment within your state. I think it best and so recommend it to you. You have registered and are holding yourself in readiness subject to the call of your country. If chosen you would have to be drafted in and be subject to the command of the National Army. The call would be compulsory; no telling where you would be stationed, or among what class of soldiers you would have to train. It would be vastly more satisfactory to us at home and more agreeable to you, I am sure, to train with our home boys.
>
> President Joseph F. Smith and the general authorities recommend our Mormon boys to join the home, or their own state militia regiment or whatever division of the army they may be assigned, and do you not think it best, and better to volunteer than to have to wait to be forced into action in the service of your country? I am sure you will agree with me.

Still, despite this public invitation to volunteer, Spencer felt it better to wait for the draft.

He had aspirations to be a teacher. He badly wanted an education. He had spent more than two years away while most of his friends moved ahead with school or marriage. He returned home in July when his father wired him about a good-paying job digging a water well with his stepbrother Wallace Jones on the Gillespie Ranch. Each night they would dynamite, then work all day shoveling and lifting out the rubble.

Spencer later recounted that one evening at the ranch he picked up the *Graham County Guardian* and a photograph in the upper right-hand corner held his attention. It was of Miss Camilla Eyring, who was returning to be the new home economics teacher at Gila Academy. He had met her once, three years back, at a dance in Snow's barn, but hadn't even danced with her. He read and reread the article. "There's my wife," he said aloud to himself. "I am going to marry her."

Years later his son, having looked in the newspaper files, pointed out that the *Guardian* carried no such picture but just an article about registration at the school, listing the nine faculty members' names. Had he any idea what made him so sure he had seen a photograph and an article especially about Camilla? He jokingly brushed the question aside: "Why should they go to all that trouble, reprinting the whole newspaper just to leave that picture out?"

In late August Spencer left the Gillespie job to move home. Early in September he would be leaving for Provo, Utah, to attend Brigham Young University. Meanwhile he lost no time, but immediately asked around about Miss Eyring. She lived with her parents in Pima, several miles down the valley. She rode the jitney bus to Thatcher daily to teach at the Academy.

It just happened that Spencer's buddy Lawrence Holladay lived in Pima. So at 5:00 P.M. after faculty meeting at the Academy let out, Spencer arrived at the bus stop. He introduced himself to Miss Eyring, who remembered him. He let her know he chanced to be on his way to visit Lawrence, and asked about her classes. When the bus came, they sat together in the back seat. For the whole way to Pima, Spencer talked about Shakespeare and art, certain that was the way to a teacher's heart. When he asked if he might call on her she invited him to do so.

But she did not expect him to call unannounced. When he arrived at her home one evening soon after their bus ride she was dressed in a kimono, hair up in curlers, preparing to go dancing with a boyfriend and some other friends. Camilla did not know what to do. So she sat with young Mr. Kimball on the porch and talked, expecting his visit to end at any moment, until it became obvious he had no intention of leaving.

"I was in a pickle," Camilla later said. Though she wanted to favor Spencer, she already had a date, so she fudged. She told Spencer that a crowd was going dancing. Did he want to come? Spencer, delighted with his good luck, said yes, so when Alvin drove up in his car with the others, Camilla asked if a friend could come along. The two piled in the car and Alvin let his rage out through his foot. He drove, said Camilla, "like the devil was after him." By the time the car pulled up to the dance hall in Layton, Alvin was through with Camilla. He wouldn't dance with her again for fifteen years. "I played a shabby trick," Camilla admitted.

They had time for only a few dates before Spencer left for Provo. Camilla attended stake conference with him when he reported his mission and sang in a quartet. (When he came back from the stand after singing he sat down on his straw boater.)

When he caught the train for Provo, Spencer took with him a box of Camilla's chocolate fudge and a strong feeling that this girl was right for him. The night before he left he kept her, a working girl, up outrageously late. *He* could sleep on the train.

They corresponded regularly while he was away. His letters suggest a sense of loneliness in his new surroundings as well as a growing feeling for Camilla. His first letters were addressed to "Dear Miss Eyring." (By the second letter his signature had graduated from "Spencer W. Kimball" to Spencer.") One written on the train en route to Utah, after a short stay with Clare in Los Angeles, read:

> Dear Miss Eyring,
>
> The train is very unsteady, rocking like a steamboat but I will try to scratch you a few lines.
>
> We are near the Cal-Nev. line and I think crossing an edge of Death Valley. It all looks like death valley thru' here for our Arizona deserts cannot compare with this for barrenness. . . .
>
> Last night I took my sister to hear Billy Sunday. I enjoyed the service very much but was quite disappointed in the evangelist. I had always heard so much about him I guess I was looking for too much. His voice was rasping.
>
> I am still enjoying the candy you so tho'tfully sent with me.
>
> We arrive in Salt Lake 11:45 a.m. tomorrow. We may go out to SaltAir and I do hope so for I have never been there.
>
> I have been sitting here thinking of you and wondering why your letter didn't reach me and decided I'd drop you a line. . . .
>
> Write soon to
>
> Just
>
> Spencer

His letter three days later from Salt Lake City, where he stayed with relatives, visiting and seeing the sights, was signed "With Fondest Memories, Spencer," and referred to a picture of Camilla:

> The picture came to me here in Salt Lake last night and I laughed as you requested HaHa. It was fine. I promptly cut off the head (ugh!!) and pasted it in my watch as I demonstrated for you "That Last Night." My cousins actually accuse me of keeping *too* strict watch of the time since. They all say: "Isn't she pretty?" "Isn't she sweet?" and one cousin just graduated from West Point said: "Some swell Fem?" I hope you won't be offended at their remarks.

His Woolley cousins, he commented, "do not seem at all ashamed of their clod hopper cousin from the country." A cousin from his father's side of the family distinguished himself during Spencer's visit:

> Last night a 16 yr old boy (a cousin, also, he is Pres. Smith's son) was walking across a vacant lot when he was accosted by two men, thugs, who tore a flag from his coat saying "take that d____n thing off." He grappled with the one and prevailed, and as he arose Fielding gave an uppercut which rendered the fellow unconscious. The second thug advanced with an open knife which Fielding kicked out of his hand. He came home with his blood covered shirt riddled into carpet rags.

Cousin Thelma Woolley remembered that with ten around the table Spencer took out the watch attached to his vest with a chain rather too frequently between bites. Her father, Uncle George, pointed at a wall clock just above them and said: "You know, Spencer, you don't really need that pocket watch out. We have the time right above us." But it was not the time that concerned Spencer.

He arrived in Provo on September 17, and wrote two days later:

> I am registered and attending my first classes today. I shall take theology under Pres. Brimhall.
>
> I think Provo a fine little college town and the people seem to be quite hospitable.
>
> I won't say what were my impressions of the school *as a school* but I do hope to like it. I appreciate the social feeling and good will. . . .
>
> If you see anything in the papers about the drafting that in any way pertains to me would you kindly mention it. You see if I am to be drafted, I should like to know long enough ahead that I might visit at least a week or so before leaving home. . . .
>
> I wish you were here. I feel like a stranger in a strange land, tho' I am meeting some nice young people. . . .
>
> With Admiration,
>
> Spencer.

Spencer told Camilla nothing of his arrival in Provo. He had stepped off the train, peered up Center Street, and caught sight of an impressive building far up the street at the base of the mountains rimming the valley. Without asking directions, he set off on foot with his baggage for the university. When he finally neared the building, exhausted from carrying his heavy luggage, he was startled to see odd-looking men, all dressed in drab clothes, tending the grounds. Two or three seemed to peer at him from behind bushes. He remembered hearing that the state insane asylum was at Provo. Mortified at his error, he dropped his bags behind a shrub, pulled himself together, and strode into the building like he "had come to inspect it or to buy it." He took a drink at the water fountain, then gravely walked back out of the building, reassumed his bags, and headed back to town. "It was a long time," he later remembered, "before I could tell of my stupidity and laugh about it."

On Sunday the twenty-third he wrote:

> I have been lonesome today, Sun. always is the longest day when away from home. I didn't have a soul to recognize me. I walked around the blocks and wished, oh! how I wished I were down on the little hill across the track near the cemetery and were listening to your musical voice telling me of your college pranks or your school difficulties or your ideals and ambitions. I'd love to meet you in the Domestic Art room again or to have you up here, too, I must wait wait wait I guess. I will come home Christmas holidays. May I call upon you then? . . .

> Two weeks tomorrow since I left, does it seem that long to you? It seems more like two years or months to me. Yours are the only two letters I have received so I know nothing of the doings or conditions of my home folks. I had a terrible dream concerning Father last night which, if I were a believer in such would worry me, but I tried to put it away.

> I am getting along fine, taking English Grammar and Composition, Math, European History, Philosophical Mormonism under Brimhall, Public speaking (2 in class) and phy. training. Hope to succeed. Please write soon. I *love* to hear from you.

And in a P.S.:

> Mon. noon. Just rec'd summons to appear for examination so I may see you soon. Will advise you further as soon as I learn and can plan. SWK.

Later that same Monday he wrote again:

> In the letter today I told you of my receipt of my summons to appear for physical examination at Safford Sept. 28th. I immediately telegraphed the Graham Co. Board and rec'd answer that I might be examined by the Utah Co. Board here. I have sent

off a night letter asking if this is just to get all of us examined or if it really means that I am to take a place in the first quota. Lawrence's was 545 mine 589. I wouldn't care now if I had to go about the middle of Oct. for that would enable me to attend the Conference at Salt Lake and visit you all briefly before I go. The Doctor here said I could leave from here and go to American Lake, Wash. My brother Del is there. I have half a notion to do it, it would be so pleasant to train with him. (I haven't seen him for years). What do you think about it? I would like to visit at home *once more* though.

I shall file no exemption claims and I'm positive I can pass the physical test.

I can't study tonight. I can only think. Pardon me for bothering you with my troubles but I tho't you might be glad to know. If I am to leave soon I am not unwilling to go but of course it is hard to have one's plans so broken into that's all. . . .

I was the only member in the public speaking class so I get individual instruction. I can now breathe clear down to my toes, can roar like a lion or squeak like a mouse. I can gesticulate till you'd think I was hammering or pitching hay or etc. etc. There were two of us in Math. 4 in Hist., about 6 in Theology. . . .

I like all my Profs fine but _____ and I can't hardly stand him. Today he had a dirtier shirt than mine and wore the trousers and shoes he wore while milking the cow.

I wish I had a class under your uncle [Carl Eyring] for he is the swellest Prof in the whole faculty.

Two days later:

Provo Cy, Ut.
9/26/17

Dear Camilla,

Just a word today. Rec'd telegram that I am to leave Safford on Oct. 3rd if possible or if not then with the next contingent which leaves soon after.

1 p.m. Am just waiting for the examining Dr. and my heart goes pit-a-pat. I hope he doesn't throw me out on a weak heart. haha

Just rec'd your letter of 23rd and it was comforting and cheering. I am so glad you appreciate my letters for I was so afraid they would not be just right. . . .

Pres. Brimhall put his arm around me and said he was sorry to lose me. I felt good for I felt I had already made some friends.

There is nothing much to write. One subject is ever on my mind and you have had so much war war war that I'm sure you wouldn't appreciate any more of it.

I do hope to see you soon and once more enjoy your association for a brief while.

Sincerely

Spencer.

2:30 p.m. Physically perfect. Not a single defect that would throw me out. There is some consolation in that isn't there?

Will let you know later when my plans develop, just what I shall do and when I shall get home.

As ever

Spencer.

On October 1 Spencer wrote that he had been to Heber City and to Nephi, visiting with former lady missionaries. He did not bother Camilla with the fact that his trip to Nephi to see Fern Riches had a serious purpose. He was still checking on other possibilities, though he had pretty much made up his mind.

Spencer left BYU but stayed in Salt Lake City to attend October Conference before he returned home.

I have been up late nights and up early mornings so I am rather sleepy and worn out so yesterday I stepped in a 5¢ movie and had a good nap, but even that did not keep me awake when the parents and I were in the Strand last night to see Clara Kimball Young play "The Easiest Way." . . .

Yesterday Pres. Bennion came up to me, put his arm around me and said, if I could get released he would put me in his mission as Secretary. Oh! that I could.

I look forward to the reunion tomorrow night with a great deal of anticipation, hoping to meet many of my old companions.

In his next letter he indicated he would arrive home on Friday and that he had cut off his moustache.

Monday I shaved off my old friend Charlie Chaplin and I look like a monkey. It seems a mile from my nose to my mouth. I hope I don't look like that to you tho' for it might prove disastrous to me.

After conference he left for Thatcher.

Los Angeles, Cal.
Oct. 9, 1917

Dear Girl,

I am doing as you asked, hurrying home. Will likely be there Fri.

Yes, indeed, I do care and am sorry that you had cause to be provoked at me for not writing for a few days. Again, I was glad in a way, for, then, I did feel like you cared a little. Pardon me. I can hardly wait till I can see you once again.

I wish I only knew how long before we leave for Ft. Riley. I had an opportunity to go up with my parents to American Lake, Wash. to see our brother and son Del, who is in training there. I wish I had gone and taken chances on getting back in time but it is too late now.

Your invitation to dinner next Sun. settled the question and made my plans conform with yours. I know we shall have a splendid time. . . .

Spencer's father and stepmother had come to conference and seen him there. Andrew felt firmly convinced of the rightness of America's entering the war and of his son's obligation to serve, but sending first Del and now Spencer to war saddened him. He took Spencer aside and gave him a blessing, "set him apart for his going to the front." Spencer set off to return to Thatcher just four weeks after leaving there, his college education disrupted.

No date had been set for the departure of Spencer's contingent. In September, when Spencer was ordered in for examination, it looked as though there might be difficulty in filling the quota of 114 more from the county. In October, just before Spencer arrived home, all but sixteen places had been filled and the contingent sent off. Spencer then expected to go with the group of sixteen, but no date was set for his leaving. He was told just to sit tight.

Unable to take a job or register in school, just waiting to go off to war, Spencer picked up where he had left off with Camilla. She was not unwilling. She had stayed with Jessie Bird in Thatcher on Friday night, so that she could see him when his train came in.

Camilla's father, Edward Eyring, was a polygamist. He had first married Caroline Romney; then, ten years later, he had married her sister Emma. The families had lived in the Mormon settlement in Colonia Juarez, Mexico, southwest of El Paso. Many families there were refugees from U.S. marshals who had hounded them out of the States in the 1880s and 1890s because of their involvement in plural marriage. That practice was not illegal in Mexico.

In 1912 a band of Mexican revolutionaries under Salazar began to rob Americans, plunder their shops, and threaten them. The whole colony pulled up roots and fled north to El Paso, where they were harbored temporarily by the city in stalls in a lumber yard. The Eyrings ended up in the Gila Valley, still polygamist but untroubled by the law in that remote country among largely Mormon neighbors. There was little or no stigma on polygamy entered into in Mexico after the Manifesto, as evidenced by Edward's serving on the high council, but he was by nature a retiring man and this suited well the community interest in his remaining relatively inconspicuous.

Each of Edward's two wives bore nine children. Eight of each family lived past infancy. He housed them in a rambling farmhouse, adding rooms as needed. Caroline's half lived on the north side, Emma's on the south. The two sections were joined by a huge room with a stone fireplace. Strict equality was Edward's approach to plural marriage, so each Saturday he packed his leather valise and moved from one half of the house to the other. Peace at any price was his wish, and each wife cautioned her children against quarreling when Papa was there. A mild man, with a reddish Van Dyke beard, he was the perfect patriarch to make such a family system work out. This was Camilla's family, and she the oldest child of the eighteen. Spencer managed to fit right in.

At the time Spencer returned home, Andrew and Josie were travelling back east, representing the county and the state at several national and international farm congresses and expositions. The new Chevrolet sat idle at the house. Spencer polished it up, filled it with gas, and sat parked outside the Academy every afternoon as classes let out. The girls in her class would giggle as Camilla glanced out of the window and blushed. Spencer didn't miss a day; he drove Camilla to the Eyring ranch in Pima over five miles of chuckholes, dust and gravel.

While Spencer courted Camilla, the entire Eyring family courted him. Mother Eyring was his strongest ally. She invited him every night to stay to dinner, then served him special cream pies. She made a fuss over him. If Camilla criticized Spencer to her mother, she had an argument on her hands. Caroline, Camilla's sister, loved to listen to Spencer play the piano and sing. Little Rose, then just five, later remembered seeing Spencer and Camilla parked in his car outside the house. Curious, she wandered out, snooping, until Spencer opened the car door, set her on his lap, and taught her to sing "I Saw A Little Elf Man." Camilla, the big sister, was mortified.

Papa Eyring had objected to Camilla's first date, back in Mexico: "My girl, that isn't a good family. I wouldn't be seen dead in a turnip patch with that boy." Only tears got her the date, on condition she see him no more. Her sister Catherine didn't get off so easy. When she mentioned a date's name to Papa two hours before the dance, he told her to "cut him off at the pockets." That meant, break her date and go to the dance with her sister. Another boyfriend parted his hair down the middle. That was all the proof Papa needed that he came from poor stock. Catherine was ordered to give him the "grand bounce." But Papa had nothing to say against Spencer Kimball. Nobody did. The family united in approval.

For thirty-one days he courted Camilla. There were some picnics, some shows, some dances. One weekend they drove the car to Roosevelt Dam with another couple. At the dam the girls wanted to rent a room for themselves and one for the boys, but the boys arranged for the party to stay at a sister-in-law's home nearby. Camilla learned later that the boys did not have enough money to rent a room.

But mostly the couple just swung on the wide front gate and talked, or after dinner walked along the railroad grade in the moonlight until one or two in the morning.

"It would be a bit late when I'd get home," admitted Spencer, "so I'd sleep until about noon." But Camilla had to rise early to teach school in Thatcher. Her father thought they stayed up too late. Spencer thought the same, at least in retrospect. But that didn't get them to bed any earlier at the time, and Camilla started dozing at school.

Spencer's status with the draft see-sawed back and forth. One night Camilla hosted a farewell dinner, complete with American flags, and invited two other couples. The next night word came that Spencer's departure was delayed. The only thing that seemed sure was that he would go.

One night at the Eyring farm the moon rose bright over the hills to the east. "At least it was bright for us," wrote Spencer. They walked along the railroad grade, then stood between the rails and talked of engagement and early marriage. That would mean an end to their exhausting courtship.

Camilla's father gave Spencer his consent. Spencer joked that he had become such a steady boarder, eating at the Eyring table night after night, that Father Eyring "gave consent to get rid of me."

It would have to be a civil marriage, they agreed. Camilla's teaching and Spencer's impending draft call tied them to Thatcher. Anyway, they had no money for train tickets to Salt Lake City. Regrettable as it was to both of them, the circumstances dictated a postponement of the temple sealing.

The wedding was planned for Friday, November sixteenth, allowing the weekend for a honeymoon. The next week, they expected, Spencer would be drafted and sent to war.

Spencer and Camilla did their best to keep the wedding a secret until it was over. As they rode into Safford for their wedding license they feared being spotted by friends and their secret guessed. They desperately wanted to avoid having their wedding spoiled by a shivaree. Only the parents and the adult children at home were invited to it.

It was Wednesday when Andrew and Josie returned home from their extended trip east. They had missed the whole whirlwind courtship. But Andrew had to leave on Thursday for Phoenix to attend the meeting of a state commission. It was an important commitment he could not change. He wished Spencer and Camilla could wait for his return, but he understood their reasons. He raised no fuss over Spencer's cavalier use of his car. If he had any reservations about the hasty wedding, he raised no barrier.

Spencer, in the last few days before the wedding, sent messages to Camilla at the school by his sister Helen:

11:40 a.m.

Lover,

Just returned from depot where I took Father to the train and while waiting for the same I had a good talk with him. He is a *Brick* and is just as good as tho' I had been true to him [by consulting him about the wedding before it was all planned]. He is wonderful. He says if we want to spend the week-end together, he will not be put out if we go on without him. So if you prefer we can still plan for Fri. night.

So far as I know I can meet you at 5:30 and take you home.

Have been at the typewriter this a.m.

Spencer and Camilla Kimball
at time of marriage, 1917

Mother suggested that Fri. was a bad day. Are you at all superstitious? I am not, but if you are, we will respect that.

Father went off and did not mention a single unpleasant thing, tho' he could find fault with me in a thousand places.

Better *annihilate* this note or put it in safe keeping ha! ha!

If you think of Fri. night you can make some excuse if they JB and Ray insist on some adventure.

> Time drags heavily.
> Mit viele Gelieb
> Spencer.

P.S. I told Mother too. Tho't best. See? Don't worry, keep your mind on your school work as much as possible, for your sake. Till we meet. SWK

On Friday Spencer drove Camilla home then went back to Thatcher to bathe and dress for the wedding that night. Nervously he undressed and stepped into their number three metal tub. But he had forgotten the water and had to call Josie to bring him the bucket and hand it around the half-opened door.

Camilla, overwhelmed by the suddenness of it all, panicked. In her bedroom she sobbed and wondered if she was ready to marry. She had ambitions to train at college as a hospital dietician and hated to give up her chance. She and Spencer had courted just weeks. He had no job and was about to leave for the army.

She worried about the shabbiness of her home and declared she could not stand to have Mrs. Kimball see it like that. With her mother she had gone through the house room by room to find one that would do for the ceremony. They had picked the living room. As the wallpaper was ragged and peeling, her mother had helped her gather tree branches and stand them against the wall over the worst holes, in the guise of decoration.

On the tiered wedding cake, so lovingly made, the white seven-minute icing had sugared.

Camilla worried about her clothing, a pink party dress she had made at school, thinking it the wrong thing to wear.

At seven, Spencer, dressed in his khaki uniform, arrived at the Eyring house with his stepmother, Josie, and his sister Helen. While last-minute preparations were made, Camilla's brother Henry, sixteen, wandered into the room where bride and groom waited. Spencer had Camilla on his lap, kissing her. Flustered, Henry rushed out, exclaiming, "I'll be as silent as the tomb." Spencer delighted in teasing Henry with the story, though adding sometimes, "That was about the first time we kissed."

Bishop Merrell, a quiet, dignified man, performed the marriage ceremony simply but impressively.

The Kimball family status in the community produced an unusual front-page news story on the wedding in the weekly *Gila Valley Farmer:*

Popular Young Couple Married

Spencer W. Kimball of Thatcher and Miss Camilla Eyring, this place, surprised their many friends when they took the matrimonial oath Friday and were joined in wedlock.

The bride is the daughter of Mr. and Mrs. E. C. Eyring of Pima. She is at present a member of the faculty of the Gila Academy. Mr. Kimball is the son of President and Mrs. Andrew Kimball. He is one of the drafted boys from this county and is certified for duty in the National Army. His name appears among those called for service in the next contingent from this county. At present the young couple are living in Thatcher.

This item followed immediately after a one-and-one-half-column story of Andrew Kimball's having reported on the glories of Arizona to a Boston convention audience two weeks earlier.

6

Bank Clerk, Stake Clerk

— "I guess it is time we bought you
an engagement ring"

On his wedding day Spencer
had less than ten dollars in his pocket and no job, since he expected
to leave for war at any time. Camilla still owed fifty dollars she had
borrowed to come home from Salt Lake City when she started to teach
at the Academy. They had no cash to rent a room, so they moved in
with Spencer's father and stepmother in Thatcher. Half a century
later, as an apostle, Spencer would warn newlyweds: "There may be a
temptation to economize by living with the parents on either side. Do
not make this serious error." It was Camilla who suffered most, thinking herself an imposition on her in-laws. In her own mind, she couldn't
please Josie, which made that time "anything but comfortable." In
Josie's mind, teaching at the Academy didn't excuse Camilla from a full
load of chores at home.

A week after the wedding Spencer and the other three Thatcher
boys waiting to go in the army were called on in stake conference to
speak briefly in farewell. Then another week passed. Spencer still was
not drafted, so he and Camilla moved in next door with Alice,
Spencer's younger married sister. Alice's whole house was just a back
porch and one long room. Spencer and Camilla rented part of the
porch and part of the room, their portion being partitioned off from

Alice's household with a flannel curtain. That seemed better to Camilla and Spencer than staying at the Kimballs. But the nervous strain caused by the incessant screaming of Alice's five-month-old baby, who was sick with colic, plus the effect which the baby's need for extra care had on the housekeeping, made the situation very difficult, even depressing for an idealistic domestic science teacher just out of school.

A month after the wedding Camilla became pregnant. Naturally she and Spencer wanted children, but the timing here would bring its problems. First, how could Camilla now finish out the school year as she was contracted to do? Then also, she felt embarrassed at how close the baby's birth would come to her wedding, afraid people would count the months on their fingers. Such concerns, combined with the housing problem, caused some tears of frustration.

The army contingent, needing only sixteen more men, filled without Spencer and it began to look as if he would not be called up until after the baby's birth.

The couple had borrowed a hundred dollars to get started on, and Spencer had been doing some miscellaneous farm work, digging ditches, pulling corn and irrigating for farmers at two dollars a day. Now he found a steady job. William McRae, cashier of the Citizens' Bank at Thatcher, offered him work posting entries for seventy-five dollars a month, the same amount Camilla received at the Academy. Spencer had friends earning twice that much, but this was steady work, and with the draft hanging over him he had been having difficulty in finding work. Besides, he joked, the smallness of his salary only made it easier to pay his tithe to the Church. One of the first things he did with his salary was buy Camilla a wedding band for seven dollars.

Spencer had no thought of a career in banking; he had no special preparation for it; but he had done a good deal of work with his father, typing letters and keeping records, he was by nature a meticulous, dogged, diligent worker, and he was smart too — not bad qualifications for a banker. McRae risked little in employing Spencer.

Before long he had made himself at home in this realm, keeping books, paying and receiving, posting accounts. He liked the work. Though at first there seemed so many ways in which the books could become out of balance, he soon identified the most likely ones; he had a knack for finding errors and balancing the accounts.

The bank building stood right in the center of the tiny business district of Thatcher; the establishment consisted of one room, three

employees. Spencer took on more and more responsibility, working
the time locks on the safe and making loans. Camilla's teenage younger
sisters had the job of cleaning the bank at night. It would have embarrassed them to be known to do janitorial work, so they hid when
someone passed by the windows.

By March Spencer and Camilla had paid off their debts and moved
into the unfurnished Wakefield place, a tiny house two blocks from
work, which they rented at six dollars a month. For them, compared
with their curtained-off rooms at Alice's, it seemed a spacious palace.
Mother Eyring donated a bed and the Kimballs offered a few odd
pieces of furniture. The young couple bought a tub, a rug, a dressing
table, some dishes, an orange box for a cupboard, and a coal-oil lamp.
With that the couple set up housekeeping. They had no running water,
no inside toilet, but a huge mulberry tree for shade and a place for a
garden plot. Then every week Mother Eyring brought from the Pima
farm four quart jars of milk wrapped in wet towels; she also brought
grapes and butter and eggs, along "with much help and encouragement. We were so happy," Spencer said later; "we didn't know we were
poor."

Then again, they knew they weren't rich. But they had work and
ability. They knew how to manage their own money, living within their
income, saving for the future. McRae boosted Spencer's pay to eighty
dollars. He became a teller and then assistant cashier. As soon as the
debts had been paid off the couple started buying thrift stamps and
Liberty Bonds, investing in these more than 10 percent of their income. They lived very simply, but with Camilla working, keeping
house, sewing and gardening, they had all they really needed.

In March Spencer had smallpox. Camilla counted 125 pustules on
his face, but even so his case was not very serious and he bore no scars.

By June the couple had scrimped enough money to buy tickets to
Salt Lake to have their marriage sealed in the Temple, before the baby
was born. "By this time," wrote Camilla, "I was big and ugly and my
nerves were worn to a frazzle. I hated meeting Spencer's relatives and
friends for the first time looking like I did, and I made matters worse
by being irritable." Everything exasperated her. On the trip up, a party
of scruffy Mormons boarded the train heading for Salt Lake. Some of
them stopped in Las Vegas, got drunk, then reboarded. It annoyed
Camilla to be classed with such loud, uncouth Mormons.

By the time they returned to Thatcher two weeks had passed and she was exhausted and miserable. Spencer, who seldom mentioned discouragement, acknowledged that "Camilla was uncomfortable" but wrote of their Salt Lake vacation as "a pleasant trip and visit in Utah with relatives and friends."

During the last month of her pregnancy, into August, Camilla completed her school contract by visiting her students over the county who were involved with home projects. This meant bouncing over rough dirt roads in a Model T Ford with the county agent day after day.

Nine months and nine days after their wedding, Camilla went into labor. A neighbor with a Model T Ford was sent out to Pima for Camilla's mother, while a Mrs. Lindsey stayed by her bedside, driving her into a frenzy by calling her "Sis" over and over. Camilla screamed so terribly with pain that she was hoarse for a week. "Such agony is indescribable," she wrote. The man next door complained to others in town, "That Kimball woman kept me awake all night with her screaming." Spencer held her hand through the whole ordeal. The doctor, fresh out of school, seemed helpless to prevent injuries to her. From all this suffering she delivered a baby boy.

A month afterwards she was still miserable; and at this point, when she was slowly recovering, a close friend came to visit her one Sunday afternoon, kissed her, then fell sick that night with one of the first cases of the terrible flu epidemic of 1918. Three days later Camilla was sick with flu. Desperately ill for weeks, she later marveled that she ever survived the flu when so many others died and she was so weak to begin with.

Camilla was to be in misery for six years. She did her housework, made friends, taught sporadically at the Academy, but all the time felt ill. She later wondered how Spencer ever put up with it and concluded that she was blessed with a patient husband. Even through this trouble he seemed optimistic and continued to be the life of every party.

But Spencer remembered this year, 1918, as a hard one. Later, in counselling people suffering from depression, he would tell them of this time when he had pitied himself because Camilla was pregnant or ill and they had no money. He had to take hold of himself, he would say, and consciously try to be cheerful.

Against this backdrop of nagging worry and illness, there were bright spots. The baby seemed bright and healthy. He was a delight to his parents. They named him Spencer LeVan and called him LeVan, thinking it an original name. They were chagrined years later to drive through a Utah town of that name.

Before the next quota from the county was sent to war in the spring of 1918, the board gave Spencer a changed status and assigned him to a contingent which was to be mobilized later. Then in November the armistice was signed.

Spencer and Camilla rejoiced with the rest of the world. The dirt road into town burst with noise, horns honking, whistles screeching, men cheering. The war was over. Spencer had worried that someone might think him a slacker or that he had married just to escape the draft. His father, who was firmly convinced of the rightness of America's entering the war, had declared in stake conference, "No person can be a slacker and maintain his standing in the Church." Spencer shed no tears at missing training camp and the war, but he had expected and been willing to go.

Having a child now and needing more income, Spencer "succumbed to the temptation to play again." He played the piano for the Williams Orchestra and the McDonald Orchestra for $2.00, $3.50, sometimes $5.00 a night, and at church benefit dances for nothing. They played for most of the dances in the valley after a while — in the church basement at Thatcher, on an outdoor concrete slab in Solomonsville, in the tottering upper story of the Lines Mercantile store in Pima. (The upstairs hall in Pima finally had to be closed because it was ready to collapse; when the dancers did the Chicago Lancers, in which at a certain point in the routine everyone slid to one end of the hall, the building swayed noticeably under them.)

Spencer and Camilla found other ways to augment income. They wrote as stringers for the local weekly paper, covering items about weddings and socials and visitors from out of town; they were paid so much an inch for copy that the paper used. Spencer's father had been an agent for Brown Herb Pills, a laxative whose advertising claimed it was good for all sorts of ills; after Andrew died in 1924, Spencer continued for at least ten years to carry a supply for the dwindling number in the community who wanted the pills. A few extra dollars came in this way.

Spencer also kept books for the People's Department Store. And soon after Spencer's marriage his father called him as clerk of the St. Joseph Stake. In those days that was about a half-time job, since nearly all the services now provided by the Presiding Bishop's Office were then handled by the clerk; consequently the clerk received fifty dollars a month. At the end of the year, with the annual reports due, it burgeoned into a full-time job, consuming every evening from the time Spencer got off at the bank until well after midnight. "The house was completely taken over by reports," said Camilla. Camilla worked, too, filling out forms. Part of the job was an annual audit of the ward records of all twenty-one congregations in the stake, which then included units as far away as El Paso, Texas, and Chihuahua City in Mexico. In addition Spencer trained new ward clerks to keep the complicated records.

A year after they rented the Wakefield place Spencer and his little family left it for the McRae house. Camilla junked the orange crates and bought a dining table and some better chairs. They bought a first car, a used Buick open on the sides. Financially, things were improving.

A few years later, with four jobs, working sometimes twenty hours a day, getting too little sleep, Spencer's eyes started giving him trouble; he had to get glasses. And "I got to be very obnoxious around the house. I found myself getting cranky with my children and cranky with my wife. I was kind of a mean father. I was just overdoing it. Nobody could work that hard that many hours. So I gave up the orchestra. After that my wife began to love me again." Though that account of it was tongue-in-cheek, Spencer did remember feeling that life was too short to drive himself to a breakdown.

In 1920 Spencer made $175.00 a month at the bank, $62.50 as stake clerk and $20.00 in other income. But after deductions he had net taxable income for the year of only $123.00, on which he paid tax of $5.00 — the first time he had been bothered by the income tax. The rate was 4 percent, down from the 6 percent wartime rate.

Spencer began to tell LeVan that he would soon have a little brother or sister to play with, too. But at five months Camilla miscarried the child. The loss shocked them with a terrible grief. Months of physical misery followed for Camilla. Then she became pregnant again, but miscarried at six weeks. She recalls that she dragged around the house, exhausted by the strain.

Troubled by chronic tonsilitis, Spencer finally had his tonsils and adenoids out in 1920. When he came out of the operation bloody and in great pain, he concluded that the surgeon, Dr. Slaughter, had been aptly named.

Spencer's first venture into public service saw him named for a two-year term, in the spring of 1920, to the Common Council of the Town of Thatcher. After only a short while in that position, however, he moved away.

In 1921, when LeVan was three, the Citizens' Bank where Spencer worked went through a change. With grand ideas the bank management built a new building in Safford, the county seat, and made that the headquarters, with the Thatcher bank a branch. The enlarged bank had a new name: Arizona Trust & Savings Bank. They also established a second branch in Pima. Spencer worked briefly in Pima. Then the bank transferred him to Safford as assistant cashier and raised his monthly salary to $225, which seemed to him a small fortune.

The bank had a basketball team. His journal for March 2, 1923, reports: "Bankers vs Pima YMMIA in basketball in which I was fortunate in making the greater part of our 34 points to their 24." And on March 6, 1923, he wrote: " . . . Bankers played the Fireman team basketball. We won."

Financially things looked good. Spencer and Camilla bought a new car, a Light Six Studebaker. And with a down payment and $25 a month they bought a neat small frame house on Central Avenue for $2400. This house had three rooms, a bath and a sleeping porch. In back stood some pecan and fruit trees and grape vines. Spencer built a corral for a cow and a shed for storage behind the garage. This home was their own and they were proud of it. Spencer planted two palm trees in front and watched them grow up with his family in the hot Arizona sun.

Camilla was pregnant again, but with the sweeping and scrubbing and interior painting she wanted to do on her new house, she fell ill of exhaustion and was threatened with miscarriage. Spencer called in a physician and together they put Camilla in bed, where she stayed much of the time until after the fifth month. When finally in the summer of 1922 a girl was born, with blue eyes and a reddish tint to her hair, Spencer's father wanted her named Olive, after her grandmother. They named her Olive Beth, but often called her Bobby.

After the baby came, Camilla couldn't seem to get her strength back. For two years she suffered back aches and pain until, in desperation, she made a visit to Dr. Bacon at the hospital in Miami, one hundred miles toward Phoenix. Shocked at what he found, the doctor exclaimed, "_____ _____, woman, if you were forty I'd say you were

Spencer and Spencer LeVan, 1920   *Spencer with Spencer LeVan, Olive Beth, and Andrew Eyring, 1927*

Camilla, Andrew, and Spencer LeVan, 1927

full of cancer!" He urged an exploratory operation. Frightened, Camilla agreed. Dr. Bacon cut off a piece of tissue the size of her palm and sent it to the laboratory, which found no cancer but only ulcers. She spent two weeks in the hospital, a lonely, dark time far from home.

Two months later she came back to be checked. Somehow the catgut knots on the incision had worked loose, so Dr. Bacon insisted on sewing her up again. He gave her a local anaesthetic while he restitched the wound. A week after her "dreadful ordeal" she was put on a bed in the train and sent home, soon to be well at last. For the first time in six years she felt really good.

The Arizona Trust & Savings Bank where Spencer worked edged in on a situation of strong competition. At the main business corner of the little country town there now stood three banks, Valley National Bank, the Bank of Safford, and the newcomer, all competing for their shares in the deposits from local farmers, ranchers, and merchants.

After a short-lived postwar boom, a serious economic depression hit the country between 1920 and 1922. Business at Arizona Trust fell off sharply and the employees voluntarily took a cut in pay. Spencer's income dropped first to $175, then to $150. He felt fortunate to have a job at all, since unemployment dogged the community. Bankruptcies nearly quadrupled between 1919 and 1922 across the nation. Banks closed by thousands.

Early on a Monday morning, December 17, 1923, William McRae phoned, asking Spencer to stop by his house. With red eyes and tear-choked voice he said that the bank examiners from Phoenix who had been checking the books for a week had decided to close the bank. Almost disbelieving, Spencer hurried to town and found the bank doors locked and a large "Closed" sign posted. It struck like a thunderbolt. The bank had been struggling, but not more than others. Slow market and low prices made it difficult for cattlemen and farmers to pay their now-delinquent notes, but Spencer had thought his bank was getting along about as well as others. Now the bank was liquidated, its doors closed forever. Camilla thought the end of their world had come.

Though the depositors received most of their money back, the stockholders of the bank lost all their stock investment and interest. Not only had Spencer worked in the bank, but he and Camilla had invested heavily in it. Spencer had been flattered when offered a chance to buy stock in the new Arizona Trust and Savings Bank. His father subscribed five hundred dollars and many other public-spirited men bought shares partly to help the new venture. Spencer, however, subscribed twenty-five hundred dollars, more than a full year's salary. He considered the investment the safest and soundest possible. He paid out his subscription monthly, as fast as he could. Shortly before the bank failed he had also bought his father's five hundred dollars in shares. When the doors closed he and Camilla lost all those hard-earned savings of six years. The investment evaporated overnight.

Spencer owed the bank $825. Luckily he was allowed to pay that by offsetting deposits which he was able to purchase at large discount from people who lacked faith in recovering much through the liquidation process. Spencer's ability to pay the debt at discount helped a little, though the loss of three thousand dollars in what he thought the soundest possible investment hurt.

When the bank closed, Spencer faced questioners. A poor widow whose savings stood endangered asked, "Why didn't you tell me the bank was going to fail? You must have known." Another said, "Why didn't you give me a hint?" His answer: "Don't you suppose if I had suspected trouble I would have moved to get my own savings out and to unload my stock?"

A frenzy of speculation had filled the air in the heady days of boom. Oil gushed in Texas and Oklahoma; the press reported instantaneous millionaires. The secret was to get in on the ground floor. Spencer and Camilla bought stock for twenty-five dollars in one company and more in Jaggers-Wallace and still more in mining claims. The gorgeously printed gold and green certificates they carefully cached. Then a brother in the Church told Spencer confidentially of a rich gold vein located in Aravaipa. "Because I love you I will let you in." The fifty dollars Spencer gave him for the worthless stock represented a lot of labor. Spencer lost all this as well as his bank stock.

Fortunately his reputation was better than the bank's. After he had helped the bank examiners for two weeks, he had a job offer at the People's Store, and the management of the two competitor banks also each offered him a position. He chose the Bank of Safford and was back to work within a week as chief teller at the same salary of $150. He and Camilla had lost savings, but the setback proved only temporary. "We were in no different position than others around us, except that maybe it hurt us worse. There was no sense of panic, but a lot of sadness."

At the Bank of Safford, after an initial period of worry, he enjoyed the work, learning new phases of banking. He made loans to customers, secured loans from correspondent banks in San Francisco, Chicago and New York, reconciled the accounts with precision — all this in addition to the routine teller work. The hours were better, the pay the same.

There were three windows, three tellers. Spencer soon found that the other two had a "petty cash box." When Spencer asked what that was, they explained it was the "over and short" box, in which they put any excess money at the end of the day and from which they drew if short. "Why don't you balance exactly?" Spencer asked. They laughed, "No one could handle so many transactions without being off sometimes." He accepted the challenge, on condition they never take change from his window without his checking it. He balanced to the penny; they could hardly believe it. When he did it day after day, they, too, found they could if they were careful enough. The "over and short" box disappeared. Spencer also made a study of accounts and worked out a system of service charges for unprofitable small accounts, especially those frequently overdrawn.

In order to become more efficient he taught himself to type. Years before that he had worked with two fingers at his father's machine, but now he bought a book of instructions and came early to work each morning to practice. Doggedly he worked at it until he could use all his fingers and type rapidly. During his later life he often typed his own letters, particularly during years when his voice became a scarce and precious commodity. As an apostle he often worked as he travelled, his typewriter perched on his knees in the back seat of a car.

At the bank Spencer met a wide range of people; businessmen and pensioners, depositors and borrowers, the plunger and the miser — they all needed banking services. This, coupled with his Church work and his singing at funerals and playing at dances, made him as broadly acquainted as anyone in the valley. He always chatted with customers. "How are the children? How are the crops this year? What does the livestock market look like?"

In addition to all the time and energy invested in his job and in his own little family, Spencer worked closely with his father from the time of his marriage. As stake clerk and stake president they met almost daily on Church business. No son could revere a father more.

Both father and son struggled with a dilemma arising from active service to the Church. In his thirties Andrew had written a little essay in which he said:

> When home, I should give my time to my darlings, but, because of foreign cares and responsibilities, instead of that my moments are so limited on account of so many letters to write, so many accounts to be kept and so many occasions to prepare for, that when my loving wife Ollie speaks to me I have not time to answer only as I do two things at once. My loving girl climbs on my knee to love and be fondled, I put her down and say I have not time; when my darling boy becomes weary after a long day's task of self-entertainment and frets, he annoys me, when my folks call in to see me they must catch me on the go, and in fact I only have time to do my duty when away from it. God and darling ones forgive me. I will try and take a little heaven as I go by making it heavenly for my loved ones.

Andrew knew what affection his family desired, but he had himself known no father close at hand to set the pattern. His strong sense of duty, cultivated by long years spent as mission president and stake president in urging others on, dominated his life.

Andrew and Josie were often separated by his travels. She suffered from leakage of the heart valves most of the time she was married to Andrew and became semi-invalid in about 1917. When others suggested there were stresses in the marriage Spencer rejected criticism, countering that Josie was a fine woman who had not had an easy life.

On October 12, 1922, Josie died at sixty-two, after fifteen years as Andrew's wife and as a major figure in the community in her own right. The junior college and public schools marched their 640 pupils past her as she lay in state at the Kimball home.

In a life sketch in the *Gila Valley Farmer* Andrew characterized her:

> Josephine Cluff Kimball was a highly intellectual person, possessing a wide range of information; she was a great reader and industriously kept herself up with the times. She was also scrupulously honest nor could she endure insincerity or dishonesty in anybody; she, like her God, hated a liar. She never owed a cent, always paying her way nor did she lose a moment in idle gossip or foolish conversation. She was exceptionally clean in her person, thoughts, and conversation, having no use for light or slighting or vulgar talk. She was exacting as she was willing to be exacted of. She

loved dearly and was a true friend, but woe unto one who deceived her or was not loyal to her devoted friendship.

Josephine, dressed in the finest handworked clothing her Relief Society friends of many years could stitch, was carried in W. C. Rawson's hearse to the cemetery in Thatcher and laid in the gravel plot up above the river floodplain. They laid her with Olive, leaving space for Andrew between them, where he would lie two years later. Spencer, ever the assistant, helped his father with the funeral arrangements.

After the funeral Andrew sat alone in the big home he had built twenty-five years before, no one to take care of him, no one to help entertain his numerous guests. Of the children, only Spencer and Camilla lived near. They rented out their home in Safford for the twenty-five-dollar monthly payments and moved back to Thatcher, into the family home with Andrew.

Andrew was getting on in years at sixty-four. Spencer and Camilla worried that the children's fussing bothered him. He rose at five to work in the garden before going to Church and business duties, while Spencer and Camilla stayed up later and got up later. Spencer was out until 1:00 or 2:00 A.M. playing at dances several nights a week.

Though Andrew loved his family dearly, they could not fill the vacant place in his life. When Mary Connelly came to the stake representing the General Board of the Young Ladies MIA as editor of the *Young Woman's Journal* in Salt Lake City, Andrew found her attractive. She was in her late forties and had not married. He went to Salt Lake for April Conference in 1923 and courted and won her. They announced their engagement, married a few weeks later, and in August returned together to Arizona. Spencer and Camilla then moved back into their own home in Safford.

Andrew and Mary lived happily together, to the pleasure of the family. Mary, a gentle, highly intelligent woman, quickly drew the deep and continuing affection of the children. They felt comfortable with her, especially Spencer and Camilla, who lived near.

But only a few months after marriage Andrew's health began to fail him. His knees and other joints hurt. He could get little relief from his miseries. He had hardening of the arteries, his teeth became infected and poisoned his system, he suffered from a nervous condition.

In search of better medical care Mary took him to Salt Lake, where they stayed at her father's home. From March 1924, things deteriorated. An energetic, determined man, Andrew refused to give in to his illness and underwent painful manipulations of the afflicted joints in treatment. Though he wilted physically under the pain, he suffered patiently.

By August the condition seemed critical. Mary sent for the sons. Gordon arrived first. Spencer asked for leave from his bank. His boss was a rough, profane man, but he always treated Spencer with respect, and extended his leave without question.

In Salt Lake City the August sun beat down mercilessly; no rain fell, but the lawns and gardens stubbornly clung to life, hanging on, dying slowly. Spencer wrote home:

> Poor Father. We are giving him drugs now but he suffers so in spite of it. Ever since yesterday he has been so nervous he could hardly stand it. Just moaned and cried all night long and throws his arms and twitches. He knows very little, at least he cannot follow his tho't thru. It is pitiful to see him. I am glad I didn't have to leave him at this stage of the game tho' it would really be a great relief. I average about 5 hours sleep, broken sleep each day but I am eating with an appetite so I am keeping up fine. . . .

> Sat. 7 a.m. Del did not arrive so Aunt Mary remained up till 12 and I have had the rest of the night. That was 1 hour troubled sleep for me last night and 4 the night before, but I am getting fat on it. Can't possibly understand how Father can get any worse, but he does. We gave him paregoric, whiskey and drugs and in spite of it he never rested a minute till 4:30 when he quieted down for about 20 min. He is all unstrung. His nerves are unhinged. He throws his hands and pounds the bed and wrings his hands and runs his hands thru' his hair and straightens out and draws up his left leg, the only one he can move and moans and yells with all his strength. All night long every 10 or 15 seconds he goes thru it all then quiets down for 5 or 10 seconds and repeats it. He cries O! My! over and over and sometimes O My God! How long! for hundreds of times then O! My! Father let me die.

> It is the most pitiful thing I ever saw. And still he lives on and his heart beats in spite of everything. Begins to look like he must starve to death. . . .

> Tell people he gets weaker and worse every day but his vitality was so strong nature is wearing it out with difficulty. Dr. Tyndall, I think, has about decided he knows very little about it.

Two days later, August 31, 1924, Andrew died.

At the funeral, held September 2, 1924, in the Twenty-seventh Ward chapel, President Heber J. Grant paid tribute. Andrew, he said, gave the best that was in him and never hid his light, always wearing his colors where everyone could see them.

President Grant and his wife and Andrew's twin sister Alice accompanied the sons and Andrew's body to Arizona for a second funeral service.

As the body lay in its casket in the family home, all the Primary children of the stake were brought to Thatcher for a viewing. They stood lined up in the hot sun to wait their turn to see this man who had been stake president for twenty-six years. Their teachers impressed on them that this was an occasion they should never forget.

On Andrew's sixty-sixth birthday they laid him in the neatly raked gravel cemetery on the hill, between Olive and Josie.

The terrible strain, physical and emotional, of tending his dying father and burying him ripped at Spencer. He broke, clinging to Camilla, sobbing almost uncontrollably at the graveside. His Aunt Alice said: "Now, Spencer, you perk up. Stand up."

As the people returned from the cemetery they gathered at the special conference President Grant called to reorganize the stake which Andrew had led for twenty-six years. He called Harry L. Payne, a music teacher at Gila Academy and Andrew's counselor, as the new president. John Nash, for seventeen years a counselor to Andrew, became first counselor. Spencer, twenty-nine years old, became President Payne's second counselor.

Spencer learned later that his brothers went to President Grant and asked him to choose someone else, arguing that it was a mistake to take so young a fellow and make an old man of him with that big a job. President Grant closed the discussion, saying, "Spencer has been called to this work, and he can do as he pleases about it." Reared as he was, Spencer never considered any answer but yes, though the calling surprised and awed him.

His acceptance of the call meant a change in plans. Camilla, at least, had thought she could go back to schoolteaching and support Spencer through college, so that he could become an accountant or a teacher. He had had some trouble in seeing this as a realistic possibility, but he did obtain from the University a report on his credits. His accepting the position as counselor made thought of further formal education impossible just then.

Though being a counselor involved major responsibility, no new stake clerk was called. President Payne said, "Spencer, you know the books, why don't you keep on with them for a while?" For years he carried both responsibilities in one of the largest stakes in the Church, which spanned the 350 miles from Miami, Arizona, to El Paso, Texas. He became very nearly the indispensable man. To many he seemed an extension of his father, who had provided leadership for almost all of their lives.

Trelva Wilson, then just a tiny girl, later remembered Spencer while he was still stake clerk as "so very young, and so handsome." She spoke of his "great charm, almost magnetic." People took to him easily. His brother-in-law, Henry Eyring, said that in Gila Valley you just didn't say anything unkind about Spencer Kimball, because you'd be saying it to one of his friends.

In his new Church position he made friends all over the far-flung stake. Grant Mack and his parents, visiting from Miami, a hundred miles west, were walking along the street in Safford on a hot day. Spencer caught sight of them, recognized them from his stake visits, and asked if he could treat the three of them to lemonades in the drug store.

Harold Turley, from El Paso, first met Spencer in the big central room of the Eyring house. Someone suggested: "Let's sing. Spencer, why don't you play the piano?" No one had to coax him. He livened the room up immediately, said Harold.

Spencer was important to the musical life of the valley. Right after his marriage he became stake Sunday School chorister. When he was made ward Sunday School counselor, he also led the ward choir. His journal notes in 1923: "Drove my load of singers back up to the rendition of the 'Holy City' oratorio at Layton. I sang a solo and assisted in three quartets and the choruses." Though a baritone, he often sang tenor, for tenors were always in short supply.

He and Camilla attended adult evening classes at the Academy; Camilla studied literature and Spencer took a music class. In the course of the first evening he, Frank Wanlass, Evan Madsen and Harold Mitchell formed a quartet and at the close of the first evening performed for the assembled groups. They continued to sing for a dozen

The Conquistadores: Evan Madsen, Spencer Kimball, Frank Wanlass, Harold Mitchell

years, with occasional substitutions. The quartet performed regularly at Rotary. They sang in *The Pirates of Penzance,* staged by the Academy at Red Knolls, a natural red clay amphitheater northwest of Pima. They sang at nearly every funeral in Gila Valley.

Spencer had a "very lovely voice," said Harold Mitchell. When he lost his voice to cancer while an apostle, many of his friends thought first of the "beautiful melody," gone now. "It rang like a bell," said Camilla's brother Henry. Spencer performed all over the valley, solo, quartet, chorus, leading a group, accompanying someone else on the piano. He was ready at a moment's notice. In World War I during the great flu epidemic from which Camilla suffered so heavily, Spencer sang in a quartet at many graveside funerals, held outside to prevent contamination by the dread virus. Some years later, while at a dance with Camilla, Spencer saw George Felshaw, a cowpuncher, fall dead to the floor, right in the middle of a dance. Felshaw's family asked Spencer's quartet to sing for the funeral, "Get Along, Little Dogie, Get Along." When the day came and the quartet launched into their song, the whole front row of calloused, strapping cowpunchers broke into tears, boo-hooing like babies.

There was a tradition in the valley dating back to prophecies by Jesse N. Smith, president of the Snowflake Stake, and John W. Taylor the apostle in 1898, that a temple would be built there. When the building of an Arizona temple became a serious matter and Mesa was chosen as the site in 1921, the decision disappointed many. They reasoned that the Gila Valley was much more nearly central in location for the Mormon population in Arizona, New Mexico, and Old Mexico, while Mesa fell at one edge of the Mormon settlements.

Even so, when the call came to contribute to the building, valley residents pitched in, some gladly, others dutifully. Spencer was made secretary for collecting temple funds from his stake. In addition to the extra labor this entailed, he and Camilla contributed $150.

As the time would approach for the temple dedication in October 1927, a stake choir, in which Spencer sang, would practice for weeks, some choir members driving from Virden, New Mexico, to Thatcher, one hundred miles round trip, a dozen times for rehearsals. When it came time for the dedication itself, the choir members and the many others who attended traveled in caravans. On the steeper sections of the fearsome highway over the mountains, drivers had to help one another push their cars, blocking the wheels with rocks when they rested, mended tires, or cooled the overheated engines.

On a September day in 1924 Camilla, now a pretty woman of twenty-nine, walked into the Safford grade school principal's office holding the hand of Spencer LeVan, who had just turned six years old, and persuaded the principal to start the boy in the second grade. Ambitious for her unusually bright child, she had already taught him to read well.

In her own family Camilla, as the eldest of the fifteen Eyring children who survived childhood, had led the way to college. She loved to read and kept up with new books, giving reviews and serving as volunteer librarian for the Safford library.

Camilla carried a large share of the home tasks so that Spencer could spend the time necessary to succeed in business and devote major efforts to Church and civic duties. She spent half her lifetime waiting supper for Spencer, it seemed. Like his father, Spencer was too busy to fit into rigid schedules easily; demands on his time came from all directions. Camilla played a large role in establishing the intellectual and spiritual climate of the home.

She made the kitchen the heart of the Kimball home. There she cooked, baked cinnamon rolls and bread, bottled fruit, ironed. There a child could find a ready listener in a patient and loving mother. With sweat dripping from her face, Camilla scrubbed clothes on a washboard. An excellent seamstress, she made certain that Olive Beth had nice clothes, anxious that her daughter never suffer the embarrassment she herself had felt as a college girl with nothing nice to wear.

When Laura Blake had looked at Spencer and Camilla as newlyweds, she had guessed that Camilla, with her strong will and college education, would run the house. She changed her mind quickly, however. Camilla came from a household where Papa, however mild, always drew respect and received the best. To her son Andrew it always seemed slightly incongruous that his strong-willed mother subordinated herself so much.

There were occasional disagreements, of course. One summer when Camilla wanted to save their extra cash for a new house and Spencer wanted to travel, they simply did not come to agreement. So Spencer loaded the car and took the trip alone and had a good time.

Camilla had a seven-dollar gold wedding band, but she had never had an engagement ring. One time when she and Spencer visited in El Paso on Church business they were shopping in a Kress variety store. Camilla spotted a toy "diamond" ring for ten cents. She said, "Oh, Spencer, I'm going to get myself an engagement ring." At a Church member's home for dinner, one of the women spotted the new ring and cried out excitedly, "Oh! You've got a new diamond." She went on about Spencer's generosity. So as not to embarrass her friend, Camilla let it go. She and Spencer laughed about it, but when they got back to Safford Spencer said, "Come on, Mama, I guess it is time we bought you an engagement ring." And he did.

7

The Great Depression

— "business is OFFF;
we are still hanging ONNN"

Bishop Joseph W. Greenhalgh saw
in Spencer a talent for business and pressed him to joint business
ventures. In 1925 they began making small loans as a sideline — what
they called their "securities business." Out of his small salary, paying
for a home and supporting a family of four, Spencer set aside what he
could and Bishop Greenhalgh matched it. By May each had put in
$350. They used $453 of this capital to purchase an installment contract which the local Ford dealer did not want to carry. Other such
loans used up their funds, but they added more and soon payments
and interest came back in. Spencer kept the books. The two men
screened the contracts carefully, so that only once, in the depth of the
Depression, did they have to repossess a car. They loaned money on
old cars, new cars, washers, ranges, radios, bicycles, almost anything
which people insisted on buying on time. No cash was ever taken out of
the small loan business. All profits were reinvested. Wives and children
also put their savings in. The first year the investments returned 23
percent, with no overhead. The money doubled and redoubled over
the years.

By year's end 1926 Spencer was earning $175 a month at the bank
as an assistant cashier. He had started in a bank nine years before,
posting entries at $75 a month. But even the hundred-dollar increase

seemed tame after a decade. With bank and stake clerk work and miscellaneous earnings, he made three thousand dollars that year. He was thirty-one years old, full of energy and ambition, but with no room at the bank to move up. Camilla was six months pregnant with their third child. Spencer told his neighbor, Ben Blake, that he had his family to think of. They could get by on the bank's wages, he said, but not very handsomely. So when he learned that the term of the Safford postmistress expired in January, he talked about applying for the position. Because of local dissatisfaction with the postal service, Spencer thought the chances were good that Senator Cameron would be responsive to the idea of Washington awarding the post to someone new. Spencer's brother-in-law, John H. Udall, in Phoenix, wrote to Cameron, who wrote back that "if Kimball is successful in passing the examination, I shall be pleased to appoint him." But meanwhile Spencer had had second thoughts. Willard Pace thought the job paid $250 a month, but someone else told Spencer it was just $200. Spencer wrote Udall again asking if the post required Sunday work, to supervise mail distribution. He explained to Udall: "If I had to be in the P.O. every Sunday *A.M.* and *P.M.* it would be difficult for me to handle my stake work."

About this time Bishop Greenhalgh came to Spencer with a different proposition. He, Oliver Larson and Harry McCarroll had formed a little insurance agency, putting in fifty dollars each and hammering together a table and counter for a one-room office in back of the bank across the street from where Spencer worked. The business had struggled and scrabbled, producing insufficient income for three families. One partner had withdrawn and taken a bank job in California. The other had become ill and wanted to get out. The bishop wanted Spencer to join him and buy out the other's share. The price was $150. Spencer now knew nearly everyone in the valley, and those who did not know him had known his father. That made a difference in a business like selling insurance.

Spencer went home and thought about the idea. He fretted at abandoning the relative security of his bank job, in which he felt some satisfaction. He had a growing family to feed. Nearly five years after Olive Beth's birth, Camilla had just borne her third child, Andrew Eyring, "with real joy." Now five depended on Spencer.

But banking looked to him like a dead end, whereas a business of his own could become whatever he had the wit and energy to make it. He talked it over with Ben Blake. Ben urged him to risk it and rise or fall on his own talent. He thought Spencer could get rich with Joe Greenhalgh. Camilla, who had always been ambitious for Spencer's success, sometimes having more confidence in him than he had in himself, reassured him that she would support his decision.

With some misgivings he tendered his resignation to the bank, effective May 1, "if satisfactory adjustments can be made by that time." Spencer drew on his savings to pay $150 for a partnership in the business. He later wrote, "It may be that $150 was too much for it since there were only a few books, a very small amount of good will and a very few policies on the books."

Once the decision was made, Spencer turned his full energies to the business. The total income for the first month was $300; Spencer's half was $150. Over the long pull he fared clearly better than he would have in the bank. Though some times were lean, particularly during the Depression of the 1930s, he never made much less than he had made at the bank — some of the time he made much more.

The firm occupied the room at the back of the bank which had been a directors' board room, but which the bank gladly rented to them. Entrance was from a side street. They had an old desk and some second-hand chairs and a lumber counter. But they boasted that from the very beginning their business "operated close to a million dollars," since the bank vault formed the north wall of the office.

The new partners hung a sign out over the sidewalk:

Kimball-Greenhalgh
Agency
Life   Fire   Casualty
Insurance
Bonds   Real Estate

From the outset Spencer managed the office and drew a salary; Bishop Greenhalgh, who had other interests and was semi-retired, helped out mainly by getting business. At the end of the year they divided the net profits, if any. Except for the very worst of times there was always something to divide.

In some ways Spencer was quite his older partner's opposite. For instance Spencer typed fast, with his hands raised high over the typewriter. He couldn't stand dawdling. When he sat down to help devise an advertisement with Carmen, his secretary, he would have the letter-

Safford, Arizona, in the Gila Valley under Mount Graham

First office of Kimball-Greenhalgh Agency, Safford, Arizona

ing and sketch laid out in three minutes. He moved about a room quickly, from one chore to the next.

Joe Greenhalgh on the other hand had arthritis, Carmen said later, that slowed his walk and made it painful for him when people squeezed his hand in friendly enthusiasm. He talked slowly. In his last years he quit trying at desk work, since Spencer could do it so much faster. But he was so honest and respected that when he asked someone for insurance business it was hard to turn him down. "Mr. Greenhalgh would swear a little bit," remembered one secretary. "You never heard anything like that from Mr. Kimball. The two were quite different."

But they were good friends. Bishop Greenhalgh used to say: "Here I am a Democrat and Spencer a Republican and our interests are the same. I think if we get a Republican president we'll go to pot and Spencer thinks if we get a Democratic president we'll go to pot. I guess that is what politics is all about." Joe's son, Grant, remembered that the year Joe died, in 1941, Spencer "was like part of the family." Spencer treated Mr. Greenhalgh like a father. Neither secretary later could imagine Spencer criticizing his older partner. Even when the bishop faded in ill health, there was no move to dissolve the business, now incorporated, nor to redistribute the profits. Spencer still took out a moderate salary and took his pro-rata share of the net income.

Spencer never took on a job halfheartedly. He expected of his secretaries the same kind of dedication. If they were at the office early and left late, in his book that was not extra. "The commonest recollection I have of him as a youngster," remembered his son LeVan, "was that I saw him relatively little." Spencer's brother Gordon said of him once, "He'll die with his shoes on."

At the start things moved slowly. About four thousand people lived in the area around Safford, about ten thousand in the valley. One competing insurance agency existed in town, outwardly cordial but unhappy at having to share business with the newcomers. Spencer made connection with some of the strongest insurance companies, acquainted himself with their representatives and benefited from their tutelage. He vigorously contacted all his friends, asking that at renewal time they would give him their insurance business. He put to use his broad acquaintanceship gained from banking and Church work. But selling was not easy; even willing friends often had policies with years to go before renewal. The agency sold enough insurance, mostly fire and casualty, to keep afloat, however. In addition they began to sell an occasional piece of real estate. And they still had their separate loan or "securities" business.

They sacrificed to make the business grow. For many months Spencer and Camilla lived on as little as $62 a month, including tithing — putting up fruit, milking a cow, buying frugally. Spencer plowed back into the business the rest of the $150 he drew as salary. Some of their friends lived better by spending their earnings but never moved ahead much. Spencer and Camilla had the patience to wait.

Within a few months of Spencer's getting into it the agency hired Val Webb full-time to help in the office. A secretary came in once or twice a week to take dictation.

Times were good; the U.S. economy puffed and swelled to the bursting point. Easy credit and rampant speculation led people into debt. But not all of this seeming prosperity showed its face in Safford. Farmers had been caught during the 1920s in a cruel scissors of steadily rising costs and sharply cut prices for farm products. Cotton prices, livestock prices, grain prices, all had dropped 50 percent between 1919 and 1921 and they never fully recovered thereafter. A farming community struggled even in years when false optimism infected the country.

The agency diversified. The partners bought some lots and built some small cement-block houses on speculation. They tried some rental properties but abandoned that as too much trouble in management. Spencer became secretary for several canal companies in the valley, eventually keeping books for nearly all of them at a monthly fee of $15 or $20 each. He also served as secretary of a cotton-growers association. Each such activity brought income to the agency and also broadened the range of potential customers.

The major business endeavor was the development of a subdivision. In 1928, for what seemed a fortune of twenty thousand dollars, they bought twenty acres of farmland almost surrounded by homes. LeVan remembers going with Spencer before the purchase to measure the property at night, so no one would know of the agency's interest in it. They had it platted in eighty-two lots.

Prospects had never looked so good; men were getting rich on paper, playing the stock market. But in the summer of 1929 the Federal Reserve Board raised its discount rate in order to dampen speculation with borrowed money. When Britain followed suit in October, that triggered sharp selling on the New York Stock

Exchange. The market broke, and in a month stock prices had dropped 37 percent. The volume of buying on margin had more than doubled in two years, and the crash left a large number of investors — really, speculators — stranded.

Some farmers in the valley had mortgaged and remortgaged their property to buy more in an expanding market. They ended with less than when they started. The bubble had burst, stocks tumbled, the wealthy became penniless, and mortgaged property slipped away. Real estate would not sell. And Kimball-Greenhalgh sat there with an investment of more than twenty thousand dollars in their subdivision lots for which there was no market.

They advertised an auction, hoping to move some of the lots on an easy-payment plan to relieve the financial pressure. They planted ash trees, poured sidewalks and curbs. They hired a band and bought prizes and refreshments. They advertised heavily to get a lot of people attending, all in hope of making a few sales. When the time came, the usually blue Arizona skies loosed a downpour. The band could not play, the decorations faded and blew away, the crowd stayed home. A few came to take home the prizes. Not a single lot sold. The auction plan failed miserably, and Kimball-Greenhalgh had additional costs to pay. The gloomy partners went home deflated.

What cash business remained was a godsend in those terrifying times. For years the agency could not sell a single lot or house, though they brokered a few trades. No one had money, no one had confidence. Captive business in insurance, that is, the protection which mortgagees demanded of properties on which they had loaned money, helped keep the business going.

But the canal companies and the cotton-growers association still paid, and people occasionally bought cars on contract, which Spencer and his partner then bought from the car dealers. With these and other miscellaneous sources of income the business limped along.

In September 1930 a fourth child came, Spencer and Camilla's last. Red-haired and blue-eyed, he reminded them once more of his grandmother, Olive. In a father's blessing when the boy was eight days old, Spencer named him Lawrence Edward. The name *Edward* was after Father Eyring. Then Camilla's sister Caroline pointed out that putting *Edward* second might seem a slight to their papa. After all, the other boys were *Spencer* LeVan and *Andrew* Eyring. Spencer responded to the suggestion and switched the order of names. Father Eyring blessed the baby in church that month as Edward Lawrence.

Business for Kimball-Greenhalgh got worse and worse each year until 1934. Things were on a downward spiral.

With cash scarce, much business turned to barter. Merchants were willing to give credit in exchange for insurance. Camilla, needing shoes for one of the children, would ask Spencer, "Which shoe store owes you credit?" She bought groceries this month from one store, next month from another — whoever owed Kimball-Greenhalgh. They traded milk for piano lessons for their children and thought longingly of the $150 cash salary Spencer had brought home when employed by the bank. Camilla often said, "Oh, for the days when I could walk into a store and buy with money what I wanted."

The crash reverberated through the whole economy. Between 1928 and 1932 national income fell by half. Growing unemployment reached 10 million in 1932 and at least 13 million in 1933. Wages of those fortunate to have work were cut. Farmers suffered even more than others.

In those days of loose regulation, banks in the United States failed at a rate of about seven hundred a year in good times. In 1930 the rate doubled. In 1931 it tripled. In 1932, with the weakest already weeded out, nearly fifteen hundred failed.

Spencer's stepmother, Mary, wrote from Salt Lake City in 1932 that she, her father and her two sisters had lost twenty thousand dollars in the Deseret Savings Bank when it had closed that week. A run on Zion's Savings Bank, where the rest of the family's money was, scared her, but President Heber J. Grant's assurance that the Church stood behind the bank, telling the people "to leave the funds there and be happy," stemmed the run and the bank survived. Mary, a consistently optimistic, cheerful woman, wrote with a strange mix of gloom and hope, "Everything that can be shaken is being shaken, isn't it? . . . Isn't it lovely to have spring? . . ."

Spencer wrote back that sometimes he felt everything was slipping away. Properties had so depreciated that lots people had bought on contract from Kimball-Greenhalgh were turned back. "I suppose we have already lost $2000 on properties turned back which we must hold or re-sell at the greatly reduced market price."

Spencer had much of his money in the Bank of Safford, where previously he had worked for over three years. Though rumors floated through town about the bank's shaky condition, Spencer stuck with it. The bank's directors, good friends of his, assured him of the bank's health. He later wrote to Gordon, "Partly out of unadulterated loyalty

we hung onto this bank." But on May 28, 1932, it failed, delivering still
another blow to the community and to the Kimballs.

The failed bank took with it a hundred dollars Spencer and
Camilla had saved for a trip to the Rotary Convention in Seattle, seven
hundred dollars in Rotary funds intended for the Boy Scout camp,
canal company funds, Church funds, estate funds — the funds of all
the organizations for which Spencer was secretary, nearly nine
thousand dollars in all, besides the children's savings accounts.

In a letter to Camilla's sister Rose, Spencer said: "You know, of
course, of the bank failure. We lost a little, about $1600
plus. We haven't missed a meal yet and are still alive ... ; times
are really getting worse and worse here." Having learned to be wary,
Kimball-Greenhalgh put some of their eggs in the Valley Bank basket,
so that they had just enough cash on deposit there to cover the $1400 in
outstanding checks drawn on the Bank of Safford, which were now
worthless. They also held checks of others which they could not collect.
Their reputation improved by their immediate ability to make their
own checks good. A sound credit rating helped when things got tight.

Shortly before the Bank of Safford closed Spencer reconciled the
Kimball-Greenhalgh statement one month and came up six hundred
dollars short. He worked it over again and again; all the checks were
listed and all the deposits correct. He struggled and sweated and finally
concluded it was "in the air." He took the statement to the bank, to one
of the men with whom he had worked, and said: "It is the strangest
thing. My account is short six hundred dollars and it is in the air." The
man glanced it over, ran up the figures on the adding machine, expressed great surprise and credited the account with six hundred
dollars. Pleased, Spencer thought no more of it until some months later
when the same teller faced charges for embezzling twenty-three
thousand dollars and ultimately spent a year in prison. It had not
occurred to Spencer that dishonesty might be involved.

He wrote to Harold Mitchell about the fact that the teller continued to take badly needed money from the bank right up to the time
of its collapse: "The more I think of it the worse I feel about it, to think
that he could be living high and spending our money and causing an
entire community to suffer by the falling of their air castles."

When Camilla's sister Caroline forgot about a sum of money she
had entrusted to Spencer, he wrote her, explaining the whole business,
including what interest had accrued, then joked: "I am quite surprised

that you would so easily forget your money, and if I were a little more like [the dishonest bank teller] maybe you wouldn't now have any to worry about. You'd better not tempt me, though, sis, I don't know what you'd do if you didn't have honest brothers and sisters. Ha."

Friends recommended Spencer to be one of the three receivers to liquidate the defunct bank, but he had not supported the incumbent governor and the appointments were political. Spencer aided the state banking department in some bank examinations. He wrote Gordon that the "big bank had lost some $4,000,000 and the Valley Bank some $10,000,000 in deposits since the first of the year." Within a short time ten Arizona banks failed. The Depression took its toll; all suffered. Taxes fell in arrears, and state payrolls could not be met out of current tax income, so the state withdrew public funds from the banks, leaving them vulnerable. Newspapers published pages of delinquent taxes and at tax sales a man with a little cash could buy valuable property for a song.

The deposits in the Bank of Safford ultimately stood to be worth thirty cents on the dollar. But people who could not wait sold their claims for less. A friend, Harold Mitchell, wrote from Parowan, Utah, that he had lost every cent he had in the world. "I appreciate your advice to be cheerful, and I halfway believe that if I were there with you that it would help. . . . I have thought for a long while that you were a 'big' man, and that is only another evidence of the fact." Spencer replied: " . . . You asked about your warrant. . . . I have asked a great many people whom I thought might be interested in the warrant but so far have not been successful. . . . I have just now talked to _____ and he said he would take it and discount it 10%. . . . If you can deal with anyone else, I know you won't want to deal with this buzzard. . . . I'm still trying to be cheerful but it is not so easy."

He wrote to someone else:

> You said that I was mighty fortunate to have a business of my own. I do feel fortunate in that the business is still solvent and a going concern though business has been steadily getting worse and worse until it is a mighty difficult matter to keep ends meeting. There is still a bad feature in owning a business. We must continue to pay sewer, water and other assessments and taxes in spite of the fact that the property is unproductive. There is a constant drain and little or nothing to drain. We have cut our own salaries down to a mere getting-by wage. And each month as the income reduces we cut again and again. It is just a matter of time with most of these

small town businesses. If the depression lasts very long it will get them too. Here's hoping that we can outlast it.

It is hard to keep optimistic. After a good night's rest I rush down to work all pepped up and ready for anything. In the first couple of hours about 6 or 8 policies are returned (can't pay for them) and down drop my feathers. And by night time you feel like everything is gone to the bad. But while conditions are certainly at a low ebb, and prospects look mighty gloomy and unfavorable, yet so far we have not actually been stinted in food, so we feel mighty thankful for that. . . . All the mines in Globe-Miami district and Clifton-Morenci district are closing now and in July so that not only affects them but deals us another hard blow as we depend on those camps largely for a market.

But life did not stop. Spencer wrote a friend that he thought he might be able to collect some accounts of people who had moved to California if he saw them personally. He thought it would pay for the trip and permit him to take the family for a few days' vacation at the beach. The worries and pressures of the time made some relaxation the more needed.

He wrote Al Pfalzer, an insurance friend in Los Angeles, "Business is offff, as you know; we are still hanging onnnn."

School districts had to pay teachers with certificates of debt, payable in sequence as money became available. The teachers sold them at discount. Spencer had to take certificates in payment for insurance and for house payments and wait for the cash. He could remain afloat so long as his reserves and credit allowed him to keep a flow of business in the stagnant economy. He bought certificates when he had cash. LeVan remembers Spencer's being critical of teachers who had no savings to tide them over even a short wait.

To Harold Mitchell he wrote: "The town is deserted and no one is doing any business. Our insurance business is falling off terribly and no one would talk real estate; in fact, they look at you as if you were crazy to mention land sales."

At the end of 1932 Spencer closed a letter to his brother Gordon with a mix of disappointment and stubborn hope: "Our Christmas will be very light this year but we will all the more hope and wish for our folks a happy and pleasant Christmas and oh! How we do wish for us all a Prosperous New Year!!!"

But 1933 proved even worse than 1932. Spencer was no longer stake clerk, and from the business itself he derived an income averaging only $130 a month. Limping on, things continued to decline when it seemed they could go no lower. By February 1933, with widespread uncertainty as to the effect of the incoming Roosevelt administration, chaos reigned in the banking business. State after state declared banking holidays for days at a time, when no withdrawals from banks could be made. By inauguration time, nearly half of the states were doing this, and scarcely a bank in the country operated normally.

Franklin D. Roosevelt's inaugural address, inaugurating the "New Deal" he had promised in his campaign, coined the phrase "the only thing we have to fear is fear itself — nameless, unreasoning, unjustified terror which paralyzes needed efforts to convert retreat into advance." He instilled confidence that something would be done. As his first act he issued a sweeping executive order suspending all banking transactions except under new government regulations.

The move appalled Spencer. He wrote his brother Gordon that it was the "craziest thing in the world according to my way of looking at things. If I can analyze the situation, it means a serious reaction against all banks and almost ruin to the country and state. It will mean a diversion of money from banks to hiding places and a loss of confidence."

Spencer saw the issues accurately but guessed wrongly as to the consequences of Roosevelt's action. Drastic as it was, it proved the first step up out of the morass. Reopening the banks under tighter regulations, however, provided no magic. The key was public confidence. Continued hoarding of money and runs on banks would precipitate new crisis. Roosevelt met the situation by going directly to the people, explaining to the common man in the first of his "fireside chats" what the banking measure meant and assuring them that the banks were safe.

It worked. Within a few days most larger banks reopened. By April 12 three-fourths of the banks again operated. Hundreds had closed forever, but after this drastic purging people trusted those that remained; hoarding ceased and money flowed back. Deposits increased by a billion dollars between the moratorium and mid-April.

The threat of total collapse, which had been real, dissipated, but the problems of depression continued on and on, ameliorating only gradually. Unemployment continued as a major problem. Temporary setbacks in the recovery sent out waves of gloom. Spencer wrote in fall 1933 that his business had been losing capital at a rate of about a hundred dollars a month.

Credit for farmers enabled agricultural areas to start moving again. Federal Housing Administration's insuring of mortgages stimulated building construction. A 1936 letter mentions "at least 60 new homes in Safford within the last year or two." Spencer qualified as an FHA appraiser and earned a few additional dollars in that way.

Despite all the cries of socialism and boondoggle and dictatorship, things turned around.

In the subdivision, which had been such a great disappointment in 1929, lots began to sell. The trees had grown, the Kimball children had chopped weeds. Eventually every lot sold and the Kimball-Greenhalgh Addition proved the finest residential section in the valley in its time, a monument to the men who saw it through. They bought other farmland and subdivided it, too. Some of it they kept for speculation, letting local farmers till the soil on shares.

In 1933 Val Webb took a job with the state and Spencer hired Emil Crockett to help him in the office. Soon thereafter he hired Blanch Tyler as full-time secretary, a move reflecting the improvement of business. Kimball-Greenhalgh moved from the back of the bank onto Main Street, replacing a cafe. When they attempted to put up wallpaper it came off because of grease impregnating the walls.

The new assistant, Emil, found that Spencer was a shrewd businessman but highly ethical. "I remember one time we had a house listed for quite a while and it would not sell. Spencer told the owners, 'I think if you paint the house we can increase what it will bring by quite a bit.' 'No,' they said, 'if you want to paint it, go ahead; we'll sell it to you.' So he bought and resold it, making about fifteen hundred dollars for a couple of hundred dollars' painting."

With the idea that a man who is in your debt holds it against you, Spencer made it policy to keep after debtors until they paid. Emil remembered "one man who owed him quite a bill and Spencer went after it. The man avoided him and said, 'I'm not going to pay it.' Spencer said, 'I'm going to see that you do,' and kept after it. As quick as the bill was paid this man started coming in the office again."

Spencer's shrewdness sometimes failed him. He sold his half interest in one property for five thousand dollars; within a few years, with rerouting of the highway, it was renting for two hundred dollars a month. And he later let go an option on some Las Vegas property which would have made him rich.

*Climbing Mount Graham
on snowshoes, 1938*

*Parade float for Kimball-Greenhalgh Agency, 1930:
Andrew, Olive Beth, Camilla*

Spencer kept the agency open six full days a week and worked hard to make the business succeed. He practiced thrift. He had his secretary reverse the adding machine tape and use the other side; he always saved for use as scratch paper sheets still blank on one side. He was not stingy, but he was selective in how he spent his money both in the business and at home. For example, early in his marriage, when he and Camilla watched every penny and recorded every tiny purchase, they paid $525 cash for a piano at a time when they were paying eight dollars a month rent.

At the agency he worked out front, where he could greet people. They liked doing business with him. But he did not feel obligated to them on that account. His secretary later recalled hearing a farmer start to tell him a vulgar story. As soon as he saw what was coming Spencer interrupted, saying he had heard that story before, and changed the subject. Neither were social considerations allowed to dictate his conduct. At a club luncheon some years later someone at his table launched into a questionable anecdote. As the story came to its punch line Spencer deliberately put a bite into his mouth so it would be obvious that he was not sharing the story. The others, seeing that, moved on to a different line of conversation.

In his business he was a perfectionist. He checked over the work done by others to be sure it was right. He was quick at figures, good at detail. In such a person little lapses of memory seemed amusingly out of character to his office staff. A secretary later remembered that after Spencer had bought a dictating machine he absent-mindedly picked up the telephone receiver and began dictating to the startled operator. Another time he attended a Garden Club meeting upon invitation, assuming it had to do with his stake position, only to discover later that the invitation had been addressed to Mrs. Spencer W. Kimball.

Despite all the problems of running the business, Spencer often remarked that rather than work again as an employee he would set up a peanut stand on the corner. He enjoyed the freedom to work at his own pace and assign his own priorities. He valued the flexibility it gave him. He could run to the hospital, speak at a funeral, or leave for days at a time to attend general conference.

A major celebration occurred in 1933, on the golden jubilee of the organization of the stake in 1883. Plans had been afoot for months. Spencer was general chairman. There was a priesthood banquet for 820 men and boys, with the President of the Church in attendance, a half-mile-long parade, two dances, a pageant presented before two thousand people, and two days of Church conference meetings. In the darkest days of the Depression the Church members celebrated growth and progress.

As counselor in the stake presidency, Spencer spoke at the conference. After one session Eli Abegg and some relatives were discussing the conference and the speakers. He clearly remembers saying in an unpremeditated way, under the influence of the meeting, "I want to tell you in the name of Jesus Christ that Spencer Kimball will one day become an apostle of the Church."

Few could see as far ahead as that, but Spencer was recognized as a man of spiritual strength. In 1927 he ordained Ray Ellsworth an elder before he went to South Africa as a missionary. As the elder recorded it, Spencer said, "You will be called upon to lay down your life for your church, but if you are faithful in the discharge of your duties, your life will not be required of you." While later serving on his mission the missionary knocked on a door in Cape Colony and a man answered and said, "Wait a minute." Shortly the man opened the door again, shoved a revolver into the missionary's stomach and pulled the trigger five times. The gun did not fire. The man then brandished a knife and the elder backed away.

The next day a Church member who lived next door said that the man, who had been threatening to "get" the Mormons, went down to the beach and killed five gulls with the bullets that would not fire the night before.

One time as Spencer visited the Eden Ward and sat on the stand, he noted five boys sitting on the front row who, all in unison, crossed their legs, put their hands on their faces, uncrossed their legs, scratched their sides. After a while he realized they were mimicking his movements. It reminded him that if he were to be taken as an example he must be cautious in what he did.

In a few years the Depression drove most of Spencer's close friends out of little Safford, many of them to hunt for work in Phoenix or Los Angeles. But in the early years there was a group of about twelve couples that did things together. They almost all had summer cabins on Mount Graham, responsible Church positions, young children, and high spirits.

The Saturday before Easter the whole group would take their children outside of town in the desert for an Easter egg hunt. At community dances they would put their children to sleep in bedding in the back seats of their cars out in the parking lot. A couple of times a year they rode hayracks up west of Safford into the black rock country. Adults, children, babies, all bedded down around a campfire in cots and sleeping bags, singing, joking, playing. During hunting season the men went quail shooting, then, back at camp, roasted the birds in dutch ovens over the fire. Except Spencer. He stayed in camp and gathered wood, tended the fire, then helped clean the birds by the stream when they were brought back, and cooked them. "Spencer would never shoot the birds," remembered Jessie Killian. "He was such a kind-hearted man."

There were parties every week or two, hosted at different homes. Usually they played Rook, at which Spencer was nearly always a winner. LeVan later laughingly rued that his father's only card game was Rook. "Dad was a very skillful gamesman," he said. "If he had taken up poker as a young man he could have supported the family on it." Camilla remembers him as the most popular one of the group. "He was always the life of the party," said Lela Udall later. "His mirthful laugh just kept us all laughing." Once at a birthday party as refreshments were served, he came out of the kitchen with a shoe on his serving tray, taking orders for fillet of sole.

He liked to dance. He and Camilla belonged to a square dance club. After a hard day at the office, handball, Church meetings, he could still enjoy a couple of hours of square dancing. The couples in the club bought matching clothes, to enhance the effect. Social dancing also pleased Spencer, and in his youth, and later with Camilla in his early married life, he danced often. He was a good dancer — not exceptional, but the sort of partner women liked a turn with.

In a nearby town where he visited often there was a young woman who had suffered from a serious blood disease which left her with blotched skin and stiff joints and clawlike hands. At dances Spencer always danced with her. Others did so, too, but he had a special knack of letting her forget her handicap.

On New Year's Eve Spencer and Camilla would party with their group until the sun came up next morning. There was a traveling banquet as the whole swarm raided iceboxes. At midnight the men shot off guns. There were party hats, whistles, horns, screams. After midnight they sat around the telephone and called any friends they suspected might be sleeping to wish them a Happy New Year. "Sometimes long-distance," remembered Camilla. "Collect," said Spencer. "Oh, yes," agreed Camilla, "always collect."

One year, one of the men dialed Vie Fuller, a neat, fastidious woman. (She and her husband weren't at the party that New Year's.) "Is this Mrs. Fuller?"

"Yes."

"Do you wash?"

"No, of course I don't wash."

"My, you must be dirty by now."

Every year Spencer telephoned his friend, Lee John, who lived on the main road east of Safford.

"Is this Mr. John?"

"Yes."

"Do you live on the highway to Solomonsville?"

"Yes."

"Well, you'd better get off because we're coming down it."

Mr. John fell for that one every year.

If any couple in the group went home early on New Year's Eve, the rest of the crowd might serenade them out of bed again. Once after a couple had been gone an hour, the party-goers piled in autos and drove to their home in Pima. They knocked at the front door, knocked at the windows, but couldn't get anyone to open. Don Pace found an unlocked window, slipped through quietly, unlatched the front door, and let the whole crowd in. The wife hid under the quilt, but her husband rolled out and hid under the bed. The men just lifted the bed off and exposed him there, shivering in his night clothes.

Another New Year's Eve the group learned that Jay Green had an expensive selection of wedding dresses unsold at his clothing store. Alma Tate got on the phone to him and made up a story about a girl who had decided on the spur of the moment to marry and needed a wedding dress so she could leave on the next bus. Mr. Green couldn't resist the chance to unload one of his special stock of dresses, even though it was past midnight and he was in bed, so he said he would unlock his shop in fifteen minutes and meet the caller there. Fifteen minutes later the whole crowd huddled in the cold outside Green's shop door while he unsuspectingly unlocked it from the inside. The door opened; they all crowded in and wished him a Happy New Year.

Almost any time the group was together socially, there were high spirits. Once when Spencer was at the pool at Indian Hot Springs, he and Jesse Udall dried off and dressed while Harvey Taylor stayed in the pool. Then they hid Harvey's clothes and went on into the restaurant to wait for their friend. All he found when he walked dripping wet into the dressing room was a blanket, a large safety pin, and a note telling him to pin on the blanket and come out for lunch. So he did.

The Kimballs were good friends with their neighbors. Next door on one side lived the Killians. After dinner they could sit inside and listen to Spencer's kitchen door bang as he sang his way out back to milk his cows. On the other side of the house lived the Ellsworths. Nola Ellsworth remembered mowing her lawn before the sun rose one morning. Spencer, already dressed, stuck his head out the window and asked Nola why she was pushing that mower, pregnant as she was. She answered that his lawn was mown and Ellsworths wouldn't be outdone by Kimballs. Spencer mowed her grass before breakfast.

When Spencer went out of town once on Church work, the Killians took charge of his cow. The cow died. All the neighbors showed up with shovels and dug a pit for the cow in the Kimballs' back yard. When they had finished, Wick Mendenhall, who was county agricultural agent, insisted on planting asparagus on the cow's grave. None better, he argued. All the wives vowed they would eat none of that asparagus. But the men later swore it was the best asparagus they'd ever tasted.

Wick Mendenhall, along with Jesse Udall, Harold Mitchell, and Spencer Kimball, played handball at the National Guard armory off just two walls. Spencer's daybook for 1939 mentions twenty-six times he played; sometimes they followed up with volleyball. He always played hard, to win. Every winter for seven years Spencer and Harold Mitchell hiked on snowshoes to the Kimballs' cabin on Mount Graham, the drifts being so high in spots that they could walk right over the cabin. Some years they had to dig down to find the cabin door. They would stay several days. "Under Spencer's direction," remembered Harold, "we never missed our prayers."

Nearly every summer the Kimball family took an extended trip together by car. Spencer and Camilla loved to travel. They could see new places for little more than the cost of gasoline if they put up at inexpensive tourist cabins. In the summer of 1928, when baby Andrew was just a year old, Spencer and Camilla took their children in the old Studebaker and motored north. The baby had a bad bout with diarrhea, and they couldn't stop it for several days. Every night after they found a cabin, Camilla took out the bag of dirty diapers and scrubbed.

The family visited June Conference in Salt Lake City, the friendly bears of Yellowstone, the beaches along the west coast. At Victoria, British Columbia, Camilla grabbed a souvenir pair of ceramic penguins just before the stores closed, then nearly threw them into Puget Sound when she had to pay duty on them on the boat back to Seattle.

Camilla's brother Ed and his new wife, Evelyn, lived in San Francisco. Since Camilla had never met Evelyn, Camilla insisted Spencer park the car outside San Francisco and rent a motel room so she could scrub the travel grit and summer sweat off her children and press out the wrinkles in their clothes. The next day they drove into town to meet the new sister-in-law. The journey continued down the coast to Tijuana and then east to Safford.

In 1929 Spencer and Camilla and eleven-year-old LeVan took another vacation, typical for them. They spent nearly six weeks touring the United States. They traveled from Safford to the Rotary Convention in Dallas, then to Louisiana, Chicago, and Detroit, where they picked up a new Dodge car they had ordered; then on to Toronto, Niagara, and Palmyra. They slept in the Joseph Smith farmhouse in the room where, they were told, the angel Moroni had appeared (actually the house had been built by the family later than the angel's visit). Then they journeyed to Vermont, Boston, on down the east coast to Washington, D.C., and back across to Carthage, Illinois. There they slept in one of the cells downstairs from that where Joseph Smith had been martyred by a mob. Then it was west across Missouri and Nebraska, and to Colorado where they rode up Pike's Peak. They visited friends and relatives all along the way. Spencer and LeVan climbed every hill, monument and church steeple from Arizona to Boston and back.

In 1923 the LDS Academy dropped its high school program and was renamed Gila College. Spencer served on the governing board. In the 1930s the Church withdrew further from the educational field and concluded that after June 1933 it would no longer support Gila College, but that it would convey the entire plant, worth at least $150,000, to the public, on condition that the property continue as an educational institution. Spencer and other community leaders stood thunderstruck. The college meant a great deal to the area.

They first tried and failed to get the state to take it. An election was scheduled to determine whether the county would take over the school's operation. Spencer, college president Harvey Taylor, and others stumped the valley in favor of the transaction. Opponents doubted the Church's motives, fearing there must be a catch since this occurred in 1933, in the depth of the Depression; others saw no use for a local junior college; others feared the additional tax burden. Still, after all the hard work, the election proved successful by a wide margin. But Spencer made some enemies who thought he was sacrificing community interest on the altar of the Church's policies.

The college changed status and after nine years Spencer left the governing board. Under public auspices the institution, ultimately named Eastern Arizona College, continued to flourish. It counts Spencer Kimball as one of its most illustrious alumni.

8

A Young Family

— "we have had our joys
and our sorrows"

The year 1933 brought the lowest ebb of the Depression so far as business went. It also brought personal disaster.

No child was ever more adored than their fourth child, two-year-old Eddie. One of Spencer's business associates later wondered "why Eddie made such a fine man. His mother spoiled him. I spoiled him. Everybody in town spoiled him." Spencer wrote in a letter: "Eddie is cuter every day. He is the sweetest, prettiest, jolliest, smartest, huskiest, red-headed-est, lovingest and most attractive child that was ever created." And "Redhead Ed is a darling and thinks his Pa is O.K. I am trying to keep him blinded as long as I can."

On September 5, Tuesday, shortly before Eddie's third birthday, he came inside from playing and complained of a sore throat. He vomited and his temperature shot up. By Thursday he had difficulty in standing. On Saturday, when he stood up from his chair, his leg collapsed under him and he fell to the floor. As he slept his muscles twitched. Fully alarmed, Camilla rushed him to a doctor, who diagnosed the problem as arthritis or possibly diphtheria.

The fever and restlessness waned; by the next Wednesday Eddie seemed well except for soreness and a paralyzed right leg. He continued to improve generally. On the following Monday Camilla took him for several recommended treatments to a chiropractor, who massaged and worked the leg so painfully that Eddie screamed when he came in sight of the office. After four days the chiropractor suggested the problem might be polio. Spencer and Camilla talked with Mrs. Gietz, whose daughter had had polio. The symptoms matched.

At five next morning the parents and Eddie were in the car. They drove through that day and night and reached Los Angeles by early morning. Dr. Lowman at the Orthopedic Hospital took one look at the medical history and Eddie's leg and recognized polio. He broke into a fury at Spencer and Camilla for trailing possible contagion across two states and into the hospital itself, instead of staying home until the three-week quarantine period was over. He did not understand that they had had no useful medical advice and had acted as best they knew.

He raged at what he considered the stupidity of massaging Eddie's leg. So far as he was concerned they could have done nothing worse. He put Eddie's legs into splints, then moved him immediately into isolation for the remaining few days of the quarantine period. As Eddie was carried out he screamed in terror for his mama and daddy. It was his third birthday.

For three days Spencer and Camilla paced the grounds outside the hospital in anguish, barred from their baby, listening to him scream and cry, "I want to go home," "Daddy," "Mama," until his voice grew so hoarse they wondered whether it would ever recover. During visiting hours Camilla talked to him through the crack of the door, amusing him with stories and songs. He screamed pitifully again when they left exhausted, distracted, their hearts aching. They rented a room across the street from the hospital, to be as close to Eddie as they could. Camilla wrote a few days later: "No one can know the anguish of that experience without having something at least similar. To know that your baby is actually torn from your arms and you cannot go near him under any circumstances." Eighteen years later she wrote, "The heartache of that experience is still devastating."

In the shadow of Camilla's terror, Spencer wrote home to the three older children on the first day in Los Angeles: " . . . Send a letter from you all every day as it will help Mother a lot. Don't fail. She can hardly stand it to be away from her baby — and it isn't so easy for Dad either."

LeVan must apologize to the neighbors, he wrote his oldest son. Eddie might have exposed their children. "Tell the good neighbors we are terribly perturbed over the matter." His letter went on talking about the drive west, then veered back again to the same dread fear. "We certainly hope that there will be no spread of the disease and certainly are grieved to think anyone should have been exposed through us even though innocently." And he wrote the neighbors directly of his concern.

Spencer had to get back to Safford after ten days, but Camilla stayed on with Eddie another two and a half months, until the doctors let him go home. Camilla wrote Spencer that she had never experienced such unending days. She thanked him for a letter, observing, "Funny how I so like to be told that you miss me and need me." Spencer wrote to her from Safford every day, so that she dreaded the weekends, when the mailman didn't come, but welcomed Monday, a "feast day" of piled-up letters. She wrote to Spencer begging "to hear about your trip home and *all* the news. . . . Tell me about everything. You know how lonesome I will be." She wrote Olive Beth, quizzing her about the clothes she was wearing and who was ironing them. She wrote home that the Halloween masks were in the front closet, that LeVan's new shirts were stowed in the bottom dresser drawer, that Olive Beth must practice her music. One Monday night she wrote to her "darling family" that "Eddie was very much distressed because I couldn't help crying while I read your letters. After I'd quit he kept saying 'Are you going to cry anymore?' and seemed relieved that I had quit."

The long weeks drained Camilla. Eddie's condition sometimes improved, other times deteriorated. Spencer urged her to have the child administered to by elders in Los Angeles. Spencer's brother Del visited and stood on his head for Eddie. Six-year-old Andrew mailed Eddie an elephant that squeaked. Eddie's Aunt Catherine paid for a box of blocks. Someone sent him a jack-o-lantern rattle; the fruit man gave him a bunch of grapes, the ice man an ice chunk, an old lady some potato chips. But the brunt of caring for Eddie fell on Camilla. "If he just wasn't such a calf for his mama," Camilla wrote home. She told what Mr. Lytthaus had said to her that day: "My G—— how many times a day does he say mama? I tried to count them and it's thousands." But Camilla excused Eddie — "My little leech" — of everything difficult he did and followed one story with another story or song or rhyme, day-long after day-long.

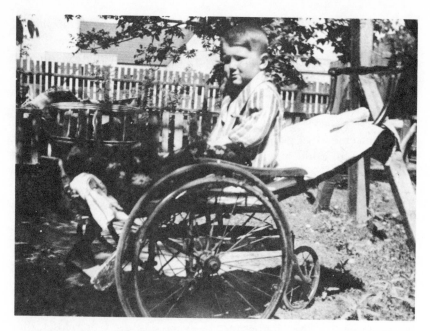

Edward, recovering from polio, 1934

Their separation gave Spencer and Camilla occasion to express their feelings toward one another.

Nov. 14, 1933

My beloved Husband,

The day you receive this note will mark the sixteenth anniversary of our wedding. Our first separation on that day. I wanted to tell you again as I perhaps do too often how much I love and appreciate you. Every year increases my love and respect. This separation is bitterly hard but it has made me realize more than ever before how much I have to be thankful for. The fact that never once in the time of our acquaintance have I found cause to doubt or mistrust is I consider one of the foundation stones upon which real happiness and contentment in marriage is built. The attraction of sex and other things of course combine to make the perfect union but without confidence there can be nothing lasting.

I feel that our trouble has drawn us even closer together in spirit though temporarily we are separated.

My constant prayer is that God will preserve the unity of our family and that we may soon all be together again. The joy of that day will be unmeasurable.

How I long for you and the strength received from your beautiful character. There is no other so fine and so true.

Your devoted wife,
Camilla

Tuesday morning

My darling wife,

. . . Sixteen years is a long time for a girl to put up with one man and especially such a poor excuse as I am so I honor you on this anniversary. It has been an extremely happy sixteen years. We have had our ups and downs, our disappointments and our surprises, our joys and our sorrows, and it has been a wonderful period. I want you to know that I love and appreciate you. You are the finest wife in the world and I am not unmindful of it even though I do seem thoughtless at times. . . .

Affectionately,
Spencer

From home the children wrote faithfully. LeVan's letters were filled with sports and church activities, reading, and public speaking. He earned his football letter even though, because he had been put ahead of his class, he was younger than his teammates.

Olive Beth, eleven, wrote: "Andrew is like a stubborn mule. He would not come to eat supper with me at Mitchells although he was invited." She was the only student in the two seventh-grade classes to get a perfect score in arithmetic. "I played marbles with Andrew last night. He beats me all to pieces."

Six-year-old Andrew wrote: "I sold six Digest this week. . . . I have thirty eight marbles." He and Olive Beth built a dog house for a new pet.

Grandma Eyring came to do the mending and the neighbors fed the family royally.

Spencer wrote: "Business is very slow but collections are good. We have collected a lot we had given up for lost." His letters are so rarely critical of others that the exceptions stand out: "Garth [Nelson] is sick again. He has had a fever of 102 and 103 all day and night and they haven't been able to break it. He has no sore throat or other symptoms that indicate what can be the matter. They are much worried. Dr. _____ thought it was his throat but it seems foolish since he hasn't even a sore throat. Anyway that is pretty close for him, maybe." The

Spencer and Camilla with Spencer LeVan (16), Olive Beth (12), Andrew (8), Edward (4), 1935

doctor was the one who had rejected the diagnosis of polio for **Eddie** even when it was suggested to him.

More typical:

> Confidentially, _____ is in bad again. He and _____ have hundreds of dollars of their checks in for cash and when the examiners came in a false entry was made. This came to me from a good authentic source. He will be asked to resign. It is quite serious I think. I'm sorry for him. It means the end of him I'm afraid, and he is a fine fellow, too, in his way.

Finally, in December, Camilla brought Eddie home.

Over the next eight years Spencer and Camilla did a lot of travelling in the cause of Eddie's recovery, fifteen trips to California, and more. The first time, while Camilla stayed with Eddie, Spencer returned home to tend family and see to the business, such as it was that year. Two months later he came to Los Angeles on the bus. In downtown Los Angeles he saw her in the middle of the street in a large crowd of people and threw his arms around her. She was taken by surprise and dropped her packages.

The prospective costs of their son's treatment staggered them. Four days after Eddie was hospitalized Spencer wrote that the doctor had quoted a cost of $1200, payable at $100 a month. At the time Spencer was drawing a monthly salary of $125 and had mortgage payments of $20 on the house and six people to support. He wrote to his partner that if someone should request information on his financial status it would be no favor to him to exaggerate his net worth, as might be true if it were a credit check. He hoped the medical charges could be scaled down so he could meet them.

Spencer arranged for treatment on a clinic rather than private-patient basis, which brought costs more within their reach. Eventually the March of Dimes came to the rescue and paid the doctor and hospital bills for Eddie's illness and subsequent operations. Spencer and Camilla incurred substantial additional expenses, but those they could manage. They felt deep gratitude to the March of Dimes and ever after contributed liberally to that fund.

One of their friends, commiserating with them, asked: "Why did this have to happen to you? You've always lived such a good life." But Camilla saw no punishment of God in the illness. Nor did it occur to her that it came to test her faith or to make her stronger by overcoming adversity. Perhaps those concepts were true, but so far as she could see it was a matter of infection and too little resistance; that was all.

The next year, when Elder Charles A. Callis the apostle came, the family asked him to administer to the boy. Spencer recorded that Elder Callis blessed Eddie "that he would recover rapidly and that he would eventually recover completely." But administration and all Camilla's work and prayer, and a series of half a dozen operations between 1936 and 1940, left Eddie still substantially handicapped. Finally he could walk without braces or crutches, but awkwardly. Though this was not the complete recovery the family had hoped for, he had been small enough when polio struck that he grew up with the condition and felt little self-pity.

When Eddie started school at six, his legs just recovering from the first series of operations, he was just out of braces. At recess he walked in front of the slide as a schoolmate came flying down, knocked him to the ground and broke his right leg just above the ankle. Camilla felt this an undeserved wallop for Eddie, on top of all the others. She nursed him again. Years later she thought of the adage "Whom we serve, we love." It was true for her, "for this youngest son is a very real part of my heart."

Spencer and Camilla worked at expecting Eddie to do all he could do. He had much the same chores as the other children had had, including milking the cows and working in the hay and cutting the lawn. Occasional adjustments had to be made. When in school the other children ran and played more active games, he worked at a horizontal bar, strengthening his upper body. He could not run with the others, but he could do more pull-ups or push-ups than they.

Despite treating Eddie without pity, their hearts were soft toward him. Spencer recorded compassionately the little boy's prayer, "Bless me so that I can run and play and climb trees like the other children and fight."

Spencer made the best of the long trips to Los Angeles every summer. The family went along. Although most of Olive Beth's girl-friends had never set foot out of the valley, the Kimballs went somewhere every summer.

To pay for trips the family worked at saving in little ways. The children learned not to ask for soda pop or candy bars. The automobile was not started up to drive to church or the store if they could walk easily. Those nickels and dimes were saved. Now with Eddie needing operations or checkups in Los Angeles every summer, the trips were to the California coast. The family would set out from Safford, the car crammed with six people and all the baggage. Along the way they stopped at roadside picnic tables and ate out of a big sack, mortifying Olive Beth and Andrew, who thought this low-class.

In the car Spencer might start the family singing the Arizona state song or "My Darling Clementine," or a cowboy ballad:

> Billy Vanero heard them say
> In an Arizona town one day
> That a band of Apache Indians
> Were upon the trail of death. . . .

He paid five cents each for memorization of the Articles of Faith in English or Spanish, or for scripture memorization. The miles passed with repeating these memorizations, with contests at estimating how far it was to a distant landmark, and with word games.

After Eddie had been checked into the hospital, the rest of the family would rent a cheap motel room in Los Angeles or a run-down

Family vacation, Long Beach, California

apartment in Long Beach, near the beach and near the amusement park where the children spent their carefully hoarded money. Long Beach was the scene of the "kidnapping." The three older children went to a show alone right after lunch. By mid-afternoon the parents started to worry. Later Spencer walked the streets and looked in all the shows and could not find them. Hours passed and they still did not come home. It might be a kidnapping, or something crazy. Spencer went to every theater within range and tramped up and down every aisle. At nine o'clock he notified the police. He rushed back to the room, really frightened, to find the three children just coming in. "The show was so good" that they had seen it over and over, three times. Poor little Andy had been ignored and soaked his pants. Always an eager tourist, Spencer was the first one out of bed on a trip. Olive Beth remembers walking the streets and beaches with him in the early mornings. When motoring across country, he often detoured from their route to sightsee a local attraction.

The family had many other ways of enjoying time together, too. Several times a summer the family swam in a broad slimy pool at Indian Hot Springs, then ate on a wobbly picnic table under some tamaracks nearby. On other evenings they drove up Mount Graham, where the air was cool.

Occasionally, when the children could catch Father at home, the family held home evening, a program only informally recommended by the Church at that time. After each family member had performed, there were games and food. The main games were Rook and Mah-Jongg. Spencer had a knack of doubling and redoubling his score at MahJongg. In Rook he liked to "shoot the moon" or bid "nullo," that is, bid to take all or no tricks. He generally won the game, or good-naturedly took his ribbing when he lost. He always competed with jovial earnestness.

Spencer could be a tease. He would read between the lines of the newspaper: "The 24th of July parade in Safford Friday was attended by an estimated 2000 people (including handsome red-headed Eddie Kimball and his delightful family)." Eddie would come running, "Where, where?" Or Spencer would remind Camilla, in the family's hearing, about the neighbor who had named a heifer calf Camilla, in her honor. Or when Olive Beth had boyfriends who had left gifts under the Christmas tree, Spencer in handing out the presents would leave them for last. "Well, I guess that's all," he would say, pretending not to see them until Olive Beth pointed them out.

Spencer read little for pleasure, not more than a handful of novels in his mature years. His diary for 1939 noted, on a trip to California, "I read The Citadel, Young Dr. Galahad, and Magnificent Obsession, more than I had read in years."

Movies provided one of his relaxations. All the winter Spencer bought a monthly family ticket for a dollar to the Thursday night movie at the Ramona Theater. The shows were mostly second rate, but a bargain. The better theater was over on Main Street. (Spencer ever after teased Andrew about the time a freckle-faced girl from Cactus Flat sat on his lap by mistake in the dark.) When Spencer found himself in a city waiting for a train he often went to the theater. He had gone to the silent films (and even sung at intermission) in the "Cozy Corner" in Thatcher as a youth. He and Camilla had marveled at the advent of talkies, seeing their first in Los Angeles in 1930. They loved films.

In 1939 his diary, though incomplete, mentions thirty-eight movies. One day in 1938, while on vacation, he saw two double bills: *Tom Sawyer, No Time to Marry, Tale of Two Cities,* and *Naughty Marietta.* Particularly in the early years as an apostle, when travel by train often meant layovers, he took advantage of the chance to catch up on movies and went, occasionally even to two or three, after not having attended at all for months. In 1949 his journal notes fifteen movies, in 1950, twenty-nine. During much of this time he was on enforced vacation, recovering from his heart attack. He noted a little apologetically, "We see many shows when away like this and resting, since we see so few when at work normally."

Every Sunday afternoon after church and on holidays the whole family drove to the Eyring grandparents' home in Pima, even those teenagers who occasionally had to be coaxed. Once they arrived Spencer pulled on a pair of overalls and headed for the barn to help milk the cows. It ran counter to his instincts to just relax and be waited on.

Spencer loved the Eyrings. And the Eyrings loved him. "No blood brother could have been kinder," said Joe. Mother Eyring gave him some of the mothering he had missed; she always praised him to the skies, beaming. Henry Eyring more than once commented on how alike his mother and Spencer were. They both moved quickly and got things done. They had the same quality of selflessness.

To Emma, Mother Eyring's younger sister raising Edward's other family on the other side of the house, Spencer seemed especially sweet. He showed a kind of sympathy for the strains of her situation that she didn't often get. Camilla's brother Henry remembered the Eyrings' awe of Spencer. "Spencer was the kind of person you just knew was doing the right thing."

Like his father and father's father, Spencer was away much of the time. Like Andrew Kimball he traveled the long distances across Arizona and New Mexico as far as El Paso, Texas, on Church work. As with Andrew, his job did not require conventional office hours, so he picked his own: he started work earlier and stayed later than other men, taking time during the middle of the day to attend to necessary Church affairs. At supper he was in and out of the house in under an hour. On little sleep he drove himself hard. In the summer Camilla and the children sometimes stayed at the multi-colored family cabin eight thousand feet up on Mount Graham while Spencer tried to come from Safford on weekends.

He didn't take much time to play. What his sons learned from him, they learned by watching him work or by working with him or for him.

"There were a lot of jobs I was unhappy doing," recalls Andrew. He dug irrigation ditches, chopped weeds, picked pecans, fixed fences, scythed and pitched hay, fed and milked the cows, shoveled out the corral.

LeVan from an early age had magazines to sell door-to-door, the *Literary Digest.* He hated the task and one time ditched the magazines behind the barn. When later Camilla discovered them, watersoaked, she shed such a flood of tears that LeVan hoped never again to cause that. Later Andrew fell heir to the dreaded job. His parents used both club and carrot. At age six he wrote his mother in Los Angeles: "They sent 15 Digests and I sold 7 of them. If I sell all of them next week daddy will take me to the show." When the magazine went out of business after predicting victory for Alf Landon in 1936, Andrew wore no black in mourning.

LeVan remembers building a corral and a small barn with his father. Neither one cost them a cent. LeVan pulled nails out of scrap lumber from some old barn or fence posts from a property Spencer had bought; and with the straightened nails Spencer hammered together his barns. He had a dirt farmer's approach to the task. He wanted to build something useful, however crude, for the farmer's work. He wasted nothing. On the half acre back of their second house Spencer planted fruit trees; then, rather than let any piece of land sit idle, he sowed alfalfa between the trees. Every day he took to the dairy in town the cream separated from his cows' milk.

To encourage his children to work and save, Spencer paid them for working around the home — Eddie's account book as a child shows ten cents for catching a mouse, twenty-five cents for a gopher, five cents for each half-hour practicing the piano (and a deduction of ten cents for missing daily practice), twenty-five cents for learning to play a hymn without a mistake, fifty cents an hour for cutting the lawn and working around the place, five dollars for pulling all the nails out of a large stack of scrap lumber, and so on. What the children did not need for gifts or movies or other personal pleasures Spencer encouraged them to invest in the business. He would take the dime or quarter or dollar and invest it along with his and Bishop Greenhalgh's money. Often the amount the child invested would not, in economic terms, justify the trouble of making the bookkeeping entries, but Spencer had other objectives in mind. Over the years this money, compounded with its earnings, added up to a considerable sum. The boys saved enough in this way to cover a large share of their mission expenses.

Kimball-Greenhalgh offered a number of ways of employing the children. Olive Beth would type and do office work. The boys would clear vacant lots so they would sell more easily, or they would fix up a house left in a shambles by a renter.

When a son had finished his chores, Spencer found him some more. But Andrew at fourteen had more spare time all summer than Spencer could provide for so he talked a Rotary Club friend who managed Sears Roebuck in Safford into offering his boy work. Since Andrew was legally too young to work for the store, the manager paid him out of his own pocket at a rock-bottom twenty-five cents an hour.

Sometimes LeVan forgot to milk the family cows. There were no harsh words, he recalls. Sometimes his father would just milk them for him without any comment. When LeVan left on a mission and Andrew took over his post as milker, there were nights when the family would drive home late from a picnic, Andrew in an agony at the thought of trudging out to the corral to milk. "Dad exhibited his humanity," says Andrew, "by letting me pretend sleep and go right to bed while he milked the cow at eleven at night."

Not one of his children ever had any doubts about what their father expected of them. Olive Beth knew that if a party let out at ten she was to be home at ten thirty. If it went on till twelve she had till twelve thirty. She never went to a movie on Sunday; this rankled at times, since the theater usually showed even its best films for just a one-day stand and often this occurred on a Sunday. Olive Beth remembers that her girlfriends' mothers would sometimes ask if the Kimball girl was allowed to do such and such; if yes, then the girlfriend was allowed to also. Just once did her father object to a boyfriend Olive Beth had, but even then he didn't forbid her to date him; he just suggested to her the boy wasn't suitable.

To pay to the Church a penny out of every dime earned, to pray at bedtime, to attend meetings — such things were never matters of argument but were just expected. Similarly the parents always assumed that school grades would be high. It was hard to disappoint parents who had that attitude. "I just couldn't," says Olive Beth. "I just had to do well."

Spencer LeVan felt his father's influence so constantly that he struggled all his life to be someone separate. It worked against this first son's grain to be known, no matter what he did, as Spencer Kimball's son. Of course, it was not all bad. LeVan remembers, "Spencer Kimball's son was thought to be a good risk, for the loan of a dollar, for a job, or even for a husband." At seventeen LeVan was eager to state his preference for going to a foreign mission so he could pick up another language. But he knew his father's strong view that mission assignments were a matter of inspiration and no prospective missionary should presume to suggest his destination. In self-enforced obedience to his father's feelings, LeVan expressed no preference on his form and was sent to Canada.

It was just assumed that LeVan would go on a mission. It would never have occurred to him to question going. Andrew didn't remember his father ever even raising the issue with him, but the expectation always existed. On his release from the Navy in 1945 Andrew wanted to marry, balking at the idea of a mission. Spencer said little, just let him come to his own decision. Ed remembers his father asking, without pressure, how he would feel about going on a mission, pointing out that some missions would not require a lot of walking. No big to-do was made of the question. All three sons went.

His sons do not remember ever arguing much about religion with their dad. He could not comfortably debate this with them. He would typically turn away from an argument, change the subject. As adolescents, thinking things out, they bombarded their mother, contesting accepted ideas with her until they ran out of breath, but not so often with their father. He was a good source of information but no fun to bait with heretical argument.

Camilla was free to admit it when she had no answer, giving the advice that she put such matters on a shelf to be taken down from time to time for review. Sometimes upon review answers had become apparent, sometimes answers seemed no longer important, and sometimes the questions had to be returned to the shelf for another day.

There was little anger in Spencer. The only time his son Ed ever saw it flare was once when his father was milking a balky cow. The cow stuck her foot in the bucket and spilled the milk. Spencer began again; the cow kicked the bucket a second time. When it happened still a third time Spencer kicked the cow in the ribs and damned her.

As to discipline, neither parent relied on spanking. The approach they both took was to discuss the child's offense with him with an air of disappointment. Olive Beth recalls just one occasion when her father spanked her. She was small and Spencer came home to find her wearing two of his hats — on her feet.

Another time, when Olive Beth was asked to help with the dishes, she answered her mother, "Just a minute," and turned back to reading. Spencer snatched her book, flung it across the room, and scolded her. But that, Camilla consoled Olive Beth later, was only the steam from a bad day at work.

When LeVan drove two miles with a flat tire and ruined it, his father, though strongly displeased, did not berate him.

Ed recalls a scolding which resulted in his stomping off to his room boiling with indignation at the perceived injustice. When his father came into his room after a while and apologized, the anger had to melt away in tears.

The style of both parents was to leave much responsibility with the children for their own conduct. Ed recalls a time in his teens in Utah when some friends came from Arizona to visit. It was Sunday and they wanted to go to the state fair before they left the next day. Ed desperately wanted to go with them. Though his mother advised him against it, she left the decision to him. He went and felt uneasy the whole time, particularly when he met someone at the fair whom he knew well.

When, after a Sunday dinner in 1948, the boys began to play table tennis, a prospective daughter-in-law asked Spencer, "How come they play on Sunday?" Spencer replied: "I don't do it, but they must decide for themselves."

Intensely proud of their children, Spencer and Camilla pushed them forward. When the parents returned from the Rotary Convention in Mexico City in 1935 they brought back sarapes and Mexican straw hats for Eddie and Andrew and taught Andrew to play the guitar in accompaniment of "La Cucaracha" and "Cielito Lindo." The boys performed for church groups, clubs, and parties up and down the valley, with their parents proudly present.

"I believe we should do a little more for the children in their cultural development," Spencer wrote in a letter to Camilla. "If LeVan would take to a cornet or violin or Bobbie either I believe we should get them one and give them lessons. At least they should go on with their piano work. I believe we have been a little careless in the matter as the years are flying and they will never accomplish themselves unless done early while we can insist upon it."

Though Spencer had not himself been able to finish college after marriage, he had the highest regard for the benefits of education. His father's long championing of the Academy, later named Gila College, made involvement in education a family tradition. Josephine was a teacher. Camilla was a teacher. Spencer's ambition as a child had been to be a teacher, though he never admitted it when people asked, "What do you want to be when you grow up?" because his small friends thought of teaching as women's work.

As his children grew, they expected to go to college. Though none of Spencer's own family had graduated from college, Camilla's younger brothers and sisters followed her to college. While she had gone into teaching when she obtained a certificate, without ever quite finishing her degree, the younger ones took the next step. The *Graham Guardian* in 1933 ran an item, "Eyring Family of Pima Holds 23 College Degrees." And other degrees followed after 1933.

LeVan learned to read as a little child. Camilla pushed him hard, sure that her boy had genius. His quick wit responded to her urging. He graduated from the University of Arizona at twenty-one, after serving two years on a mission in Canada. When Spencer and Camilla attended his graduation they puffed with pride; the University president told them that LeVan's record in earning his mathematics degree was the highest in the school's history. He followed his father into the insurance business for a time, working as an auditor in San Francisco. Then, after the war, he went to law school, obtaining his first law degree from Oxford as a Rhodes scholar. Thereafter he served as law teacher or dean at the universities of Utah, Michigan, Wisconsin, and Chicago.

Olive Beth graduated from the University of Arizona; she, too, was a good student. At Gila Junior College she had received the scholarship award (as well as a music award, debating award, student organization award, and special service award as a school officer). After Olive Beth's family was largely grown, she returned to the classroom as a grade school teacher in Salt Lake City.

When Andrew graduated from junior high school, Spencer wrote: "Last night we were mighty proud of Andrew. . . . About fifteen others were cited for being outstanding in one field or another — art, music, athletics, etc. — but Andrew topped them all. Was I proud?" Andrew obtained a master's degree in business from the University of Michigan and worked as a middle-level executive for General Electric.

Edward graduated from law school at the University of Utah, at the head of his class, then took additional degrees at the University of Pennsylvania and taught law at the universities of Montana and Wisconsin, and at Brigham Young University. Thus all the children responded to their parents' high expectations.

Spencer valued academic achievement, but not to the exclusion of other things. When he thought Ed was concentrating too hard on his studies in high school, Spencer pointed out how important it is to have friends and spend time with them. He said he would be content if his son got some Bs, if necessary, in order to avoid becoming too narrow. Similarly, to a nephew who bragged that his daughters were doing well in school, upholding the Kimball family tradition, Spencer replied with a compliment coupled with the observation that there were other things just as important.

9

A Force in the Community

— "master of every situation"

In 1935 Louis Long, with the backing of the Chamber of Commerce, applied to the Federal Communications Commission for a radio station license for Safford. Long had been a long-time friend of Spencer through the Rotary Club. He ran a string of theaters, the local weekly newspaper, and now the radio station.

A financial plunger, he was most of the time in debt. Spencer warned him he was too much of a dreamer, that he lacked caution. But Long kept expanding and bought new movie theaters all over the state. He got into legal trouble with film distributors, but he always settled the disputes out of court. Jesse Udall saw in him a certain bigness of character. When his second wife, a divorcee, ran off and left him with her children by a past marriage, he reared them himself. If anyone was hard up and out of work, he always took them on. Someone stole from him, but he would not file charges.

Long talked Kimball-Greenhalgh into putting up a small amount and lending their names to the radio station project. Jesse Udall did the legal work. The four had primary ownership in the station. The call letters KGLU represented the four — Kimball, Greenhalgh, Long and Udall. Long wanted the others associated with the venture especially for the prestige their names would add.

None of the men had any idea how to run a radio station. Spencer served, as always, in the role of secretary, seeing to it that the station had enough ready cash to operate. Long did the major overseeing. Active managing was left to an employee manager.

The station opened in July 1938. At the dedication the mayor sounded a grandiloquent note: "To you, KGLU; may your benignant rays spread gently and graciously over our domain and even reach out into the vast expanse beyond our realms to tell others of our previously untold and unheard potentialities."

When broadcasting started, Camilla was again in California with Eddie. Spencer wrote:

> I wish you had access to a radio and could get KGLU 1420. I have never seen anything happen in Safford to create such a sensation. Nearly every store or businessplace on Main St. has a radio and you can go down the street and hardly miss a word or note. We hear it from 8:00 a.m. on. The programs are very good. It seems to me that the Arcadians are as good as the average orchestra over other stations and some of the other programs are excellent and I thought they were all good.

Amateur hour on the station drew a lot of local talent. Spencer accompanied his niece June on the piano and she "made quite a hit" with her singing. Spencer tried to interest Olive Beth and Andrew in performing. One Sunday morning he had Eddie sing "Give, Said the Little Stream." The boy received one postcard of "fan mail" from a family friend, which he treasured.

Letters and calls began arriving from shut-ins and others expressing appreciation for the window on the world opened to them through the local station. KFI in Los Angeles and KTAR in Phoenix could be heard on good receivers, but they lacked the personal local touch.

For two years the station played records interspersed with local programming. Harry L. Payne presented a daily program, reading poems and homilies. Occasionally Spencer gave a Sunday talk or went on the air with Rotary news or with his quartet. Camilla gave an occasional book review. In 1940 KGLU joined the NBC network.

Long later recalled the Sunday-morning incident over which the station was threatened with the loss of its license. When Long arrived at the studio to broadcast live a Jehovah's Witness service, the minister insisted on removing the studio's American flag, as being in conflict with his group's principles. That rubbed Louis the wrong way. He told the minister that the flag stayed. The minister stormed out of the studio irate and complained to the Federal Communications Commission, which threatened to convene a hearing.

Worried that Long might lose the license, Spencer told him, "You may lose everything you have put in." Long answered, "I don't want to hear any more about it. That flag is going to stay there. I don't give a damn whether you like it or not." "Well, you're running it," said Spencer. He never did say whether he agreed with Long's stand or not. The FCC did not withdraw the license.

Spencer's dogged devotion to Church duty amused Long. Whatever Spencer was doing, he dropped it for Church business. Long never did see him at any KGLU board meeting that conflicted with a stake assignment. Long got so annoyed by it one day, or so he said years later, that he told Spencer, "The way you're working they'll make you head man up in Salt Lake soon." Spencer replied, "Oh, no, I don't have that kind of ambition." But Long remembered and later called himself prophetic.

In 1923, as a young fellow working in the bank, Spencer had received an invitation to join the Rotary Club in Safford right after it had been chartered. They needed someone who could play the piano, and Spencer could play almost anything they'd be likely to want to sing, with or without music, chording his way through the song. He joined. He enjoyed the fellowship. He sang in the club quartet and with Camilla attended nearly all the annual conventions within reach.

On his leaving Arizona twenty years later, the Rotary newsletter would pay him tribute:

> He's been so faithful and so "on the job" all the time, we often accept him as a fixture — like the president's gavel. Ponder the past of the club for a moment. Who'll be ready to play the piano on call? Who'll put on a program on short notice? Who'll direct community singing for our parties, and what good will a party be without Spencer to be master of ceremonies?

In 1931-32 Spencer was elected club president. As president he promoted particularly the Boy Scout movement. Club members fined themselves for all kinds of "derelictions," including lateness, new children, a cent a pound for weight. In this way the club raised four hundred dollars during 1932 to build a scout building on Mt. Graham, but the fund was swept away in the bank failure and money had to be raised again.

Rotary was coming to mean more to Spencer "than merely kind associations and the good fellowship and the business contacts that have been found there." In a way it was an extension of aspects of his Church work, for "I have realized that when I was teaching and furthering the Rotary cause I was at the same time teaching the fundamentals of Christianity, for the great mission of the Saviour of the World was founded upon service." Over the years his club donated thousands of dollars and countless hours of service to the Boy Scouts. And during the Depression it provided thousands of free lunches to children.

With forty-two members the Safford club was one of the larger ones in the district, which covered approximately the state of Arizona. It had tried unsuccessfully twice before to push a candidate for district governor. A year in advance of the May 1935 district convention in Prescott the Safford club announced Spencer as its nominee and began sending out publicity. The Glendale club started promoting Harold Smith. Smith had an edge because his club was situated in the Salt River Valley, near Phoenix, where many large, strong clubs were located. But he had already been defeated twice; some considered him an easy mark.

No Mormon had served as district governor. Mormons as a group were not overly popular. Some seemed self-righteous: "We don't smoke and we don't drink, thank you." Louis Long, a non-Mormon, took on the task of convincing men from other clubs that Spencer was neither prudish nor smug. When his non-Mormon friends got drunk, as sometimes happened, Spencer managed to help them without a lecture. One man commented that Spencer could have a better time sober than others could drunk. That might have given excuse for a sermon, but Spencer just laughed.

After a year of vigorous campaigning Spencer arrived at the convention only to learn that the president of the Glendale club, who was Smith's campaign manager, had just died after teeing off at the golf course. Everyone naturally felt sympathetic toward the man's family and his club.

Spencer and his backers huddled. Someone suggested conceding the election. Spencer agreed that it would be the right thing to do. Louis Long wondered whether throwing away a year's effort in campaigning made sense, but he supported the decision.

On Monday morning when the Rotarians gathered on the floor of the theater building where the convention was held, there was excitement and speculation about the race. Many of Spencer's friends thought he could still win.

The district governor called for nominations. Spencer jumped up and was recognized. Spencer withdrew his candidacy and himself nominated Harold Smith and moved he be elected by acclamation. The Safford club president, Ben Blake, seconded the nomination and, as a practical matter, the election had ended. Said Spencer, "That was like a bombshell." A thundering ovation signaled the Rotarians' approval of the gesture. They swarmed about, congratulating him. Some said it was the best example they had ever seen of the fellowship for which Rotary stood. "I became somewhat of a hero all at once without meriting it," noted Spencer.

The state's major daily newspapers reported Spencer's action without any explanation of the background. His friends at home and around the state were dumbfounded.

LeVan, seventeen, said he did not know why his father had ceded the election but it was right or his father would not have done it. Of all the compliments, Spencer treasured that most.

Just the same, ceding the election was a real disappointment. To be district governor was a great honor. And it would have included a paid trip to the international convention in Mexico City.

But that summer, Spencer had decided to run again. Though they could ill afford the trip, Spencer and Camilla went to Mexico City anyway, feeling it essential to his candidacy for the next year. Money was tight, so they cut corners when it would not be noticed.

Spencer felt comfortable out front in public, but Camilla disliked the limelight. She greatly appreciated small attentions — flowers, a token gift acknowledging her presence, a word of welcome — she noted them all down. She recorded the surprise of women that she had an eighteen-year-old son. "You seem too young," they said.

After the events of 1935 Spencer had no opposition for election the next year, and he went into service as district governor.

Being district governor brought some small status. In Needles, California, the hotel keeper insisted on moving Spencer and Camilla to a better room when he learned who the clerk had stuck away in a second-rate room. But at the district governors' convention, Bill Manier from Tennessee, the international president, had counsel for

District governor of Rotary, 1936

the assembled governors, many of them young and self-confident. He told them to expect a great time that year, to expect their clubs to applaud when they walked in and out, to expect to be feted, dined and praised. "But remember," added Manier, "it is not you they are applauding; it is your position. Any of you who don't believe it, try visiting the clubs next year, after your term ends." That stuck with Spencer; he thought of it when people praised him and honored him in Church positions.

To Spencer, receptions where coffee was served were occasions to let people know something of the Church and its standards. In the planning for the next district convention the entertainment committee proposed that, as usual, the district should provide a free bar. After thought, Spencer indicated that this year no liquor should be provided by the district itself. If men wanted to drink, that was their right, but he could not see why the organization should furnish the liquor. His wishes prevailed; and he never felt he had lost by his action.

As the year drew to a close, Camilla wrote:

It was a very pleasant experience but I really do not crave publicity. I am satisfied to go quietly my own way. I do feel that

much worthwhile development has come from the contacts
through Rotary this year and I have appreciated it as an opportunity to grow. I have a real ambition to learn to be quietly at ease
under any circumstances and in any company, to take my place in a
dignified yet simple manner. I dislike a pompous air and I do seek
to be genuinely cordial.

She added: "I never expect to come as near the center of the stage
again."

Spencer had diligently visited all twenty-three clubs during the
year and Camilla had accompanied him most of the time. She had
developed toward becoming the kind of person she aspired to be. And
he had displayed the kind of leader he was. He had sacrificed time
from his business and had nearly worn out his automobile. He had
organized four new clubs in a single year, a record recruiting job in
district history.

The unexpected reward for his unusual record was that his district
voted to pay his travel expenses to the International Convention that
year in Nice, France. He jumped at the chance. He and Camilla took
enough out of their savings for her expenses, too.

To Europe! No one they knew well had been to Europe except on a
mission. The Rotary Convention offered what might be their only
chance in a lifetime to see those far places. Spencer was forty-two, a
small businessman, and the rest of his life appeared clearly mapped
out in Safford, Graham County, Arizona. He had lived as much of his
life as he could remember in the valley. He had travelled a great deal in
the United States, but never abroad.

This was to be the great adventure of their lives. They recorded it
meticulously, brought back a gigantic scrapbook full of every theater
stub and tourist guide, and lovingly collected memorabilia of a glorious
trip.

As Spencer and Camilla left the house, Andrew continued ab-
sorbed in his baseball game in the vacant lot, waved and continued with
his batting as they loaded up the car. Between innings he ran over for a
goodbye kiss. His parents travelled often, and this longer trip seemed
no different to him. A dozen friends saw them off at the train station,
including Bishop Greenhalgh, who would carry on the business while
Spencer was away. Spencer carried off the keys to the car and mailed
them back at the first stop. He wrote just a few minutes from home on
the train, "Will be a good bronco buster by the time we reach Bowie.

Visiting LeVan in the Canadian Mission
on the way to Europe, 1937

Andrew, Olive Beth, Edward, 1937

We've had a glorious trip so far but don't feel very foreign yet as we're still in sight of Mt. Graham, or is it the Alps? We nearly got seasick as we came up the San Simon River so we'll be prepared for the Atlantic."

No one used an umbrella much in Arizona, but Spencer and Camilla took one on this trip, not willing to be cooped up by rain.

At every railway station they explored the town and stores when time allowed. From Chicago they rode chaircar to save money.

In Montreal, a city of a million inhabitants, they met LeVan, now six feet one inch tall, a mustachioed missionary in the Eastern Canadian Mission. They met with the Church members; Spencer sang and talked. They were intrigued with the French atmosphere in the city and with the omnipresent Catholicism, evidenced by the general celebration of the festival of Corpus Christi. One of LeVan's companions remarked how pleasant it must be to grow up with such young parents. Spencer took a group of missionaries and members out for ice cream and had a jolly time.

After a week of sightseeing in Montreal they boarded the *Duchess of Athol*. "The day long looked forward to!" Camilla wrote.

More than two hundred Rotarians travelled on the same ship. A newlywed couple from Oklahoma, a widower and his new bride, shared the Kimballs' dining table, beginning a friendship lasting forty years. Eating elegantly, served six-course meals — fresh flowers on the tables — dancing to an excellent five-piece orchestra, playing games, visiting, relaxing, they had a grand time.

On the open ocean they saw whales spouting and six icebergs. On Sunday they attended the ship's services. The crossing took a week. As the weather became rough, fewer and fewer people came to dinner; Spencer and Camilla watched what they ate but managed not to miss a meal.

Upon landing in France they travelled from LeHavre to Paris by train, arriving at midnight. With friends they then went out to see the sights, returning to their hotel at daylight giddy with sleeplessness and catching the train for Nice at seven. It was hot and crowded. They were annoyed at having to pay fifteen cents for a glass of water when wine was only ten cents.

At Nice, the convention city, Camilla and Spencer enjoyed themselves — the comradery of thousands of Rotarians from around the world, fireworks over the beach, a speech by the President of France (in French), dancing, socializing, sightseeing. Spencer had no difficulty in

In Pompeii, 1937

bypassing the seven goblets of wine which routinely accompanied his convention meals. He had long since made that decision.

They watched the gambling in Monte Carlo, saw the home of Columbus in Genoa, passed the Tower of Pisa, and landed in Rome. No city they would see had such impact. The monuments, standing or ruined, intrigued them. The Colosseum impressed them with its immensity; the Catacombs, five stories under ground with seventeen miles of passageways, brought back poignantly the suffering of the early Christians; St. Peter's, with its wealth of art treasures and its grand sweep, represented the sacrifice generations had offered to God. Words failed.

Mussolini's works made modern Rome also something of a showplace — clean and quiet with signs everywhere of prosperity and industry. But his state also was typified by the numerous soldiers in evidence, many in colorful uniforms, and by the fact that one of the tourists near them was stopped when he tried to take a photograph of Il Duce's private residence.

Pompeii had special meaning for Spencer. He vividly remembered reading *The Last Days of Pompeii.* Now he and Camilla walked the streets rutted by chariot wheels nineteen centuries before, saw meals left on the tables when deadly volcanic ash rained suffocation, noted the brothels that signified to them a decadent society. They climbed Vesuvius, where for a fee two men fished up a blob of molten lava from a crack under their feet and formed it with an iron bar around a coin, to show it had been captured live.

Florence disappointed them after Rome — everything was less grand. Gone from home a month, and having had no word from the family, Camilla felt pangs of homesickness. But Venice, on the other hand, delighted the two travelers. The city built on islands, criss-crossed with waterways, proved the most romantic stop of their trip. Spencer recorded: " . . . We had a grand gondola ride. The rain had subsided and the moon broke through the clouds occasionally. How romantic to sit cozily in a comfortable upholstered seat under a canopy with someone you love and glide smoothly through the water, down little side canals, under bridges, hearing voices from the houses as you pass along. It was a never-to-be-forgotten experience."

In their enthusiasm, they rode the train by night to save the day for more interesting things. They traveled to Budapest, then to Vienna.

Vienna brought them back to earth a little. Here their guide, Mr. Schmeltz, mentioned to them an ultimatum Germany had given Spain, and the war fear in England and France. They had been out of touch with politics for a month.

In a whirlwind day, Mr. Schmeltz, for $2.60, gave them the grand tour. The next morning when they left he came to the train and bade them goodbye. For years after this they corresponded with him, mostly by Christmas card, and in 1955 when they toured the missions in Europe they looked him up and took him to church.

Through Switzerland they enjoyed the Alps, the ice caves in the Rhone glacier, the waterfalls. After seeing Frankfurt am Main, they took a riverboat down the Rhine.

Holland impressed them with its multitude of bicycle riders and the picturesque costumes in the fishing villages. More than anywhere else they had been, Belgium seemed studded with reminders of the terrible bloodshed of the First World War.

Returning to Paris on the crowded train they had another chance to tour the city, ascend the Eiffel Tower, and see the World Fair under construction before crossing the Channel to the White Cliffs of Dover.

After all the exciting sights and sounds of the Continent, in London Camilla wrote in her diary:

> For the last hour and a half I have been waiting in the hotel while Spencer has been looking for a less expensive hotel. I am so downright homesick tonight I just had to cry a bit. I wish I could fly home. I have seen so much I have reached the saturation point. Nothing seems interesting anymore. Our expenses are so high I am quite in the dumps. Went down to Trafalgar Square and I sat on a bench overlooking this much-talked-of stretch of cement for about an hour while poor Spencer continued the search for a hotel. It rained a bit and I sat on with the rest of the bums, not a woman in sight, just loafers.... I have seen so many tourists all herding around trying to see the same places and do the same things that I am quite fed up with them. I shall be most happy to go home to my own little niche and let the rest of the world go by.

They found a cheaper hotel, tanked up for the day on breakfast that came with the room, and set off again, feeling better. The museums, and the government buildings in London, Stratford on Avon and a performance of *Hamlet*, Brighton (a great disappointment), Mormon services in the South London Branch, plays, shopping for gifts — these occupied the last busy days before the *Berengaria* sailed.

The cruise back was much the same as going. Again they made lifelong friends with other passengers. They noted how closed some of the passengers were. They themselves met people easily and enjoyed new companions.

After a long week, the New York skyline rose gradually into view. "The skyscrapers of New York are like nothing else on earth," wrote Camilla, "so high and thick together. The Statue of Liberty with her light of welcome held high was a real thrill."

After eleven weeks away, "the biggest thrill of all was to be at home again with our three little children. Edward had had whooping cough and was dreadfully pale and thin. Both the boys had hair like lions' manes. They had done remarkably well. Mary [Camilla's sister] takes mighty good care of them. And so the end of a wonderful journey and back to the daily tasks."

European travelers were scarce enough in Safford that Camilla and Spencer had a number of occasions to give travelogues up and down the valley. Even with all the traveling they did later in their lives, no trip ever meant more as a personal adventure than this first trip abroad.

They had seen the major cities of ten countries with the intensity of zealots. They had kept track of every nickel they spent — $1,576.23, plus $251 for a new car purchased in Detroit on the way home. They had made friends. They had stored up memories which Spencer would call up later — experiences with icebergs, the sight of the Statue of Liberty, the decadence of Pompeii, and others — to illustrate his sermons. Now it was back to keeping house and tending business.

In the years since 1924, when Andrew had died at the Connelly home in Salt Lake City, a strong, continuing relationship had existed between Spencer and his stepmother, Mary, whom he called Mother. As he attended Church conferences in Salt Lake City he never failed to visit her. They wrote to each other often; she visited in Arizona. With no children of her own, she felt especially close to Andrew's children and to her own grandniece, Agnes. Mary gave to Spencer her deep affection; he gave her the allegiance of a son.

In October 1937 Spencer received word from Mary's unmarried sister, Lillian, that Mary's cancer of the stomach was progressing very swiftly, that she had to stay in bed and a nurse had been obtained to tend her. Spencer hurried to Salt Lake and stayed with Mary for a week. While he took care of her, she gave him several thousand dollars to distribute to Kimball family members after she was gone. In addition, she gave him a handwritten will which stated: "I give and bequeath to Spencer Kimball $4,877.52 and to Agnes G. Lunt $3,200.00 and also give to them all my personal effects of every nature to be distributed by them as I have instructed."

Mary insisted that Spencer return to his business, desiring that her illness not be a burden on him. He wrote almost daily to her and corresponded also on these matters with her father and sister and Agnes and the bishop and his own brothers and sisters. Her welfare and the carrying out of her wishes mattered greatly to him.

In the time they spent together in October, Mary had outlined in detail what arrangements she preferred for her funeral, which included that Spencer be among the speakers. She lingered on in pain or asleep until the end of November. Her father, eighty-four and himself in almost constant pain, and her sister Lillian tried to see to her welfare. The father wrote to Spencer:

> . . . If anyone deserved the blessing of health, it's my dear daughter because she was faithful in everything and to all. There she is lying down in bed so quietly. . . . She is suffering but keeping as quiet as she can because she knows I have had another attack that drives me out of my mind . . . I just read your letters to Molly [Mary]. Three of them just arrived just now. She was very pleased to get them and just as I was leaving she said, 'Don't write Spencer to come as there is no necessity.' . . . Yes, my daughter has always been self-sacrificing."

A week later Mary's illness had gone so far that with the drugs she no longer had interest even in having letters read to her. Her father continued miserable, too. "We all know here how Molly feels about you. You have always been her favorite . . . If there has been anything in my letters displeasing to you remember it's the strain I am under all the time. Molly always loved you as a son. . . ."

Spencer continued to write, in the hope that Mary would regain interest in life. On November 22 Lillian wrote that her father thought Mary so near death that Spencer should come. By the time Spencer got this word Mary was gone.

At the time of her death, Mary was serving on the Relief Society general board and as editor of the *Relief Society Magazine*. At the funeral Spencer spoke, as she had requested, along with President Grant and other General Authorities. They all paid her warm tribute. She was laid to rest in the city cemetery.

Most of her stepchildren attended the funeral. Afterwards the family met with Mary's father and sister concerning the will. Recriminations flew against those who came from far off "to take away what did not rightly belong to them." Father Connelly, sick and grieving, was pushed to make accusations; he gave them an armload of Mary's clothing, nothing more.

For the Kimballs, this scene stood in stark contrast to that of a few years earlier when Andrew had died. Mary had then urged the children to keep his property; she had a home and money enough. She took only a few keepsakes. Distribution of the personal property posed a problem, the problem of who should choose. Each urged the best on the others. "You take that, Clare, it will fit into your home." "You should have that rug, Del, you can carry it easily in your car." The books, rugs, clocks, souvenirs, bedding, and personal belongings carrying sentiment were parceled out without bickering or envy, leaving a lifelong good feeling among the children, unlike the distribution of many other estates Spencer administered during his years in business.

On December 7, Agnes wrote to Spencer:

> Your love and devotion to Mother was beautiful. I don't think any of us will ever be able to know fully how much it did for our blessed Mother, to have a family and to be called "Mother." . . . How I wish I could be master of every situation, Spencer, like you, and be so dear and gentle in the face of such accusations as Grandpa made.

Spencer sent to Gordon and others of the family the designated share of money Mary had given him in October to hold until her death. "I know you will realize that much love came from Mother with it and her greatest concern was that she could not have made it much more. . . . She was a beautiful character."

And he wrote to Father Connelly: "It is our great hope that you have continued to mend and that you have been relieved of your discomforts. . . . I shall greatly appreciate a letter occasionally as I think the world of you and am much concerned in your wellbeing. May you continue well. With love, Sincerely, Spencer."

At the same time, Father Connelly was writing Spencer enclosing two hundred dollars for each of three grandsons as mission funds from Mary, in accordance with her request. He also mentioned that he had given money to the Church and to various individuals as Mary had asked. But he kept the other money and valuable belongings which Mary had intended for the Kimball family.

Spencer's aunt Alice Kimball Smith in Salt Lake City heard of the problem from Clare and wrote to Spencer. He replied:

> It is gratifying that Grandfather finally decided to comply with Mother's requests and distribute the funds as he has done. I believe he will be happier now. . . . We have not been given [the personal effects] but expect to say nothing further regarding the matter. I never have suffered so in my life. The accusations made and the threshing I took, no one will ever know. It was *her* father, and I knew he was strongly influenced and it was her request there be no trouble, so I *took* it and have been trying very hard to forget the whole unpleasant situation.

Aunt Alice, I have been honorable in this matter. I would face Mother today with my every word and thought in connection with this matter. I know she would approve. Her only disappointment would be that her wishes have been only partly carried out. . . .

I would appreciate it also if nothing further were said about it. . . . In spite of it all, I still have affection for Grandfather, and desire to keep in touch with him and help, if I can, should he become ill and ever need me. Mother and we had a perfect understanding. . . . How heavenly this old world would be if everyone could have the same beautiful spirit of love and service and unselfishness as she. . . .

When Spencer became Harry L. Payne's second counselor in 1924, President Payne said: "Spencer, we would like you to continue to handle the books as stake clerk for a while. You know the books and records. We'll get someone to replace you soon." Three years later, in December of 1927, Cleone Payne, the president's son, was called as stake clerk. Spencer helped him with the annual reports, since he was too new in the position to do them alone. In about a year, Cleone moved to Tucson and Spencer had the records again. The following year Ray Killian became stake clerk, again at year's end, so that Spencer helped with the annual reports. Ray moved to Mesa in 1935 and Spencer once more became acting stake clerk.

In the fall of that year he had written to his stepmother, Mary:

A few weeks ago Brother Ellsworth came to me and suggested that the Clerk work was so tremendously important and that they would have the benefit of my help and advice anyway and would then have four instead of three, if I were retained as Stake Clerk and another were appointed in the Stake Presidency. I have been quite puzzled. I told him I thought so and that I would be glad to be released as Counselor and keep the Stake Clerk work. He was very careful about it and gave no offense, and yet I have been wondering a lot about it, wondering what would lead him to make such a suggestion. I can hardly think of any selfish motive on his part. If there is one, it is well hidden, at least I have not been able to fathom it. The strange thing about it is that I rather like the idea myself and fell in quickly with the plan. He spoke to Pres. Payne about it and while he remonstrated, I rather think that he is not averse to the idea. As I think about it a lot, I seem to feel a great relief from responsibility and it seems good to contemplate that there will be few or no more funerals, no more responsibility in manning the organizations, signing recommends, attending meetings, etc., and I welcome it. The Clerk work is more in my line and I like it, and have the work well organized now so that much of it is done by my stenographer at the office. Still I wonder how I shall feel shorn of the honor and responsibility and all, to which I have become so used. I am wondering just how I shall feel when the change takes place. Of course it will not be done without my urging it a little now, but the change will likely take place at Conference time....

Just how he served made little difference to Spencer. When in 1928 the first counselor, John Nash, had moved away and had had to be released, President Payne had proposed to make Spencer first counselor and William Ellsworth second counselor. But Spencer had dissuaded him, urging that Brother Ellsworth, twenty-three years his senior, should have the first counselor position.

In 1936, a few months after the letter to Mary, Elder Melvin J. Ballard the apostle came to stake conference. He and Spencer discussed the situation. Spencer remembered beginning the conversation:

"It is hardly right, is it, for one little man to have two big jobs?"
"What do you mean?"
"I'm both stake clerk and a counselor in the stake presidency."
"Which position would you like to keep?"
"It doesn't matter. I'd like to serve wherever I am called."
"But if you had a choice, which would you rather do? We won't hold it against you. You tell us which you'd rather do."

Spencer answered: "I'd rather be stake clerk, because I have a secretary in my business and I have an office. I have typewriters and a telephone and files."

Apart from any expressed preference, it may have appeared easier to find a counselor than to keep a good clerk. So Spencer became stake clerk again and Jesse Udall replaced him as counselor.

After the switch was made at the conference, Spencer received a letter from an acquaintance who drew her own conclusions from the fact that the stake clerk received a salary, however modest. "Spencer, I'm disappointed in you. To think that you'd accept the money calling instead of the spiritual calling." She predicted that within six months Spencer would apostatize.

10

Stake President

— "an estate where we would
end our days"

In 1938 Elder Ballard returned to
divide the growing St. Joseph Stake. St. Joseph Stake was to retain the
wards from Thatcher westward. The new Mount Graham Stake was to
include the wards from Safford east. Elder Ballard called Spencer as
the first president of the Mount Graham Stake. Spencer's reaction was
one of gratitude and concern.

He prayed that night that when the time came for him to be
released from the stake president's position he could accept it gracefully, knowing how difficult it was for some to do this. He also thought
wistfully that his parents were no longer alive to share with him this
new experience and honor. He felt inadequate to the calling but set to
with a will to organize the newly formed stake and get it functioning.

He had told Brother Ballard that he could not be president of the
stake because he had enemies who hated him. The apostle had passed it
off lightly, saying, "You can take care of that all right."

His first act, that Sunday evening after he had been set apart, was
to go with Camilla to those with whom there had been some trouble and
clear the slate so that he could go forward with free conscience.

Spencer called to the high council one of his neighbors with whom
he had had a dispute over water, putting behind him a feeling of hurt

Spencer Kimball (center) as stake president with his counselor Vernon McGrath (left) and El Paso Ward Bishop Arwell Pierce and (standing) Trenial Pauly, Vernon Turley and Mark West of the El Paso Ward bishopric, 1942

and injustice and recognizing that there may legitimately be two sides to a disagreement.

To visit each ward and return home would take 1,750 miles. Spencer and his counselors did that repeatedly. He initiated a stake bulletin which kept missionaries and members of the scattered wards informed of Church-related news.

Responsibilities as a new stake president sometimes seemed overwhelming. Spencer wrote to Camilla, who was in California again with Eddie: "Tomorrow is a heavy day — I dread it and will be glad when it is over. I find I am weak and too small and too lazy and too inefficient. Maybe they will release me after a year or two. I really hope so. I could step out today with the best of feelings and no misgivings, but I guess I'll have to go on at least until an Apostle comes down to see how poor it is."

Much of Spencer's work was organizational, but much also involved people directly. Spencer stood by while the doctor amputated Martin Stewart's leg. They cleared off the kitchen table and laid the young man on it. The doctor anaesthetized him, bared the bone and sawed through it. Spencer took the leg outside wrapped in newspapers.

Spencer stood by in the hospital when Ethelyn Rawson had a gall bladder operation without general anaesthetic. Family members could not get there in time, so Spencer talked with her all during the surgery to keep her calm.

Spencer's interest was not only in his own Church people but in the whole community. He wrote in a 1940 letter: "Am going out to Lebanon tomorrow. They have new chairs. I Okd a graduation exercise in their chapel for the colored school yesterday and there is some opposition, I find. Maybe I will have a race war to settle tomorrow."

And he wrote in his daybook:

I offered prayer for a family over 5 year old boy deceased. They wanted no funeral, but just a prayer. Just 4 of us present. They seemed appreciative. Cotton pickers. . . .

Nov. 21. At the hospital twice to administer to Dan Flowers — non-member.

Nov. 22. Administered to Dan Flowers with Bishop Maloy at noon and at 7 p.m. with Pres. Payne.

Nov. 23. Blessed Dan Flowers and at his request I stood by while the doctors amputated his right arm. 2 hours. Called again and administered with Pres. Payne.

Nov. 24. My boy at the hospital was worse today. The nurses shook their heads. A little better in evening.

Nov. 25. At hospital Dan Flowers a little better.

Nov. 26. Hospital. Dan better.

Nov. 27. Two visits to Dan Flowers at hospital — better. Everyone delighted. Doctors and nurses were shaking their heads on the 24th.

Nov. 28. Dan is improving.

Dec. 2. Hospital visit — 2. Dan asked me to baptize him.

Dec. 4. Visited the hospital.

Dec. 5. Took Flowers out to his home from hospital for ride.

Dec. 13. Took Dan to see his folks.

Dec. 14. Dan went home today from hospital.

Weddings, too, for non-members came to him. As a new stake president Spencer recorded: "Went to family show. During show I was called out to perform marriage ceremony over the radio. I did it but think I shall never again. It is too sacred to me to handle thus."

Often cotton pickers and transients would come to his office to be married. He did not charge them, but if the husband insisted on paying, Spencer asked five dollars and then gave it to the bride as a wedding present. He always took time to talk to the couple about the responsibilities marriage entails.

Spencer had a way with people. As neighbor, businessman, and Church leader he knew practically every man, woman and child in the valley — Mormon and non-Mormon. Decades later he would still demonstrate phenomenal recall for Arizona people he had not seen for thirty years. And if he did not know those he met, he surely knew their parents or grandparents, frequently knowing their genealogy and family ties better than the young people themselves. "It comes from all the funerals I attend. If you sit on the stand and see the family groups, you associate people."

"I was asked to speak at a Follett funeral in Pima," he once recalled. "Then I saw come in and sit on the front row the man whose funeral I thought it was. That was a shock. I quickly inquired and found that there were brothers who looked somewhat alike."

He and President Harry Payne between them had long covered most of the funerals in the valley. President Payne had a way of making one almost envy the deceased, about whom such fine things were said. Spencer had a different style; as much as anything, his son LeVan thought, his success here resulted from his extraordinary capacity to demonstrate sympathy for people.

Some years later Spencer preached the funeral sermon for an elderly man whose daughter said before the funeral, "Well, Spencer, just think, we used to play together when we were little children and now you are an apostle and I am an apostate." But after the sermon, which was warm in its appreciation for her father and loving toward the family, she said, looking him straight in the eye, "I had thought of you as a stuffed shirt, but now I have changed my mind."

Added to that was his willingness to extend himself for people, as a journal entry indicates:

> Attended the funeral of Aunt Ida Allredge [near Phoenix] and sang her song: "I Would Not Part the Curtains." After a most difficult time, I got a ticket at 12:00 midnight on the bus and sat on the jump seat to Globe, and a better seat to Safford, arriving at 6:00 a.m. Went directly to work at the office.

Business and Church work mixed because Spencer saw to it that both got done; whatever the cost in hours, neither was sacrificed to the other.

Two years after his call to be stake president, Spencer was in attendance at general conference in Salt Lake City, away from his family. Twenty years before, it would have been his father, seeing to Church affairs, regretting the constraints upon his time. Now it was Spencer who wrote home:

October 4, 1940

Darling Wife:

> With little to do till 10 and my habits waking me at 5:30, I have been lying here in comfort thinking how much I love you and my family — how much I appreciate you all and how little time we seem to have or take at home to think about it and express it. Maybe it is a good thing to get away for a few days and have a chance to think.
>
> What a shame that we are so completely occupied with all our outside interests, our business, church, clubs, school activities that we see so little of each member of the family and then so hurried.

As the children are developing in school, church and social activities, they are gone more and more. . . .

You, dear, have been a wonderful wife — considerate and patient with all my faults, understanding in my eccentricities and sympathetic with my crankiness. You have slaved, sacrificed and been loyal to me. I write this letter to let you know again I love you, darling.

Devotedly,

Spencer

His love of family would soon be extended into a further generation. The next year Spencer and Camilla's first grandchild was born — Barbara, daughter of LeVan and his wife Kathryn. Spencer and Camilla dressed up as old folks, complete with cane and shawl, and hobbled around to their friends' homes to announce their graduation to a new status.

All through stake conference in September 1941 it poured rain. People shifted in their seats, wondering when it would stop and how they would get home over inundated highways. The Gila River, usually a foot or so deep over the rock and sand bed, rose and rose. At Duncan, where the river passed through the narrows, word came Monday from a high councilor who lived upriver that a crest was coming which could flood the town of a thousand inhabitants.

The river had been high before, but never enough to reach the town itself; so the people assumed the warning exaggerated. But the water rose, up and over the railroad tracks, a new river coming down the main street, ever deeper and swifter. "Leave the cars and things and get the people out!" was the cry. Men and boys pushed into the torrent, waist deep, holding hands to maintain their balance, helping women and children to high ground. J. Vernon McGrath, Spencer's counselor, found a woman in a tree and helped carry her to safety. Her sick husband was put in a car which several men pushed, floating, to high ground. Adobe houses melted, frame houses shifted on their foundations. The telephone girl stayed at her post until she was sitting in water, then left. With darkness, people slept on cots or on the floor at the high school or in homes higher up. The river took over most of the town.

On Tuesday morning the flood remained at its height, and Spencer, in Safford, learned of its full extent. He managed to reach his counselor over a makeshift telephone connection through New Mexico, filled his car with food from the interstake welfare storehouse in Safford, and drive the forty miles to Duncan. The bishop and Brother McGrath had handled the short-range needs of getting many families taken into homes in Franklin. Government agencies and the Red Cross brought emergency supplies of water and food and blankets for those still in Duncan.

Going on to Virden, the Mormon settlement eight miles upriver, Spencer had to walk through swift water on the approaches to the bridge, thought unsafe for cars. The devastation of the valley spread before him. Whole farms had been washed away, the rich fields gullied and converted to sand and gravel; crops in the fields had been swept clean. A thousand sacks of onions floated downstream.

The farmers had suffered the greater long-term loss, but the problems of homeless families in Duncan, a fourth of them Church members, seemed more acute. The members had mostly been taken in by other LDS families, but their homes stood deep in muck as the water receded leaving furniture, bedding and clothing fouled, utilities out, water contaminated, and morale low. When two missing children turned up, it was evident that at least no lives had been lost. Spencer met with federal and state relief agencies to correlate a program of rehabilitation. There seemed more bureaucrats than victims. The Mormons came in for some criticism that few of them ate at the emergency feeding station. Spencer explained that the Mormons were happy they could take care of one another. The Methodists had similarly pooled their resources and had a communal kitchen at their church.

Spencer gathered up muddy clothing from the members, who had water only for drinking, and had them cleaned by the laundry in Safford; clean clothing lifted spirits. He arranged for the bishops to buy water-soaked grain from the cooperative mill owned by Church members and distribute it to farmers whose livestock had no feed. A careful survey of the members' needs took place on Thursday. On

Saturday morning a truckload of food and clothing, and mattresses (made from Welfare Program cotton), left Safford for Duncan. Quilts, shoes, fruit, honey, flour and other supplies got people started again. By the end of the week, utilities were reestablished and people could begin reclaiming their homes and cleaning up.

Conservative estimates of loss among Church members ran to a hundred thousand dollars — shockingly high for a small rural community. Men tended to minimize their own losses and dwell on the losses of their brethren. Spencer was deeply touched by the courage and unselfishness. One family of nine had lost its home entirely; the Welfare Program bought land for a new home, one ward contributed cement for the foundation, the Church Welfare Program provided other building materials, and quorum members supplied the labor to build a new home. Other wards in the stake and surrounding stakes contributed cash, hay, grain, equipment for leveling land. Primary concern extended to Church members, but help also went to non-members.

Spencer noted the good spirit:

> When one of our brethren from Virden was loading hay at a barn in St. Joseph Stake, he came to a few bales of poor hay. Noticing it, the donor said:
>
> "Throw that out; we'll feed that poor hay to our dry stock."
>
> The Virden brother jokingly said:
>
> "That's all right — beggars cannot be choosers."
>
> To which the donor quickly came back, and meant it:
>
> "We want you brethren to understand that we do not consider you beggars. We are happy to give you this feed and help out a little and we want you to have the best."

Bulldozers from the Soil Conservation Service were obtained for the cost of fuel and operation, and through the winter thousands of hours of work by the machines helped restore the land.

Spencer's effective work in coordinating the emergency response of the Welfare Program and the long-term rehabilitation efforts received favorable notice among the General Authorities. He had kept the General Church Welfare Committee, of which Elder Harold B. Lee was chairman, apprised of the situation, but had chosen to handle the problems locally and regionally without recourse to Salt Lake, except for some cash to be used in the process of restoring the farms.

Spencer wrote a description of the flood and its aftermath which was published by the *Improvement Era,* accompanied by photographs he had taken of the scene. He saw it as a great tribute to the spirit of cooperation embodied in the Church Welfare Program.

In late 1941, Hoover Long heard of some investment property in Las Vegas. He and Lawrence Maloy, Bert Hatch and Spencer traveled to Las Vegas, driving through the night, to inspect the property. The vacant property was the triangle at the juncture of two roads leading out of Las Vegas toward Los Angeles. Six hundred to one thousand feet long, it was a block wide at one end and narrowed to a point on the other end. It would have space for a number of business buildings or a motel.

The men talked with an attorney who was handling the property and found it was available for twenty thousand dollars. They obtained a thirty-day option and drove home.

Spencer talked it over with Camilla, and she did not feel comfortable about it. Spencer concluded that getting involved in a gambling town like Las Vegas was not a good idea for him and that, though there was money to be made, he did not want his last two sons to grow up with that background.

Before the option expired, the Second World War broke out. Las Vegas enjoyed a wartime boom, and Spencer later said: "It is good we didn't buy that property. We'd unavoidably have been multimillionaires and I don't think I could have stood it." After his call to the apostleship he also mused about the likelihood of his having been chosen if he had himself been distracted either by wealth or by involvement in the wrong kind of business.

Spencer once asked his nephew, "Are you making money?" When the answer was yes, he said, "I hope you don't make too much money."

December 7, 1941, Camilla's birthday, was memorable. In Duncan, clean-up from the flood continued. The Lebanon meetinghouse, where Spencer was visiting meetings, buzzed furiously with the news that the Japanese had attacked Pearl Harbor. From church, people scurried home to put their ears to the radio. The shocking news crystallized sentiment. Whereas before many had been reluctant for the United States to embroil itself in another war across the sea, sympathies for European peoples' suffering under Nazi attack joined with outrage at the Japanese perfidy to mobilize immediate fighting spirit. Another holy crusade began like the First World War, in which the United States fought to Make the World Safe for Democracy. The country had been shipping aid to the Allied countries, but had not fully mobilized. With the United States now in the war, men hastily trained as the Japanese swept over much of the Pacific. The draft pulled in boys from the farms and towns and soon sent them overseas to fight in Europe and the Pacific. LeVan, married and with one child, tried to enlist but could not qualify because of his eyes. Andrew, the second son, was only fourteen.

Spencer watched "his" boys from the stake begin leaving, either drafted or volunteering, young men who would rather have been on missions or in school or rearing a family. At one time, 250 men from his stake served in the military. Spencer felt great responsibility for them. In addition to the contacts families and wards maintained, the stake kept in touch with the servicemen (and the few servicewomen) through sending copies of the stake bulletin. Every month, Spencer individually signed copies of the bulletin and usually penned a brief personal message to each serviceman. Notes of appreciation came back from all over the world. Young men leaving often called on him for a blessing; parents losing sons to death leaned on him in their grief.

Much of the cost of the war had to be met by governmental borrowing. Just as Andrew Kimball had been asked to promote sale of Liberty and Victory Bonds in the First World War, so now on top of his other responsibilities Spencer received the assignment to run one of the United War Fund campaigns in the valley. "I realize the responsibilities you are under. Our Board, however, has extreme confidence in you," wrote Delbert Stapley. The goal for the campaign was $4250. Two months later, Spencer reported donations of $7000 for war relief. He also aided in war bond campaigns and scrap metal drives.

Over the years Spencer served the community in countless ways. Emil Crockett thought perhaps no one else had done as much. "When they wanted something done they would come to him because of his capability." Spencer served on the Safford city council, on the board of the Chamber of Commerce, in the Boy Scout organization, as secretary for the fund-raising project to build a new gymnasium at Gila College, and on the board of the Red Cross. He worked for the continuation of Prohibition and he expressed particular disappointment when Utah voted wet instead of dry. He lobbied in the legislature for a bill requiring the schools to teach about the dangers of alcohol. He served as a director of the Arizona Association of Insurance Agents, as a member of the governing board of Gila College, as chairman of the local United Services Organization. He belonged to the governor's Fact Finding Committee for Education in Arizona. He was named by the governor a member of the Arizona Teachers Retirement Board. There had been some talk of his running for the state legislature, but that had not ripened before he left Arizona. He served the Rotary Club as president and as district governor as well as continually on club committees. He organized a chorus; he performed musically both vocally and on the piano. He served faithfully in his various Church callings. All this, in addition to his work with Kimball-Greenhalgh, the cotton growers, the canal companies, and an active social life with square dancing, entertaining, travelling, and occasional athletics such as hiking, snowshoeing, handball and volleyball.

With this dizzying round of activity and responsibility it is no wonder that he felt extreme pressure. In addition to the more predictable activities he spoke or sang at many funerals — at twenty-two in 1934, for example. His journal reflects the strain. "April 9: Spent the evening at home. Hurrah!!!!" After speaking at a funeral, he wrote, "I was so fatigued mentally and physically, that I made a failure, I fear." "16 hours continuous today without a moment relaxation — 7 a.m. to 11:45 p.m." "Worked annual reports till 1 a.m." "Heavy day. Some disappointments. Meeting with Safford Building Committee. Something wrong with me, I guess. Feel like I could scream. Maybe I 'can take' it after a night's sleep. Bed 9:30." "Meeting with Layton Ward Building Committee. The work and strain continues. I feel I might explode. It will ease up after Union day perhaps." "Nov. 16. Had a bad scare today. Felt like might be going to have a stroke. Feel pretty worried. Will get a chiropractic treatment tomorrow." "Nov. 17. Had a treatment today. Feel better a little but quite worried and distressed. Am on a tension from 7 a.m. till 11 p.m. every single minute every day. I know I'm working too hard but there seems no place to stop." "Nov.

18. Feel better." "Spent balance of evening with my family. My boys had not seen me since Sat. 2 days before." "A day of a thousand duties as usual. My head whirls. I am bewildered in the impossibility of doing all I must do." "After 11:30 I prepared my 7th talk for the week."

One year Spencer sent Emil in his place to the state insurance agents convention. When Emil arrived he was met by a group who proposed to elect Spencer president of the state association. But though they phoned Spencer long distance now, it was too late for him to come. Emil suspected that Spencer had learned of the proposed draft and, never able to say no to a plea for his service but too busy to say yes this time, had avoided the convention on purpose.

In spite of the strain, Spencer kept up his breakneck pace year after year.

On top of it he suffered from boils, a plague which began about 1932 and continued for many years until he began to bring them under control with miracle drugs developed during the Second World War, the sulfa group and penicillin. The first came on his nose and lips. Camilla returned from June Conference in Salt Lake City to find Spencer wearing a handkerchief over his face, like a bandit.

At one time he had twenty-four boils around his waist where his belt rubbed. The infectious sores spread from one location to another.

In 1943 he wrote: "I am really low today. Can hardly drag around but the carbuncles will eventually go as some 50 have gone before them. (I hope.)" "The three are just where I cannot let my pants hang on my hips as they hurt the two on my hips and if I pull up the trousers above the hips it catches the one on my stomach, so you see what a fix I am in." "My nose with its boil was devitalizing me. I tossed all night with but little sleep." Spencer jokingly compared himself with Job, whom the Lord allowed to be tested by pain and personal loss.

In 1943 a rash of fires set people in the neighborhood on edge. First a lumberyard caught fire mysteriously at about 2:00 A.M. In the next two nights, hay barns burned. At supper Spencer said, "Well, it is about our turn tonight." That night around two o'clock Spencer woke to the fire siren and jumped up and went to the window. In the field behind the house his hay barn burned brightly. He and Andrew rushed out and threw such hay down from the stack as they could to save it. But four tons burned or was ruined by water. He and Andrew slept in the barn for the rest of the night, since fire continued to break out in the bales. Luckily insurance covered most of the loss.

The police had been sleuthing, checking footprints in the freshly plowed field. They identified and confronted a fifteen-year-old boy at the school, who confessed that he set the fires and then pumped his bicycle to a safe distance away and stopped to watch the scene. He said tearfully, "If I had known that barn was Brother Kimball's I would not have set it on fire." After being found delinquent he was committed to the reform school and later paroled to relatives in Utah.

In 1930 when Spencer was still a counselor to President Harry Payne in the old St. Joseph Stake, Spencer's uncle J. Golden Kimball had been the General Authority to visit the stake conference. President Payne's suggestion that the Kimballs put Uncle Golden up during his stay pleased Spencer, though it presented a problem. Their house had only one real bedroom and a small added-on room made by enclosing a front porch. Since Camilla had a new baby, they put their guest in the little front room, with a three-quarter bed. After a pleasant evening sprinkled with his stories and salty language, the tall man stretched out cater-corner in the bed, placed his hot-water bags about his aging, thinly covered bones, and tried to sleep.

Spencer had bragged what an angel his new two-week-old baby was. But no sooner had Uncle Golden got settled than the baby began to scream. Nothing would stop him. Spencer grabbed him up and carried him to the farthest point in the little house from the front bedroom and walked with the baby long and impatiently.

Next morning, when Spencer was driving Uncle Golden to the conference, the visitor said, in his high-pitched voice, "Spencer, why don't you take your guests down to the hotel where they will be comfortable?" He liked Camilla's cooking and came to the house for all his meals, but the next night he slept at the hotel.

Uncle Golden's frankness had always been a prominent characteristic. He wrote to his brother Andrew once, after a severe reprimand from one of the apostles of the Church: "It may result in keeping my mouth closed. However, this would seem to be an utter impossibility. I may, however, close my mouth, burst and go up in smoke. . . ." He once said he figured that no other Kimball stood a chance of high Church office, since the Brethren would not risk the chance of another one like him.

Ten years later, Spencer and Camilla were able to move into a new, larger home. As a real-estate man, Spencer had for years kept an eye on a tract of sixteen acres southwest from Relation Street and Eighth Avenue. It seemed an ideal place to build and good for subdividing. Spencer's inclination, after his experience with banks, was to put his money in real estate. When Lester Bingham indicated in 1938 that he was ready to sell, Spencer wanted it so much that he paid the asking price of six thousand dollars in cash and was happy to own it. This was more than farm property would bring, but Spencer saw its potential as residential property.

About 1939, Spencer added twenty-four contiguous acres, to make a forty-acre farm, which he and a renter planted to cotton and alfalfa. Others saw the desirability of the location for building and Spencer sold off a number of lots along the street. The farm paid its own way as farmland but turned a good profit as residential property.

He and Camilla began to dream and plan for a new home, to be built on the Bingham property. For several years they had talked, settling on pueblo style. As they traveled they took pictures of houses with features they liked. As business got gradually better they actually got down to drawing plans. Off and on through 1939 Spencer worked on the house plans.

In 1940 they let contracts for the house, so lovingly planned. The bids ranged from $4,685 to $6,850. In March construction began and in June they moved in. No house ever represented more thought in its planning. To Camilla, the house, six rooms and a bath and a half, "was a mansion and built of love and dreams." The shower, complete with ceramic tile, represented real luxury.

They bought a special guest book in which they had guests — prominent and humble — sign their names. In this home in November 1942 they celebrated their silver wedding anniversary, inviting friends with a unique home-made photomontage card showing the changes of twenty-five years. They carefully specified they did not want gifts; they wanted, and got, the warm affection and appreciation of friends they had made over half a lifetime. They sent out more than six hundred

SPENCER KIMBALL — CAMILLA EYRING
MARRIED NOV. 16 1917
25 ANNIVERSARY

—

AT HOME TO ALL THEIR FRIENDS
SAFFORD, ARIZ.
SATURDAY, NOV. 14, 1942

—

NO GIFTS PLEASE.

1917.      1942.

Invitation to silver wedding reception: newlyweds, first Safford home, family members, new home built 1940

invitations, staggering the times so they could accommodate the crowd. But nearly everyone came and stayed. Inside the house people could not move; sitting down to visit proved unthinkable.

Spencer and Camilla looked back in satisfaction upon twenty-five years of married life, living in their small corner of the world. They had planted an orchard behind the new house and expected to watch the trees blossom and bear fruit year by year. Spencer and the boys built barns and tended livestock. "We loved the feeling of permanence and security our new home gave us," remembered Camilla. "In fact, we felt we had established an estate where we would end our days."

11

The Call to Apostleship

— "the Evil One has tempted me
a thousand times"

In 1943 business thrived. It seemed
that everything Spencer touched turned to money. Deals fell into place
so quickly he hardly had time to attend to closings. His income nearly
quadrupled what he had ever known before. The business in which he
had invested $150 in 1927 had now skyrocketed to $100,000, "almost
like a fairy tale."

On the streets in Safford he had trouble in walking a block without
friends stopping him to chat or to ask for advice. When the *Guardian*
polled its readers as to the most prominent man in the Gila Valley,
Spencer came out on top.

In April Spencer walked onto Temple Square in Salt Lake City in a
surge of hundreds of bishops, stake presidents and stake patriarchs.
Joseph F. Merrill stopped him at the gate and asked him to open the
113th Annual Conference with prayer. Spencer took it as "a signal
honor." Other attentions followed. He ate dinner at Elder Stephen L
Richards' "rich and lovely home." He had to turn down invitations to
dine with Elders David O. McKay and Antoine R. Ivins. His cousin
Elder J. Reuben Clark, Jr., President Grant's counselor, invited
Spencer to stay with him through the conference period. That they
were especially gracious in their greetings pleased Spencer greatly. He

assumed they appreciated his skilful use of the Church Welfare Program in handling the Duncan flood.

After a Woolley family visit on the Sunday night of conference, Spencer's cousin Preston Parkinson took him back to his hotel. Preston insisted that if Spencer moved to Salt Lake the Brethren would make him an apostle, but that they would never find him down in Arizona. Spencer answered: "Preston, that's silly. They would never pick me, with all the great men in the Church."

Back in Safford, Spencer was chosen to present Gila College's graduates their diplomas. In June Governor Osborn appointed him to a state board on the strength of his insurance experience. After the years of struggle, things began to look promising.

Then, on July 8, 1943, when Spencer had gone home for lunch the telephone rang at his office. The operator said, "Salt Lake City is calling for Spencer Kimball."

The secretary responded, "He isn't here right now."

The caller broke in: "I'll speak to whoever will speak to me. Where is Mr. Kimball?"

She replied, "He's gone home for lunch, but hasn't had time to arrive there."

"This is J. Reuben Clark. How long until he'll be home?"

"It only takes him five or ten minutes, unless he had another errand. I think you can catch him in ten minutes."

Spencer describes the events which followed:

> It was noon and I was just entering the house for my luncheon at my new home on Relation Street and Eighth Avenue, Safford, Arizona. As I pushed open the door I heard my little 12-year-old son, Eddie, saying, "No, Daddy is not here. Oh, yes. Here he comes," as I pushed my way into the room.
>
> "Daddy, Salt Lake City is calling."
>
> I had had many calls from Salt Lake City through the years but today an overpowering feeling came over me that instant that I was to be called to a high position in the Church. Why I should think so, I do not know. If ever that thought had entered my mind in times past, I had quickly thrust it from me as being most unworthy.
>
> It must have taken only a few seconds for me to cross the room to the phone, grasp the receiver and say, "Hello," but it seemed that an hour's thinking and retrospection coursed through my mind with lightning rapidity. I realized I had no unfinished business with Salt Lake City. I knew that there were two vacancies in the

Quorum of the Twelve but I had given it little concern, knowing that the Brethren would take care of it in due time and it was still some ten weeks before the Conference, at which the vacancies would most likely be filled. There was no reason in the world why I should be called. I instantaneously convinced myself that it was impossible, that I was not capable or prepared or worthy, that no one would be called away from the headquarters of the Church and that there was no reason whatever for the feeling that came with the announcement that Salt Lake was on the wire, but I still had that short premonition that an announcement of great portent was coming. Much happened in that short second. I was upbraiding myself for permitting such a thought to enter my mind; I was proving to myself that it was only an ambitious dream, unworthily presumptuous, and that it was impossible, when the clear pleasant voice of President J. Reuben Clark came:

"Spencer, this is Brother Clark. Do you have a chair handy?"

"Yes, Brother Clark," I answered with a quivering voice.

His words came with strength and power unmistakable.

"The brethren have just chosen you to fill one of the vacancies in the Quorum."

I heard the words ringing down into my consciousness, but it was unbelievable.

"Oh, Brother Clark! Not me? You don't mean me? There must be some mistake. I surely couldn't have heard you right." This as I sank past the chair to the floor.

"Yes. The Brethren feel that you are the man. How do you feel about it?"

"Oh, Brother Clark! It seems so impossible. I am so weak and small and limited and incapable. Of course, there could be only one answer to any call from the Brethren but —"

A complete panorama came before me of the little, mean, petty things I had done, of the little misunderstandings I had had with people in business and with people in the Church whose feelings I might have hurt. It seemed that every person that had ever been offended because of me stood before me to say, "How could *you* be an Apostle of the Lord? You are not worthy. You are *insignificant*. You shouldn't accept this calling. You *can't* do it." I must have hesitated a long time, for Brother Clark said:

"Are you there?"

Catching my breath I said, "Yes, Brother Clark, but you've taken my breath. I am all in a sweat."

"Well, it is rather warm up here also," he said good-naturedly, sensing I am sure, the tense emotional strain through which I was passing. It wasn't the warmth of the summer day and he knew it well.

"Does this mean that I am to sell my home and business and all my belongings and move up to Salt Lake City?" I asked.

"Yes. Ultimately," he said.

"Do I get a little time to think this thing through?" I asked, almost pleadingly. "My mind is such a blank. I am so confused. By the way, my wife and I are leaving Saturday for Boulder, Colorado, to see our son and his family. Why couldn't I fly over to Salt Lake and talk it over with you?"

"Alright," he said. "I will not be here but Brother McKay will be and you could come over. They have overnight service between here and Denver."

There were other things he said, inquiring about the welfare of the family and other pleasantries, but my mind was going so fast I was only partly conscious of them. As the two receivers, a thousand miles separated, clicked I turned to my wife and the two boys, Andrew 16, and Eddie 12, who had been standing where they were when my first exclamation put wonder in their minds.

"They have called me to become an Apostle," I announced with an unsteady voice, and there was only silence in their faces — bewilderment.

"Are you sure that you were to be an Apostle?" my wife asked finally.

"No, I am not sure now," I answered. "It seems that is what he said, but that is so impossible. Perhaps it was to be an Assistant or something else. It couldn't have been that. I am not sure. I am so bewildered."

Little was said, but in a daze the four of us found our way to the table where the noonday meal was cooling. Without a word we sat and one of the boys asked the blessing on the food. We took helpings but the food didn't reach our mouths. I looked off into space and ground my teeth. The boys went outside to their work. I lay down on the floor for a moment of relaxation, as was my custom, but not to relax or rest.

"I must, of course, accept it and do the best I can," I thought. Then the opposite: "I can't do it . . . there is the new home with all its luxuries and comforts to give up. True there are other homes, but this one has embedded into its very structure our hearts and lives. There is the business, my life's work for all these years. My heart is there also, and it is now so prosperous and fast making us independent. How could I give up that? There is the farm property which we have finally accumulated after these long years of striving. How can we leave that? And our people and friends and dear old Arizona in which we have our roots so firmly embedded." Then would come the thought: "When the Church calls, we obey." But the predominant thought was my own limitations and incapacities and weaknesses and I was overcome. The tears came then, an inexhaustible flood. It had been years since I had shed a tear. Scores of funeral sermons I had preached, I had closed eyes in death, I had seen mothers taken from their little ones and yet I had reached the point where I had perfect control of my emotions. But now uncontrollable, I wept and wept. It seemed that all the conflicting thoughts of my mind were trying to wash themselves clear with tears. I was in convulsions of sobbing. My wife was sitting by me on the floor, stroking my hair, trying to quiet me.

Finally came a lull in the storm. I washed my face with cool water and went to the office. Some routine things I was able to do, but I went about in a daze.

The night, but no sleep. Both of us rolled and tossed and wept and walked the floor through the long hours that lengthened themselves out into an eternity. Finally came the dawn and with it some definite things that must be done. What a boon! Things that forced my thoughts from the revolution coming in our lives. Friday the 9th was a hectic day, never-ending. And the night was a repetition of the first. How I prayed through those long dark hours, prayers for forgiveness of my weaknesses and imperfections, prayers for strength to do the right, prayers that the family would all make the necessary adjustments in their feelings, but above all, prayers that I might feel that I was called by the Lord through His Servants and an assurance of acceptance. My wife was my salvation. She comforted me and encouraged me and continued to say there was only one road to follow.

We needed no alarm clock to get us up early this morning for our trip. We had wished all night for 5 o'clock to come so we might get on our way. We started off in the Buick car for El Paso, the four of us (Olive Beth was in San Francisco working and LeVan was in Boulder, Colorado, in a Navy language program). It took us seven hours to make the trip and we had a seven-hour family council meeting. What to do, how it would affect us, the changes that would come to the boys and girl, their schooling, their friends, our life.

Two of the brethren and their wives took my wife and myself to the El Cortes Hotel for dinner and it seemed they insisted on discussing for the whole hour the very topic so worrying me, that of the filling of the vacancies in the Quorum.

"Brother Kimball," they said, "do you have any idea who will be called?" And I hope I will be forgiven for the answer I gave, for the secret was not yet to be divulged. I swallowed, shifted a bit and said, "No. I can't tell you." There was a meeting of the Stake Sunday School Board that evening, followed by another sleepless night.

Sunday was a most busy day. Little time for deep contemplation, but vagrant thoughts continued to get away from the business at hand to worry about the call to the Apostleship. At 10:30 we bade goodbye to the boys who were to return on the train to our home in Safford, and we boarded the train for the North. Our berth was comfortable, but there was little sleep. All night long I was upbraiding myself for not having better prepared myself for the great work, for my weaknesses and imperfections, praying for strength, for an assurance from the Lord that "All was well," and that I was acceptable to Him. I continued to tell Camilla that I was not sure what I would do, though I knew all the time there was only one course. She continued to encourage me and insisted that acceptance of the call was the only thing. We arrived in Albuquerque early in the morning and had a 14-hour lay-over. We went to restaurants, but the food didn't taste very good. We went to shows and I don't know how much she saw, but there was little of the pictures that penetrated my thoughts. We tried to read books but it seemed only pages and pages of words, meaningless words that my eyes were seeing, but my thoughts were hurdling.

We reached Denver on the 13th of July and were met at the station by our son, Spencer LeVan, and his wife and baby. They thought it strange that I should be seeking reservations on a plane to Salt Lake even before I left the railroad station. We dropped no hint of the impending crisis in our lives. We caught the train to Boulder, arriving there in the late evening. By this time we had been through five nights and days; it seemed years since that telephone conversation the previous Thursday. I was weak and tired. I knew I could sleep from sheer exhaustion, but not so, for this night was no exception and very early it was a relief to leave the bed.

It was just breaking day this Wednesday, the 14th of July. No peace had yet come, though I had prayed for it almost unceasingly these six days and nights. I had no plan or destination. I only knew I must get out in the open, apart, away. I dressed quietly and without disturbing the family, I slipped out of the house. I turned toward the hills. I had no objective. I wanted only to be alone. I had begun a fast.

The way was rough, I wandered aimlessly and finally came to the top of the hill. I nearly stepped on a snake coiled on my path. An unexplainable sudden strength sent me into a high jump over his striking head. Could this be symbolic of my other worries and problems? I stopped to rest, thinking that here I was alone, but cows were near and people stirring in the homes below. Over the little ridge was a sloping little valley and on the other side the high mountain rose rapidly and farther up almost precipitously to a high peak far above. Without thought I found my way down and started up again on the other side. The grass was ankle high and the seeds fell into my shoes. The lower reaches had been pastured by cattle when it was wet and it was pitted with deep hoofprints. The rocks on the hillside increased in quantity and size.

My weakness overcame me again. Hot tears came flooding down my cheeks as I made no effort to mop them up. I was accusing myself, and condemning myself and upbraiding myself. I was praying aloud for special blessings from the Lord. I was telling Him that I had not asked for this position, that I was incapable of doing the work, that I was imperfect and weak and human, that I was unworthy of so noble a calling, though I had tried hard and my heart had been right. I knew that I must have been at least partly responsible for offenses and misunderstandings which a few people fancied they had suffered at my hands. I realized that I had been petty and small many times. I did not spare myself. A thousand things passed through my mind. Was I called by revelation? Or, had the Brethren been impressed by the recent contacts in my home and stake when they had visited us, or by the accounts of my work in the flood rehabilitation which reports I knew had been greatly exaggerated in my favor? Had I been called because of my relationship to one of the First Presidency?

If I could only have the assurance that my call had been inspired most of my other worries would be dissipated. I knew if the Lord had revealed to the Brethren that I was to be one of His leaders, that He would forgive all my weaknesses and make me strong. I knew full well that He knew all the imperfections of my life and He knew my heart. And I knew that I must have His acceptance before I could go on. I stumbled up the hill and onto the mountain, as the way became rough. I faltered some as the way became steep. No paths were there to follow; I climbed on and on. Never had I prayed before as I now prayed. What I wanted and felt I must have was an assurance that I was acceptable to the Lord. I told Him that I neither wanted nor was worthy of a vision or appearance of angels or any special manifestation. I wanted only the calm peaceful assurance that my offering was accepted. Never before had I been tortured as I was now being tortured. And the assurance did not come.

I was getting higher and the air was thinner and I was reaching some cliffs and jagged rocky points. I came to a steep slide area and it was almost impossible to make the grade. I stumbled over an old oak stick which I picked up. I broke off one end and it was exactly the right length for a cane. It was rough and a little crooked and worm-eaten in places, but it helped me climb. I stopped to catch my breath in a protected cove behind some large rocks but unsatisfied I continued to climb, up steep jagged rocks made the more difficult of scaling by my tear-filled eyes.

As I rounded a promontory I saw immediately above me the peak of the mountain and on the peak a huge cross with its arms silhouetted against the blue sky beyond. It was just an ordinary cross made of two large heavy limbs of a tree, but in my frame of mind, and coming on it so unexpectedly, it seemed a sacred omen. It seemed to promise that here on this cross, on this peak, I might get the answer for which I had been praying intermittently for six days and nights and constantly and with all the power at my command these hours of final torture. I threw myself on the ground and wept and prayed and pleaded with the Lord to let me know where I stood. I thought of my Father and Mother and my Grandfather, Heber C. Kimball, and my other relatives that had been passed from the earth for long years and wondered what part they had had, if any, in this call, and if they approved of me and felt that I would qualify. I wondered if they had influenced, in any way, the decision that I should be called. I felt strangely near them, nearer than ever in my life.

I mentally beat myself and chastised myself and accused myself. As the sun came up and moved in the sky I moved with it, lying in the sun, and still I received no relief. I sat up on the cliff and strange thoughts came to me: all this anguish and suffering could be ended so easily from this high cliff and then came to my mind the temptations of the Master when he was tempted to cast Himself down — then I was ashamed for having placed myself in a comparable position and trying to be dramatic. I looked out over the beautiful world below, stretching out to the horizon, with its lovely homes, fertile fields and prosperous businesses and I was reminded that I had had a small part of that world and was in a position that I could get more and more of it, and that I was asked to give up a part of it; then I was filled with remorse because I had permitted myself to place myself again in a position comparable, in a small degree, to the position the Saviour found Himself in when He was tempted, and I was filled with remorse because I felt I had cheapened the experiences of the Lord, having compared mine with His. Again I challenged myself and told myself that I was only trying to be dramatic and sorry for myself.

Again I lay on the cool earth. The thought came that I might take cold, but what did it matter now. There was one great desire, to get a testimony of my calling, to know that it was not human and inspired by ulterior motives, kindly as they might be. How I prayed! How I suffered! How I wept! How I struggled!

Was it a dream which came to me? I was weary and I think I went to sleep for a little. It seemed that in a dream I saw my grandfather and became conscious of the great work he had done. I cannot say that it was a vision, but I do know that with this new experience came a calm like the dying wind, the quieting wave after the storm is passed. I got up, walked to the rocky point and sat on the same ledge. My tears were dry, my soul was at peace. A calm feeling of assurance came over me, doubt and questionings subdued. It was as though a great burden had been lifted. I sat in tranquil silence surveying the beautiful valley, thanking the Lord for the satisfaction and the reassuring answer to my prayers. Long I meditated here in peaceful quietude, apart, and I felt nearer my Lord than ever at any time in my life.

I finally looked at my wrist watch and discovered that it would soon be time to leave for Salt Lake. With my cane, which now seemed an important part of my spiritual experience, I went down the mountain, not down the steep difficult precipitous way, but down the other side which was easy and gradual. I had found a path that was easy to follow. I felt I knew my way, now, physically and spiritually and knew where I was going.

Spencer took a United Airlines flight to Salt Lake, still fasting, to finish his search for confirmation. He spoke at length with President David O. McKay, second counselor to President Grant, who reassured him of his call to the Council of the Twelve Apostles: "The Lord has spoken and the brethren of the Council are all pleased." Spencer told him that "every fibre of my being bore testimony to the divinity of the Lord Jesus Christ."

Within hours the First Presidency released the news and like wildfire it spread. Spencer's cousin Preston Parkinson accompanied him to the train, stopping in every office along the way where his friends worked and introducing them to "the new apostle." Spencer felt a mix of gratitude and acute embarrassment.

Now that the decision had been irrevocably made, he could begin to relax, but the shock took time to wear off. In two months he lost eighteen pounds. His sleep continued fitful all summer. He "fasted and prayed and prayed and prayed." Still the call seemed somehow unreal. He wrote friends, "Each morning as I get up I seem to think it was just an impossible dream from which I will soon awaken." It seemed impossible he could measure up. "I have worshipped all the brethren of the Quorum all these years of my life and then to try to visualize and place myself in that group frightens me."

Returning home through Colorado to pick up Camilla, he noted that LeVan "seemed genuinely pleased and proud." Relatives in El Paso "were quite reverential." To his Eyring in-laws in Pima he wrote: "My emotions are so touchy, my tears so near the surface and the ducts so full that I can hardly mention the matter without the loss of my voice and the blurring of my eyes. I hope I can get the tear ducts empty by the time I get home." Each time he met relatives and friends and retold the events of the past days his emotions overflowed in tears again. He felt the assurance his call was from God, but he still felt unworthy.

In Safford friends streamed into Kimball-Greenhalgh to express their congratulations, non-Mormons as well as Church members. They saw the calling of Spencer as an honor to the Arizona community; the Church for the first time had looked outside the tight circle around its headquarters.

John F. Nash, who had been his father's counselor and had served with Spencer for four years as counselor to Harry L. Payne, wrote his congratulations: "You suit me 100%. Surely the Lord is managing this work on the earth. He knows where his servants are even in the out of the way places, even in far off Arizona. Your grandfather and father have had something to do with it for they have been close to you all of the time and they have interceded in councils in heaven for you, knowing that you were worthy of the place."

Orville Allen, who had been Spencer's deacons adviser, stopped by. He told Spencer for the first time of an evening he remembered from about thirty-three years before. He had sold a load of pumpkins to Andrew Kimball for pig and cow feed. As the two men unloaded pumpkins in the corral they heard Spencer singing as he milked. "Your boy must be happy," said Orville. Andrew turned to him and answered: "Yes, he is always happy. He is a clean and obedient boy and always minds what I ask him to do. I have dedicated him to the Lord and to His service. He will become a mighty man in the Church."

Spencer set to work cutting the ties that held him in Safford. Within a week he had resigned from the USO fund, the United War Fund campaign, the Teachers' Retirement Board, the Board of the Arizona Association of Insurance Agents and the Board of Trustees of Gila College. His stenographer marveled that one man had held so many jobs. He quit the Scout Council, Rotary Club committees, the Gila Valley Irrigation District, the Union Canal, the Graham Canal, the Brown Canal, the Highline Canal, the Montezuma Canal, the San Jose Canal. His share of the business he sold for sixty-five thousand dollars. His home, which he had built three years before for five thousand dollars, now, in war-time, brought ten thousand dollars. He sold his bonds, real estate, truck, hay, corrals, barn, the furniture in his home.

The prospect of uprooting the family after living in the valley for a generation finally started to become real. Giving up the business, with its burgeoning success, led him into "weak moments when I can hardly keep from counting the temporal things."

Spencer's worst worry was how to live up to his call. What about people he had offended? Would they resent him? He started visiting every man he had done much business with, to explain his new situation: "I've been called to a high position in my Church. I cannot serve in good conscience unless I know my life has been honorable. You and I have had dealings. If there was any injustice I want to make it right, and I've brought my checkbook." Most shook hands and refused to hear any more. A couple of men fancied that in fairness they should have got a few hundred dollars more on certain sales. Spencer wrote the checks.

He visited a neighbor. The two men had had a difference over use of the irrigation ditch that ran past their home lots. Spencer knocked at his door and apologized. "I felt very definitely that he had been the offender largely and that he had hurt me terribly, but I knew that no quarrel was one-sided and therefore I was willing to forgive and forget everything if he was willing to." A week later Spencer sent a dozen carnations. He wrote to Camilla, "I hope they were received in the spirit they were sent."

A clerk in the stake whom Spencer had once taken to task for carelessness in keeping some Church financial records had been cold toward him ever since. Now Spencer looked him up and said he could not begin his apostleship with bad feeling between them. They talked it out.

There was a woman in his stake so bitter she would cross the street to avoid him. She had never told him why. Spencer's stenographer remembered him fidgeting in the Kimball-Greenhalgh office one morning, a folder under his arm, tapping his car keys against the counter. Finally he said: "I hate to go. I never did anything so hard." But he went. He asked the woman, "What have I done against you?" She thought he had intervened with the governor to oppose her husband's being named to a state office.

"Who told you that?"

"My friends."

"They were mistaken. I wouldn't do that. And I don't have that kind of influence with the governor anyway."

Their talk patched things up between them.

Congratulations were still piling up on Spencer's desk. "I never knew I had so many friends." Well-wishers stopped him on the sidewalk. Many declared it had been inevitable, that they were not surprised at all. Evans Coleman, from Thatcher, an old cowpuncher, plunked himself down in the office. He drawled, "Well, Spencer, so you're going to Salt Lake to be one of the Twelve Apostles, are you?"

"Yes, Evans, I guess so."

Evans leaned back, eyeing the boy he had watched grow up. "It's clear the Lord must have called you — no one else would have thought of you."

Spencer laughed delightedly. It was a relief to have someone share his feelings.

For two months he attended farewell parties and some testimonial dinners. At Layton Ward they eulogized him extravagantly; he felt uncomfortable but gratified. There were tears at Lordsburg and at Morenci. When the Chamber of Commerce proposed a major banquet, to draw men from across the state in tribute to him, he persuaded them to postpone and subsequently to cancel the dinner. He already knew they were his friends; they did not need to prove it again in that way.

Spencer decided that by conference time he should be moved to Salt Lake, available for full-time service. But time slipped away. Everything seemed in an uproar. Business still stacked up on his desk — sales to close, files to cut through, property to dispose of or move. On top of it Camilla was sick, and her doctor suggested an operation. They

Spencer, Camilla, Kathryn holding Barbara, Spencer LeVan;
(standing) Olive Beth, Andrew, Edward, 1942

decided to move the family to Salt Lake ahead of schedule. Spencer would come back alone to finish up.

On August 26 the family piled the car full and left, homesickness tugging as Mount Graham disappeared behind them. Spencer determinedly shifted his loyalty to their new home. Tired of his sons' complaints about leaving Arizona, he told them: "Now, boys, we have come to Salt Lake to live. We have left Arizona. From now on Utah is the best place in the world, the finest people, the best climate, the most wonderful schools."

In Salt Lake the first task was to find a place to live. The five of them crowded for days in a small room at the Temple Square Hotel and looked urgently for a house that would do. But wartime shortage had bloated house prices beyond their worth; apartments had long waiting lists.

After several days they arranged to rent a house, though it would not be free until late October. Meanwhile they would double up with cousin Vie Woolley, living in the family home Spencer had often visited as a boy.

The next day Camilla checked in at the hospital, still suffering the consequences of poor medical care after her first pregnancy. Two deep cysts were cut out, fissures cauterized, and radium used to stop the bleeding. The day after the operation Spencer boarded the plane for Arizona, with just a month left before conference.

The race began; day after day, Spencer got up with the sun and went to bed long after dark. He still served as president of a large stake and had all the detail work of preparing the business for transfer to others.

Camilla, still in the hospital, recuperated in an air of tension. The shock of the move, the boys' complaints, the crowded housing, and now the absence of Spencer pressed on her mind.

Spencer wrote reassuring letters:

> Darling wife, I do hope that you will take good care of yourself and not take any chances of having further trouble. A few unwise climbing of stairs or other unwise moves might bring on the major operation which we hope has been averted.... We went up early yesterday morning to Franklin for Sunday School and testimony meeting, then to Duncan for testimony meeting at 12:30, then up to Virden for 2:30 meeting. All the meetings started out as testimony meetings regular and ended in testimonials for me. I told the boys as we went late to the last two meetings that I was the first corpse I had ever seen that had three funerals in one day and was late for two of them. I needed only pallbearers and an open grave to make it complete.

Camilla: "Dearest Dad, . . . It seems harder and harder for me to be reconciled to this move. You seemed to realize it from the start so much better than I. With me it is getting worse and worse the more I am brought to face it. I am so desperately homesick I am really ill from it. I can't seem to see any recompense in all the sacrifice ahead of us.... I am afraid I forgot to thank you for the chocolates, darling. I do appreciate them and thanks a million. I do love you so much. Troubles don't seem anything when you are with us but loom to mountains when you are away."

Just as school began, a polio scare closed the schools down, as well as movie theaters, dances, churches. Ed paced from one room to the next, read a little, sat at the piano for a minute, then was up again. The boys felt uprooted from their lifetime home. Andrew, who would have been a senior at Safford High School, had been elected class president and would be a star in athletics. He decided to return to Safford alone and finish high school there. Well-meaning friends aggravated the situation by writing to offer him a home for the year. Camilla, reluctant to let him go, telephoned Spencer, in despair. To her the boys seemed like caged lions in the house.

Spencer wrote a family epistle to "My beloved children": How much he and their mother had loved them they could not know, he wrote, nor what sacrifices had been made in caring for them when they were sick. Everything had been done for the children — the new house, the farm land. "In all our ambitions for you and our efforts to do the proper thing for you, perhaps we have failed to some extent. Perhaps we have overdone for you. Maybe we have given you too many comforts and luxuries for your own good. Maybe we have made the way too easy. There has been little, so far as I know, that you wanted that you have not had. It has been our supreme joy to provide it for you. Our hope has been that it would all redound to your good."

He called now for sacrifice, agreeing that

perhaps I will get most of the glory while your dear mother and you will get the sacrifices. It will not be easy for you, but who wants an easy job? . . . You have the best blood of the generation in your veins. It is strong, vigorous blood to make powerful people. The Eyrings, Romneys, Woolleys and Kimballs were great pioneers and builders of empires — undaunted. . . . None of them would squirm or whine or hesitate as a difficult situation presented itself.

. . . I am not complaining but you must know that this is not easy for Mother and me. If you could have walked with us down the mental trails of anguish the past two months you would know what I mean. One sister told me last Sunday: "I didn't realize that there could be anything in such a call but one great joy." I have lost 18 pounds in these two sleepless months. Your mother and I have gone and are going through an unparallelled experience of our lives. I am writing this letter at 4:45 A.M. to you.

Don't misunderstand me. I am not minimizing the glory of this great call. On the contrary it is so great and glorious that I am finding it so difficult to rise to it. I feel so weak and helpless and impotent and insignificant. It is so much above and beyond me that I have felt a thousand times I could not reach it. . . . This is such a great responsibility for such a little man. You can help me so much. I promise you I will do my best to qualify and bring you honor. . . . I tell you again, the spirit of the evil one has tempted me a thousand times to not accept the work because I am weak and unworthy and incapable. But I have accepted the work. I am relying on you to help me and I am pleading that you will live for me, pray for me, help me.

The storm blew over. The schools reopened. The number of days until Spencer's return dwindled. Camilla wrote that the children were trying hard to make the best of the situation.

Spencer wrote to Olive Beth:

> You've got the sweetest mother in the world, so I hope you will save her all you can so you will have one a long time. You can never know how much I have missed my mother — what an unquenchable yearning I have felt so often, when I was younger especially, for a mother who could understand and love and appreciate and spoil me. Don't let the sun ever go down without having thanked the Lord for such a dear mother, and let her know often, too, for parents sometimes get pretty hungry for expressed affection. . . . Your old Dad dotes a lot on his only daughter. They say you are like me. . . .

As October Conference neared, Spencer had been released as stake president but he despaired of closing out his work at Kimball-Greenhalgh in time. He dated one letter, "Sunday Morning by Lamplight." Well-wishers and advice-seekers dropped into the office. Dinner invitations, socials, good-bye parties ate at the time. These people were lifelong friends.

He finally had to leave for Salt Lake, his work unfinished. On the train he wrote Camilla:

> There was not a soul came to say goodbye. I tried to explain to myself but it still hurt just a little. I think I am not so indispensable as I had imagined — life seems to go on nicely in Safford in spite of my going. . . . I had no reason to expect it but just thought maybe one or two would chance by as the train came in, to say goodbye. But they didn't — and that is that — and I have been so much honored I am ashamed to mention it, but you, knowing my weakness for demonstration of appreciation, will understand me. Now I have forgotten that. And now I am on my way to the great adventure of my life.

Salt Lake was home from now on. On his first day there, Spencer called on President Grant. The old man, too weak to stand, drew him down and kissed him. Spencer stopped in on President J. Reuben

Share in Conference Sessions

Spencer W. Kimball, formerly of Safford, Ariz., left, and Ezra T. Benson of Washington, D. C., new members of the L D S council of twelve apostles, who are here to participate in the church's 114th semiannual conference beginning Friday. Both will be sustained in their new positions before taking over their new responsibilities.

Clark, who explained to him at some length what the apostleship would be like. He visited others of the Quorum who were in that day. "I am electrified with the very presence of these men of power — these Prophets, Seers and Revelators."

Next day general conference began. Into the Tabernacle crowded thousands of Church officers and members. Six months earlier Spencer had sat there as president of the Mount Graham Stake. Now, for the moment, he held no position in the Church. He was just a member.

Spencer locked himself into his newly assigned office in the Church Office Building, knelt and prayed for the Lord's help, then walked over to the Tabernacle, where he sat on the front row in the audience with Ezra Taft Benson. Two weeks earlier he had jokingly urged Jesse Udall to show up at conference "so I would be sure to get a few votes." Today there was no joking.

In the Friday afternoon session, October 1, 1943, the General Authorities of the Church were presented to the conference for sustaining vote. When the Quorum of the Twelve was sustained

> How weak I felt! How humble I was! How grateful I was when President McKay said the voting was unanimous. I seemed to be swimming in a daze. It seemed so unreal and impossible that I — just poor weak Spencer Kimball — could be being sustained as an Apostle of the Lord Jesus Christ and tears welled in my eyes again as I heard myself sustained as an Apostle, a prophet, seer and revelator to the Church. We were called to the stand and took our places with the Twelve Apostles. I was next to Brother Lee who squeezed my arm in welcome. Thousands of eyes were upon us appraising, weighing, honoring us. . . . After some other talks I was called on for my maiden talk. How I reached the pulpit I hardly know. What a moment — a sea of upturned, wondering, expectant faces met my first gaze. I began. . . . I must have taken about 15 minutes. I lost track of time as I poured out my appreciation and gratitude and bore testimony.

> As I took my seat I felt I had failed and continued to tell myself that I had failed as Brother Benson gave his simple sweet-spirited testimony. The balance of the meeting was a blur, except I remember how Bishop Ashton and others paid tribute to the two new general authorities and their humble testimonies. At the conclusion of the meeting numbers of people commended us and numbers of strong men and hundreds of women then and later told me how they sat unashamed of the tears that came as they listened

[, many by radio]: this woman at her ironing, this one sewing —
another reading stopped short and wept — they said, as our testimonies unfolded.

The talks of the three-day conference all seemed gems to the new
apostle. "Glorious hours of new spiritual values. . . . Is it because I have
already received answer to my prayers for greater power of discern-
ment and concentration?" To LeVan he wrote that when seven
thousand hands raised in the Tabernacle to sustain him, it was the
greatest instant in his life.

The next day Spencer and Ezra Taft Benson waited upon President Grant in the big room next to the President's office. Elder Richard
R. Lyman prayed in behalf of the group; President David O. McKay
spoke briefly. Then Spencer Kimball knelt at the feet of the invalid
Prophet, who had been born before the Civil War and who now laid his
hands on his head, joined by the other apostles, and ordained Spencer
Woolley Kimball an apostle. "What rapture — What bliss and joy
unspeakable!" At home the new apostle underlined three sentences in
his written copy of the blessing President Grant had given him:
"Therefore, we admonish you to look upon this calling and this
Apostleship which we are now giving unto you as paramount to everything else upon the earth. Therefore, set your heart upon the service of
the Lord thy God. From this very moment resolve to make this cause
and this labor first and foremost in all your thoughts."

12

The New Apostle

— "I hope they will be tolerant"

In October Spencer Kimball stood at the verge of his apostleship. "It is a new world," he wrote his brother-in-law John H. Udall. Latter-day Saints revered him now as an apostle of Jesus Christ. "It makes me feel so inadequate!" Two days after being sustained, he spoke by invitation at Wasatch Ward, but the talk wasn't good enough for an apostle, he told himself. "I spoke, but poorly." He studied and worried over a special Thanksgiving talk, but it "was a flop." LeVan would complain that before 1943 his father had been "a lively and joking person," but that concern for the dignity of the new calling drained some of the spontaneity from him. Olive Beth noticed how seldom her father now shed his suit for casual shirt and jeans. He asked Harvey Taylor, an Arizona friend, to bury the old stories about their practical jokes. "That part of my life is past."

His new life preoccupied him. Firsts sprinkle his journal — a first talk, a first Quorum of the Twelve meeting, a first stake conference as a visiting General Authority, a first meeting with outgoing missionaries for their settings-apart, a first temple marriage ceremony, a first calling of a new General Authority, a first mission tour, a first winter of incessant travel in the new work. As a General Authority from Arizona he himself was a first.

Many Church members did not know him yet. In New Mexico the counselor conducting stake conference introduced him in the morning session as Elder Ezra Taft Benson. "That's all right with me," Elder Kimball began his sermon. "Just don't tell Brother Benson." In another conference session the flustered stake president announced him as Richard R. Lyman. Some in the audience tittered in embarrassment; Richard Lyman had just been excommunicated.

While he was waiting in the Salt Lake Temple, an aged man from Sanpete struck up a conversation. Learning he sat next to a Kimball, the man asked, "You related to Heber C. Kimball?"

"He's my grandfather."

"Did you know Golden Kimball?"

"That's my uncle."

"I read some on that Kimball just made an apostle. You related?"

"I'm that boy."

"What's that?"

"I'm that boy."

"You're *his* boy?"

"No. I am the man you are talking about."

The old man pumped Elder Kimball's hand ecstatically and declared those two new apostles, Kimball and Benson, were *real* LDS. "But," he added in surprise, "you don't look more than twenty-eight years old." Spencer, forty-eight, penned in the margin of his diary, "Ha."

Every Thursday the Council of the Twelve met in a room on the Temple's fourth floor. The apostles sat by seniority in twelve large oak chairs, in a crescent around an upholstered altar. Harold B. Lee played a small organ in the corner as they opened with a hymn. Then all twelve, dressed in temple clothes, formed a prayer circle around the altar. The prayer completed, they changed back to street clothes to handle the Quorum's business.

These eleven men who gathered with him around the altar became dear to Elder Kimball. George Albert Smith sat in the first chair, an apostle since he was thirty-three, the son and grandson of apostles. A frail man, with long, narrow face, goatee and glasses, "he was the sweet personality." Usually a quiet man, he would later surprise Elder Kimball in a gathering at Bishop Isaacson's by being "almost scintillating." Once at Yale Ward while the deacons passed the sacrament, Elder Smith stood, walked down front of the rostrum, picked off the rug a

piece of bread a deacon had dropped, and slipped it in his pocket as he
sat back down. To Spencer he seemed "very tender and loving." It was
said that in Wyoming, standing before the grave of Washakie, Elder
Smith had listened with tears in his eyes to an interpreter's stories of the
great Shoshone chief. At President Smith's funeral, Matthew Cowley
would say, "God is love. George Albert Smith is love."

In the second oak chair sat George F. Richards, the son of an
apostle and father of an apostle-to-be. He was so honest he circled the
block and stopped again for a red light he had accidentally run.
Spencer Kimball found him especially "kind and considerate." Once
Elder Richards came up to him, embraced him and said, "Brother
Kimball, I feel great love for you." To Spencer he was "about as nearly
perfect as men get on the earth."

In the tenth chair, next to Elder Kimball, sat Harold B. Lee. A
strong-willed man, square-faced, four years younger than the new
apostle, Elder Lee "was always more dominant than I was." "I looked to
him in a degree for leadership." Reared on a small farm, principal of a
country school at seventeen, Harold B. Lee was the youngest stake
president in the Church when called to preside over Pioneer Stake at
age thirty-one. When the great Depression bottomed, over half the
men in his stake stood unemployed. This man, "sagacious for his
experience and age," as Spencer Kimball characterized him, built a
stake welfare program, with a farm, a storehouse, a coal yard, a can-
ning factory, a clothing remodeling project. Those who drew supplies
from the stake contributed their work. The Church adapted for use
everywhere this welfare system he and his co-workers had engineered.
Elder Lee's strength came, said Marion G. Romney, from his conviction that "he lives in the shadow of the Almighty."

This group of men became almost as close to Spencer Kimball as
his own family, with affection born of their common commitment to
serving the Lord.

Within a month of Elder Kimball's ordination the Quorum reeled
under the trauma of an excommunication. Not since 1911, when for
unwillingness to abandon the principle of plural marriage John W.
Taylor was excommunicated and Matthias F. Cowley was dis-
fellowshipped for a time, had the Quorum acted against an apostle.

Richard R. Lyman was a big man, six feet four, 250 pounds, a
meticulous dresser. People said that as a boy he had never smiled. In
photographs his face had a gentle look. Years before, he had won the

only scholarship in civil engineering at Cornell, then the one fellowship, then his Ph.D. Methodical and painstaking, Dr. Lyman would
insist that his geography students study their maps with their seats
facing north. He had taught at the University of Utah until 1918 when,
like his father and grandfather before him, he became an apostle. He
had married Amy Brown, whom one friend called the most popular
girl he had ever known, just a year after Spencer Kimball was born; she
had since become the Church's eighth general president of the Relief
Society. At age seventy-two Richard Lyman had welcomed Spencer
Kimball to the Quorum with a luncheon invitation at the Lion House.
On November 12, 1943, he lost his apostleship and his membership in
the Church.

> It was a terrible experience that came to me today. I think I can
> never forget the scene. We were called to a special meeting of the
> Council of the Twelve Apostles. . . . The slow, deliberate and sad-
> dened approach of some of the brethren as they came to the
> Temple presaged something ominous was ahead of us. As soon as
> we were all seated the meeting was called to order and announce-
> ment was made by Pres. George Albert Smith, who was almost
> overcome, that there was a very serious charge against one of our
> brethren. He then directed that the charge be read.

> Our hearts stood still as we heard that Richard R. Lyman, for
> 26 years a member of the Council of the Twelve, was accused of
> immorality. His written confession was read and he being present
> did not deny the accusation nor the confession. He told also of the
> situations. He had little to say. He was as pale as could be. . . . It was
> a terrible ordeal. To see great strong men such as the members of
> this Quorum all in tears, some sobbing, all shocked, stunned by the
> impact was an unforgettable sight. No tears from him but plenty
> from the rest of us and what a heart-rending experience.

> After considerable discussion a motion was made, seconded
> and we voted unanimously to excommunicate him from the
> Church. When he retired he said goodbye and shook hands with
> each of us and left the Temple, his quorum, his Church. Still
> stunned almost beyond recovery, the members seemed to be yet
> unable to believe the terrible truth.

The Quorum provided the newspapers with a one-sentence
announcement, stating only that the ground for excommunication was
violation of the Christian law of chastity. That night in bed, painfully
awake, Spencer Kimball brooded long over Richard Lyman. Six days

later in the weekly council meeting, eleven apostles handled business under the shadow of the twelfth's fall.

Elder Kimball had an office in the Church's main office building, a block from Temple Square. In 1943 there were 146 stakes and 38 missions, with about 900,000 Latter-day Saints, a large share of them within a hundred miles of that building. Through the new apostle's door came a never-ending stream of them: men called to serve in Church positions spoke their gratitude; young prospective missionaries expressed fervent testimonies; other young men, recommended for missions, broke down in his office and confessed dark sins they could not tell their bishops; a bishop's wife sat weeping, her faith in God shattered by the death of her son in the war; a woman whose husband had always been active in the Church sought comfort when he deserted her and cast all aside in his passion for another woman; young couples, love lighting their eyes, asked him to perform their marriages; married couples came, intolerant of one another, carping, hate-filled; an eighteen-year-old girl asked if she should marry her boyfriend who had deserted his mission and was fast deserting the Church; a man stalked in, enraged at his bishop, and demanded excommunication.

Some evenings when the new apostle locked his door and drove home he was drained and almost ill at what he had heard. One evening he stopped at the Veterans' Hospital to visit a troubled, quiet young man he had been counseling. The attendants showed him to a cell where he looked in horror at the young man, now a mad beast, raging, cursing, his bare feet spotted with cigarette burns.

Some days heaven and hell intertwined strangely. In the Temple, as Elder Kimball stepped out of the sealing room where he had married a couple for time and eternity, a young mother walked up and, in an agony of remorse, confessed adultery.

In his journal one day he wrote:

> I have been depressed all day — I feel so inadequate. It seems that I am not succeeding with my work as I should like. It has been a hectic day. Everything seems to have been disturbing and disappointing. Received a long letter of severe criticism from one of my friends — and everything seemed to be at cross-purposes. Maybe I needed further humbling.

Four days later:

Oh! I am so happy today. To see just a little fruit of our labors is encouraging. One of the people who some weeks ago had confessed his sins to me and asked what he could do to get right with the world, came in this morning to express over and over his gratitude. . . . Those weeks ago, we had sat a long time. He had told me part of his troubles but had withheld the sin. As he left I felt inspired that all was still not well with him. In about 10 minutes he came back, choked with emotion and said, "You knew I lied to you. You knew I'd be back." He sobbed out his story to me and when he had finished I knew that he had opened his heart and had told me all. We prayed together and I advised him what to do.

Week after week the president of the Quorum sent apostles out to stake conferences, most of them in Utah and Idaho. In November 1943 the new apostle presided over his first stake conference alone. A Saturday welfare session and a leadership meeting, plus the two general sessions on Sunday, proved just the tip of the iceberg. The rest of the time was taken up in meeting with stake leaders, dealing with special problems, interviewing, ordaining, blessing. The work proved exhausting.

To divide or reorganize a stake greatly added to the complexity of the task. In his third month Elder Kimball paired with Stephen L Richards to find a new president for Emery Stake in central Utah. At the outset they got suggestions from the retiring stake president, his counselors, the stake clerk. Then they had each member of the high council list three choices for president on slips of paper. But after studying the recommendations they still had no assurance whom they should select; so they interviewed each of the bishops in the stake as possible candidates. Finally they agreed upon Eldon Luke, a high councilor. The two apostles knelt alone in a room to ask if their choice was acceptable and each had the impression that it was. They reconvened the high council. Eldon Luke, "a perpetual smile" in the first meeting, reentered the room with his smile erased. He told the apostles later that he had sensed he was the choice.

As Spencer shouldered his heavy load of counseling and Church travel, Camilla could offer no direct help, but she did all she could to lighten his load at home by taking primary responsibility for the house and children. She waited meals for him, concerned herself about his

health, wrote him when he was away, encouraged him when he
doubted his own capabilities.

Spencer and Camilla were careful not to assume any special
privileges from their position. Although people seemed to accept them
readily, it took some time before the two newcomers felt entirely
comfortable socially.

In December, still new in Salt Lake, the Kimballs had a wedding in
the family. Olive Beth married Grant Mack, her friend from Gila
College days. He had just returned from a mission in New England and
was about to enter the navy as a musician. Spencer performed the
ceremony himself, "a joy and a blessing." He wrote his sister Clare:

> How we wished you were present at the wedding and the
> reception. You would have been impressed as were we all with the
> beautiful, simple, sweet marriage. Olive Beth looked like an angel
> in her lovely gown and veil and Grant is so splendid.... The
> reception was a brilliant affair in our humble, simple lives . . . ; you
> would have remembered and enjoyed the numerous Woolley and
> Kimball relatives that came. About ¾ of all our guests were rel-
> atives on those two lines and the Eyring and Romney lines. Then
> there were a few friends we had met socially, and the Authorities of
> the Church. . . .
>
> Quite a change for us was giving a big party in the city where
> customs are so different . . . ; we had to buy and hire everything . . .
> the music . . . caterers . . . flowers. . . . With the wedding gown, the
> invitations and all these it cost us a pretty penny, you may know,
> and we strained a point, as we wanted this one time to do it right
> and we had only one daughter and we were somewhat "on the
> spot" and a curiosity, so you see we had to do a lot of things we
> wouldn't have thought of at home. Well, now that it is over we will
> settle down again and economize to make up for the extravagance.

The family of four children had now shrunk to two teenage sons at
home. The married children were away.

In March 1944, Elder Kimball left on his first mission tour. Elbert
Curtis, president of the Western States Mission, met him at the train in
Grand Junction. For the next seventeen days the strain did not let up.

The first day, in Grand Junction, the apostle closeted himself with
seven missionaries in a three-hour meeting. This was followed by
sessions with the mission presidency, then the branch presidency; then
there was a banquet, then a play. He had not one quarter-hour alone.
Late in the evening at the home where he was taken to sleep the mother

could not help pouring out her heart to him, asking why, nine months earlier, the Lord had allowed her son to die in the war. A patriarch had promised her boy a mission, a family. Elder Kimball had no answer for the unfathomable question. He could only say, "Sometime all things will be made plain to us." Finally he got to bed.

The second day he had a priesthood session and a general conference session in the morning. Right after lunch the group traveled more than a hundred miles to Meeker for a meeting, then fifty miles to Craig for still another meeting. They slept in the hotel while snow fell.

The next morning they drove toward Denver, up over three high passes, the snow becoming increasingly deeper. When they came to a sudden turn and downgrade, President Curtis at the wheel lost control. The car skidded off the road, off the shoulder, skirted the barrow pit for a hundred feet, and headed toward a deep gully. With only a few feet to spare, President Curtis brought the car back to the road. No one said a word; all were "silent as the tomb," wrote Spencer. Finally Sister Curtis remarked that Elder Kimball looked pale. "It's just my aftershave talcum powder," he joked.

But in his journal he wrote: "A narrow escape and how grateful I have been since the tense moment was over that it didn't end my earthly career. And I have wondered since, maybe the Lord does have a work here for me — maybe I am not so utterly inadequate and unprofitable as I often feel in this new work." He wrote Camilla, "It would have been such an easy chance to get rid of me if the Lord had wanted to."

In Denver Elder Kimball and President Curtis worked at the mission home on mission matters, then drove to Boulder for an evening meeting. The next day took them back through Denver to Colorado Springs for meetings and a banquet and on to Albuquerque, New Mexico, for the night.

The following day there was an afternoon meeting in Blue Water, a drive to Gallup, a bowl of soup, another meeting, meeting upon meeting with members and missionaries, interviews, counselling.

With all the meetings, he wrote Camilla, "I am having difficulty finding something new to say." He told congregations of their trip to Europe in 1937, when he and Camilla had stood a yard from the molten lava of Vesuvius and had toured the excavated ruins of Pompeii below, which had been buried in volcanic ash. He told of the stone roads, rutted by chariot wheels, the brothels, shown to men only, containing wall paintings portraying "all the vicious sins that have

accumulated since Cain began his evil ways." As in Sodom and Gomorrah, he emphasized, fire from above had extinguished the flames of
human sin and uncontrolled appetite, which keep man from God's
kingdom.

From New Mexico the party traveled by train back to Denver and
then to Nebraska. On Sunday Elder Kimball spoke in three meetings in
Lincoln, then rushed without lunch to Omaha, where, after an early
dinner, he spoke to three more meetings — the groups were small, 120
in Lincoln and 157 in Omaha, but meeting with a small number of
people required as much energy as meeting with a thousand. In Grand
Island he met with seventy-two. "I am being well received," he wrote
home. He worried about his talks, but "some of the people seemed to
think that some of them were all right." "I was blessed with some
freedom of expression." "The Lord has been kind to me."

At Winter Quarters in Nebraska, President Curtis drove his visitor
in a drizzling rain to the century-old Mormon pioneer cemetery. It
contained the graves of six hundred Latter-day Saints who had never
reached the valley of the Great Salt Lake. "I truly stood on holy
ground," wrote Spencer. Later the men walked two miles off the
highway up a railroad track to a wagon wheel marked "Rebecca Win-
ters." The story was that the railroad company had resurveyed the
route so as to have the railroad pass around the grave rather than
desecrate the spot. Elder Kimball gave a prayer of gratitude for the
courageous pioneers, and together the men sang "Come, Come, Ye
Saints."

Elder Kimball had brought with him from New Mexico an un-
relenting cold and he carried with him "a private drug store" to clear it
up. The illness made it hard for him even to think. President Curtis and
two missionaries administered to him, but it did not seem to help. His
cold befogged him for the rest of the tour. His work with the Saints
exhilarated him, but the steady round of speaking, dealing with problems, and traveling wore him down. He dropped dead tired into bed
each night. And it worried him that some of his talks seemed failures. "I
am the first Apostle to visit many of these places," he wrote Camilla. "I
keep hoping that they will accept my humble offering. I keep wondering always if they are judging the Church by me and hope they will be
tolerant and long suffering."

Snow interfered with travel. In Nebraska they had to go by train
rather than by car. In South Dakota all talk was of a record winter. At

Belle Fourche men dynamited the ice in the river. President Curtis' car skidded dangerously on the icy roads down through Wyoming. On the tour's seventeenth day they stopped at Casper. Snow whitened the air. Casper's mayor, said to be a "dry-land Mormon" who believed but remained unbaptized, called the Highway Department, the police, and the bus company for weather reports. When he learned that the road to Rawlins was blocked by snowdrifts, he urged the travelers not to risk disaster. But Elder Kimball knew that "a congregation would be waiting for us, having come from long distances, so," he wrote,

> we bought an ax, secured paper, matches, some wood, extra blankets and started out. The road was fair till we came to a few miles of deep drifts 15 miles out of Rawlins and a long difficult detour. We reached our destination safely, had a good dinner at the home of Spencer Williams and made the meeting on time. I spoke on tithing and I rambled and made a failure. I was so exhausted I couldn't seem to hold up my pep until the end. This concluded my first mission visit, having in these 17 days travelled some 4500 miles, slept in 17 different beds, spoken at some forty-odd meetings with numerous interviews, ordinations, administrations and special contacts.

At year's end he totaled up for 1944 thirty-one stake conferences conducted, eighty-six returning missionaries who reported their missions to him, two missions toured (for a total of seven weeks), twenty-four temple marriages performed, an estimated 148 ordinations and eighty sick people administered to, thirty-six thousand miles traveled for the Church, and an uncountable number of interviews and talks.

This same attention to detail he brought to stake conferences. He soon became known as a man who did his homework and got quickly down to rock bottom. He jarred the leaders of a Wyoming stake out of apathy with charts which contrasted their low statistics with Church-wide averages. In a Los Angeles stake he checked closely enough to discover that their statistics were artificially high because the calculations had not included a large number of inactive members in their area. After conferences he wrote with specific suggestions for improvement and asked for follow-up reports.

Underneath the statistics were individual Latter-day Saints. The apostle shook their hands, heard their testimonies, listened to their problems. At Farmington, New Mexico, he interviewed for a mission a girl crippled by polio. She brought to mind the time ten years before when his own baby, locked in isolation, had screamed from fear. "I would do anything I could in reason to favor this young girl," he wrote. "I am recommending her." At Henefer, Utah, a tall man, blinded a year before, asked the apostle to administer to him. Later that morning at stake conference Elder Kimball's gaze fixed on the same man seated in the audience on the front row. He could not forget him. He offered to bless him a second time. Two months later the apostle led the tall man, still blind, by the arm through a temple endowment, "letting him see the temple with its rooms and paintings through my eyes."

At stake conferences he met thousands of people. Though it was difficult to remember them all, he had a marvelous memory. After one stake conference in the East a young woman shook hands and said, "I thought maybe you would remember me because I am Blanch's sister." The apostle answered quickly, "I remember you because you're Julia."

People asked him for all sorts of advice. At Franklin, Idaho, a man asked whether he should buy into a bee business. Elder Kimball didn't know, but gave his personal opinion that the investment might work if the man were frugal. A Church member from Springville, Utah, wanted to know whether he would be better off in farming or in selling insurance. The apostle thought he would not go far astray in either choice. A niece pressed him to decide for her about a house she thought of buying. He appraised it for her, but emphasized that she must decide for herself. A young lady asked him whether she should continue to work in an arms plant until her wedding. He advised her to move to her parents' home and prepare for her marriage. It irked him that she left his office still uncertain what she would do, after seeking his advice.

In May 1944 Elder Kimball received assignment to stake conference in Arizona. He wrote, "How good it is to be back home, the most beautiful place in the world, I think — home, sweet home." In downtown Safford so many friends crowded around to visit that he gave up trying to finish some business he had come with. He felt honored "in his own country." In writing to Camilla he said that a certain friend "has already hugged and kissed me so much since I came I do not know if I can go through it again. He came up right in conference before hundreds of people and threw his arms around me and kissed me. I think I blushed. I may have to wear a mask, I guess."

In Mesa, Maude McDonald LeBaron, the sister of his closest boyhood friend, came to him for help. Twenty years earlier she and Dayer
LeBaron had been excommunicated for polygamy, maintaining that
Joseph Smith had secretly passed the priesthood sceptre to the
LeBaron line and that this gave Dayer supreme authority to authorize
plural marriages. Two of their sons on missions had been excommunicated and sent home. But now Maude had a changed heart and wanted
to rejoin the Church. She begged Spencer to visit her at home.

> She seemed to have a good spirit and attitude and began telling
> me of my problems when her three tall apostate sons came un-
> invited into the room. They had also been excommunicated for
> apostasy and they were very belligerent, cold, haughty, defiant.
> They demanded of their mother what she was telling me. She gave
> them little satisfaction, but said since she knew me she had asked
> for some help from me. The one boy had his shirt off with his
> garments prominently displayed. I am sure it was intended to
> impress me. I told her and later them that if they wished to see me
> further I would be at the hotel and that I would do anything I could
> for them. They followed me to the door. Never before have I come
> in such close contact with Lucifer and his devils.

Spencer was relieved to escape the room.

During these first years of his apostleship World War II continued
to occupy people's minds. At the time he was ordained, the Allied
forces had finally won the desert war in North Africa and had fought
their way past Naples in Italy. In the Pacific the Americans were
fighting their way island by island.

From the pulpit he urged Saints to link patriotism to America with
loyalty to Church by buying war bonds now to support their boys
fighting in Europe and the Pacific, which could later provide cash to
send those same boys back out on missions. Of the war he wrote in his
journal, "How outraged the Lord must feel to see his children fighting
down here like wild beasts."

On June 5, 1944, as the Fifth Army liberated Rome, Spencer
delivered the baccalaureate address at Brigham Young University. He
did not undertake elaborate "diagnosis of this global malady." To him
it was, ultimately, simply rooted in sin. "Why should we fight against

the tyranny and shackles of nations," he asked BYU graduates, "and at the same time remain in bondage individually to sin?" He reflected upon the open lewdness of soldiers and girls on the crowded trains he had to travel, they rationalizing their conduct by the fact that it was wartime.

The day after the BYU address, Allied forces landed on the beaches of Normandy and began the long last chapter of the war in Europe.

Elder Kimball toured the mammoth San Diego naval base of thirty thousand men. In his journal he noted with pride the statistics the Latter-day Saint chaplain gave him: the jail on base held only sixteen Mormon boys; just fourteen of seventy-five recruits running a certain obstacle course finished, twelve of them LDS. Elder Kimball visited LDS sailors in the base hospital, one with a crushed back, one with a hole through his knee, one with a bullet lodged an inch from his heart. One LDS sailor told the visitors he was paid to train recruits to kill with knife or fist. "If it were not for the Church, I'd go crazy," he said.

By war's end the Kimballs had some of their own sons in the service. In 1943, despite his weak eyes, LeVan obtained dispensation to join the navy. They needed language specialists, and his unusual academic credentials made him prime material for a navy crash-course in Japanese.

After a period in Hawaii, monitoring Japanese radio broadcasts, LeVan (known as Spencer L. in the service and thereafter except by those who knew him before the War) shipped on the aircraft carrier *Franklin*. In 1945 Japanese bombs started a holocaust aboard the ship, a furnace of blazing aviation fuel and exploding munitions. Listing and burning, the ship seemed doomed. Half the crew went overboard. A quarter died in the fires and explosions or drowned. LeVan was one of those who were scattered over miles of open sea, drifting chilled in lifejackets and wondering when or whether rescue might come. After three hours a cruising destroyer fished him and many others from the ocean, stiff and near freezing. The *Franklin* did not sink and its remaining crew managed, with help, to reach port safely. LeVan wrote the story fully to his family and did not discuss it again. When Japan surrendered, he served the occupying army for a time as interpreter.

Olive Beth's husband, Grant Mack, served in the navy, too, spending much of his time in Hawaii. And Andrew, after a year of college, turned eighteen and joined the navy, working in electronics. Ed, still in high school, was too young for the service, though because of the polio disability he would have been exempt in any event.

As war casualties mounted, it seemed to Spencer that "everywhere our relatives and friends weep in their loneliness and sorrow." He preached funeral sermons he dreaded. He wrote a letter which he sent from his office wherever he thought it might help. "There is no tragedy," he wrote, "except in sin." The letter spoke to grieving Latter-day Saint mothers. Was there tragedy, he asked, in Jesus' death? Life had been sweet to him, too. He, too, had been young. "He was taken from his mother, though it broke her heart." But "would we have had it different? Would we have saved his life, if we could, now that we know that he through this very circumstance brought redemption to the world? Would his agonized mother today have it otherwise as she looks back on the entire program? Would the apostles on whom the burden of the kingdom fell have it otherwise?" Trust God, then, he urged. There was meaning in the death of this mother's son, too. Her boy "was not born for a day, a decade, or a century, but for eternity." God, who is his parent also, had taken him home knowing His own eternal purposes.

On May 9, 1945, the Germans surrendered unconditionally. (The Pacific war had only a few more months to run.) Five days later Elder Kimball, touring the Eastern States Mission, was at a member's home in Elmira, New York. He was playing "Till We Meet Again" on the piano for group singing when the telephone rang with news of the death of President Heber J. Grant.

It seemed impossible for President Grant to be gone. Eighty-eight years old when he died, President Grant had already been an apostle for thirteen years when Spencer Kimball was born. Although for several years he had been too feeble for routine Church administration, his counselors, J. Reuben Clark, Jr., and David O. McKay, had continued to take major problems out to the Grant home on "A" street in Salt Lake City for his decision. But now, after twenty-six years as the leader of the Church, the prophet was dead.

As instructed, Elder Kimball cut short his mission business and made arrangements to rush home. That night he slept little: "I felt the great weight of responsibility that had suddenly come to us as a quorum of Apostles. This [is] the seventh time the Council leads the Church"; it was the first such time in his own experience. The next day he boarded a west-bound train.

Once in Salt Lake City, he rushed home, bathed, then drove back downtown to squeeze into the long double line of thousands shuffling through the corridor of the Church Office Building past the prophet's body. Many Saints could remember no prophet before this one. When the doors were finally shut, hundreds had to be turned away.

On the day of the funeral six grandsons carried the coffin, followed by the General Authorities, who walked two by two, out of the office building, down South Temple Street and into the Tabernacle. Crowds jammed the street, cameras snapping. After the funeral, thousands of the devout and curious watched the procession of cars move from Temple Square toward the cemetery.

Like Elder Kimball, President Grant had wondered at first about the divinity of his call to the apostleship. But on horseback in Arizona, four months after his call, he had turned aside from the main road to pray. Suddenly he felt saturated with knowledge, just as if it had been spoken to him. As if he had seen it, he knew he had been called as an apostle at age twenty-five because in heaven Joseph Smith and Heber's father, Jedediah, had asked for that appointment to be made. He had never wavered, through all the long years.

Now with his death it became the responsibility of the Quorum of the Twelve to designate a new President of the Church. For years, during President Grant's long illness, some members of the Church had urged that succession did not need to follow seniority and that in light of George Albert Smith's advanced years it was time for a younger man to be president.

On the Monday after President Grant's funeral fourteen apostles met in the Council room in the Temple. David O. McKay and J. Reuben Clark, Jr., despite their decade of prominence in the First Presidency, resumed their positions by seniority in the third and ninth chairs of the Quorum's semi-circle. The apostles sang a hymn, then dressed in temple robes to pray at the altar. After they had changed back into coats and ties, George Albert Smith, seventy-five, senior apostle after forty-one years in the Quorum, talked about his feelings, then asked each man to state his views, beginning with Mark E. Petersen, the most junior. Unanimously they agreed that the president of the Quorum should become President of the Church. "To see great men weep and shed tears as they evidence love and devotion to their brethren and a cause is stirring," wrote Spencer Kimball of the experience. Then the second apostle, George F. Richards, moved to reorganize the First Presidency, and David O. McKay, the third, seconded the motion. Voting was unanimous. Similarly they adopted the proposition that George Albert Smith become President of the Church. Then the thirteen apostles laid their hands on his head and George F. Richards was mouth in ordaining the new President.

They returned to their chairs, except for the new President, who now occupied one of three chairs on the far side of the altar. To fill the other two President Smith selected Elders Clark and McKay, Heber J. Grant's counselors, to be his as well. To Elder Kimball he seemed to ask after slight hesitation, probably because for eleven years these men had presided over him.

At luncheon, President Smith sat at the head of the table, a counselor at each arm and the apostles seated by seniority. It had been a sacred day to Spencer Kimball. "Here was no balloting — no electioneering — none of the cheap, petty politics. No contenders for the position."

As the leadership of the Church was reorganized, Elder Kimball marvelled at the continuity of things. Nothing changed except the individuals filling the offices. He became ninth in the Quorum. He wrote to his brother Gordon, "I get older in the work."

He continued to wonder at his call to the apostleship two years earlier. Was the Lord now pleased with his work? Was his father proud of him? Was his grandfather?

In June, passing through Boulder, he wrote in his journal:

> Boulder, Colorado. Up at 5 a.m. I began to re-live my unusual experiences at this place July 14, 1943. As in 1943 I followed my footsteps of that early morning in July, 1943, up to the hill, past the sanitarium, south and west up over the little shack home. At the top I nearly stepped on a coiled rattler. I dropped a twig on him to get him to move to ascertain if he really was a rattler. I think he sensed I was not an enemy and he slid slowly into the rocks hardly raising his tail.
>
> On up slowly, resting often up the same ridges, same caves, same rocks, all the time re-living that (now far off) morning in '43. . . . Finally at the top of my sacred mountain I found my cross of July '43 was broken. I found a cross beam and carried it up the hill (remembering the Savior as he carried his cross up Calvary) and fixed it the best I could. I found an altar for my prayers, then lay down in the same spot and slept for a while. It was a beautiful day and a marvelous view from the cliff rocks and a pleasant

morning. The valley was beautiful and green with the little lake mirrors. I came down and back to the hotel at 11 a.m.

On August 6, 1945, the bomber *Enola Gay* dropped an atomic bomb on Hiroshima, killing seventy-eight thousand Japanese in a searing flash. On the ninth, Nagasaki was similarly destroyed. On August 14, as Spencer and Camilla were in Calgary, Canada, word came that Japan had surrendered. All day, until midnight, tumult continued — flags flying, horns honking, bonfires, bells. "The dread war finally over." A month later when the formal surrender took place on the battleship *Missouri* in Tokyo Bay, Spencer wrote in his journal: "A happy day! To know that murder and blood spilling has ceased at least temporarily. And that our sons may return home and to normal lives in a reasonable time."

Some said George Albert Smith was the perfect Church President for these times. The great World War had crippled large cities in Europe. Millions had died. Much of the land lay stripped bare by bombing and plundering. Wholesale starvation threatened Europe. President Smith, with a great heart of love, boarded the train for Washington and called on President Harry Truman. He told Truman that the Church had blankets and clothing to ship to Europe. Truman "smiled and looked at me," remembered President Smith, "and said, 'Well, what do you want to ship it over there for? Their money isn't any good.' I said, 'We don't want their money.' He looked at me and asked, 'You don't mean you are going to give it to them?' " "They are our brothers and sisters and are in distress," President Smith replied. "God has blessed us with a surplus."

For the next two years the Church shipped bedding, homemade quilts, canned food, and vitamins to Latter-day Saints in Europe. President Smith, inspecting boxes of clothing being packed the first winter, took off his own overcoat and, in spite of objections by those with him, laid it on one of the piles.

The Kimball Family Organization had been drifting for years, but in 1943 with an apostle in the family it dropped anchor. One cousin claimed that Spencer's apostleship was boosting several Kimballs out of Church inactivity. Elected family president in 1944, Spencer energetically set about reviving interest. He started annual reunions and invited General Authorities to speak at them. He set moving a massive project to identify and locate all the thousands of Grandfather Heber C. Kimball's descendants and printed and sent an annual newsletter to a mailing list of five hundred families. In 1945 he set about reissuing the *Life of Heber C. Kimball,* which had been out of print for some years, hoping with this book "to bring the immense Kimball family together . . . that they will lean to the Lord and his work as they follow grandfather."

Although the many miracles, prophecies, and visions in the *Life* were thought by some to be too loosely documented and by others too sacred for general publication, Spencer decided that, except for a handful of changes, it was "wise to leave the new book in the masterful form given it" by his cousin Orson F. Whitney in 1888.

In 1946 the family presidency passed to another Kimball, but Spencer continued to be a magnet which held the organization tightly together.

As he visited the stakes the apostle often sang from the pulpit at conference a song with a moral, "O Where Is My Wandering Boy Tonight?" In his journal he wrote, "I am trying hard to keep close to my boys and keep their love and respect and palship!" It was easiest to do with fifteen-year-old Ed, whom he took bowling occasionally, who seemed to fit in well at school and in the family. A year later Spencer would devote two weeks of his brief vacation to a trip through the Pacific Northwest alone with Ed, who had just graduated from high school, in an effort to build on his relationship with this last child at home. Close ties were hardest with twenty-seven-year-old LeVan, who was engaged in a long-time struggle to achieve an identity separate from his father. It had been difficult for this eldest son of exceptional ability always to be Spencer Kimball's boy. The love and strain between the two would pain them both greatly, the father unable to let go the hope that one more plea might make a difference, the son wanting to be accepted fully for himself without reference to his activity in the Church.

The middle son, Andrew, now eighteen, wrote home from a navy base outside San Francisco asking advice on his plan to marry as soon as he was discharged. His father wrote back with strong praise of his son and allowed that "Phyllis is very pleasing to us," but suggested "another possibility which you might consider: If you and your sweetheart came to an understanding of eventual marriage, you could go on your mission and six months later she could go on one and since girls go for 18 months only, you would both return at the same time." "We could wish it," was all he wrote. "We would not like to *tell* you what to do, but would rather present all the angles so far as possible and let you, with our help and the help of the Lord, find the answers, since it is your life." In October 1946 Andrew left as a missionary to New England. Phyllis waited.

In 1946 Elder Kimball was assigned to visit Hawaii. Elder Matthew Cowley accompanied him, and the two men's wives went also. Elder Cowley was the newest apostle, two years younger than Elder Kimball.

"Matt" combed his hair straight back and was round-faced; he stood only about Spencer's height. He had heart trouble and had been sent to Hawaii on this assignment partly for a rest. When she heard this Camilla laughed, "Imagine that, sending him with Spencer Kimball for a rest!"

The Kimballs, accustomed to dry country, were overwhelmed with Hawaii's lush vegetation. The land burst with a color and fragrance almost intoxicating to the senses. The welcome from Church members proved as generous. As the ship landed, members piled twenty-six flower leis on Spencer and Camilla, who hung them about their room along with gardenias and orchids. Camilla told Spencer, "This is so heavenly perhaps I don't need to strive any more for heaven."

On this tour of the Islands the apostles' responsibility included looking after all the Church's interests — a stake, two missions, a temple, a plantation at Laie, servicemen's programs. They consulted with military officials about arrangements to send relief parcels to Church members in Japan, which was still under an occupation army. They toured the several islands, inspecting chapels, conferring on problems, meeting with members — Japanese, Chinese, Hawaiians, Samoans, whites.

In testimony meetings great emotion flowed. Thelma Hisatake, whom Spencer confirmed a member of the Church, told how for seven years she had desperately wanted to be baptized but her mother refused, heckling her "Mormon-crazy" daughter, sending away the missionaries who tried to visit her while she sat crying in the other room. Thelma wept with joy now at being in the Church; the congregation wept with her.

Three or four would rise at once, ready to speak of their faith and experiences. To Elder Kimball one such meeting was "a day of Pentecost." Testimonies often dwelt on opposition from families, personal sacrifices willingly made, miracles: A forest fire ran uncontrollable before the wind, until prayer caused the wind to die. A missionary hiked seventeen miles across a waterless desert to a meeting, to find only four people present, but ultimately one of the four received the gospel. A fifty-year-old woman was washed out to sea by a tidal wave which had struck the Islands three months earlier; she grasped a plank, then climbed onto a floating door where sharks attacked her, ripping her dress but leaving when one touched her temple garments; she had been spotted by a rescue plane after thirty hours at sea with terribly torn legs.

On July 14, the anniversary of his experience on the mountain above Boulder, Colorado, three years earlier, Elder Kimball asked two mission leaders to drive him up Iau Canyon. From the end of the road they hiked a long way up the ridge to a secluded spot. He related his experience to them and they prayed together. Then the others left him for a time, alone for his private devotions.

During this tour he had four boils developing. After three weeks he wrote in his journal, "I wish we could stop just a day or two and rest, but not so." The next day:

> I was tired — so tired. Tense all day and on strain. I have been so tired these last few days with long rides over dangerous roads and a heavy schedule. It seems that the fatigue is cumulative. I pick up 5 units of it each day and my reduced night of sleep restores only about 3 or 4 units, so that I can feel the strain now. I will be happy when I can let up a bit, though I have enjoyed it so much.

Despite the fatigue, Elder Kimball prided himself on being "the huskiest and strongest" member of the Quorum. He joined in a softball game at an outing of Japanese Saints. When he helped pull in the net at a hukelau, wading into the sea in water up to his chest, he was told that Church leaders in the past had only watched from the beach.

At place after place the members entertained the visitors, fed them, loved them. Elder Kimball wrote that the welcome astounded him, but "I realized it was not Spencer Kimball they honored but the apostle." Humble Saints expressed their love for the visitors by decking them heavily with expensive flower leis as they boarded ship at the end of their four-week tour.

On his return from Hawaii the exhausting work wore on without a break. In a letter Spencer noted that during one four-month period he had slept in his own bed only two nights. He went where he was assigned. Although boils would continue to plague him for another few years, he took no sick days off. During stake conference at Nyssa, Oregon, in March 1946, he sat on a painful carbuncle for fifteen hours. At Phoenix he tossed all night with a boil inside his nose. By conference time next morning his nose had swelled tight and red, "a pretty sight!!" In Lost River, Idaho, as he put on his tie, a neck boil burst soaking his hand and collar with blood, draining his face white. In Salt Lake he got on the train for Pocatello with three abscesses in his left ear and a carbuncle on his neck. "I gritted my teeth. . . . I was in great distress." He worried that he would be useless at his stake conference, so sick was he, "but I felt I should go as I have always tried to be 100% dependable. I was miserable in my berth, chilling, then finally perspiring." At Pocatello he transferred to a bus. "I secured a good seat but there was an old man very ill who needed my seat. I sat on the jump seat all the way to Arco in considerable agony."

Some months were particularly hard. From Denver he wrote, "I was so tired I could hardly talk or think." Near Ogden, Utah, after a welfare meeting he said, "I was so tired I could not think and I fear that I wasted an hour for those brethren." He wrote his brother from a train, "Here I am enroute again. Always enroute."

In May 1946, Quorum President George F. Richards wrote to Elder Kimball in Mexico that he had cancelled an Oregon conference assignment, as he calculated the apostle would have difficulty in getting north in time. It turned out that Spencer could have filled the assignment; but, hungry for a rest and with his assignment already canceled, he wrote to Camilla suggesting that they meet in Los Angeles for a holiday together. "Perhaps you should not say very much about our taking off these two or three extra days," he wrote her. "My conscience hurts a little, and yet I have been going pretty fast and hard these last four months and I have not had time to rest at all on this trip."

In Los Angeles they saw a play and bought furniture. They spent a day in Long Beach "honeymooning — watching the ocean, eating, bowling, walking the pike."

Elder Kimball meant to share fully in the work of the Quorum. He said once that when he saw a fellow General Authority, even across the street, his heart quickened. In his journal he entered notes from them

*Mark E. Petersen, Matthew Cowley, Spencer W. Kimball, Ezra
Taft Benson, (seated) Harold B. Lee*

expressing appreciation for his efforts. When he prepared a general
conference address he asked himself, "What would Brother Lee think
of this? or Brother Richards? or President McKay?" He said, "I've been
a hero worshipper all my life."

In 1946 Spencer was appointed chairman of a quarterly social for
General Authorities and their wives. He drafted the four junior
apostles — Elders Kimball, Benson, Petersen, and Cowley — with
Harold B. Lee at the piano, for a quartet. The *Deseret News* photo-
graphed them five days before the event, decorously rehearsing
"Teach Me to Pray." But at the social they followed that piece with a
song about a sure cure for baldness. LeGrand Richards and Milton R.
Hunter, both nearly bald, were seated on stage, doused with hair tonic
and their heads wrapped in towels as the quartet sang. When Bishop
Richards' towel was unrolled, he sported a head of frowsy red hair.
Under Elder Hunter's towel was an English barrister's wig of long,
solemn curls. "It created a good laugh and added a bit of merriment to
the occasion."

That same month Elders Kimball and Petersen cut Salt Lake City's
four mammoth stakes into six. (They had been paired off for so many

stake division assignments that some of the others called them "the butchers.") This job took half a year. Each of the six stakes needed its share of chapels, children and leaders. On a map, the two men had redrawn boundaries using streams, hills, and highways to divide stakes. After the Quorum had approved the complicated split, the two apostles interviewed 150 men in search of six stake presidents.

Two Sundays later was division day. Elder Kimball, presiding at a conference, proposed that they name the new stake Temple Stake. "Temple is the symbol of purity," he told the congregation. "West Temple, one of the first streets named by the Mormon pioneers, runs straight through the stake." The people seemed pleased. But two weeks later, at a Quorum meeting, the propriety of the name was challenged.

One apostle hinted it was sacrilege. Elder Kimball defended the name and "made as heroic a stand as I could." To him there was no sacrilege. But when it came to a vote Elders Kimball and Petersen stood alone. In good spirit Elder Kimball moved that the vote be made unanimous. "I am swallowing my pride and disappointment," he wrote in his journal, "and will be ready to do as the brethren desire at the stake conference in some three weeks." At the conference the name was changed to Temple View Stake. After all his exertions, it surprised Elder Kimball how calmly the stake membership accepted the change.

In the course of his many conferences, sermons, counselings, and interviews, the Lord's hand seemed evident many times. A year before, after having changed his general conference talk at the last second, he had received the heartiest compliments ever. "So I felt that the Lord inspired my change of heart." In his journal he wrote of successful sermons, responsive stake leaders, and recoveries from illness following his administrations. In all of these, he said, "the Lord blessed me."

In 1945 he had driven to a bishop's home to call him as the first president of the new East Mill Creek Stake. The bishop had expressed no surprise; his voice had quavered as he explained that two days earlier as he climbed the stairs from his basement a clear, distinct voice had formed the words in his mind, "You will be the president of the new stake." He had fought the idea down and told himself it couldn't be, but the sensation had remained.

To Elder Kimball, though, such clarity of inspiration could not be always expected. He wrote cautiously to Andrew on his mission: "I have come to realize that the Lord does not expect to reveal to us generally in actual daylight vision as he did to Joseph Smith in the grove. Sometimes it will come in open vision, sometimes in dreams, sometimes in whisperings, but generally His revelations will come" through a burning in the heart.

He puzzled over a dream he had in August that year. "It seemed that we were heavily laden and enroute to China and after I had awakened I seemed to continue to be obsessed with the idea that I might be sent to China for missionary service." He mulled it over for another hour in bed, wondering if it were prophetic, then finally got up and dressed, still unsure. Dozens of times he had puzzled about the prophetic in the blessings he gave the sick. Usually he laid hands on the person's head, after the anointing with oil, and asked the Lord for a particular blessing, "if it be Thy will." In some cases he unconditionally promised life, then "literally trembled in my shoes afterward when I realized what a responsibility I was under." But it seemed to him he could do nothing else except "speak what I seem inspired to say, having asked the Lord for that inspiration, and any effort on my part to curb the spirit would be rank folly and unappreciativeness and un-responsiveness to the moving of the spirit."

At a Salt Lake hospital he visited a badly burned woman who had begged her family to pray she would die. Elder Kimball blessed her to live and rear her children. On the other hand, a young man entering the military service asked for a blessing to live. Elder Kimball wanted to promise him safe return but did not feel so inspired and taught him instead not to worry about the time of death. Always he tried to feel in his mind the Lord's voice and will.

Often he did not learn the outcome of his administrations, but sometimes he received letters: A Mexican father whose son had lain with a fever of 107°, nothing but skin and bones, one lung eaten away, wrote that the boy now was as good as new. A pregnant woman whose kidney had malfunctioned reported that after the blessing her doctor had not even found a trace of the problem left. A woman suffering from cancer was blessed to live long enough to rear her small children. A retarded child developed normally. One mother wrote back express-ing immense gratitude for her child whose esophagus had been badly burned with lye and nearly closed with scar tissue. One doctor had said that a four-hour operation was the child's only chance to survive, but within hours after the blessing the baby was eating soft food with a good appetite. "That wonderful prayer was answered," the mother wrote.

He blessed many childless couples who were able to have children afterward. After eight years without children a couple lost their first baby at seven and one-half months due to a serious toxic condition. A year later, at the same point in pregnancy, they faced the same situation. Feeling helpless and depressed, they sought a blessing from Elder Kimball. During the administration they felt the greatest outpouring of spiritual strength they had ever experienced. A few days later their doctor was astounded to find no problem of any kind in the pregnancy.

A thirteen-year-old girl, bleeding internally and from the mouth with a serious disease, was brought to Elder Kimball after the doctor had said there was nothing further he could do. He blessed the unconscious girl and she recovered.

Accounts of blessings realized were numerous, yet Elder Kimball stressed that it was not always the Lord's will that the sick recover. He went to the hospital one night to administer to a child who had had open-heart surgery and lay at the point of death. The parents were perturbed and frantic. When he left they were composed. Though the child died a few hours later they felt comforted.

A young engineer who lay dying of cancer was promised relative freedom from pain, and peace in the knowledge that his family would be well cared for. He died three months later, having suffered little.

A neighbor suffered from cancer in the sinuses. In administering to him Elder Kimball promised that this malignancy would heal. He did not recover, and died the next year, but autopsy showed that the cancer in his head had disappeared; he had died of cancer and ulcers in his abdomen instead.

In the spring of 1947 Elder Kimball made his first tour to Mexico to visit the mission. He grieved over the poverty of the people, many of whom were eking bare subsistence out of rocky mountain fields, living in huts without water or sanitation. He thought how much good might be done with a little knowledge of improved agricultural technique, and of health principles.

Members singing at an MIA program near Mexico City included Indians in sandals or barefoot, a mother with her child wrapped tight to her body with a shawl, most speaking only their own dialect, not Spanish. At the Gold and Green Ball ten couples performed a special dance. It was not the finished performance he might see elsewhere, but "I could hardly control my emotions as I saw those humble Indians and Mexicans trying so hard to do their work. One little fellow had borrowed the suit of the missionary Elder Juarez in which to dance. (I didn't see the Elder during the program. Perhaps he went to bed.)"

At Atlixco the group arrived at 4:30 for a three o'clock meeting, held in a long, narrow room of a home. As the apostle came through the portico a double line of little children showered him with rose petals, while the congregation sang, "We Thank Thee, O God, for a Prophet." Tears sprang to Elder Kimball's eyes and he could hardly control himself at this expression of love for the Church. The town itself was the scrubbiest he had seen. Persecution of members was rife. Missionaries slept on a cement floor because they could not find a bed to rent.

Conditions were not everywhere primitive. The members in some city branches were prosperous and provided missionaries themselves.

In a few places there were remnants of the Third Convention, a nationalist movement within the Church, which in 1936 had drawn perhaps a third of the Mexican members into branches which sought to remain doctrinally orthodox, while refusing to recognize the authority of the non-Mexican mission president. A few of the leaders had been excommunicated. In 1946 President Arwell Pierce had effected a reconciliation and nearly all the Conventionists had returned to the Church.

In one branch Elder Kimball made factual investigation into the rumor that one of the leading families had negroid ancestry, which would have made the men ineligible to exercise the priesthood they had been given. After questioning the family and other branch members he concluded that the rumor, stemming from a time some years before, had no factual basis. In the same branch he had to deal with a question of murder. A counselor in the branch presidency had many years before killed a man after they had been drinking together. So far as the counselor could recall it had been an accidental shooting. His subsequent conversion and baptism and his exemplary life since that time supported his version of the incident and the apostle dispelled the cloud which hung over him.

At most places they were late for the scheduled meeting times, but the people waited patiently, none upset or embarrassed but Elder Kimball. In one of the branches he found it distracting to have a young man circulate constantly through the congregation shaking people or nudging them with a long stick as they began to nod during the meeting.

At another place he tried to drive into back country to visit an isolated member family. Rain had turned the roads to impassable mud. They rode the last few miles on the back of a passing tractor, and Elder Kimball ripped his trousers in jumping off. They found the members to be not home but back in the town.

The tour occupied three weeks of hard travel. Spencer was glad to return home.

His fourth year in the Quorum passed. He visited Latter-day Saints in their stakes, rode in their cars, ate their dinners, slept in their beds. On weekend assignments to stake conferences he would stay in the home of the stake president or one of his counselors. If there were a piano, he would play a song or two and sing with the children until gradually the entire family grouped around. "They'll forget my sermons," he later said, "but they'll never forget the singing." At Lost River he got back from meetings Saturday night and helped his host feed the cattle in sub-zero cold. Another time he was out repairing a shed at 5:30 in the morning.

At Rigby, Idaho, President Christensen put him up on Saturday night. When they got home about 10:00 P.M. from the chapel, Spencer asked his host for a jumper, overalls, old shoes and a hat. "Under a little pressure he agreed," said Spencer.

> I milked two of the three cows while he milked the other and did some feeding and then we went in and went to bed. Next morning I was up and dressed again in my old clothes with the milk bucket on my arm. In conference when he introduced me he told about my help. After the meeting people came up to shake hands and said, "When you come next time you can stay with us."
>
> One day in the next three or four months Bishop Marvin O. Ashton saw me at the Lion House and pretended offense and said, "Brother Kimball, I am never going to speak to you again." Of course, I was disturbed, feeling that perhaps I had given offense. Then he said, "I was the visitor to the Rigby Stake last week, and after what you did three months ago, I found as we came to the

outside gate, having driven up from the town, there on the front gate hung the overalls and the milk bucket."

He was not one to be waited on. He would insist on carrying his own briefcase or bag and would try to help others with theirs, even in later years when his health was poor.

One time his host insisted on shining the visitor's shoes. Spencer allowed him to. After giving the shoes a good polish the man said, "There! Finished!" But Elder Kimball replied, "Oh, no! Not yet! You sit here and I'll shine yours." And he did.

With all his warmth, he appreciated respect and tried to maintain reasonable dignity, but he did not puff himself up. He enjoyed telling stories about himself, such as the visit he received in February from twenty Primary children. When the teacher had asked who this man was with whom they were shaking hands, one small boy had looked at the apostle searchingly and, scratching his head, answered, "I know I've seen that mug somewhere."

As Elder Kimball matured in the work his native ability with people grew greater. To reorganize a stake, he had to select leadership from what he could surmise from five-minute interviews plus the advice of others and impressions of the Spirit. In one case he felt impressed not to release the stake president he had come to replace, but instead to give him new counselors to inject fresh energy into the work.

A high councilor to be set apart had three questions which he felt needed answering. He prayed that whoever set him apart would be inspired to give him the answers, and in the prayer Elder Kimball answered the questions so directly and explicitly that the man marveled.

A bishop, when called, expressed some reluctance because of serious financial problems. Elder Kimball felt strongly that the Lord would bless him financially and told him so. Within a few years he had prospered sufficiently for him to buy an interest in a funeral home.

One man selected for a stake position admitted to the apostle that he had a beer license. "I don't carry beer in any store but one," he went on, "because I don't feel right about it." The apostle asked if he felt right about the one store. The man said no. After a heart-to-heart talk, he grasped the apostle's hand and said, "I'll do it; I'll give it up."

A man selected for bishop said he could not pay a full tithing, he might need his occasional cocktail, he might have farm work to finish between Sunday meetings. The apostle pleaded with him for his own sake. "We can make other arrangements, call a different man. The Church will get along without you. But you cannot afford to take such desperate chances." Finally the man said he would drop every bad habit and be bishop.

Sometimes it was a whole stake that seemed down at the heels, with many leaders not full tithepayers, some breaking the Word of Wisdom, their attendance slack. Elder Kimball would do some hard preaching, tighten the personal interviews, and hope he had moved them.

In November 1947 he was assigned by the First Presidency to hold conference at a small Utah town torn by dissensions. Saturday night at seven o'clock, he later recorded in his journal,

> we went into session at the meeting house with the principals who were involved in the terrible schism which had rocked this entire community. I took charge of the meeting and let them talk. The various members were cold and tough and bitter in their denunciations of each other. I tried to hold them to the facts and what they heard and not what they imagined someone thought and meant.
>
> Accusations and recriminations continued for hours. Finally I held them and said I was sure that the guilt was almost universal; that all had been to blame for something; that all needed repentance and forgiveness and that it seemed to me there were two alternatives: first, that the bitterness could continue, each progressively hating and despising the other and the factions getting farther and farther apart and the consequent loss of the sacrament among them and their meetings and even ward organization. Second, they could all repent, forgive each other and ask forgiveness of each other. Some seemed willing to do this but others were still cold and hard and tough, demanding that the other side must admit their guilt and ask forgiveness.
>
> It seemed that there were few or no facts to verify and sustain the accusations of theft or misuse of money and other of the charges, so I told them that it was their duty now to forget and forgive each other without giving ultimatums. I quoted many scriptures: the story of the prodigal son; the forgiveness of the Savior on the cross . . . Stephen, who extended the same forgiveness for the taking of his very life, and that without any repentance by those who took his life, and many other examples and scriptures. But I found some of the group still cold and demanding. I turned to D&C 64:7-10 and read it with much emphasis and with a little pounding of the table. I was exasperated at their unwilling-

ness to yield and bow in humility. In him who refuses to forgive lies the greater sin. I told them with power which the Lord gave me and it seemed to turn the tide.

The Lord was so good and their hearts were finally touched, and about 2 a.m. Monday morning when the final prayer was offered by myself, the entire group on their knees, the group arose and began to ask in tears forgiveness of each other. It was a sweet spirit and, as some of them said, in spite of the unpleasantness of the long meeting there had been much to commend it as one of the most spiritual experiences of their lives. All seemed to feel good as they left for their homes. I emphasized that it was now a dead issue and that they must never mention it again. I told them that they must silence everyone who should wish to review any part of the whole transaction. Later in the week I wrote each couple involved and sent to each of the families a *Life of Heber C. Kimball* and a long letter urging their sticking to their determination to make this adjustment complete and permanent.

The hard traveling and weekends away from home continued. Occasionally there was a layover between train connections or assignments. The Fourth of July 1947 found him alone in Los Angeles with a day's wait, so he took the bus out to the amusement pier at Long Beach, a place with many family memories. He wrote home:

> The old giant racer above challenged me and I wondered if I had the nerve to try the fool thing now in my aging years, so I decided to prove myself. I walked up and bought a ticket for a quarter and rode the crazy thing again. It was a rough ride. It nearly jerked my head off and I was glad when the experience was over, but I had proved that I was still nervy.
>
> I walked up and down the pike and bought me a bag of pop corn, and a "mile-high" cone, and a cone of the soft, mushy ice cream, remember? and an ice cream sandwich. Then I went and heard or rather sat through a band concert. After the first number the warm sun through the slats and the little cool breeze and the music lulled me to sleep and I awakened as the musicians were putting up their instruments and the people were crawling over me from inside the long seat. I went over to the soap box corner on the pier and heard the haranguing but it became monotonous soon, . . .

That week he marked the fourth anniversary of his call to the apostleship, writing: "How well I remember the details of that day! I was so shaken emotionally and so shocked. I could not believe it." He continued to wonder why the Lord had singled out Spencer Kimball for this great honor. But to the Saints it was no mystery.

13

Apostle to the Indians

— "watch after the Indians
in all the world"

On May 31, 1945, a few days after
he became President of the Church, George Albert Smith asked
Spencer Kimball to assist in supervising the Navajo-Zuni Mission,
which had been the first modern Indian mission, established in 1943.
In 1945 the mission had about a hundred members on the rolls, many
of them non-Indians. In 1945 the mission showed no baptisms. Elder
Kimball saw in this assignment a fulfillment of his patriarchal blessing.
Forty-two years before, Patriarch Samuel Claridge had blessed him,
"You will preach the Gospel to many people, but more especially to the
Lamanites."

In his childhood, when an occasional Apache came into town
Spencer hugged his mother's skirts. In those days oldtimers still remembered the killing of Brother Thurston out at Bear Spring Flat, or
the ambush of the Wright brothers as they chased a band of Apache
horse-rustlers out beyond Solomonsville. Geronimo had surrendered
at Lordsburg just ten years before the Kimballs arrived in Arizona. So
as a boy of nine, Spencer remembered, "I was not too much elated at
the promise" of the patriarch.

For years Spencer watched the freight trains carry Indians
through Thatcher. In return for rights to build across the San Carlos

Reservation the railroad had agreed to let Apaches ride free for forty years, but not inside the passenger cars; so they rode the tops, the braves with long hair, the women in bright calico, carrying their babies, a colorful sight steaming across the hot desert.

The long years Spencer's father had spent in the Indian Territory Mission, teaching both whites and Indians, laid the groundwork of Spencer's interest. Andrew used to sing the Indian chants and show his family souvenirs and pictures of his Indian friends.

As Spencer grew older he wondered about the patriarch's promise. When at twenty-one he ended his mission in Missouri without having preached to a single Indian, he worried, "Have I failed to live up to the promises? Or did the patriarch make an error?"

In 1945 the promise finally began to be realized. For a year the assignment involved only occasional administrative work. In August 1946, Spencer dreamed one night that he was among the Indians in New Mexico and Arizona. Maybe, he wrote, he had dreamed about Indians "because I have been thinking about them much of late." A month later President Smith called him into his office, handed him several file folders, and said, "I want you to look after the Indians — they are neglected. Take charge and watch after the Indians in all the world." Now that he had received primary responsibility and a broader mandate, Spencer became deeply involved.

This new responsibility, in light of the great Book of Mormon promises to the Lamanites, caused him particular reflection following an experience he had a few weeks later. On October 19, he drove south to a stake conference assignment in Pleasant Grove, Utah, and spent the night with relatives. He awoke in his room alone. There was a strange foreboding feeling. He turned a light on, picked up a book. But he felt something horrible in the room. "I felt almost as if I were being enveloped and taken over." He remembered his grandfather Heber's vision of a great rush of evil spirits "who foamed and gnashed their teeth." Time stopped. As his grandfather had, Spencer broke into a sweat.

> It seemed that an unknown enemy was trying to destroy me. He was unseen but very real. I was not afraid in the ordinary sense of the word. It was a deep fear of the unknown, something or somebody one could not wrestle with. It was bleak and black and fearsome. I sweat and fought and fought and sweat and then remembered the temple program and for the first time in my life

invoked the power of the Priesthood in that particular way and relief came to me. As I pondered over it for days and relived it in a measure, I wondered if I was marked for destruction by the enemy of all righteousness — if I might be getting into a program which would upset the plans of the god of this world.

He finally fell back asleep, then woke at 7:00 A.M. exhausted, "not wholly my usual self."

That same month Elders Spencer W. Kimball and Matthew Cowley accompanied President George Albert Smith to Window Rock, Arizona, on the Navajo Reservation, to attend a Christian missionary meeting. Almost two hundred white ministers and government officials met in "Little Washington," in an octagonal room circled with benches, the chairs set in the center. It seemed strange to Elder Kimball that these missionary sessions began without prayer. For two days the President and the other two apostles sat on the hard wooden outer benches, waiting to tell of the Church's needs in carrying out its program for the Indians. Until the Church was recognized, the missionaries could not rent, buy or build on the reservation without permission.

During the second day the chairman gave the ministers the floor. One after another stood and attacked the Mormons, demanding that they be kept off the reservation. One complained about two elders who had visited and administered to hospitalized Indians of his flock. He insisted that missionaries be restricted to their own members. Complaints strung on and on. Finally President George Albert Smith, out on the edge of the room, stood and was given the floor.

"My friends," he said, "I am perplexed and shocked. I thought it would please me very much if any good Christian missionary of any denomination would be kind enough to visit me and bind up my wounds and pour on the sacred oil. My great, kind friends, we're all brothers and sisters, all children of our Heavenly Father. We only want to bless your people." To Elder Kimball "it was like fire and cleansed." President Smith's approach laid the groundwork for a more tolerant attitude toward the Mormon missionaries.

On the trip the group also stopped near Blanding, Utah, to look at the little chapel of rough pine being constructed by the Church for the Indians. They found an old Ute and his wife squatted beside their two dying boys. The family had an orange crate of food, some dirty bedding and a hunk of venison. They had been allowed to use the chapel, which at least had a floor and a stove. "I was almost ashamed to get back in the big warm car and go to the palatial home of President Redd after seeing their scant facilities," wrote Spencer.

A month later he went south again, into the barren land of sagebrush and cheat grass, part of it laced with gorges and dwindling streams, isolated buttes, towering needles, great washes and gullies. Here the Navajos had been for eighty years. Near Aneth, Utah, the country seemed desolate, so barren it took a quarter-section to support a single horse.

Ralph Evans, president of the Navajo-Zuni Mission, stopped the car near a hogan. A crowd had gathered for a "sing," to benefit a sick woman. The medicine men were just breaking up the ceremonial painting, dumping the sand outside the mud house. The two white men stepped inside and watched as the Indians ate a meal. Using an interpreter, Elder Kimball gave practical advice: "Send your children to schools. Store your food; don't sell it out wholesale and buy it back retail." He ended with a prayer that the Lord would please heal the woman and bless these Indian people. One Indian turned to Brother Evans and said in Navajo, "Bring the apostles here always."

By trial and error Elder Kimball learned some ways to communicate. Outside Gallup the group visited nearby hogans to invite the Indians down to the Collins house to a meeting. Twenty-eight came. They sat stolid and silent. The white men sang a hymn; the Indians watched. The apostle urged the Indians to sing a Navajo song. No response. He asked for questions. Nothing. After a moment one Indian asked what good were Nephi's brass plates. Finally Spencer tried out a song he had learned as a boy:

> I met a little elfman once,
> Down where the lilies grow.
> I asked him why he was so small
> And why he did not grow.
> Ha, Ha, Ha, Ha, Ha, Ha, Ha,
> And why he did not grow.
> Ha, Ha, Ha, Ha, Ha, Ha, Ha,
> And why he did not grow.

"It amused and pleased them."

On another trip they stopped at Sand Hills to visit Vinton Polak'a'a, a Church member, who begged them to stay. He wanted to "trade talk." So they split a watermelon, built a bonfire, and talked while the sunset flamed red and orange and then died. The moon rose as the fire burned low. Ralph Evans and Eugene Flake slept on the sand. To Elder Kimball the ground under his sheepskin seemed to grow harder and harder; he cramped himself into the back seat of the car to spend the night. "O! How glad I was we stayed!" wrote Spencer. "This one lone man with his family, against opposition, [had] to go months, almost years without anyone from the Church to upbuild and encourage him. I was truly glad we had stayed."

> I was awakened by the ducks on the pond and arose almost with the sun and shaved at the spring without mirror and in the cold water. I went for a walk in the high sand hills to the east — a regular little Sahara desert. On top of one of the highest sand dunes, I found a small rattlesnake slithering its way up the dune, over its top and down the other side. He shot out his tongue angrily and rattled his buttons, warning me that I was intruding in his domain. I found some strange sand stones. In one of the depressions between the sand hills I found an altar stone, much the height and shape of a pulpit or an altar, and I had my morning devotions all alone and far away from everyone.

Elder Kimball moved about the reservation from trading post to trading post. It did not take long to sense the Indians' distrust of Washington. Someone told him about Irene Redshirt. She was put in a government hospital with tuberculosis. Six months later, her TB arrested, she asked to go home to visit her children. The homesickness, she said, was worse than the other sickness. The government doctor refused her, but she left anyway. Winter came on. When she tried to return to the hospital the doctor, still incensed, locked the door on her. Her husband begged medical supplies and groceries and wept while she died by inches in a small hogan in front of her little children. Having heard this story, Spencer complained indignantly in his journal.

The government was blamed even for the drought by one Navajo. The Indians prayed for rain, got it, expanded their flocks, but then the government's stock-reduction program initiated the slaughter of the extra animals. "Washington is whittling on our prayers," the Navajo complained.

It bothered Elder Kimball to see the Indians cheated. Back in Salt Lake City again, he combed through articles about Indian problems. An 1868 treaty had promised the Navajos schools. But only one out of three Indian children ever set foot inside one. There were just 365 hospital beds for fifty-five thousand Indians, and just one dentist. The Navajo ate only 1200 calories a day. The fifty-five thousand had been locked into a desert reservation of 175 million acres, but only twenty-seven thousand of those acres were irrigable. The government had drafted thirty-six hundred young men to serve during World War II, but none of them were allowed to vote.

In February 1947, Spencer Kimball returned to Window Rock where he sat two and a half days in a tribal council. Seventy-four Indian delegates gathered, surrounded by 150 onlookers. Most of the Indians wore silver turquoise rings and bracelets, moccasins, bright headbands, their hair either shingled, or shaggy, or long and tied in a bob at the back with wool strings. A handful wore suits. The women dressed in blue, green, yellow, or purple velvet. Smoke clogged the room. When a council member got the floor he hashed his ideas over and over. It was tedious and monotonous. The speeches were long and all had to be translated to or from Navajo. But one idea came through clearly. The Navajos wanted schools.

Elder Kimball was there to urge the Church's right to station missionaries on the reservation. The request had been put in the council chairman's hands. But the resolution never came up; there was too much distrust of the Mormons. In fact, one woman said she was at the meeting for one main reason, to keep the Mormons off the reservation. Some Indians blamed the government's unpopular stock-reduction program on the Church because one key post in the Grazing Department was held by a Mormon. Elder Kimball felt certain that biased ministers had inflamed that misunderstanding. Discouraged, he left the meeting and sent his clothes to a cleaner and scrubbed his hair to get rid of the stench of smoke.

In July he went to Window Rock again. The Church's request was tabled, undiscussed, at the end of three more long days. Nevertheless, with the consent of President George Albert Smith the Indian missionary work was expanded from just the Navajos and Zunis to encompass all the Indians in New Mexico and Arizona, with the mission name changed to the Southwest Indian Mission.

On one trip south, Elder Kimball visited the Navajo school at Blanding, Utah. There the Church had bought an unpainted building for the school for $750. Benches were hammered together out of rough lumber. One white man in town donated a thousand feet of

*Spencer and Camilla Kimball on Independence Rock, Wyoming,
overlooking reenactment in 1947 of Mormon pioneer trek of 1847*

lumber, another gave firewood, another offered potatoes if the Indians would dig them, others gave flour, beef, cash.

The one-room school held twenty-seven Indian children. Fourteen thousand children on the reservation could not get into any school. The visiting apostle watched a mother with two children turned away at the door. After sundown twenty-seven parents came from the hogans out through the cedars for a school meeting. One man said he hoped the school was permanent; he had moved his family a long distance and built a hogan so his children could attend. When Elder Kimball spoke to the meeting he urged the Indians to keep the room swept, to cut the wood, to make their children mind the teacher.

At Tolani he found the only school closed for lack of funds. At Tohatchi, New Mexico, a large school complete with dormitories and a hospital had stood closed for five years. At Aneth, Utah, fifteen hundred Navajos asked for just one teacher for the little school. There was no money, and the school was boarded up. "It made my heart sad to realize that such a great government with such unlimited facilities would so neglect its conquered victims."

He stopped at a small school near Teas Toh Trading Post. Of three thousand children in the area the school took only seventy-five. It was the last day of school. Spencer watched the mothers who had come with wagons to take their boys home. Behind them trailed the brothers and sisters not in school, "dirty and sore-eyed and scared like little rabbits." But the ones fortunate enough to get in the school seemed well cared for. The contrast was stark. Spencer Kimball drove to the trading post for candy, gum, and oranges to distribute, then back to the school, wondering how the Church might help the Indian get what he wanted: schools.

By 1947 sugar-beet farmers in Sevier County, Utah, brought Indians in by thousands to work their fields. Some of the Mormon farmers insisted that the way they managed their workers was not a Church matter. But others were more concerned. When one seventeen-year-old Indian girl, Helen John, begged her employers to let her stay in a tent on the farm all winter so she could go to school, they called Golden Buchanan of the stake presidency to talk to her. He found the Indian girl, with four sisters, digging beets in the fields, in snow and mud almost to their knees. They were living in an old tent which was about to collapse. Helen told him, "I am going to stay. I want to go to school."

Golden Buchanan said later that as he thought about the matter, "it was as if the whole program opened up to my understanding." Why couldn't Indian children be taken into Latter-day Saint homes? He wrote to Elder Spencer W. Kimball in Salt Lake City. A few days later the apostle showed up in Richfield on his way to Arizona and spent a night with the Buchanans. He asked them if they would take Helen into their home, not as a guest and not as a servant but as a daughter. "I couldn't," responded Sister Buchanan at first. "The neighbors wouldn't like me." Two of her sons worried that their school friends would laugh at them. But everyone agreed to sleep on it. By next morning the Buchanans had agreed to try it.

They brought the girl to their home. "I don't know who was more scared," said Sister Buchanan, "she or I." When Helen disappeared almost at once they assumed she had given up. But finally she showed up again about Christmas, this time with two other girls. The Buchanans found homes for them. When school let out for the summer, Helen went back to the fields with her parents. But that fall she returned from her reservation home near Coppermine, Arizona, along with six new friends. Miles Jensen in Gunnison said he would take one. When he met the bus two girls got off. Each told him she was the assigned one. He kept both. Some Richfield schoolteachers promised to give the Indians extra help outside of class. A carpenter volunteered to take seven apprentices into his shop. A nurse offered to help with health problems.

The program grew, until by 1954 the placement of LDS Indian school children had become an official Church program. That year sixty-eight students were placed. In 1958, 253 children were being sent to homes all over Utah. A bus chartered by the Church brought them north from the reservation. They were showered, fed, given physical examinations, given instructions, then introduced to their foster parents. By 1969 the number had grown to nearly five thousand placed in seven states and Canada. After that time the Church placed emphasis on use of improved school facilities on the reservations, where the children could remain at home, but despite a temporary dip the numbers grew again.

The same bitter winter that Helen John had harvested frozen beets, Navajos on the reservation came close to freezing. At Blanding they lived in wood and mud hogans with dirty floors, or in flimsy canvas tents. The snow piled up two feet deep. Their children shivered in thin shirts, some without coats or shoes. Some lay in their tents with mattresses pulled over them.

Some families edged close to starvation, with just handfuls of dried corn or bread cakes made of dried beans. Some had only hot water to drink. Elder Kimball heard about it from Golden Buchanan. He remembered hogans in which army overcoats hung. It exasperated him that the government would let these men and their families suffer.

He alerted the *Deseret News,* which sent a correspondent south with a photographer. He appealed to the Church Welfare Committee for a truckload of supplies. He wrote Utah's Senator Arthur Watkins in Washington, begging for an appropriation for Indian relief. He wrote pleas for help to the Rotary district governor in Arizona and to Rotary International. He mailed out piles of pamphlets. He wrote a two-part article for the *Improvement Era.*

On November 25, 1947, the *Deseret News* came out front-page with a first story on the Navajo plight. They ran photos of solemn-faced children in oversized shirts, standing barefoot against a backdrop of snow, staring into the camera. The series ran for five days. The paper printed photos of two large transport trucks being packed with canned foods and wheat and clothing at the Church's Welfare Square. A two-part newspaper article on the Navajos by Elder Spencer W. Kimball gave the campaign special legitimacy. When telephone inquiries flooded the newspaper's switchboard, the *Deseret News* created an Indian Aid Caravan, inviting the public to contribute flour, bedding, old clothes, canned food.

Stories of gratitude came back. Children who had owned just a single dress now had warm clothing. An old woman huddled in a blanket at a trader's store took a heavy coat and said in Navajo: "Thank you. I will not freeze now."

By December the crisis had passed. A Red Cross official in San Francisco complained that his people had been on the reservation, too, but had missed the vision of the Indian's need. He went on that it had been the "little *Deseret News*" that went down, photographed scenes of suffering, and stirred the nation with the story. And behind the paper, he said, it was "one little man" who had wakened the country and had contacted a senator who pushed through Congress an appropriation the Red Cross had failed to get for years. "Of course this was much exaggerated," Elder Kimball reacted, "but I do feel that we have made much progress."

He saw the long-range solution as schools and roads, reasoning that with this kind of help the Indians would inevitably improve their condition, even if nothing more were done. To promote their cause, he continued to speak to service clubs, neighborhood groups, Church organizations. After one such talk a man came up to offer two university scholarships for Navajo boys. Another donated radio time to Elder Kimball to plead the Navajo case. "I am grateful," Spencer wrote, "as I realize the large number of people who have smoldering in their bosoms the same feeling toward the Indians as I." In both April and October general conferences in 1947 he spoke on the Indians' needs and their promise.

His concern for the Indians was deeply personal. One man told of watching him in a Denver meeting. The closing prayer over, the chapel began to clear. An Indian man with a woman and a boy, dirty and unkempt, walked up the aisle toward the apostle, the churchgoers parting as if before lepers. In broken English the parents asked Elder Kimball to give their sick boy a blessing. Spencer scooped the boy up, hugged him and kissed him, then blessed him while holding him close.

With Glen Spencer Charleston

Said the observer: "If I'd heard that story, I'd say he was just trying to impress onlookers. But I could see his face. I could read the love he has for these people."

When Albert Lyman told him of three Indian boys about to be arraigned in Salt Lake City on charges of operating an illicit still, Elder Kimball went down to federal court. On the word of Lyman he suggested that two of the boys were unlikely to have been involved and wondered whether they might have been framed. He wrote:

> I found that they had no legal counsel, though they were entitled to it, and discussed the matter with the commissioner and the other men present, of the terrible plight of the Indians and at what a great disadvantage they found themselves in appearing in American courts. One of the men proffered to get his son-in-law who is an attorney to defend the boys, and see that they get justice when the case comes up on Friday. I was delighted with the general attitude of these people after I explained the great handicap of these poor Indians.

A couple of times a year he was back in Indian country. After touring a well-kept Presbyterian school for Indians at Ganado,

Arizona, he "felt very kindly to the Presbyterian Church. . . . God bless these people for the good they are doing."

He listened to the stories of the white missionaries and recorded their comments in his journal. One pair of nineteen-year-old elders tracted Percy Big Mouth. One of them handed him a small card printed with the Articles of Faith.

"How much?" Percy asked.

"Nothing."

The other gave Percy a pamphlet.

"How much?"

"Nothing."

They had a long visit. Then Percy said, "How much for talk?"

"Nothing."

"Can't understand. All white man preachers pat me on back with one hand, hold out other hand for money. You come back."

One Indian tried hard to kick the liquor and tobacco habit so he could be baptized. He came in the store where Ed Lyman, a Church member, worked and asked in despair if soda pop was forbidden, too. When Lyman's house burned to the ground the Indian got his tobacco out again. He said a man might as well chew, if God wouldn't save his house for stopping.

The elders reported a blind Indian who had a dream some days after he first met the missionaries. "I saw a light come down from heaven," he said, "and I could hold to it and it brought hope."

Hope is what the apostle felt, too. In 1948 at Toadlena, New Mexico, he visited thirty-eight bathed and well-groomed Indian children. It "enlarged my vision." He imagined these people as leaders in the Church, as bishops and stake presidents. He felt a spirit of awakening among the Indians. "The red Rip Van Winkle is rubbing his eyes." He often quoted to audiences Orson Pratt's promise of 1845: "The despised and degraded son of the forest, who has wandered in dejection and sorrow, and suffered reproach, shall . . . drop his disguise, and stand forth in manly dignity."

Elder Kimball urged on whites the role of nursing fathers and on Indians that of diligent students of the good the white man has to offer, without abandoning the best of his own culture. "The only difference between us and the Indian," he told a group of Church women, "is opportunity. They are not stupid. They have a high I.Q. They are equal to us in their mental powers." He blamed the white conquerors for locating reservations on useless, barren land, while "we became fat in the prosperity from the assets we took from them." The first part of the Church Indian program, he continued, "is education of the Latter-day Saints at home, some of whom need their hearts opened, cleansed and purged. . . . Racial prejudice is of the devil and of ignorance."

"The historian has used the *white* ink to write his stories when he was emphasizing honor and integrity and honesty and glory and heroism," he declaimed in a radio address, "but when he was emphasizing terror and death and raids and scalpings and betrayals and broken covenants, always it was with bold *red* ink. . . . There has been a prejudiced historian sitting at his desk for 400 years writing the Indian story. . . ."

He so identified himself with the Indian work that among Latter-day Saints only Jacob Hamblin's name carried the same connotations. At general conference a woman came up. "Elder Kimball," she said, "every time I see some dirty, ragged Indian I think of you." He appreciated the intended compliment, while he winced at the stereotyping.

In 1947 an Indian woman near Perea in New Mexico sent word to George Lee, a Mormon elder in the area, to come quickly and bless her baby, who was dying. He arrived and asked what name he should give the boy. "Spencer Kimball," she answered. The child lived and bore the name, sharing it with many others across the reservations.

14

The Heart and Throat Protest

— "I have tried by double expenditure
of energy to measure up"

With constant preaching, traveling, and counseling, the strain of his years in the Quorum drained Spencer's energy. For all the satisfactions, there could be no real vacation from the work, no forgetting its heavy demands. Physically it pushed him to the limit of his endurance.

The pattern was insistently the same for months: out along one of the spokes from Salt Lake City on the weekend, back to the hub on Monday. Out and back again.

In May 1948 he rode the train south to Los Angeles, then drove across the desert into Arizona with Golden Buchanan to tour the Indian mission. Their auto stuck in drifted sand. To free it the two men got out and pushed hard, straining to the utmost. The car ran forward and stuck again. They pushed and ran, pushed and ran. Elder Kimball's heart pumped like a diesel. In Phoenix that night at Glen Stapley's home, as Spencer finished his bath, an agonizing pain struck him down. He sat, then lay full on the floor. The pain clutched his chest; he sweat profusely. But when the attack passed after a while, Spencer told no one but Golden. He was determined to finish this tour, despite his heart.

Golden Buchanan and he drove through the San Carlos Reservation, stopping at an Apache wickiup made of poles and thatch, with a
dirt floor and a lumber doorway. To their meeting five women and ten
children came; the men were off working.

They drove on to the Tenijieth home, where they found the
woman stretched on a filthy mattress on the floor of the little lumber
house, plagued with flies. Her husband, wearing a thin goatee of long
chin hairs, was Lizard Eyes, the Apache chief over a small area. He
watched as Elder Kimball administered to the old woman, who gazed
fervently to heaven. "I had an unusually powerful feeling as I sealed
the anointing. I do hope the Lord will find it in his Providence to heal
her or at least to stop her pain." During the visit, her five-year-old
step-grandchild, Spencer Kimball Tenijieth, played around the house.

At another meeting in Whiteriver, Arizona, only a few nonmembers came. But the apostle felt the spirit of the work coming to him with
greater power than ever before. He sensed a new attitude on the
reservations, among both the Indians and the officials.

For seven days, going from meeting to meeting, he pushed himself
into exhaustion — from Whiteriver to St. Johns to Zuni, New Mexico;
to Ramah, Gallup, Crystal; to Window Rock, Arizona; to Wingate and
Toadlena, New Mexico; to Aneth, Utah, and Blanding; to Taos Pueblo
and San Ildefonso Pueblo in New Mexico and back to Gallup; then to
Ganado, Keams Canyon, Teas Toh, Winslow, Snowflake, and Taylor
in Arizona — zigzagging through three states over rough roads. In
each place he held meetings with missionaries, Indians, government
workers, or Indian school personnel.

He finally returned to Snowflake for stake conference. There he
stretched out on a floor, too tense for sleep. Brother Buchanan massaged his back and neck, and that helped a little.

The Quorum of the Twelve finally caught up with him. Word of
the heart attack had passed from Golden Buchanan to Jesse Udall in
Thatcher, who reported it to Elder Mark E. Petersen as he came to
stake conference there, who in turn reported it to the Quorum when he
returned home. Now Elder Petersen phoned from Salt Lake City in
behalf of the Quorum. "Slow down," was the order. "I was embarrassed
to have brought concern to the brethren," wrote Spencer, "but it was
really quite a lift to know that the brethren were concerned about me. I
am so small and weak in this great work of the Lord that it had hardly

occurred to me that I would ever be missed from it should anything happen to me."

His tour over, he rode the bus back to Salt Lake City, where his congested heart stupefied him into an almost-drugged sleep. The next day he dozed repeatedly in a temple endowment session. He went in for a checkup from his cousin, Dr. LeRoy Kimball, who shook his head gloomily at the electrocardiogram and insisted that Spencer quit Church work for a month.

Stunned, Spencer begged the doctor not to tell "the brethren," to let him think about it and get adjusted to the restriction. But overnight he decided to ignore the doctor's warning. "It seemed so impossible — so silly" just to stop cold. He had exercised, kept his weight down. He thought of himself as physically the fittest of all the General Authorities. He boarded a bus for his stake assignment in Rigby, Idaho. By night his chest was heavy with pain and he began to wish he had followed advice. He stuck it out through Sunday afternoon, then hurried home by train.

Frightened, he lay for four days in bed in his pajamas, although "it seemed so ridiculous for me, so strong and well." He had his secretary come to the home for dictation. Then early Friday morning he awoke with the severe pains of another heart attack. Sweating, he woke Camilla, and through the dark hours they discussed funeral plans and family finances.

Then "we saw the dawn come lightly," the quail scurry across the back yard, the dewy trees sparkle in the first sun. "It is a beautiful and glorious world in which we live."

Determined to get well, Spencer stayed flat on his back on Friday and Saturday. Then on Sunday, after a full week in bed, he sank into depression. He felt guilty for failing to carry his share of the load. There were just twelve apostles, he berated himself, and so much work to do. What good was he on his back? Even on his feet, he felt he was the least of them. Others were smoother, smarter, more efficient, better educated.

The next week, though, the gloom lifted as he surrendered to the inevitable. A flood of flowers, get-well cards, phone messages, fruit, cakes, fried chickens and hamburger suppers began arriving from well-wishers, more "than I ever deserved." His brethren in the Quorum visited him. President George Albert Smith came and blessed him.

The weeks dragged on. In his seventh week in pajamas, Spencer began looking for an escape from his monotonous house confinement. He arranged with Golden Buchanan to shift his convalescence to the Navajo Reservation. On July 8 Brother Buchanan picked him up in Salt Lake, and they reached New Mexico in easy stages. With food and supplies, chlorine tablets for the contaminated water and a case of root beer and orange pop for variety, they pitched camp in a borrowed trailer-tent under some pines a hundred yards downhill from the large hogan of Howela Polacca.

Spencer wrote Camilla that he liked "Navajoland, far from the haunts of the white man with all his noise and chatter." An airplane overhead one morning seemed irritatingly out of place. "They have no right to clutter up our peaceful little world down here. . . . This is not U.S.A. — This is Navajoland." When a woman passed with a hoe slung over her shoulder, they asked where she was headed. She pursed her mouth and pushed her lips toward the fields west. Spencer jotted that in his journal. He noted that the Polacca boys spoke in monotones and that Navajos don't knock on entering a room, but just peer in or grunt.

Golden Buchanan had to leave. His place was filled by Edward Ellsworth, a twenty-year-old missionary with two ailing knees; he came to recuperate with the apostle for a week.

Elder Ellsworth wrote home about Sunday morning when the two of them walked out in a drizzle onto a hill to hold their devotions. They sat under a tree, where Elder Kimball opened with prayer. With his "Amen" the rain stopped. They each read a chapter of Matthew, sang a hymn, then had a closing prayer.

Restless at inactivity, the older man whittled two sticks into canes and the apostle and the missionary hiked slowly up and down a few hills. Behind one they surprised little Francis Polacca singing "Come, Come Ye Saints" at the top of her voice as she herded sheep. When she saw them she stopped, shy, and would not be coaxed. The next day, on her eleventh birthday, Spencer gave her a book, a stack of paper, colored pencils, a pillow cover, and a package of gum. Won over by this display of affection, Francis agreed to teach them to count to one hundred in Navajo and to sing a Navajo song. A few nights later, when someone suggested the white men sing, Spencer tied a ribbon around his forehead and, with the missionary, sang Francis' song to the merriment of the Indians.

One afternoon Spencer and the young elder hiked to the red cliffs north of camp, where they noticed the Polaccas' names carved in rock. They got a hammer and chisels; the missionary carved an initial E in the red cliff and the apostle started an enormous human head. He abandoned it at dusk, unfinished. But back at camp he found a chunk of white sandstone and devoted several mornings to steadily chipping out a crude three-foot bust of himself, to the delight of a crowd watching him.

At the end of two weeks, Golden Buchanan drove back and helped Spencer break camp. The Navajo vacation had been perfect. The apostle felt cured. As he climbed into the car, Howela Polacca gave him a rug and pottery and pressed an inlaid silver tie clasp into his hand. Spencer almost wept.

Back in Salt Lake City he immediately began to pick up loose ends at the office. But day by day he grew more jittery and nervous until on his sixth day home his heart pains returned. He sank back into bed, frustrated to tears at his inability to do his share of the Quorum's work.

For four days his telephone rang, his visitors stayed too long, his office work was too near and too hard to ignore. And the long days with little to do exasperated him. So when Dr. Kimball urged him to escape the city again, he and Camilla packed their suitcases hurriedly and caught a train to Long Beach, where they sought out a quiet apartment facing the sea.

Some black days followed. One night he lay for eighteen hours in agony, his chest seized with pain. For long hours in his room he thought through his life. He told Camilla what to do with the investments and property if he died. He mused that "thousands of people in the Church are measuring the Church, their Church, by me. They look at me with my smallness, my ineptitudes, my weaknesses, my narrow limitations and say, 'What a weak Church to have such weak leadership.' It is one of the things that has brought me to my back now. I have tried by double expenditure of energy to measure up. . . ."

His thoughts turned especially to Spencer LeVan, who was studying law at Oxford on a Rhodes scholarship. He wrote his son a long letter:

Last night was another of those many interminable nights when there is restlessness and sleeplessness for both the mind and body. The distress came about four o'clock yesterday and persisted unabated into the night. There have been many such nights in the past three months. And I have done much thinking. Sometimes I feel good and optimistic; then when these spells recur I get quite discouraged. It seems that my distress has been far greater the past three weeks than it was at first; certainly it is more prolonged, and it leaves me sleepless and wondering and thinking. And my thoughts seem to center around my children and my program of life. . . .

Son, there are things temporal and things spiritual. The temporal will pass away — only the spiritual eternal things will remain. Degrees given by mere man will be forgotten, universities will crumble, nations will come and go, positions and honors will fade and many things which seem so important to us mortals may shrink into insignificance. Political parties and their philosophies may flourish and succeed and benefit or damage mankind, but they, too, will pass. There is but one thing which transcends all and continues through the eternities. . . .

I hope you will know that my only interest in writing this letter is you. I shall probably never write another such letter. I may never write another letter. I do not know. . . .

Seated in a large stuffed chair watching the breakers, Spencer wrote to his sister Clare, "I can watch the sea all day without even going out; can have the sea breeze constantly by just opening the window." Camilla took care of shopping, cooking, cleaning. She "waits on me hand and foot." He mailed a letter to his doctor complaining that nothing seemed to account for the heart pains. On the days when he walked a couple of blocks down the beach, he might feel nothing. On days he stayed in bed, he sometimes suffered bad pain. So why stay down? "If you can give me any additional help along the line of advice I shall try to follow it. I must get well. I am loafing now on Church time."

Camilla mailed the First Presidency at their request a report on the patient. "Spencer is impatient to get back to his work," was the predictable news. But, she recommended, "since every unusual physical or emotional strain seems to end in distress and a sleepless night, it seems that perhaps a little longer resting now may be prudent; however he wants you to know that he is subject to your call always."

The Presidency wrote back, asking her to keep Spencer down. "We pray that the Lord will bless you as well as him and that he will harken and yield to your solicitous loving counsel. If he does, the Lord will bless him."

From presidents David O. McKay and George Albert Smith came short get-well notes; from Elder Mark E. Petersen, a long, friendly letter with Quorum news and some chit-chat.

For several days Spencer knelt on the floor in his pajamas, with a fistful of colored pencils, working on a twenty-five-foot scroll of paper chronicling the earth's secular and religious history. The long roll of paper unwinds through the tangle of history, with cutout pictures pasted on here and there — a globe at the creation, a map of Egypt at 1700 B.C., pictures of conquerors and scientists down to 1948, where secular history ends with "Russian Cold War," and religious history with "172 stakes."

While he was at Long Beach, one of his high school friends sent him a signed blank check with instructions to fill it out in whatever amount he needed. Spencer returned it with his heartfelt thanks. He mentioned it in a letter to his son, commenting that good friends are worth more than honors, and each friend that one acquires gives him so much the more strength, security, and happiness.

Three weeks passed by the sea. Spencer was frustrated by the recurrent heart pains. When Dr. Harold Hinckley, a Long Beach Stake high councilor, offered to put him through a new battery of tests, he jumped at the offer. It was a chance to find out why he was not getting well. Dr. Hinckley X-rayed the lungs and digestive tract and took a cardiograph. There was almost nothing wrong. Any angina had reduced to nothing. Hinckley insisted on it. He drove Spencer and Camilla to Laguna Beach, where Spencer swam in the sea. "I began to breathe freely! How good to know that every extra ounce of energy expended did not imperil my life!"

He spent three more weeks in California, gradually increasing his activity and feeling only an occasional pang, then returned to Salt Lake City. His doctor there thought that after three more months he could resume conference visits, but that for the rest of his life he should be more sparing of himself than formerly.

His first morning home Elder Kimball spent at his desk, eating into his piled-up mail. On his second day President George Albert Smith invited him into his office and told of his own bouts with ill health. "Don't exhaust yourself," the President urged. "As I stood to leave his office President Smith stood also and came near me and said they all loved me and the Church loved me and he drew me to him, put his arms about my shoulders and kissed my forehead."

On his way out, Elder Kimball stopped in on President J. Reuben Clark, Jr., who inquired about his health, then "was kind enough to say to me that 'you are too valuable to the Church' and urged me to take great care that I had no relapse. And as I left the room he walked with me to the door and put his arm about my shoulder."

It seemed to Spencer Kimball that he had done nothing to merit such kindness, but "I did so much appreciate the apparent good will of these brethren."

In October he asked Elder Stephen L Richards to administer to him. By authority of his priesthood Elder Richards blessed Spencer that he would recover totally. "From that moment I began to feel much better." Better, but still not well. As fall wore away he could not shake the persistent chest pains. But he tried to ignore them and bowed himself under an increasing weight of work.

In January 1949 he left for his first stake conference in more than half a year. Camilla went along to take care of him. As the train raced across the desert toward Los Angeles, Spencer watched through the window the giant Joshua trees and cacti, pillows of snow on every arm. He felt exuberant to be back at work. But in his meetings the stress built up; the old chest pains nagged. He complained to no one. If the Quorum suspected another heart flare-up, he worried, they "would immediately retire me for weeks or months until I was pronounced well, and that I could not stand. I gritted my teeth and made up my mind no one would know and that I would endeavor to take care of myself."

On top of that, he caught a bad cold. He ignored it. He returned home, but in two days he was out again; this time he went south to look after the Indians. At Richfield he drove down a dead-end street in the northwest section of town to visit eight Indian families tenting in deep snow, lying under cardboard and mattresses for warmth. "I was shocked and mortified." Though local people had already supplied two new tents, coal, and other help, the crude camp left the Indians suffering in the sub-zero weather. Spencer urged more assistance. The Shivwits near St. George he found in rude huts on a muddy hill. He arranged for nearby abandoned government buildings to be rebuilt with Church money for Indian housing and a chapel.

During all that spring, Elder Kimball felt occasional teasing heart pains. They came on worst when his fatigue built up. He arrived home many nights distressed at the problem interviews in his office, unable to

About 1950

shrug off the misery. A wife came in, abandoned by her priesthood-
holding husband. A mother asked about sterilizing her insane daughter; another sought help for a wayward daughter headed for divorce
and tragedy. One couple walked through his door with divorce papers
already filed and left two hours later in one another's arms, though
Elder Kimball wondered whether the reconciliation would last. Near
midnight he answered his door at home to an unmarried couple, the
girl pregnant and in tears, begging help. He never turned anyone
away. The accumulated stress continued to overtax his heart.

A year after his first heart attack, he set out with President Flake
for another tour of the Southwest Indian Mission.

Camilla mailed a letter after him:

> Dearest, I can count off two days of the thirty you will be gone!
> That isn't much and I am not looking forward without some dread
> of the long lonesome time. I do miss you, so very much. I can't quite
> get over the terror that you are re-enacting the tragedy of a year
> ago and while I know I shouldn't suggest the possibility of a
> repetition I do hope that you will exercise judgment and not take
> chances. I am tempted to write Brother Flake and caution him
> since you are so recreant about caring for yourself.

The two men held meetings at village after village across the reservation at breakneck pace. The apostle's chest pains came back. At one stop he lay down in the woods as the Indians prepared a picnic in a nearby field. At Phoenix he stretched out on the floor of the bishop's home until meeting-time. But the tour, mile by mile, went as scheduled. At Sacaton, Elder Kimball preached practical advice, urging the Indians to plant fruit trees, bottle vegetables, start farms. He tried to give those who were dirt poor a vision of improvement.

On the banks of the White River he urged another hundred Indians to own cows. When he went on to argue that "the Lord must think milk is the best children's food, since he provides it through mother's breasts," a cluster of Indian women giggled, which "fussed me a little." One old Indian mumbled through the whole sermon, then afterwards strode away down the dirt road as the other Indians grouped by the river for a baptismal service. Someone shouted after him that he could stay, but he called back cagily, "You no water me."

At Ramah, the apostle watched as twenty-three more Navajos were baptized in the reservoir. "I am sure that angels were not far away." He reported fabulous progress to Camilla: 124 baptisms in just five months.

In Tucson, he told a packed chapel of white Mormons the Bible story of the Good Samaritan. The robbed and beaten traveler, he said, is the Indian and we whites are either priest or Good Samaritan.

He stopped at Smith Lake, where the missionaries had beaten the bushes for a congregation of Indians to hear him. Just a handful showed up. "My name, title or personality," he wrote Camilla, "was not as fetching as was the trial over at Mariana Lake to which all the Indians in the area had gone. Someone had burned a tent." At San Felipe as he stood behind the pulpit speaking to a sprinkling of Indians and missionaries, with scores of ragamuffin children peeking in the doors and windows, he felt inspired, "if I have ever been inspired." Through the children we would convert the adults, he urged. One Primary a week was too little for idle children with no schedule. They must be taught the gospel for many hours every day, with stories and songs and games.

As they crossed Whiskey Creek, Elder Kimball remembered baptisms in that water and asked, "Why not call it Baptism Creek?"

After five hard weeks on the reservations of Arizona and New Mexico, Elder Kimball came "Home! Home!" When asked to report on the Indian work at a gathering of General Authorities, he took a half hour and did his best to pass to them his own enthusiasm. He wished they could have heard Sallie Sundust on the reservation plead that missionaries be sent to her village. He wished he had taped her message so that he could spread her fervor to others.

Spencer wondered what to do about a strange dream he had had while on the reservation. He had retired, feeling well, and fallen into a peaceful sleep. He dreamed vividly of going to the members of a family he had known well in Safford. He urged them to change their ways and devote themselves seriously to the work of the Lord. As he spoke he wept, realizing that they might reject his message and might resent his interference. One put her fingers over his lips as if to stop him, but he continued with great urgency to plead with them for complete surrender to the Lord's way.

The scene changed slightly and he and one of the women stood apart. Her deceased husband stood near them, pleased at what Spencer was saying to her. The man stood straight, clean, well-groomed, looking taller and straighter and healthier than in life. Spencer slapped him on the shoulder and greeted him. The man seemed pleased but did not speak. As the husband moved slowly away and vanished, Spencer continued to implore the wife to follow a life of Church service.

Spencer awakened from the dream and lay there under a continuing impression of serenity, reviewing the picture of his friend — peace personified, with face almost transparent, wearing a perfectly fitting dark suit. He got out of bed and recorded the dream. When he finished, his watch showed 2:35.

In retrospect the dream surprised Spencer a little. His friend had been a businesslike shopkeeper, often worried and preoccupied, a good fellow but sometimes lightminded, giving little attention to Church or religion. And after the funeral the wife had dropped all connection with the Church. Years had passed without any contact between Spencer and the family. Nothing he could recall would have triggered this dream; it came like lightning from a clear sky. Although he could almost hear the family laugh together at the huge joke and express resentment at his intrusion, Spencer felt he must contact them.

Just a month later a funeral called him to Arizona. He sought out the woman he had dreamed about and, at her invitation, met with her family. They seemed interested in the dream and what it might mean. He left with a hope that his visit might influence them.

While in Arizona, Spencer telephoned a friend he had heard was losing his faith and proposed a weekend camping trip. Delighted, his friend offered to buy provisions. Spencer suggested that instead they fast. They camped out from Saturday to Monday noon at a meadow in the high mountains. They read the scriptures, prayed, and talked out the friend's "many erroneous ideas and concepts." When his friend argued that God as depicted in the Bible was a tyrant, Spencer reasoned with him that God's only ultimate interest was man's welfare and that only men's faulty perception obscured the fact. By Monday noon they prepared to leave, but the station wagon would not run. They fiddled under the hood, but nothing seemed to help. Finally they said a prayer, and after a moment's further tinkering the car started. Both felt the Lord had answered their prayer. Over several years thereafter the friend's faith strengthened, and with his wife he served several missions.

When he came through the Gila Valley Spencer visited old friends as much as possible. One such was Elizabeth Craig, who had worked as a cook for Andrew Kimball's construction crew many years before. One day Spencer had knocked and she had hobbled to the door.

"Good morning, ma'am. Could I sell you some Fuller brushes this morning?"

Not recognizing him, she said, "No, I don't need any brushes this morning."

"Could I sell you some garden vegetables?"

"No, thank you. I have a garden of my own."

"Well, isn't there anything I could sell you today, Grandma Craig?"

She finally recognized him and his teasing and scolded, "Oh, you — you —!" They laughed together. For many years after that he greeted her with, "Can I sell you some Fuller brushes?"

The last time he saw her she was in her nineties and lay on her deathbed. She did not acknowledge her daughter's announcement of his presence nor show recognition of his voice, but when he mentioned Fuller brushes she smiled and pressed his hand as he kissed her wrinkled face.

In December 1949 the heart pains came back, so severe that the doctor urged hospital rest. Elder Kimball wouldn't hear of it. He reassured the doctor that he intended to get more rest on his own. But two days later he overtaxed his heart badly by a long day of interviews with weak and unhappy Latter-day Saints, interviews which he felt he "could not logically escape."

The only real escape was to leave the city. So on December 30 Spencer and Camilla drove south to Pima. At the Eyring ranch Spencer lounged for two weeks in pajamas or old clothes. Some nights, as the family slept, he lay in his bed starkly awake through hour upon hour of agony. He wondered if the Lord would heal him.

Spencer held the conviction that if the Lord "sees He can use us and needs us, He will heal us." But how much did the Lord need Spencer Kimball? In his six years as an apostle it seemed to him he had done too little good. And now because he was ill he was on enforced vacation.

"This very fact is nearly annihilating to me since it increases my feeling of uselessness and my inferiority complex." The previous July near Matamoros he had been amazed when a young Mexican proudly reminded him, "You blessed my baby two years ago." It still surprised and pleased him to think someone would remember.

Midway through January the pains vanished. He wrote to the First Presidency that the rest had made him well and he wanted to return to work. But their reply telegram turned the evidence neatly against him: "Have consulted your doctor. Evidence that rest is what you need is that the rest you take gives you relief. We pray the Lord to bless you and ask you to take another month."

Spencer heard from friends about a Mexican diagnostician in Nogales, said to have done wonders with other American patients. Spencer laughed it off at first, but finally, desperate to speed recovery, he sought an appointment and drove to Mexico. Dr. Guerra examined him exhaustively, then announced that his problem was not heart but chronic indigestion. Though Spencer laughed about the expensive pills Dr. Guerra prescribed he bought them and hoped they would help. That night in the motel bathroom he swallowed one of the large black capsules, turned violently ill, and suffered through the night. In the morning he phoned for two elders and received a priesthood blessing. The discomfort waned. He discarded the pills.

The extra month of rest completed, Spencer and Camilla drove leisurely home through California, getting still another medical diagnosis there. This specialist thought the heart had been weakened by an undiagnosed case of rheumatic fever in childhood. He suggested avoiding overweight and overwork.

Elder Kimball reached home in mid-February, after consultation with three doctors and eight weeks of enforced vacation. Almost at once his impatient plunge back into committee meetings and interviews precipitated a black night in which he felt at the edge of death. It convinced him he still was not well and "MUST reduce" his schedule. Two weeks later he still had the brakes on, working at half speed. He sat in the Quorum's Thursday meeting in the Temple, disgusted with his uselessness. Each apostle reported his week's activities, until it came Elder Kimball's turn: "No report — I am loafing." President Clark responded with force, "No, you aren't." But Elder Kimball blamed himself for letting the Lord down. His physical condition made him emotionally volatile.

That month, as part of the University of Utah's centennial, the university's literary magazine, *Pen,* published a centennial issue which roused his ire volcanically. To him it seemed a deliberate slap in the face of the Church. The student editor had republished pieces from earlier issues of *Pen,* but so many were pieces by authors whose later writing Spencer characterized as unflattering or actively hostile to the Church, that he saw it as an anti-Mormon gesture.

At the suggestion that there had been no intent to harm, Spencer exploded. The *Pen* had vilified the Church, and he resented that with all the power of his soul. But just as much or more it incensed him that Church members "would sit blandly down and ignore insult to themselves, their forbears and the Church prophets." It all suggested to him a dilution of loyalty and a lost sense of injustice. His view was that members of the Church should zealously foster "the Cause." There were plenty of enemies and self-appointed critics around to point out weaknesses. Advocates were needed to point out strengths. "I slept little and very poorly, having become so agitated in my feelings that it took me a long time to relax."

In 1948 Spencer's sister Helen Farr had been painfully sick for many months. He drove down to her home in Provo about once a week to sit by her bedside. Cancer had terribly devastated her face. "One could not imagine anything so horrible," Spencer wrote to his brothers.

By December she suffered spells of delirium. Spencer saw her beyond all earthly help. "I still know that the Lord could raise and heal her and to the end we still supplicate Him."

Helen died on December 18, at forty-seven. She was buried in a snowstorm, with a small turnout. The Farrs were well represented, but Spencer noted in his journal that no Provo stake leaders came, no General Authorities, none of the many Gila Valley friends resettled in Utah, beyond her immediate family no Kimball relatives and only two Woolley relatives. It hurt to watch his beloved younger sister die so little noticed.

From that winter on, Spencer felt personal fear of the black angel of cancer.

In the spring of 1950 he began to worry more about an annoying hoarseness that had hung on since before Christmas. Nothing seemed to explain it. There was no congestion, no cough. He made an appointment with Leland Cowan, a cancer specialist. Dr. Cowan examined the throat carefully, noted a spot of white on one vocal cord, and arranged a second appointment.

Spencer walked from Dr. Cowan's office in fear. That night he wrote in his journal: "Cancer! Cancer of the throat would render me useless from now on for the Church. I have done so very little in these six short years — there is so much to do — it is a black outlook indeed."

At the Thursday report meeting in the Temple Elder Kimball looked so glum that President Clark asked the cause. When told, he sympathized, "Surely you don't need anything else to worry you." But just that attitude by the Brethren plagued Spencer more. The only Church work he could get now was what he dug up on his own. The Brethren's rest policy sent him into depression.

For the next month Spencer pinned his hope to every hint of improvement. If he awoke in the morning less hoarse he brightened. But by April Dr. Cowan had sent him to Dr. Smith and Dr. Rigby, who proposed a biopsy to obtain a specimen for laboratory examination. Just that cutting of the vocal cord alone could leave Spencer with a harsh, raspy voice which could hinder his work for the rest of his life. "I am so useless anyway — I have done so little — my efforts have been so puny — my service so small — how can I face inactivity because of physical handicap?"

But on the other hand, if he refused the test, there might be cancer which would spread up from his throat into his head, ending his usefulness that way, too. He agonized over the image of his sister Helen's distorted, cancer-eaten face and wished for death by heart attack before that ever happened to him. He agreed to let the doctor cut. "My children do not yet know the possibilities — practically no one else does. I shall keep it to ourselves until it is more surely diagnosed. I hope to go on forward to the last ounce and inch. I hope to repay in a small measure My Father."

At St. Mark's Hospital in Salt Lake City he was put under total anaesthesia and operated on, then wheeled on a table back toward his room. Still drugged, Spencer sensed his table stop by an elevator and heard the orderly, angry at something, profaning the Lord's name. Half-conscious, he pleaded with labored sounds: "Please don't say that. I love Him more than anything in this world. Please." An absolute silence. Then the orderly answered softly: "I shouldn't have said that. I'm sorry."

In two days the doctor phoned Spencer at home. What he had was an infection which would need to be cauterized. But no cancer.

For that happy news, though, Spencer had paid with his good voice. He spoke into his dictaphone and played the belt back. The sounds from his scraped throat were like the grating of harsh materials. Even in a quiet place he could not be heard beyond a few feet. One day he talked in a meeting for five minutes with his raw throat and then finished, perspiring from the exertion. He prayed for relief, but he ended each prayer, "Thy will be done." He had a foreboding he would lose his voice.

But a week later he recorded a miraculous recovery. Elders J. Reuben Clark, Harold B. Lee and Henry D. Moyle had met with him, first to console him and build his faith, then to give him a priesthood blessing. As they left a calmness lighted his mind, and when he awoke next morning he could talk with strength. Jubilant, he refused to listen to his doctors, who still insisted he have his throat infection cauterized. In two days they agreed with him that there was no hurry. By two weeks they concluded there was no need at all.

By June Spencer could sing again, and in his exultation about the healing of his throat he almost forgot he had a heart problem. But in the summer the chest pains began again. It drained him to exhaustion and left him on some mornings barely strong enough to dress. But he did dress and did drive to his office and did beg the Quorum president for regular assignments to stake conferences.

In June 1950 North Korea sent troops and armor stabbing across the 38th parallel. Within two days President Truman committed United States forces to aid South Korea. More than 54,000 American boys would die in Korea, including one of Elder Kimball's next-door neighbors.

At Fort Sill, Oklahoma, he spoke to about a hundred green Mormon soldiers who had marched to the base chapel in formation, armed and carrying their equipment. He shook hands with each one; some wept and embraced him. From the service they marched directly to entrain for battle duty in Korea. He watched them go with an empty feeling. "It was cold and heartless. I saw the two trains pull out and went away with a heavy heart. Why, oh why?" He imagined what these same boys, clean and brave, could do if they were leaving instead on missions to preach the gospel of peace. It seemed so senseless to thrust them into death and destruction. The missionary work slowed. Draft boards bled the communities of the young men who would otherwise have gone on missions. They proved so suspicious of Mormon requests for deferments that the Church nearly stopped calling missionaries of draft age for a time.

Whatever his own troubles, he found others with greater ones. He met with a deranged woman brought in by her friends. She told him of fabulous and strange religious experiences. Spencer sensed an evil darkness in the room and with his hands on the woman's head gave her a blessing, rebuking Satan.

An Indian woman came to complain of the hatreds and insults of white Latter-day Saints. Questioning whether a Church containing such people could be true, she struggled for faith. Elder Kimball listened to her problems and those of others, trying to help, but he kept his own troubles to himself.

As they had been counseled to do for years, Spencer and Camilla stored a year's supply of food. He wrote to Ed with reference to a surge of hoarding at the start of the Korean war: "The Church people ought to be ashamed. They have been warned over and over. . . . They have paid no attention to the Prophets, but the moment a little war scare comes they get busy. One of our High Councilors in one of the Stakes hurried right down and bought 100 cases of canned goods. Said he had intended all the time to do it. The word of the Leaders did not jar him, but one or two newspapers with screaming headlines jarred him loose."

While the war raged in Korea Spencer's private inner war went on, a fight against pain and worry as he endeavored to fulfill, without slackening, the demands of his calling.

15

A New Era of Church Leadership

— "we can create a style of our own"

As the 1951 April Conference approached, Church President George Albert Smith, who had been ill for months, was taken home from the hospital. He preferred to die in his own house. His counselors, J. Reuben Clark, Jr., and David O. McKay, visited his bedside on April 2. The dying man, who was surrounded by weeping daughters and others, did not remember them. Two days later, on his eighty-first birthday, he died. His daughter, remembering how much her father had wanted to attend April Conference, said that now he could be there, unencumbered by a decrepit body.

The fourteen apostles, including the two counselors from the dissolved First Presidency, met next morning in the Temple to talk about the funeral arrangements. David O. McKay, the senior apostle, occupied the first oak chair in the semicircle arranged about the blue altar. J. Reuben Clark, Jr., assumed his place in the sixth chair. The chairs for the Presidency stood empty. As the senior apostle spoke, a strange feeling came over Elder Kimball. He saw David O. McKay in his majesty and power. "I saw him as the President of the Church. . . . There was no doubt in my mind. It was a soul-satisfying feeling. It was hardly a light — it was more like a sudden flood of warmth and into my

mind came the thought: 'A PROPHET'S MANTLE.' " The experience
stood for him as a testimony that David O. McKay was the Lord's
choice. But beyond that, it seemed a special mark of favor to himself.
"It gave me the feeling that perhaps the Lord might be pleased to a
small extent with my work, attitudes and myself to be so kind to me."

On Sunday afternoon the apostles met again in the Temple.
Joseph Fielding Smith, second in seniority, proposed that David O.
McKay be President of the Church. Stephen L Richards, third in
seniority, seconded the motion and it carried unanimously. President
McKay then chose Stephen L Richards as first counselor and J. Reuben
Clark, Jr., as second counselor. There was stunned silence for a moment. Elder Clark had been first counselor to two presidents, for
seventeen long years. Then Joseph Fielding Smith moved approval
and the apostles voted unanimously to sustain the President in his
choice.

> Not until we started down the steps of the temple did I come to
> realize that I was not alone in my bewilderment and devastation.
> All the others of the Twelve seemed to be alike stunned. We had
> been wholly unprepared for this shock. President Clark had stood
> and accepted this call and in this order like a god. What a man!
> What fortitude! What courage and self control! What self mastery!
> How could any mortal take a blow like that and stand? But he did.

> I had slipped into the room where he was changing his clothes
> and whispered to him with my warmest feelings and a tight hand-
> clasp: "President Clark, my love and admiration for you knows no
> bounds." This was all I could say. I think he knew my heart was
> breaking for him. We had all re-dressed in silence. We walked back
> to the office building numb. The other brethren from Brother Lee
> down came together at the corner of the building and commiser-
> ated together. We realized that the President had a right to choose
> his counselors in or out of the Twelve, but we had not expected this
> arrangement. We knew that nothing incorrect had been done, but
> our hearts were breaking for that stalwart who for two regimes had
> carried the major load.

The next morning at the Tabernacle, in a specially convened
solemn assembly as President Clark presented for sustaining vote each
General Authority, Elder Kimball could detect no trace of self-pity or
complaint. In his remarks President Clark gave ringing testimony that
David O. McKay was the chosen prophet of God and said: "In the
service of the Lord, it is not where you serve but how. In The Church of
Jesus Christ of Latter-day Saints, one takes the place to which one is

duly called, which place one neither seeks nor declines." Elder Kimball said in evaluation: "He did more in his perfect reactions perhaps to establish in the minds of this people the true spirit of subjection of the individual to the good of the work, more than could be done in thousands of sermons. How I honor and appreciate and admire him. Surely he is one of God's greatest noblemen!"

President McKay spoke feelingly to the assembled members and explained there was no rift, as some might suppose, but the greatest of harmony. He had prayed and prayed about the matter and, having the privilege of choosing, had felt the arrangement of his two counselors to be right and hoped the people and the Twelve would sustain him. He spoke and bore testimony with emotion unusual for him, and an additional testimony came to Elder Kimball that he was the Lord's prophet on earth.

In his journal he added:

> To my readers: I want you to know that I know this work is true and the work will roll on and God is at the helm. . . . I am positive that the appointments of His Twelve by the Lord and the subsequent deaths control the Presidency of the Church. No man will live long enough to become President of this Church ever who is not the proper one to give it leadership. Each leader in his own peculiar way has made a great contribution to the onward march of the Church. No one of the nine Presidents had all the virtues nor all the abilities. Each in his own way and time filled a special need and made his great contribution. This I know. This I know.

The Church was being built worldwide by a new generation. A handsome, vigorous man, President McKay at seventy-seven seemed, after his invalid predecessors, to be youthful. His personal presence had great charm. Half a foot taller than Spencer, with a "wavy white mane of hair," President McKay impressed Spencer as "positive and dynamic and powerful." One man described his eyes as "fiercely tender." An Oregon news editor wrote that he looked like a prophet "stepped out of the Old Testament."

In his first years as President he toured Europe, the South Seas and South America. Under him Church membership would more than double to 2,800,000. The most repeated phrase in the Church would be his slogan, "Every member a missionary."

To the Quorum of the Twelve at a Thursday temple meeting, the President said that God's kingdom was growing at a time when other

Christian sects were disintegrating. This Twelve today, he told them, was as pleasing to the Lord Jesus as were the eleven with whom he broke the sacrament in the upper room before Gethsemane.

The bonds among the twelve brother apostles were strong. Elder Kimball felt special respect for those senior to him in the Quorum, since he might live to see any of them become the prophet of the Lord. He did not know which. In 1949 he had helped administer to George F. Richards, then eighty-eight and president of the Quorum. "I had a rather bold impression come to me as we placed our hands on the head of President Richards that he would recover and live to become President of the Church." Elder Richards did recover and live more than a year longer, but he did not survive George Albert Smith to become President.

Because the four apostles senior to Harold B. Lee — Joseph Fielding Smith, John A. Widtsoe, Joseph F. Merrill, and Albert E. Bowen — were all much older than he, Spencer thought Elder Lee "would surely be the President and I would sustain him with all my heart."

Elder Merrill died suddenly while on a stake conference visit. As Spencer stood at the wintry graveside he thought of the gravelly hill in Thatcher, sunnier and drier than this Utah soil, where his parents lay buried. And he thought of buying a cemetery lot for Camilla and himself.

The next year Elder Widtsoe died. And shortly afterward, during the quarterly meeting of the Council of the Twelve, Elder Cowley started at the sudden sagging of Albert E. Bowen's face. Half a dozen apostles ran to Elder Bowen's chair to help. They carried him into the lounge, where Elder Kimball loosened his tie and rubbed his wrists and ankles to keep him conscious until the ambulance arrived. A stroke had left Elder Bowen badly paralyzed. Spencer visited him in the hospital. "I was shocked at his apparent condition," wrote Spencer. "It almost haunted me — he looked so nearly gone. I dreamed about him much through the night. Could hardly get my thoughts off of him." He faithfully visited "beloved Brother Bowen" until the older apostle's death a year later.

With each death Elder Kimball advanced in seniority, but his bad heart made it impossible for him to conceive he would outlive Harold B. Lee. When he woke one morning in July 1951 with extreme chest pain he wondered whether he would even survive the day. In his journal he wrote: "I might hope that my children will take from my many journals and write a simple story or biography for me. I would like for my posterity to remember me and to know that I have tried so hard to measure up and to live worthy."

The chest pain proved a false scare, but Camilla lived in terror that Spencer's heart might kill him at any time or any place without warning. Any telephone call could bring the message. The doctors urged him to cut back, to save his heart. So he and Camilla left again for California. They located a room overlooking the ocean, where they "could hear and see the waves dashing upon the rocks." And for three weeks he rested. He made a project of carving a likeness of Camilla's face in the sandstone cliff by the beach. On other days he organized boxes of his father's papers and journals and started typing a rough draft of a biography. His father, he thought, was "one of the greats in this kingdom." He hoped to preserve a record of his greatness.

He ended his vacation revitalized. And for the next several years there was little change in his health. There was the see-saw of alarms and lulls; the same tendency to overwork, bringing on stress and forced rest, followed by a gradual acceleration into another cycle of intense effort and then distress.

In 1947 when Elder Charles Callis had died, President Clark had asked Elder Kimball to help fill the gap. There began for him a disturbing flow of interviews with Church members involved in fornication or adultery or homosexuality, cases which formerly had been directed to Elder Callis. He never got used to the tide of grief day after day, over long years. A teenage girl, eight months pregnant, came in with her aunt to ask what to do with her fatherless baby. The aunt, "a lovely young woman," had once been in the same spot, had given her baby away, and now could have no more children. Elder Kimball offered to contact the boy responsible and try to get him to marry the unwed girl. A shattered husband came, shocked that his wife had deserted him. The apostle dropped everything and with another man along as a witness drove to the wife's apartment to persuade her to leave her "libertine" lover and go back to her husband and four children. He wrote often in his journal, "I hope I was helpful." He tried. There were no limitations on age or race or social class. Hundreds poured out their troubles to him.

The heartbreak in these lives haunted Spencer. The theme began to surface often in his sermons.

In 1951, assigned to address Brigham Young University's student-body of forty-five hundred, Elder Kimball spoke on modesty. "A woman is most beautiful when her body is clothed and her sweet face adorned with her lovely hair," he told his audience. "We can create a style of our own." The world had styled the costume for college baton-twirlers, he went on. The world had designed the strapless evening gowns and body-revealing sweaters. "They are an abomination in the sight of the Lord." The place for women in shorts "is in their own rooms in their own homes. Shorts are immodest." He wondered why any Latter-day Saint girl would exhibit her body in a bathing suit to a panel of men judging a beauty queen contest. "Abominable!" He ridiculed "scholarly research" at the University of Washington which photographed college girls nude. He called again for "a style of our own."

The talk created a sensation on campus. The university paper reported student reaction ranging from those planning to remodel their formals to those who predicted that after a few months of wearing "Kimballized dresses" things would revert to normal. One of the faculty, though, wrote a long letter, accusing Elder Kimball of offending the school's baton-twirlers needlessly and objecting to his statement that God had buried Pompeii beneath ashes to punish the people for sexual wickedness. When Elder Kimball's reply letter brushed aside the objections the man could not forgive what he saw as a belittling of his complaints.

In another talk Elder Kimball told of an unmarried couple who had knocked on his front door late one night, the girl in tears that they had slipped gradually from flirtation and touching into unchastity. To his congregation Elder Kimball urged the unchaste to confess their sins to the Church authorities and repent. Over the next few days dozens of single students and couples called on him at his office to confess. One boy telephoned him at home and asked for an appointment for himself and his girl, explaining, "We're in the same fix as the couple in your talk."

The apostle longed to preach to all the Church the bitterness of unchastity. Heartsick for the disrupted lives, he grew impatient at the carelessly and stylishly immodest. "I was disgusted," he wrote in his journal after attending a Salt Lake wedding reception, "with the number of women with strapless gowns and bare upper bodies and with frothy formality." He criticized the brides-to-be, scheduled for temple marriage, who displayed photographs of themselves in low-cut dresses on the society pages. Why, he asked, would any girl want that printed? When he spoke to 264 high school graduates at the Jordan school district seminary in 1954, he noted that not one girl there was immodestly dressed. Probably, suggested a friend, because everyone knew that he would be the speaker. That, answered Elder Kimball, was a compliment.

Against the harsh background of recurring heart pains, his throat troubled him again. He had recovered suddenly and remarkably in 1950 after a blessing, but the trouble returned a year and a half later. Every few months he had his throat checked for cancer. The fear never totally left. One Sunday he stood in Moore, Idaho, to speak to a congregation, when the public address system went out. What should he do? To raise his voice might damage the throat he had carefully nursed for two years. But to sit down would disappoint the faithful Saints waiting to hear him. He hesitated, then strained his voice hard enough to be heard in the rear of the chapel. "I felt sure My Father, knowing my predicament, would bless me."

A week later, his voice still hoarse and broken from the terrific pressure of that experience, Spencer fasted three full days for faith to heal his throat. By noon of the third day he had dehydrated badly and could hardly speak through his dry lips, but he kept his vigil because he felt so much the need to be blessed. That night, though his voice remained hoarse, he broke his fast with a calm assurance that the Lord would bless his life. His voice gradually improved.

In the Tabernacle at general conference Elder Kimball delivered a pleading, scorching sermon which he began by quoting an anonymous letter. A woman had written: "I never dreamed I would live to see the day when the Church would invite an Indian buck to talk in the Salt Lake Tabernacle — an Indian buck appointed a bishop — an Indian squaw to talk in the Ogden Tabernacle — Indians to go through the Salt Lake Temple.... The sacred places desecrated by the invasion of everything that is forced on the white race." This roused Spencer to fever pitch.

At Brigham Young University he decried to the young white

students and the white faculty that there were "too many Pharisees among the white men"; too many who worry about "unwashen hands; too many 'superior' ones who call, 'Unclean! Unclean!' ... too many who ascribe the degradation of the Indian as his just due. ... too many priests who 'pass by on the other side of the road' ... too many Levites who pull their robes about them and pass by with disdain ... too many curiosity seekers and too few laborers." He ended his speech with an impassioned plea, "not for your tolerance — your pitying, coin-tossing tolerance —" but for Christian help born out of love.

He pleaded with a congregation in New Mexico to accept the Indians and Mexicans "with open arms and hearts and meetinghouses. God will bless you if you do; God forgive you if you don't."

When any major Indian problem arose it was given to Elder Kimball. One Tuesday the president of the Quorum of the Twelve took an urgent call warning that at noon the next day the Navajo Tribal Council would try to outlaw Mormon proselyting on the reservation. An hour and a half later Spencer and Mark E. Petersen headed south from Salt Lake City by car. At eleven o'clock the next morning they reached Tuba City and went into a huddle with three Tribal Council members. A Mr. Goodtooth accused Mormon missionaries of baptizing Indians by force and converting their children at school on the sly. Elder Kimball phoned the school on the spot and the school personnel denied any missionary interference. The air cleared. The Indians and the Mormons parted friends.

In August 1951, Spencer represented the Church at the Pan-American Indian League Conference in Independence, Missouri. It had been billed as drawing up to three hundred delegates from many tribes. What he found was twenty Indians from a few tribes and a program so informal that the fourth day was completely cancelled; for lunches someone would collect everyone's loose change and go to the store for bread, cheese, meat and coffee. Spencer offered prayers, accompanied their singing on the piano, and visited with each delegate and presented him with a copy of the Book of Mormon. When given the floor, he urged them to think beyond appeals to Washington for compensation for broken treaties. He saw education as the quickest and best route out of their wasteland. The delegates, however, kept on arguing about how to get redress of grievances.

On the first night, Elder Kimball received initiation into the Washoe tribe of northern Nevada. He mailed home his ceremonial feather. Camilla wrote back: "The feather arrived safely. Hope your being a chief doesn't affect your personality."

From Independence Elder Kimball left to tour the Eastern States Mission. From Syracuse, New York, he wrote to Camilla: "Yesterday as we got in the elevator to come down, two little midgets came down with us. I certainly got a lift when I, the scrubbiest of the scrubby, could look far down on grown men so much smaller than I. I frequently find men thinner, but seldom find them shorter."

He often joked about his small stature, but it bothered him. He would say that he was a Woolley — he sat tall but he stood short. When seated on the stand he looked as tall as any, but his short legs reached him only up to five feet six inches. Even at that he was six inches taller than his mother had been. He would say that his brothers had stunted his growth by making him carry the five-gallon cans of swill to slop the hogs.

One time he said, "I remember that once one of the Brethren, who's tall and handsome, said as we were considering a man to be the president of the stake, 'Well, he's a good man, but he's such a little runt.' " And Spencer was only half jesting when he added, "I've always held that against him a bit."

Autumn passed and with it Spencer's eighth year in the Quorum of the Twelve. It was Camilla's eighth year, too. Spencer passed long weeks on mission tours away from her, as she usually preferred to stay home out of the spotlight. On weekends all year around she rarely saw her apostle husband. Even the frantic Arizona years seemed good to Camilla beside these multiplying meetings, interviews, trips. Sometimes her husband seemed like a human engine, never relaxed, never casual.

But she never questioned Spencer's deep love for her. After thirty-three years of marriage he still glowed whenever he heard her complimented. In El Paso he accompanied her downtown and together they picked out a red hat, a red purse, and red shoes, to match Camilla's red suit. "She is very pretty," Spencer wrote in his journal, "and looks very well in red. She is a lovely lady." And, he concluded, "she adds so much to my peace and well being."

But sometimes the constant waiting for a preoccupied husband strained her patience. She needed reassurance. When Spencer traveled on assignment in Alberta, Camilla poured out to him in a letter her mixed feelings:

> .... Sometimes I almost feel in the press of your many responsibilities that I don't matter very much any more. Any one who thinks being the wife of one of the general authorities is a bed of roses should try it once, shouldn't they? Theoretically I realize and appreciate all the blessings and advantages but sometimes I selfishly feel it would be nice not to have to share my husband with a million others. I do love and appreciate you, dear, and admire your sterling qualities. I wouldn't have you be one whit less valiant in the pursuit of your duty . . . , but it is comforting to be reassured once in a while that you realize I am standing by. . . .

He bought her gifts for her birthday and Mother's Day and Christmas, though his impatience in shopping often produced presents which she took back. One time he bought her some expensive jewelry which she returned to the store. Recognizing the travail for him in shopping at all, she accepted the gesture for the deed.

This fall, 1951, they traveled together through the Central States Mission. Spencer relived the past. Wherever he went he saw places and met people that brought back memories. In Independence, Missouri, was the chapel he, as a new missionary, had helped prepare for dedication by President Joseph F. Smith in 1914. He had helped sod the lawns, lay the sidewalks, put down the seats, and wash the windows. In Jefferson City he reminisced that thirty-seven years before, on Thanksgiving morning, he and his companion had begun their first country tracting without purse or scrip, walking southeast into the wilds of Missouri. In Richmond he visited the graveyard where Oliver Cowdery, David Whitmer and others lay. At Liberty he walked through the old jail, now in disreputable condition, where Joseph Smith and other early Saints had been imprisoned for months awaiting trial.

The countryside blazed with reds, yellows, greens and browns as Spencer and Camilla went south from St. Louis through the flamboyant forests. Near Van Buren, Arkansas, they visited the monument marking the site where Parley P. Pratt had been assassinated in 1857.

In the Oklahoma backwoods, in Cherokee country, Elder Kimball remembered his father's long, faithful missionary service, in which he

*Near Menard, Oklahoma, by cabin believed to have been built by
Andrew Kimball in the Indian Territory Mission*

had trekked through these hills and roadless areas, wading swamps on
foot or on horseback, preaching, from 1885 to 1897. In Fort Gibson he
inquired about the Hendricks home, where Andrew had stayed. In the
scrubby town hall a man dribbling tobacco juice said, between spits in
the general direction of a bucket in the corner, that a man down the
street might know. That man, shabby, unshaven, and tobacco-stained,
referred him on to an old woman who had been postmistress in 1897.
The old lady remembered the missionaries and directed Spencer to the
Hendricks place.

About eight miles away they found the house they were looking
for, back through the fields about a half mile from the road. Near the
house was a little cemetery, now overgrown, containing the graves of
the Hendrickses, who had died in 1903 and 1911. They had been most
kind to Andrew. Spencer gave the present owner money to clean the
plot, repair the fence, and set up again the one tumbled monument. A
small building two hundred yards from the home, 12 by 15 feet, built of
logs on a rock foundation, fitted the description of a house built by
Andrew and his companion in 1885. The first mission home in the

Indian Territory, its dirt floor and unchinked logs and newer tin roof now sheltered the walnut crop.

But the here and now pressed loudly for attention. A boil inside Spencer's right nostril swelled so painfully that he continued the mission tour only from sheer will. At times the pain grew almost unbearable. He got through his talk at one meeting, he believed, only due to the prayers of the people there.

The mission president took him to visit a man and wife who were in apostasy. Elder Kimball pleaded with them not to throw away their exaltation. He bore his testimony with all his heart. But they remained "cold and hard. They seemed immovable."

Back in Salt Lake City, Elder Kimball wrote individual letters to the families of the dozens of missionaries he had met. The letters were necessarily similar, but each included a personal touch. This was his regular practice. The sheer volume of his correspondence was staggering. He wrote long letters of encouragement — to a sister who was sick, to a nephew in the military service, to a niece who had been abandoned by her husband, and to thousands of others. One Christmas a group of fifty Indian children each sent him a letter. He responded with fifty long, individual letters of thanks and of admonition for the children to prepare for their future.

By letter and in person he concerned himself with those who needed help. A boy whose father was apostate, and whose deaf mother was divorced and struggling to support four children with Church help, expressed his bitterness at life's hardships. Elder Kimball wrote him a four-thousand-word letter, pleading with him to get over his bitterness. "I have gone through many of the experiences which you have suffered," he wrote the boy, and he described the poverty of his own youth. He urged the boy to behave "brilliantly and gloriously" and to make his Church and mother proud. To an inactive member whose father was excommunicated and whose other family members were straying, he wrote at length charging him to save them all through his leadership. "Perhaps you were born for that very purpose," he encouraged him, "to be the sealing, welding factor in bringing this family together."

Camilla once received a bouquet of roses with an anonymous note: "Yesterday afternoon while ... waiting for the pedestrian light to change I heard a voice beside me say, 'Let me carry that box across the street for you.' Turning to that voice I saw your husband. His offer was appreciated and accepted because I am on crutches and the box was awkward to carry. He also insisted on carrying the box to my car. . . . Since he is the type of man who would appreciate a gift to you more than to himself, it pleases me to send you these roses in gratitude for you and your husband's lives of service. . . ."

In April 1952, after a general conference priesthood meeting at the Tabernacle, Elder Kimball offered his hand to a tall young man near him in the crowd. The man shook hands, then asked who he was.

"I am Brother Kimball."

"Which Kimball?"

"Spencer W. Kimball."

"Oh! Well, I am the great LeBaron."

The apostle's mind shot back to his confrontation with the LeBaron boys in their mother's home in Mesa, and he stiffened. He looked up at the large apostate looming over him and said sharply: "You were not invited to this meeting. In fact, you were invited *not* to come. You hold no priesthood. Leave the Tabernacle. Don't ever come to such a meeting again. If you can repent and get back in the Church, you had better do it, while there is still time." Spencer Kimball's seemingly infinite patience had boiled over.

LeBaron shrugged and said, "It's your building," then left.

In that same month Elder Kimball left on a four-stake conference trip north to Canada. After a conference session he wrote back to Camilla that a bishop at Lethbridge complained, "He talks like Joseph Fielding Smith and I don't like it." In his letter Spencer talked of "itching ears" that prefer to hear easy things rather than true things, and wrote that he was proud to be thought "a sitter at the feet of President Joseph Fielding Smith." But, the letter went on in a lighter vein, it seemed he had indeed nearly killed one woman in the Canadian congregation with his severe preaching. She had blacked out as he was speaking, and a doctor had rushed in with great commotion. "It must have been a stiff!!!!! sermon!!!"

He wrote in his letter that he had met there two of Spencer LeVan's former missionary companions, both of them now bishops' counselors. "How proud their fathers must be of their spiritual progress!" Already Dean of Law at the University of Utah, father of three girls and one boy, Spencer LeVan was an unusually talented and hard-working man, much in his father's mold in that respect. He was already well launched on a successful professional career.

That fall, 1952, Elder Kimball was sent with Elder Bruce R. McConkie of the First Council of the Seventy on a five-week tour of Central America. They were assigned to contact the various governments about starting missionary work there. They drove by car through the seven tiny Spanish-speaking nations, sometimes along dirt highways up sharp canyons, vapor seeping out of the hothouse jungle on either side, past fabulous vistas of high waterfalls and lush orchids and banana trees. In Honduras the government representative welcomed missionaries, he said. In fact he added with a smile that if the Church brought polygamy back he too would be baptized. In El Salvador the Minister of Interior claimed that his country was tolerant of all religions. So it went in all the countries.

Satisfied, the two General Authorities established the Central American Mission, with headquarters in Guatemala City. At a testimony meeting, during the opening hymn a line formed of Church members anxious to bear testimony. After twelve had spoken it was announced that only those already in the waiting line could be heard from. But Elder Kimball noticed that every time he glanced at the line it was longer. The leaders had no heart to turn the people away, so eager were they to testify. Elder Kimball watched one man get into line, then wave his wife over. When it came her turn to speak, she trembled like a leaf and wept through her testimony. After five hours of testimonies in Spanish the meeting ended.

The two General Authorities spent several more days working with the new leaders in Guatemala, then drove back up through Mexico visiting the Saints. Every spare minute in the car Elder Kimball studied his Spanish, anxious to be more effective in his work. He was certain the Lord was helping him learn it. They arrived at Monte Corona in a rainstorm. As they walked into the chapel the singers stood and burst into "We Thank Thee, O God, for a Prophet." A woman in braids and a long dress rushed up to embrace the apostle, then grasped his right hand and placed it on her baby's head, then on her two-year-old's head. These were "dear, sweet people!!" to Spencer, who was touched to tears.

At Mexico City Elders Kimball and McConkie took off their suit coats in the heat while they relaxed on the chapel lawn. When it came time for the meeting inside, they playfully picked up the wrong coats

With Indian family in Mexico

*Spencer W. Kimball and Bruce R. McConkie
exchanging coats, 1952*

and pulled them on. Elder Kimball's coat reached just halfway down the taller man's forearm. Elder McConkie's swallowed the shorter man's hands. All the missionaries around raced for their cameras. Later at Oaxaca the two authorities were shown a round column. There was a legend that if a man reached his arms around the column, the number of finger widths still left between his hands was the number of years he had left to live. Elder Kimball discovered he had sixteen left. But Elder McConkie, with his huge arm-span, encircled the column and overlapped a little. Elder Kimball told him that meant he was already dead and didn't know it.

The visiting apostle met with the high council in Mexico City:

> When we were through, Brother _____ arose and said perhaps he was not worthy of membership in the Council because he was not paying his tithing. He wept as he told that his business was slipping from him and his expenses high and that he was losing out and having a very hard time. Another brother said that he was being persecuted at his employment because of his Church work and that his wages were small. Another Brother rose and said perhaps he should be released also as he could not pay a full tithing since he worked as a watchman at the Museum, his wages were very little (probably not over $30 or $40 a month), and he had six children and a brother that was in distress whom he had helped. He could not pay.
>
> My heart bled for them. I told them that it would be much easier if I could tell them to forget the law of tithing, but since it was not my law, I had no right to waive it, also that since great blessings were predicated upon faithful living of the law, certainly it was these good folks that needed the blessings and I KNEW THAT IF THEY WOULD TRUST IN THE LORD AND RENDER TO HIM THEIR TITHING THAT HE WOULD BLESS THEM. They must make the first gesture. They should never use a penny of the Lord's money no matter how much the apparent need.
>
> There was some weeping. I told them stories of sacrifice — of Grandfather Edwin D. Woolley — of Abraham. I told them that the blessings did not come till their faith had been tried and until they had proved faithful. It was a warm farewell between us and them.

The years passed. Spencer still suffered from heart pains and rawness in his throat. He still was on the road to stake conferences almost every weekend of the year. The interviews piled up. "Broken families, distressed lives, frustrated lives, sinful lives." He spent seven hours with one married couple, fighting to keep them together, then dragged home almost four hours late for dinner, exhausted. A young father stopped in his office and told how he had been awakened by his four children climbing over his bed, asking, "Where's Mommy?" She had slipped off in the night, abandoning her marriage. A woman came in to complain that her husband, to whom she had been sealed, was spending his vacation in another city with a girlfriend. Another woman's husband was in the penitentiary.

Every night Spencer went home to a happy, unselfish marriage. Some nights it seemed that his was the only good marriage left; there were so many troubled people.

A middle-aged couple came by his house with their fifteen-year-old daughter. She was pregnant. Elder Kimball urged them to have her marry the boy. Another night he invited his own married children to dinner, but halfway through the meal he left in response to a frantic phone call from a family about to split apart. When he returned near midnight his own family had gone home.

He urged couples to cement their marriages with continual expressions of love, yet he knew that some, now obviously in love, would end their marriages in bitter divorce. On a mission tour he told one congregation, "When they fail to take care of their marriage they'll come to the point of divorce and sit in my office and say they don't love one another, that they never did." He went on heatedly, striking the podium, "That's a damned lie!" Later he said to the mission president, sheepishly, "I said something today that I haven't said in a very long time."

He had much satisfaction in meeting with competent, faithful stake leaders on the weekends. From them he could draw strength. When he ordained a bishop in Reno, for example, a friendship began. Spencer would occasionally mail a postcard: "I looked down as my airplane passed over Reno today but didn't see you out and around. . . ." or "Thought you might have been at the depot as my train went through at five this morning. . . ."

Yet occasionally even the leaders presented problems. In one stake Elder Kimball called the second counselor to be the new stake president. The first counselor, asked to continue in his position, refused, bitter at having been passed over for president. When the Saturday night meetings ended, Elder Kimball drove to his house. Both the man and his wife complained that he had been treated badly. The apostle stayed on, explaining that there was no succession in stake offices, that a president was selected only as the Church authority felt impressed by the Lord. He pleaded with them not to destroy themselves by turning down the call. Finally the man accepted the position. By next morning in stake conference the darkness had passed. The counselor's wife hugged Elder Kimball and thanked him and rethanked him that he had not let them hurt themselves.

In another stake Elder Kimball called as stake president someone other than the obvious choice. The apostle made occasion to ask the man not chosen to drive him somewhere in the city and, as they drove, asked him whether he was disappointed. The man shed a few tears and felt better. He expressed appreciation at the opportunity to talk about his feelings and to receive reassurance.

Spencer wrestled over an assignment to his home stake in Salt Lake City. He remembered a testimony meeting with few members speaking and a sacrament meeting in which secular songs replaced hymns. In his journal he wondered, "What is the matter with our people? Are they getting too sophisticated and rational? Are they losing their enthusiasm?" He wanted to avoid offending his own neighbors in their stake conference, but after earnest prayer he decided to simply confront them with their worldliness and lack of spirit. In his talk he told them to stop addressing one another as Doctor, Colonel, Judge; in the Church everyone was Elder or Brother or Sister. He told them to support one another. By statistics their stake looked good, he conceded, but they needed to enter into the spirit of the Lord's work more. To his surprise, the stake returned in record numbers to the afternoon session for another scorching and poured scores of thank-you's in afterwards for the visiting authority's directness and practicality.

By 1953 Elder Kimball had spent over nine years in the Quorum. In that time seven apostles had died and one had been excommunicated. Conscious that he, too, might die at any time, he described a typical day for "those who might someday be kind enough to read" his journal after his death. Perhaps his grandchildren and great-grandchildren would be interested, he thought.

January 26, 1953, a Monday. He spent three hours in his study at home dictating letters into his dictaphone. Then he drove to his office, closed his door, knelt, and prayed for guidance through that day's problems. The problems began at once. The phone rang and the people began to arrive in the foyer asking for interviews. First was a returned missionary who wanted a recommend for temple work, but masturbated. "This habit has fastened itself upon him like an octopus. He earnestly desired to do right. I talked to him long and earnestly and believe I built up his determination and strength and gave him a blessing and sent him away happy. He will keep in touch with me until he has gained total mastery."

Next came Clark, another returned missionary. Clark had started smoking, met Mary, an unmarried girl with three babies, moved in with her, married her, then contracted gonorrhea. Scared, Clark pawned his watch and clothes for cash and deserted her. For a long while he fled from one city to the next, hating himself, trying to escape his past, a cheap tramp. Just weeks before, he had finally arrived back in Salt Lake, ragged and filthy, his fingers yellow, his clothes saturated with tobacco smoke. He made up with Mary. An old missionary companion directed him to Elder Kimball's office. That had been two weeks ago. At that meeting Clark had paced, "with his eyes to the floor, his face twitching, and agony written over his face," Spencer remembered. "I had him sit and assured him I was his friend, that I had time to visit with him and disposition to help him. He paced the floor, he chided himself, he cursed himself. He said he had offered himself to the asylum." Elder Kimball calmed him, then handed him fifteen dollars to tide him over and promised to help find him work. He flushed but reluctantly accepted the money. On his latest visit Clark had come to give a progress report.

After Clark there were two interviews with men who wanted blessings, a third with a *Church News* writer who needed information, another with a bishopric to be set apart in their callings, and one with a young woman from Idaho who was being pressed by a nonmember boy to marry him. She went away determined to follow the apostle's advice and either convert her boyfriend or find another.

Next came a middle-aged woman crazed with fear over a non-malignant growth the doctors had removed. Spencer told her of his throat and the miraculous healing of what he was sure had been cancer. He urged the woman not to let fear unnerve her, but to "settle down, accept the doctor's diagnosis and enjoy peace for herself and her family." He was gratified, after giving her a blessing, to see her wrinkles vanish.

Next a man asked Elder Kimball to come to the hospital to administer to a woman who thought she had mouth cancer and to her husband who faced brain surgery in the morning. The apostle stopped at the hospital on his way home.

At home, after "a simple dinner," he opened his stack of letters, among them one asking him to marry a young couple; one from Duchesne Stake reporting the attendance of Indian children at state schools; one from a bishop reporting his work with a young girl "about whom we had written him and asked him to look after"; one with a check for his Safford farm's cotton profits. There was a letter from a man who had committed adultery and confessed to Elder Kimball in his office. He reported that he had followed the apostle's suggestion to confess to his wife and together meet the other couple and "make adjustments." A letter came from the other couple involved in the adultery case. There was a letter with genealogy data from a cousin in Portland. A boy whom the apostle a week back had turned down for a missionary recommend, wrote that he had resisted petting with his girl, and was determined to justify the apostle's confidence in him. And a young girl wrote him thanks for his counsel the week before, continuing: "I couldn't have gone to a kinder person than you when I was in trouble. I know with your blessing and your prayers I will overcome my weaknesses. Pray for me, please. It seems easier to have some help. I hope there are few in this world like me. I often wondered why the Lord didn't destroy me for all the things I've done."

As his tenth year in the Quorum went by, Elder Kimball often wondered how to evaluate his work. In 1951 he had been introduced in the Port Arthur, Ontario, chapel to an old lady from Norway. Someone explained to her in Norwegian that this man was an apostle of Jesus. The old woman asked twice to be sure, then pulled him down to kiss his cheek. Others, with damp eyes, lined up to shake an apostle's hand. By contrast, in St. Paul the same week he met by appointment Governor Youngdahl of Minnesota. The governor, cold and rude, greeted him formally and found quick opportunity to dismiss him with, "I am glad you called." Spencer had not even been invited to sit. Someday, he told himself, the governor would beg for such an interview with the Lord's servants.

In his journal, for himself, he summarized his work with caution and hope: "My work is glorious. My accomplishments are few and small. I love my work and am trying mightily. Surely none of the brethren try harder or work harder. I am sure they accomplish more and are more powerful and more influential. I am enjoying my work and hope and pray that my puny efforts may count."

He wondered sometimes. Hundreds of people came to him for help. Not even a tithe ever wrote back thanks. In Ogden he interrupted a trip for two and a half hours to work desperately to patch a shattered marriage. As he finally boarded the train he wondered if the couple now would hold together for eternity, for a year, for a week.

In his journal on July 8, 1953, Spencer noted the tenth anniversary of his call. "I HAVE HAD TEN GLORIOUS YEARS. I HAVE BEEN HONORED BEYOND MY DESERTS." He had told the Quorum that if a business offered him a quarter-million dollars a year to work for them instead of the Church, he would answer, "Don't bother me with it." When he met an old school friend who was making enough money in his dental practice to dress his wife in mink and work only four days a week, Spencer congratulated him, then added pointedly, "Unlike most men, you now have three days a week free to serve humanity through the Church." Replied the friend, "I thought you would say that."

At a Thursday temple meeting in February 1955, President McKay "made an announcement which was a bit startling but very pleasing to me."

Rather than maintain a General Authority in Europe to preside over the ten missions there, periodically a General Authority would be assigned to tour the missions. For the first of these visits President McKay recommended Elder Kimball, to leave immediately after April Conference and finish in time for the dedication of the Swiss Temple in September.

Delighted at his first major overseas assignment, Elder Kimball plunged into preparations. He mailed instructions to the missions and asked for a proposed schedule of meetings for him. When the schedules came he returned them with the request to "double the number of meetings."

In April, he and Camilla boarded the train, being seen off at the depot by a crowd of well-wishers. From New York they sailed on the *Queen Mary* to England, then flew to Frankfurt. They were struck by the changes which had taken place since their trip through a tense, explosive Europe eighteen years before. The marks of a devastating

President Kenneth Dyer (West German Mission), Camilla Kimball, Spencer W. Kimball, Sister Dyer, President William Perschon (Swiss-German Mission), Sister Perschon at Berchtesgaden, Germany, 1955

With interpreter, Odense, Denmark, 1955

Catnap during European mission tour, 1955

war faced them at every turn. Block after block of rubble, ten years after the war's end, marred Frankfurt, Munich, Nurnberg and other cities. In Rotterdam a grotesque statue of a writhing figure with a gaping hole in his chest symbolized the city's devastation by German bombs. Spencer and Camilla's situation had changed, too. Earlier they had been a young couple on holiday, giddy with high spirits. Now they were sixty and tied to a grueling schedule of meetings and interviews with members and missionaries.

From Germany they flew to Norway. Church activity there had flagged. Proselyting brought in few new members, while the long-standing members only waited for the time when they would emigrate to "Zion" in Salt Lake City. Elder Kimball tried hard to change their minds. He spoke of the new temple just finished in Bern. That meant some permanence. He urged them to build up Zion in their own cities.

The mission president drove the two visitors by car from branch to branch through Norway. Elder Kimball held conference sessions for members, for priesthood leaders, and for missionaries; inspected the chapels; evaluated record-keeping practices; met with members who needed counsel; gave blessings to the sick or troubled; interviewed each missionary; and contacted Norwegian officials and newspapers to gain favorable attention for the Church.

His heart pains began again. He told no one, determined not to cut back on his schedule but to push a little less hard.

From Narvik, well above the Arctic Circle, where it remained bright all night, Spencer and Camilla took the train into northernmost Sweden and began to travel south, visiting almost every branch in the country. In two weeks the visiting apostle held forty meetings and dedicated eight chapels. He often worked eighteen-hour days, noting in his journal his increasing weariness.

The mission visits continued through Finland, Denmark, England, Scotland, Ireland, Wales, the Netherlands, France, Austria, Germany. Camilla wrote home: "I don't know how Dad stands the strain and holds up under the burdens that are placed on his shoulders. He is doing a wonderful work with both missionaries and Saints. I stand amazed at his power and know the Lord is blessing him far beyond his natural strength."

In the Netherlands he left the mission home before six o'clock one morning to stroll across the sand dunes bordering the North Sea and pray. An hour and a half later the missionaries saw him come back with a young man on a bicycle. Although the boy spoke halting English and Elder Kimball knew no Dutch, the apostle had made a friend. As he gave him a pamphlet of the Joseph Smith story, Elder Kimball said, "That is the man I told you about on the beach."

In Bristol, England, a missionary had told Elder Kimball that he was eager to meet Sister Kimball so he would know what kind of girl to marry when the time came. Spencer repeated that remark to another group and added, "I have brought Sister Kimball with me so you will have something to shoot at." He could tease her, but in his journal he said about Camilla's presence: "How glad I was to have her . . . by my side! She is so strong and splendid! How I love her!"

In the French Mission a misunderstanding had resulted in no time being scheduled for missionary interviews or testimony or instruction meetings. To provide the necessary time, Elder Kimball scheduled interviews and meetings starting at 7:00 A.M. and running until after midnight, "and was I weary!"

The tour moved into the Swiss-Austrian Mission. In Salzburg they looked up John Schmelz, seventy, who had been their guide in Vienna eighteen years before and an occasional correspondent ever since. They drove him to all their meetings. At the end he shook Spencer's hand long and warmly: "What can I do to help? Could I be baptized?" Elder Kimball urged him to study with the missionaries.

A tour of the German Mission began. As elsewhere, the apostle told the mission president that as long as the missionaries ran the branches, local members would not develop leadership. He jotted notes: "_____ , handsome blond Austrian. Wife was in operetta. Has possibilities. Watch him for leadership." "_____ , convert of two years . . . , homeland is in Jugoslavia. . . . We may have need of him!" Before leaving, he made to the mission presidency a thirteen-page single-spaced report consisting of evaluations and suggestions for change and emphasis. He spoke again and again in conferences of the approaching temple dedication, carefully explaining to the members the standards that would be expected of those who would make temple covenants.

At Dachau, near Munich, Spencer and Camilla took time to see the World War II gassing rooms, the crematoriums, the mounds in which the ashes of untold thousands of victims had been interred, the range for execution by shooting, a drainage channel for the human blood, the slab where the gallows had stood. "We walked as living dead," Spencer wrote. In his journal he expressed his feelings:

> The silenced cries of tortured dead kept
>   ringing in our ears.
> We fancied haunting sighs, and moans kept
>   whisp'ring through the tears.
> Oh, Father, please this scene erase,
>   Thou Holy One so kind.
> Let us return to pleasant thoughts;
>   remove this from our mind.

As they drove on their way Spencer thought, "I should not like to live in a town by the name of Dachau."

The mission president drove the Kimballs by car through the Russian-occupied zone into Berlin. After the devastation he had seen elsewhere, it was hard for Spencer to conceive that there could be worse, yet Berlin was worse. Early in the morning he walked the city alone, in reverie. He strung together fragmented images of the shattered city.

> Rusty fences
> Naked walls
> Jagged chimneys piercing the sky
> Little trees growing from basements and
> vegetation from the walls
> Pockmarked trees, gaping wounds healed over
> Empty windows
> Green ivy trying to hide the naked walls
> An iron bedstead hanging from a chimney
> Plumbing pipes hanging into space like dragon
> claws
> Ghosts of yesterday
> Deformed giants slumped in misery and shame

In the Russian zone fear continued. A district Sunday School superintendent had simply disappeared three months earlier; the counselor in the mission presidency had received a notice to appear before the authorities the next day — for what he had no idea. When the door opened during a missionary meeting, all turned in obvious anxiety to see who entered. They had a sense of being watched. As Spencer's car stopped at the train station for the trip back to West

Germany, a young soldier he had never seen before stepped up to him
and addressed him by name: "Mr. Kimball, let me see your permits."

Back in West Germany again, weary from the killing pace yet
enjoying the work, Spencer tried to evaluate his efforts:

> Arose very early, about 5 a.m. It looks like a busy day ahead of
> us with meetings and travel from 7 to midnight. I am somewhat
> depressed and wonder if my work is going well. I fear I am not
> doing so well. But oh how I have tried. I believe no one ever tried
> harder to do a job well. I have felt some resistance on the part of the
> missionaries. Their work is not up to par . . . ; my pressures seem to
> antagonize sometimes, and yet sometimes they have been accepted
> with such good grace.

The next day he wrote again:

> I was much upset, very low and feeling bad. I had difficulty in
> stirring myself to a satisfactory effort not to disappoint the people
> who came. I was so weary and nervous and I wondered if I was
> about to break. Went to bed as soon as the meetings were over and
> felt a little better in the morning.

A German approached Elder Kimball after a meeting and said
things Spencer did not understand. He assumed it was a greeting and
responded: "Gut. Gut. Das ist gut." A missionary then told him that the
man had been saying his wife had died, and that he himself had been ill
and beset by poverty.

In the West German Mission, the last of the ten to be visited,
because of the press of time the Kimballs hardly averaged two meals a
day. Sometimes they ate only once a day. With only a week of the tour
left, Spencer again began to feel heart pains.

About half of the thirty-six thousand Church members in Europe
had heard him speak. He had met a thousand full-time missionaries
and from them "heard a thousand testimonies, sweet, resonant, glorious testimonies." At one meeting, though, a lady missionary stood and
told the group: "I can't go along with you. I do not have a testimony."
In his journal Elder Kimball wrote with unconcealed disapproval that
"in conclusion of her rambling evasive talk which ended without a
prayer or testimony or in the name of our Lord she said if anyone could
help her she would be glad so I attempted it for a half hour talking
about 'testimony.' I did it most kindly. She seemed to appreciate it and
said, 'I'll try.' "

On September 11 Spencer and Camilla returned to Switzerland to participate in the dedication of the first Mormon temple outside of North America and Hawaii. Assigned to be one of the speakers, Elder Kimball spent the noon hour alone in the temple, preparing his heart and mind for his part. "President McKay seemed pleased," he said of his speech. "I hope the Lord was also." During the several days of dedication services he greeted again Saints and missionaries he had visited over the past few months. The people he saw seemed to him no longer Norwegians or Germans or French, but simply Latter-day Saints. "The confusion of Babel is being overcome," he wrote. Endowment sessions ran through the night. In order to help the pressed temple president, Elder Kimball stayed up all night, after having risen at 3:30 A.M. the previous day. After a few hours' sleep he traveled to Paris, where the Tabernacle Choir, which had sung at the dedication and on a tour of Europe, gave its last concert.

The next day he wrote, "Today my mission is ended and my cold came." After all the abuse his body had stood since April, with no illness, "I cannot complain at a bad cold today."

Despite feeling miserable he still had energy for enough sightseeing to do any tourist credit — monuments and museums in Paris, the opera, a river trip, hiking the streets of Montmartre. He had trouble in unwinding. Homebound on the *Queen Elizabeth* he slept fitfully, writing and rewriting his impressions of the past few months, preparing the general conference address to be given a few days later as a report to the Church on the faithfulness and sacrifice of the members and missionaries in the European missions.

On the second day of conference, Spencer gave his address. He arrived at the Tabernacle with what he felt was too much undigested data, "a handful of papers." Behind the pulpit his enthusiasm carried him, breathless, five minutes over his allotted time, describing the trials and faithfulness of the Latter-day Saints in Europe. He recorded the immediate approval that followed his talk:

> I felt two great arms from the rear. They enveloped me and closed in front, and there was a tight embrace and it seemed to me his head was pressed against mine. I looked up to find the Prophet of the Lord embracing me and saying, "That was a masterpiece." What ecstasy! In my silly sensitiveness I had felt that my intense work of the past months was not known nor appreciated — that it was more or less passed over or ignored — that it had sunk almost

into oblivion under the glare of the more spectacular choir tour and the temple dedication. I whispered to him, "Thank you President McKay. I shall never forget that." And later wrote to him: "If I could live to merit the smiles of my Lord so that sometime in the far future He might shake my hand or embrace me in His arms, then and then only would I ever be lifted up to greater ecstasy than I was on Saturday afternoon when I felt your strong arms around me and heard your word of approval."

Many people spoke appreciatively of my talk; many talked of my diary page which they thought was poetic. A few suggested that another Carl Sandburg had arisen. I was so grateful for all the kind thoughts expressed, but I realized that the Lord was kind to me and gave me the expression.

Another year passed, much the same as the twelve before. Into his complex schedule of stake conference assignments, mission tours, Quorum report meetings, marriage ceremonies, funeral sermons, and interviews, Elder Kimball fitted committee meetings. Over one four-year span he served all or part of the time on more than a dozen committees — the Statistics Committee, the Budget Committee, the Expenditure Committee, the Student Loan Committee, the Temple Committee, the Missionary Committee and two subcommittees on stake missionary work and on mission methods, the Indian Relations Committee, the Publications Committee, the Music Committee, and committees to revise the Priesthood handbook, to evaluate an insurance plan, to keep track of single girls working in cities, and to deal with problems of delinquent youth. As the Church grew larger the problems of administration occupied even more time.

Spencer was sixty-one years old. As he put on his tuxedo one evening for a formal reception he found "it has been shrinking a bit since I wore it years ago." He knew he ought to lose ten pounds. But there were inner changes, too. He had less tolerance for the ways in which the world found pleasure. There were fewer movies and plays he could sit through and enjoy. A stage presentation in San Francisco disappointed him and Camilla. "It was crude and vulgar," and its irreverence made him uncomfortable.

Even more than before he struggled desperately to help Church members in transgression. He could not say no to their pleas for his help. Often spouses had despaired, exasperated bishops had given up, and sometimes the individuals themselves had little hope, but Elder Kimball had a gift for believing in the possibility of repentance, in the miracle of change.

One woman, excommunicated for adultery, he shepherded back through repentance and rebaptism. He was sure the change in her was genuine. But when her request for restoration of temple blessings came up in a temple meeting he could not attend, the request was turned down. Elder Kimball wrote, "I screwed up my courage and presented to the Brethren her request a second time at the next Thursday meeting." He offered additional information, showing extenuating circumstances. "They agreed to permit her restoration. I was very grateful."

In June 1956 Elder Kimball received a call from a woman in California that her husband was at a seedy Salt Lake hotel and needed help. He had his secretary call the man and make an appointment for that afternoon. When the man did not arrive, Elder Kimball waited for an hour and then went to the hotel.

The man came to the door of his room near naked and staggering. He was overwhelmed and much abashed to see his visitor, who had been a missionary in St. Louis when the man was just a boy. Elder Kimball asked where his liquor was. The man replied, "I haven't got any," but he finally pointed out a bottle under the mattress and let Elder Kimball pour the liquor into the toilet. He babbled his appreciation about Elder Kimball's saving his soul and wept over his sister's death. The visitor got him into a cold bath and plied him with tomato juice.

When the man had sobered somewhat, the apostle walked him down to Western Union to cash a twenty-dollar money order from his wife, who had borrowed on her car to raise the funds. The man asked the girls in Western Union whether they were Mormons and, as he staggered out, to their embarrassment told them loudly who his friend was.

Elder Kimball supported his wambling companion to Alcoholics Anonymous, where he arranged for help, and the two men staggered back to the hotel to pack the man's bags. But while the apostle was checking him out he disappeared. Up and down Elder Kimball looked, in the alleys and the corners, but could not find the man; so he took the bags to AA and then started searching again. He was suffering from a bad back and every step was torture, but he hurried because he had a train to catch. He tried every pool hall, tavern, cafe, alley, movie house in the area, to no avail. Finally he had to leave.

When he returned from California, where he attended a solemn assembly at the new Los Angeles Temple, he went to AA and found his friend, clean and looking like a new man. Two years later, though, the man turned up again in the apostle's office, destitute. Elder Kimball found him a job and sent him out with some cash, but the man disappeared again without ever showing up for work. Two years after that there came a call from the wife telling where her husband was, and the apostle went to a flophouse hotel to find him stuporous with drink. Elder Kimball arranged with a doctor to try to help the man. A few days later he drove to the doctor's home to visit the man ("one of my problem boys") and found him, for the moment, much improved. But over the years the collect calls from faraway cities, begging a loan "for the last time," kept coming. Elder Kimball never gave up.

Elder Kimball refused to indulge himself in discouragement. In his Indian work, although the process was slow and somewhat unsteady, he stubbornly kept at it. In one meeting of the Quorum he "found it necessary to defend vigorously the Lamanites" against calls for reduction in the missionary effort among them. In admiration President Clark wrote him in a note: " . . . you are able to shut your eyes against many of the disadvantages and problems which are incident thereto, and which are too much before the eyes of many of the rest of us."

In April 1956 he drove south with Elder Petersen onto the Navajo reservation in Arizona. This time the two apostles took a petition that Church buildings be allowed on the reservation and they sought out four tribal councilmen they hoped would sign it. They followed almost impassable roads up and down gullies and and dry washes across a desert of sagebrush and sand. They had to get out and push the car free from drifted sand a half-dozen times before they finally found the hogan of the first councilman. He was not home. But after following other nearly impossible trails they found him. He refused to sign their petition until others had agreed. Disappointed, they looked for the district chairman, in their quest getting stuck in deep sand again. They finally located him and he willingly signed the petition. Efforts to find another councilman failed, so after a full day of driving over four hundred miles of the most primitive roads, they had only one signature of the four they had hoped for. The next day, after much difficult driving, they finally made contact with another man, who signed the petition. The council chairman advised them on how to get approval for the building sites.

Some months later another member of the Council of the Twelve, after a quick tour of the Southwest Indian Mission, reported to the Quorum that he had seen no headway being made in the mission and went on in pessimistic terms critical of the Indians. Furious inside, Elder Kimball complained in his journal that, while he did not question the honesty of that view, he believed it did not at all take into account the difficult circumstances under which the mission operated. In general conference he spoke again on the Church Indian program. It needed constant reinforcement.

He visited Indians in Montana and North Dakota. The groups there felt neglected. Where there had once been some twelve hundred Indian members, numbers had dwindled with the passing of the first wave of enthusiasm among the non-Indian members for the often-difficult Indian missionary work. Elder Kimball shored up the sagging effort.

At Brigham Young University he met with the thirty-three Indian students there, the Tribe of Many Feathers. Only a few years before, the Church had struggled to keep even one or two Indian students at the university from dropping out. He saw reason to hope, and even when others seemed discouraged he stubbornly continued to lavish his energy and time on the Indian work. It was a gift he had, to believe in the possibility of change in people.

In June Elder Kimball and Camilla, Harold B. Lee, and mission leaders drove from El Paso to Monterey and then, after seventeen hours of breakneck travel over incredible mountain roads, finally reached Mexico City. The trip was made for the purpose of dividing the flourishing mission. At Ermita twelve hundred people attended a meeting. From the original Mexican Mission the Spanish-American Mission had been split off in 1936, then the Central American Mission in 1952, and now in 1956 the Northern Mexican Mission was created. In ten years the population had grown from thirty-four hundred members to more than nine thousand.

With the division made, the two apostles separated, Elder Lee travelling through the Mexican Mission and Elder Kimball through the new northern mission. In some communities the Saints in the new mission seemed prosperous, but often they lived at starvation level. Some suffered terribly from lack of rainfall; in other places the water stood in muddy streets. The heat was almost unendurable.

Elder Kimball undertook to make arrangements for a crippled girl to get aid from the Primary Children's Hospital in Salt Lake City. In one branch there was only one sister who could read, and when she did not attend Relief Society there was no one to read the lesson to them. In another little branch Elder Kimball played the piano, since no one else could. After the meeting the usual potluck dinner was spread out. The apostle ate food he could not enjoy, but he would not refuse. As they finished the dinner the branch president notified them that an old sister, eighty-two, had prepared a dinner for them, too. Rather than offend her the Kimballs left and ate a second meal of beans and mole in a dirt-floor shack swarming with flies.

In December, Camilla drove with Spencer to the St. Joseph Stake Conference in Thatcher. They fought snow all through Utah and up over the Kaibab forest in northern Arizona. Past Jacob Lake, they drove cautiously through three or four inches of new snow. As the road wound down it became icier. They came around a turn to find that a truck was stuck in the road. Their car began to skid and struck the left front of the truck and rebounded down a steep hillside. Spencer had presence of mind to guide the car straight down, so it would not roll. They bounced down over rocks, caroming off a tree, landing fifty feet down in the bottom of a ravine. Spencer, though shaken, was unhurt. But Camilla had been thrown forward hard by the impact with the truck and lay on the floor writhing in pain. Spencer thought she was screaming for fear and said, "Well, Mama, I guess we are all right," and she answered, "No, I am dying."

Spencer heaved open the caved-in door on his side and got around to wrench open her door. He dared not move her for fear her back was broken. With a tire iron he tried to bend the crushed fender away from the tire, but could not. The truck driver came to help and with bars and jacks they freed the tire. A passerby stopped and said in frightened voice: "Brother Kimball, I am a member of the Church. Should we administer to her?" As they prepared to do so, Spencer in the car and the other man reaching through the window, the man pulled back and said: "Maybe I shouldn't. I don't keep the Word of Wisdom." Spencer urged him to assist and they blessed Camilla. Another passerby and a highway truck helped them to get the car along a wood road and onto the highway again, pulling them through a snowbank with a chain.

With Camilla in intense pain, the car frame bent, the tire cut, and the emergency brake locked on they struggled an endless thirty-five miles to Kanab, stopping often to check the damaged tire rubbing on the fender. Finally the brake released itself and the crippled car made it to the hospital about four hours after the crash.

At the hospital they treated her for broken ribs, a punctured lung, and cuts and bruises. Spencer stayed with her all day and then, at her insistence, caught a bus to Arizona at 2:00 A.M. to fulfill his assignment. He had not been hurt, but he was jittery and worried.

When he had completed his conference he returned to Kanab and found Camilla miserable. Their son-in-law, Grant Mack, took her back to Salt Lake City in a bed made in the back of his station wagon and delivered her to the larger hospital there.

Twelve days after the accident Spencer brought Camilla home from the hospital, still in pain but glad to be out of the hospital. Camilla's sister Mary, who lived with the Kimballs, had recently broken her hip and still hobbled on crutches. Then Olive Beth started labor pains and delivered a son at the hospital even before her father could locate and notify her husband. What more could Christmas bring? Luckily Spencer had no stake conferences, so he spent time nursing Camilla and caring for Olive Beth's children. "Billy slept with me and kept getting his feet in my face," he wrote in his journal.

Though still uncomfortable, when Christmas came Camilla was on her feet and prepared a turkey dinner for twenty-three family members.

Several months later Spencer told his son Ed: "I have felt that the accident in December was my fault for not having heeded what I felt was a warning. I felt very strongly that we should go the other road, through Zions Park, down through Las Vegas and over to Phoenix. But for a few miles just before we reached Kanab we had had almost dry ground, so that my spirits soared and I thought we would have no more deep snow; so I disregarded my rather strong feeling and we went merrily on to our dive in the canyon."

There had been a dozen other near-accidents in the years since his call to the apostleship. The year before, Elder Lee, driving them to a conference, had come to a sharp curve fast and put on his brake, which locked. The car had skidded off into the barrow pit in one of the few places along the twenty-mile stretch of mountain road where that could have been done without calamity. Elder Kimball had sat in the car, knees shaking, thankful for the Lord's protecting care. And a few weeks before the December incident, Elder Sterling W. Sill had been driving Elder Kimball at seventy miles an hour through a Utah canyon to make a conference on time when a truck stopped suddenly in their way. Elder Sill swerved around the truck just as a second one came from the other direction. Though it seemed that there was not room, they squeezed through.

Elder Kimball speculated on how great the odds had been that he might have been killed in any one of these situations and decided that perhaps the Lord still had work for him to do. "I wondered what it could be, and I prayed that I might find it and fulfill it." He recalled the night in 1946 when he had felt an evil power trying to possess him, and again wondered, "Am I destined to do something important enough to cause the Evil one to desire my death?"

16

Preaching with a New Voice

— "I fell among cutthroats"

At about Christmastime 1956 Spencer's throat began to bother him again. The earlier hoarseness, which had disappeared after a blessing in 1950, recurred. He woke one morning with blood in the back of his throat and a weakening voice. Dr. Cowan, alarmed by the inflamed vocal cords, urged him to see Dr. Hayes Martin in New York, the best in the world for throat cancer. Spencer was scheduled to visit the New York Stake in February and he hoped to consult with the specialist then.

His fear of cancer, stilled for years, troubled him again. At night he lay sleepless as his mind wandered restlessly back to his boyhood in Arizona. He followed his life forward until it came to the disquieting vision of his sister Helen's death from cancer. He had watched "the octopus literally eat away her face" and now imagined the "horrors and deprivations" he might expect if he had cancer in his throat.

After these thoughts, however, as he later recalled, "I came to myself." He thought of the thirteen years of service he had given and his children all married and settled. He began to face possible death without self-pity. He wrote, musing: "So what? You have had a long and abundant life. You have had bliss, been granted privileges and opportunities far beyond your deserts. Suppose your time has come! What if your mortality does give way to immortality, is it so bad?"

A calmness fell on him and through his mind passed vividly "a hallowed experience when about a year ago my own beloved father, Andrew Kimball, came to me" in a dream. In the dream it had seemed he was in a room, tying a ribbon onto a child's braided hair, when his father appeared. "I dropped the child's hair and called loudly, 'Father, Father, oh, Father.' His smile was radiant as in life. It warmed me. I was pulsating with gladness. . . . Then he drew away further and I followed him across the room still calling so happily: 'Father, Father, I'm so glad to see you, Father, oh, Father.' It was very real. I seemed fearful that he would leave me. At the far side of the room I was still near him and reaching toward him and calling him when . . . Father faded out of the picture. I awakened." He had lain in bed, reliving the dream, not wanting it to end. Now a year later, enveloped again in the feeling of his father's love for him, "somehow a new peace filled me and my fear of death began to leave me."

In February Elder Kimball and Camilla went to New York for the stake conference, where he took opportunity to visit the United Nations and listen to sharp debate in the General Assembly concerning Israel's continued occupation of the land from the Gaza Strip to the Gulf of Aqaba. He then presided over the stake conference in Washington, D. C.

On Monday morning, March 4, 1957, Spencer had an appointment with Dr. Martin in New York City. "It is dark and gloomy outside, drizzling rain and the sun has not been out today. I wish I were as sure my own sun would come up." Dr. Martin prescribed an immediate biopsy and thirty days of complete silence.

Spencer marvelled that, whereas he had been frantic about the suggestion of cancer the first time the possibility had come to him, in 1950, this time he felt great calm. "I pray only Thy will be done. If my work justifies my continuance of it, I pray my life and my voice may be extended and strengthened. If my work is done and others can fill in now to better advantage then I am resigned to whatever He wills."

That night he played MahJongg with his son Andrew's family, who lived in New York. "It is hard to keep one's silence. We say so many inconsequential things."

The next day "was a sad day. I entered the hospital with a voice and came out the next day without one." The hospital personnel and the

doctors lacked warmth, making Spencer feel just one of a herd of cattle
being inspected. Before the operation he asked the anaesthetist how
long he would be unconscious. "Just enough," was the curt reply.
Spencer fought the sedative until Andrew could come and give him a
blessing. He then passed out and woke up sixteen hours later to a nurse
scolding him because she had trouble in changing his sheets. His
tongue was bruised and cut and was swollen so large as nearly to fill his
mouth. When the doctor came he looked and said only, "We did what
we went in to do." He brushed aside questions about the tongue.
"Perhaps they thought I would never have use for it anyway." Spencer
was released from the hospital and unsteadily got to Andrew's home,
his eyes still affected by the anaesthetic. Of the whole experience
Spencer wrote, "I cannot imagine anything so impersonal and in-
human."

Almost his entire voice was gone. It might come back after the
biopsy, but for the present it was gone. "I am treading deep waters. I
see a dark cloud." He went to Church meetings with Andrew. His
presence was acknowledged, but he could not respond. In the Sunday
School class things were said he felt needed refutation, but he could not
challenge them.

"Monday, we shall know if the growth is malignant," he wrote in his
journal. "If so, I think I'll not let them cut on me any more. I think I
shall just go on and use my expendable voice till it phases out or till I
phase out."

To his other three children he wrote: "Don't know just when we
shall be home. Really doesn't matter much for I will be as useless there
as here. The doctors didn't paint a very rosy picture for my future even
if there is no malignancy."

On Monday he and Camilla returned to the hospital to hear the
verdict, but they were told the laboratory tests were not finished and
they would have to come back two days later, changing their plans to
return to Salt Lake. Their convenience seemed of no moment.

On Wednesday the verdict was still uncertain, the condition borderline as to malignancy. Dr. Martin suggested letting Dr. Cowan
watch it further. Spencer asked again, jotting his question out on a note
pad, what they had done to his tongue. One young doctor standing by,
joked, "We stepped on it." "Yes," Spencer scribbled back, "and with
hob nail boots."

From Salt Lake City many of the Twelve wrote letters of concern.

Elder Lee told of a deeply stirring Quorum meeting in which there had been a united pleading in the prayers by the Brethren that "the Lord heal you, if necessary by his miraculous power. All I know, Spencer, after what we experienced today, is that if He does not listen to that plea it will be an evidence that He has plans for a greater mission that we know nothing about. Somehow there seemed to be expressed with all the brethren a feeling that because of the magnificence of your service, and because of the greatness of the mission you are now performing, that as measured by all human understanding, that mission is still uncompleted."

While recovering, Spencer with Camilla paid a visit to their son Ed, in Montana. There Spencer had a dream about getting a team and wagon stuck in a tunnel, going off to get help, but then forgetting the problem so that when he finally remembered it worried him terribly that he had forgotten something important. As he awakened he thought it might be a reminder that he had not gotten his financial affairs in shape for his wife and family in the event he might die of cancer. Was the dream a warning he would die soon?

He needed to talk to someone. "What I am going to write you may be crazy as a loon," he warned Ed, typing his half of the conversation. But "when I look out into the future, there seems to be none. Even though my voice gets better, it seems that the road is dead-end."

He told Ed of the dream of his father which had so comforted him and wondered whether it had been a warning that his father would soon come from the other world to bring him home. "I may be wrong," he typed on,

> I may live for a long time. I do not know. I felt like I should tell you these things. If I go it is all right. I have had a rich and delightful life and many joys and blessings, far more than I deserved. I have never been able to understand why such honors should come to me.... I realize that I do not go to my Maker perfected. I have tried. I have many limitations and weaknesses but my hope is that when I stand before the bar to be judged, which I know I must, that for every serious error or weakness of my life that there may be a few dozen second-mile offerings and contributions on the other side of the ledger.... I leave with my children and others my testimony. I know. How more completely could I know anything? I know that it is true and divine. And as I face the end of my days I say it again and again without fear and in total honesty....

Back in his office in Salt Lake City he conducted what business he could. He drafted letters on the typewriter for his secretary to copy. He conducted interviews by typing his questions. But although in one exhausting interview he typed nineteen pages, he found that when he was obliged to use this method people did not open up their hearts as they otherwise might have done. They tended to answer yes or no.

Even in this trial his humor survived. When he had to write out his side of the conversation he found that people labored, hesitated, eventually froze up. Most assumed that because he was dumb, he was deaf, too. A store clerk who knew him seemed puzzled when he asked in writing how much a book cost. She held up five fingers and seemed relieved when he left. A giant of a man with a deep bass voice became confused when Spencer wrote questions out. He came close and shouted. Spencer's five-year-old grandson Bill looked him over strangely, then whispered in his ear. Camilla's sister Mary, who lived with them, was deaf but could speak; Spencer could hear but not speak; Camilla had difficulty in keeping things straight.

People who found it hard to talk with him pressed his hand more warmly than usual, an alternative way of expressing their feelings.

Some found him a wise counselor. They told him their troubles without interruption, he nodding encouragement. Eventually, having it off their chest, they would run down and go away feeling much better.

At a dinner club a friend looked at the silent apostle for a long time and finally said, "Well, at least you can eat."

Camilla's father, Edward Christian Eyring, died in Arizona and Spencer and Camilla attended the funeral. Spencer could not speak at the service, though that had been requested. On the way back to Utah they stopped to pick up an Indian woman and her children along the highway and drove twenty miles out of their way to deliver her to Tuba City.

After a while Spencer began to whisper lightly, ending the period of total silence, but he was still not able to carry on a conversation. The silence, which had at first involved some novelty, grew increasingly frustrating. When President McKay asked whether his whispering had an adverse effect on people, it was a new thought to Spencer. He reacted by not setting apart missionaries, for fear his whispering might detract from the occasion for them. He wrote: "I seem so useless. I find myself withdrawing, becoming almost anti-social, quite opposite to my normal nature."

By June 1957 Dr. Cowan was worried that Spencer's raw throat was not healing. He urged a second consultation with Dr. Martin in New York. Dreading to put himself back on the operating table, Elder Kimball wrote out his fears to President McKay and delivered the note personally. He apologized to President McKay for having allowed the biopsy in March without permission. "Since I feel that I belong to the Church with every moment and energy and power I possess, I felt I had no right to take things in my own hands, but it was over before I realized it and my voice went down the drain in the Memorial Hospital." President McKay commented, "I had wondered." Now Elder Kimball promised to follow President McKay's advice.

His typed message went on: "President McKay, I seldom presume to take your time, as much as I enjoy every moment in your presence, so many make demands on your precious moments. I wish to assure you again that I have a great admiration and esteem for you, amounting as nearly to worship as I would dare permit it toward any human being. And as the Prophet of God, I stand in awe, and my admiration and affection know no bounds and you have my undying loyalty and devotion. . . ."

With tears in his eyes, President McKay asked for time to think and pray. The next day he advised Elder Kimball to follow the advice of his doctors after consulting with Elder Harold B. Lee, who would be in New York to join in the decision. He felt that a complete laryngectomy would probably not be necessary, but that if it were, Elder Kimball could still serve.

Spencer made preparations for the trip, not knowing just what the future would bring. He talked long and earnestly in his office to two of his granddaughters, "trying to alert and fortify them against evil and weakness and gentile courtships and out-of-Church marriage. They were serious and listened intently."

Learning that Dr. Martin was about to leave on vacation, Dr. Cowan urged the necessity for speed. The two apostles and Camilla hurried to New York and went for the examination. Dr. Martin sized up the situation quickly and prescribed immediate surgery, even though it meant postponing his own departure for another day. Elder Kimball and Elder Lee explained to the doctor the unique importance of his patient's voice to Spencer and to the whole Church and obtained from him a commitment to remove as little tissue as possible. It was determined to remove one vocal cord entirely and part of the other, but not to remove the larynx.

The suddenness of the operation, just two days later, found Spencer and Camilla unprepared. Spencer had made up his mind to it, but his spirit rebelled at the near certainty that he would never again in this life have a real voice. Over that weekend he spent his voice. It would be gone on Monday, so he spent the coin he had hoarded over months of silence. As he talked over the telephone, people who had only heard him whisper for months expressed surprise. He did have a voice and could even sing a few notes.

> I talked, talked, talked like the cracked and parched soil drinks in the long awaited rain. . . . I talked across the table — I raised my voice — I spoke above the noise of the hubbub of diners in the room — I talked above the noise of passing trucks. I talked. I must enjoy it while I could. Monday it would be gone — gone forever! Only till death, of course. Maybe I can preach again after the resurrection!

Sunday, intellectually accepting but still struggling in spirit, Spencer finally yielded to Camilla's scolding, arguing, pleading. He relaxed and was ready. When Elder Lee administered to him on Monday he felt at peace — no fear, no resistance.

At the hospital the staff took blood, gave injections, listened to his heart, took more blood — more than a dozen different doctors during his time in the hospital, and dozens of nurses.

When it came time to be taken to surgery, he received two anaesthetic injections. He thought, "When I wake up, it will be gone." Up the hall on the truck, up in the elevator and to the surgery room. He wanted to see that room. The lights, the instruments, the masked doctors and nurses. "Just to satisfy my curiosity, what are you doing?" The doctor answered that he was sewing soaker towels to the skin of his face, from ear to chin. As Spencer was losing consciousness he said, "Is that you, Dr. Martin?" And after his nod, "There are thousands of people praying for you this morning that you will be blessed in your decisions." Then the patient gave up the light.

Four or five hours later he began to wake and they wheeled him back to his room, his neck cut down the front with an incision four inches long. A tube extended out of his windpipe, through which he breathed and through which the nurse with a suction device cleared blood and mucus from inside. She demanded he cough, cough, despite the pain and ache. When he tried to speak, his breath gushed out of the tube, like "a wheezy old horse." "Now go to sleep, Mr. Kimball," she commanded, as though sleep could come just by willing it.

She gave him pills. He took them. Later she brought two more and he took them. When she brought a third set he gasped, "What am I taking?" She would not say. He hesitated, then wheezed, "Put them down on the table." But the nurse insisted, "You've got to take them." She did not know her patient; he never took the pills.

Finally Camilla was admitted and he felt immediately more secure in her presence. On the day after the operation he ate a little. The food tasted good after his two-day fast.

The days merged. It seemed years between sunup and sundown, eternities from the time Camilla left at dark until she came again the next morning. Pain killers had little effect. He walked the corridor, tried to read, thought of the future, tried to sleep, but no sleep came. He had a beautiful view of the midtown skyline. Far down among the tall buildings a sign in lights showed the minutes. It showed 3:46. He counted sixty very slowly and saw it change to 3:47. He closed his eyes for what seemed a long time and looked again. It was 3:49.

The pain in his neck and chest and throat, and a constant dull headache, continued on and on. In an effort to divert his mind from the pain he wrote down his memories, wrote of his childhood, bringing back the world of sun and shade and pigs and cows, of missionary days and courting, of Church service and finally the prospect of voiceless- ness. The nights seemed endless, each turn of the clock an eternity, each minute a thousand seconds long, each hour a thousand minutes.

After six days he left the hospital, still weak and miserable, and moved to the Eastern States Mission home, where he occupied a room. He and Camilla insisted on going out for their meals so they would not burden the mission president's family. Spencer explained, on his note pad, that he did not want to be "a pain in the neck."

Spencer attended Church meetings, covering the ugly, meaty wound with a scarf when in public. The doctor wanted it kept un- covered otherwise. The agony gave way at last to distress and then to mere discomfort. But the incision flamed with infection, bringing fever and new pain, then sleepless nights, hotpacks, painful probing and cleaning by the doctor, who took his pincers and scissors and knife and whittled and trimmed. I couldn't yell or might have done so. He cut and whittled and pulled and pressed, then when I thought I could stand it no longer, he said, "Did I hurt you?" I meekly said, "A little," but I wanted to say, "Of course not. This is delightful, just like getting an itching back scratched," but I didn't. He laughed about it. This was probably nothing compared to what he had helped do at the *"opening up party,"* and so it seemed simple to him.

"Insomnia is my trouble," Spencer wrote to his children. "Why, I couldn't even doze in Sacrament meeting yesterday." Another week passed, with continuing infection which was not much affected by the antibiotics, it seemed. To a friend he wrote: "I have had two hectic weeks, rugged ones. . . . Camilla has been an angel through it all."

Gradually the ugly slash closed and healed on the outside. The inside healed more slowly.

As the doctors allowed him to try his voice, to see what was left, Spencer found to his delight there was a bit. A weak, rough rasp, but it was something and he would make the most of it.

As soon as they would let him he sought out voice trainers, who coached him in proper breath control and sound production and gave him drills, but warned against taxing his voice.

After nearly three weeks he began to sleep again for several hours at a time. And after nearly four weeks the doctors released him to return home.

He and Camilla visited their children in New York, Michigan and Montana on the way home, then returned to Salt Lake City, where Elder Kimball reported for duty. President McKay insisted he follow Dr. Cowan's advice, which Elder Kimball thought too conservative, and limit his talking to a little at home and in a closed room. After eight weeks the wounds still had not completely healed, but they continued to improve.

Elder Kimball wrote hundreds of letters, catching up on the backlog of correspondence, responding to expressions of concern, writing several grandchildren long letters of advice about setting high ideals and choosing friends carefully and determining to be happy and to follow the Lord.

He watched cancer waste away one of his nieces. When she died in October, after saintly patience through the last weeks, she weighed just fifty-eight pounds.

His voice seemed to grow thinner and thinner. A special battery-operated amplifier in which he had placed great hope proved useless.

On a trip to San Francisco he and Camilla went to the theater, to a play highly recommended. "The curtain was raised at the time appointed and six professional actors and actresses took us on a journey that left us red in face and filthy in mind. . . . How much more corrupt was Sodom? How much more degenerate Gomorrah?" They left the theater feeling defiled by the blasphemy and smut which a sophisticated audience applauded and enjoyed. This widespread acceptance of evil provided him with the basis for a later general conference sermon.

At priesthood meeting in Berkeley Ward the rationalism of "some self-styled intellectuals" shocked him. He almost burst, but dared not use his voice yet.

In Salt Lake City a woman came up to him in the railway station and said, "I guess you do good to a lot of people, but you broke up my marriage." He gathered from her rambling talk that she had mental problems, but it hit hard that even such a person would feel that his best efforts could do damage.

He felt depressed and lost, outside the rhythm of stake assignments weekend by weekend. Then in September he received his first assignment since the operation. He aided two other Brethren in division of a stake. For nine hours he participated in meetings and interviews, though in constant and intense pain from a major carbuncle on his stomach which had eight or more heads. He gave no hint of the discomfort, lest there be reluctance to return him to full service soon. He reveled in the sensation of being back in the work.

He remained mostly at home, but so many people came to the house to see him that he might almost as well have gone to the office. Still, freedom from regular assignments did leave him with some more leisure. He played with his grandchildren, cut their hair, hiked in the hills, did some research and article writing, painted part of the house, worked several days helping Olive Beth with painting of her new house, even went shopping with Camilla. On his wedding anniversary he wrote, "How glorious have been these forty years with the sweetest girl in the world."

Finally, in November, Dr. Cowan pronounced Spencer's throat

fully healed and freed him to use his voice as he could, so long as he did not strain it or subject it to fatigue.

But he had still not spoken at a conference with his gruff, unfamiliar voice, and he feared the experience.

In December Elder Kimball attended stake conference in the Gila Valley. Elder Delbert L. Stapley, the appointed conference visitor, offered him a chance to speak. Elder Kimball was tempted to pass the opportunity by, but he decided that if ever he were to speak in public again he would have to brave a first time and there would be no more sympathetic group in the whole Church for him than this one. He started by telling the congregation that he had gone to New York and fallen among cutthroats and thieves who had slit his throat and stolen his voice. The audience laughed heartily and both he and they relaxed. He was home, he was back at his work again.

He spoke briefly three times that day, with no apparent harm, and he found that with good electronic equipment he could be heard reasonably well. The doctors had told him that to keep his voice he must now use it, with restraint but regularly. He appealed almost plaintively to the First Presidency to allow him to take regular assignments again. "My service, my time, my energies and my life are in your hands. Please command me." They agreed. He felt "like a resurrected person."

In January he was assigned, with Elder Harold B. Lee, to divide the Dallas Stake and organize a Shreveport Stake. It was a hard week. He had a cold, diarrhea, two boils starting in his nostrils, some nosebleeds, and an excruciating back pain. Elder Lee, who shared his bedroom, asked him several times if there was anything he could do for him.

After denying any difficulty until three in the morning, he decided that Elder Lee must know perfectly well from his twisting and turning that something was wrong. He then admitted he had been in constant pain for two days. Elder Lee gave him a sleeping pill and a blessing. Then Spencer slept a few hours and the pain was gone and did not return. "The Lord is so good to me and so far beyond my deserts."

At the Houston conference Elder Lee, the senior of the two apostles, announced Elder Kimball as the next speaker. He stood, opened his mouth, but only an ugly grating noise came out. He swallowed and gulped and tried again, with the same sickening feeling. The thought came: "Better quit — you can't do it — you can't impose on the people like this." But he tried again, this time found his voice, and delivered his short sermon. Then he turned to Elder Lee, shrugged helplessly and sat down. Elder Lee put his hand on him and said, "Thank you, Brother Kimball."

The next day there was another meeting in Houston. Elder Lee, in charge, announced Elder Kimball as the next speaker. He stood and "made the most terrible sound you can imagine" until finally he found his voice and gave his sermon. Then he sat down, buried his head in his hands and mourned. "I was crying gallons of tears inside. I don't think they showed. But I really thought I was through, that I'd never preach again, that I wouldn't even try."

Three days later, driving by car to Texarkana, he passed Elder Lee a note: "I hope you won't embarrass me again." Elder Lee jovially responded, "Oh, I'm sure we'll call on you again. I think it's important for the people to hear your witness." Elder Kimball answered nothing. He knew he would do anything Elder Lee, his senior, asked. But inside he rebelled at the thought.

The conference at Texarkana was held in a long, narrow Methodist chapel. True to his word, Elder Lee called on his companion apostle to speak. It seemed impossible. The public address system was out. The chapel was huge. Outside the window was the highway, with trucks climbing a hill, grinding and shifting gears. Elder Kimball stood and began, "Brothers and Sisters. . . ." He prayed silently, he strained, the words came. For ten minutes he bore his testimony. Every person in the chapel heard him. He sat down and Elder Lee put his arm around him and said, "That's right, Spencer."

Spencer wrote home to Camilla: "I realize I cannot quit for anything, though the temptation is terrific when I stumble and stammer and halt."

In the 1958 April Conference he spoke in the Tabernacle, on missionary work, and reactions from listeners reassured him he need not worry too much about his raw voice. Indeed, Elder Lee had earlier observed that when he spoke people leaned forward and listened with special intentness. President Clark asked about a boil on his neck and Elder Kimball said he was so glad to be able to speak that he could not be bothered by anything so minor as a boil.

That summer a nephew, talking about frustrating dreams, asked him, "Have you ever been in a dream and tried to scream, but just couldn't get it out?" "Yes," answered Spencer immediately, "for a whole year now." They both laughed.

Elder Kimball's attention turned again fully to his work. During the Christmas period he had sorted through his files. The mass of letters relating to people's troubles — marital difficulties, moral transgressions, struggles with faith — he burned. He had kept their confidence sacred and he now destroyed the record. "As I watch the letters of confession of ugly sins curl up and become gases, I somehow wish the pernicious sins could be as easily destroyed." In his office, at home, as he visited the stakes and missions, in hotels, or by the roadside, people sought him out with problems, asking him for help. He could not turn them away, and would not, though this aspect of the work often left him heartsick.

A returned missionary had lost his testimony; after a long interview "his apostasy melted away and he changed from rebellion to humility." A girl about to marry outside the Church came seeking justification. The mother of a pregnant girl came, referred by a doctor of whom she had requested an abortion for the girl. A bishop came to confess some early misdeeds he had concealed when interviewed for his position. A couple who had had sexual relations before their temple marriage wanted to make things right. A man on a downward course came for advice; he was faced with jail for bad checks, had lost his job, lost his family, was locked out of his hotel room. An Indian boy, smelling of liquor, asked for a bus ticket to St. George.

A woman had let her husband go out of town to work and now found he wanted a divorce. A serviceman had married a fifteen-year-old girl; now at eighteen she wrote she would divorce him. A man imprisoned in San Quentin for arson found his wife and six children cutting free from him and wrote for advice. A young man with whom Elder Kimball had worked for some time had taken a girl into the hills and come near raping her. A man who had invested unwisely found himself wiped out financially and twenty-five thousand dollars in debt. Two stake officers maintained a feud which upset the stake. A Navajo missionary, bright and qualified but somewhat spoiled, wanted to terminate his mission early. A father of four confessed adultery with a married woman who had several children.

But for all the pain, many of the interviews yielded positive results. A missionary who had been disfellowshipped for earlier immoral acts which he had confessed only on the eve of his release from an honorable mission, was reinstated four years later through Elder Kimball's intervention. A man who had left his family returned to them again.

Many of those who entered the apostle's office with troubles left with lightened hearts, on the road to repentance. They left their burdens with him.

President Clark wrote Elder Kimball a loving, scolding note, urging that he should not use up his energy on individual problems that local leaders should handle, but should save it for tasks he uniquely could do. Intellectually Elder Kimball might agree, but temperamentally he could not stop himself. He helped because he had to.

His service to others all seemed paid back in kind, though, one day when he visited his older brother Del, who had been inactive in the Church since boyhood. Their father had not been able to reach Del in this respect, and over the years Spencer, with patience and love, had "made many trips and written many letters and . . . tried with all my might to bring him to his senses," but without effect. Now as Spencer visited Del he found him hungry for the gospel. "I could hardly believe this was the same brother." In the end it was not the apostle but a pair of full-time missionaries, "two fine young men," who had succeeded.

In January of 1959 Elder Kimball and Camilla were assigned to visit the three missions in South America, in Argentina, Uruguay and Brazil. They boarded a ship in New York which in nine days carried them more than six thousand miles by sea to Buenos Aires. Rough weather made the cruise less pleasurable than it might have been. They dressed for dinner; "that is, the men do," wrote Spencer, the women on board "mostly undress."

In South America the apostle found the affection of the people unrestrained, almost adulatory.

> After the meeting at 9 p.m. the people rushed me for autographs. I never have been in such a crush before. I could not get down from the stage until the brethren took a hand and insisted that the people back up. I went downstairs where there was a little more room and in front of the fan the people crowded around. I think most of the 250 people present came for me to write my signature in their Bibles or song books or on their printed programs. My arm nearly gave way as it has been lame for a long time. President Pace asked me if I wished to be relieved of the pressure and I told him No, that if it gave the people pleasure I was happy. I would shake hands with the individual, sign the paper, then they

On horseback at Isla Patrulla,
Uruguay, 1959

wished again to shake hands and wish us felicidades and bon voyage. . . .

A little boy stood in front of me almost smothered by the larger people around. I finally noticed him and shook hands with him. He had no paper to sign. He reached up and kissed me on the cheek and slipped away.

In another city, " . . . the people were so sweet. Tears in some of their eyes, occasionally they kissed my hand, one man fell to his knees and kissed my coat and made me nearly drop with humility. They brought their little ones to shake hands and be kissed."

They criss-crossed the continent, visiting Argentina, Chile, Uruguay, Paraguay, Brazil and Peru, crossing some national borders several times. Their visits ranged from the major cities with large congregations to mountain villages where the people literally dressed in rags and tatters and the little chapel had electricity only when the missionaries ran the generator. Elder Kimball wished to establish the basic patriotism of Church members to their country, so he asked

With mission leaders at Machu Picchu, 1959

occasionally for the playing of their national anthem in the Church gatherings.

In light of the Church's generally strong opposition to divorce, Elder Kimball faced a puzzling question. In the Catholic countries divorce could not be obtained. As a result an innocent person, whose marriage had been destroyed, could not legally remarry. Some set up new households without legal sanction. Though the arrangement fell technically outside the law, the officials were completely unconcerned. When such people wished to join the Church the missionaries would not baptize them, since technically they lived in adultery. Three years before, one of the General Authorities had authorized baptism of one such couple. Elder Kimball helped to establish as Church policy that such couples could be baptized if they showed that they had done what they could to legalize their relationship, had been faithful to one another, had met responsibility to their previous family, and had conformed to the expectations of custom.

The practice of not conferring the priesthood on blacks posed questions in areas where a number of blacks and persons of mixed blood belonged to the Church. In one branch the Relief Society president was black and seemed well accepted. A man with about five percent Negro heritage said, "I can't even be a doorkeeper, can I?" "Yes," Elder Kimball replied, "you can serve wherever priesthood is not a requirement." "My heart wanted to burst for him. I think I helped him with tithing and drink and . . . I think he went away less perturbed, more sure of himself."

The visiting apostle spent much time with the missionaries. "I hope I have given them enthusiasm, charged their batteries, helped them get peace." He warned them that too much missionary time disappeared into supervision of branches when local members could just as well assume the responsibility and would grow from the experience. Too many missionaries ended up playing the piano, leading the singing, ushering, passing out song books — all things which could be done by others.

He talked to elders about the moonlit night after returning from a successful mission "when you ask that one individual to be your companion." Marry her in the temple, Elder Kimball urged, and be sure she is "better than you are. I would never be in the Council of the Twelve today if I had married some of the girls that I have known. Sister Kimball kept me growing and never let me be satisfied with mediocrity."

One of the missionaries he had talked with in Uruguay wrote home: "He is such a loving person that I just can't explain it. He gave a personal interview to every missionary in the mission. We stayed over after convention for two days extra for instructions. We were in meetings for eleven and twelve hours. And besides that, when we had little ten-minute breaks between meetings, he would go out and start giving interviews. I've never seen anyone who works the way he does. When he speaks there is no question but what he speaks with authority."

All told, during their eleven-week tour Spencer and Camilla traveled thirty-five thousand miles and held a hundred meetings, meeting with nearly all of the nine thousand members in South America. Four General Authorities had previously visited South America, but not during the time of any of the current missionaries or of most of the members. Elder Kimball recommended that more frequent visits be made.

Returning from South America, Spencer had a checkup on his throat. Dr. Cowan saw no evidence of further cancer. The throat looked healthy, and as sometimes happened with operations such as his a fold of tissue had developed in the larynx. "The false cord had grown to where it vibrated somewhat like a normal cord, though of course not comparable to it. What a miracle it has been."

In May 1959 Elder Stephen L Richards, first counselor to President McKay, died. When the Twelve met with the First Presidency two days later, President McKay, now eighty-five years old, "looked very old and haggard and grief-stricken . . . ; he talked about Brother Richards. Their association for all the years had been like Jonathan and David. He indicated that it would not be long until some of the others would follow him into eternity. As the meeting proceeded towards its end President McKay, more cheerful, considered the many things that came before us and by the end of our association was reasonably cheerful."

In June President McKay reorganized the First Presidency, calling President Clark, eighty-seven, as his first counselor now and Henry D. Moyle, seventy, as his second counselor.

Spencer W. Kimball, twenty-one years younger than the President, still occupied the third chair in the Council. When both Joseph Fielding Smith and Harold B. Lee were absent at the same time, he presided for the first time over the meeting of the Twelve. In contrast with some of the Brethren, he felt generally healthy and energetic. A year later during the summer vacation he had four of his grandsons with him for several days at the beach. At age sixty-five he climbed hills with them, played games in the sand, swam with them, hunted seashells, tramped through the zoo.

He did have one episode of great heaviness in his head, which he feared might presage tumor or stroke, but he asked for and received an administration and the feeling passed.

That summer one assignment held special interest. Thirteen years after his exuberant tour of the Hawaiian Mission in 1946, Elder Kimball returned to hold two stake conferences and visit the mission again. The years had changed Hawaii. Now airliners arrived often, disgorging hundreds of people; the more leisurely approach to life was waning. Spencer realized after he had been there for nearly a week that this time he had not heard a single Hawaiian song nor seen a Hawaiian dance. Worried that the traditional culture was in danger of being lost, he charged a district president, a native Hawaiian, to record the fast-disappearing chants which preserved the traditional genealogies of the people.

But the people were still warm and hospitable and tolerant. In other communities Elder Kimball had had to prod and preach to Latter-day Saints who were intolerant of other races, urging acceptance of Indians and Mexican-Americans. But he was delighted to see the mixture in Hawaii. Of one stake he wrote: "One counselor in the Presidency is Hawaiian and the stake clerk Chinese. In the High Council is a Filipino, a Samoan, a Japanese, and five Hawaiians, the balance being from the mainland. The Patriarch is Hawaiian. Five of the bishops are Hawaiian, one Portuguese, one Japanese, one Samoan, and a larger percentage of the counselors are of the other races."

After Hawaii Elder Kimball continued his work pattern of interviewing, committee work, and stake conference visits. One night at a stake conference he stayed in the luxurious home of a high councilor, where his hosts insisted on his staying in their bedroom. Upon opening the closet to hang up his coat, he was so impressed with the clothing arrayed that he counted thirty suits and twenty pairs of shoes and boots, with other clothing in proportion; he had too much delicacy to open the wife's closet. The bed was "wide enough for a family." The high councilor "is a good man," was Elder Kimball's reaction to the abundance, "and I am happy to see his family so comfortable."

In another stake, though, he drew limits to the pursuit of abundance, as he often did. In calling as counselor a man the stake president had requested, Elder Kimball discovered that he sold beer and wine in his grocery store and stayed open on Sunday. He discussed the matter frankly with the man and indicated they would not be able to use him in the position under those circumstances. The prospective counselor then volunteered to discontinue the practices, despite the financial sacrifice.

As he ended one meeting with stake leaders, Elder Kimball overheard a man say as he went out of the door, "He certainly lays it on the line." That seemed to him a compliment. It surprised him, though, to learn that some Church members thought him humorless. It was true that he thought of his responsibilities as serious, but he often used his good-natured wit in an effort to establish a warm atmosphere. When he arrived at the stake center in San Fernando on Sunday morning in brown socks and a blue suit he was embarrassed by the mismatch and gratefully allowed the stake president's wife to bring him a pair of her husband's socks. In the conference meeting he told stake members,

"I'm not filling the stake president's shoes this morning, but I *am* filling his socks."

People were always his first concern. As he visited one stake conference a young father sent word through his bishop that he would appreciate a blessing. Between meetings the bishop drove the apostle to the hospital at top speed. They ran up the stairs and down the hall, fighting for seconds. But as they entered the room, the bishop related, "there was an amazing change. Elder Kimball seemed to have all the time in the world. He sat by the bed and unhurriedly talked about life and death and testimony and faith. Finally he said, 'I understand you would like me to administer to you.' After the administration we left. The moment we were outside the hospital room the pace changed and we ran to the car and sped back across the city to the conference, arriving just after the meeting had begun."

On one occasion a stake begged him to stay over an extra day, returning home Monday evening so that he could speak at a Sunday night MIA meeting. "They filled the time and when they introduced me there was only five minutes left. I had spent 24 hours just to be almost wholly ignored. I was provoked — I had so much to have done at home."

A member of the General Sunday School board wrote Elder Kimball of his observations over a period of eight years out among the stakes. "No one save President McKay is more highly respected nor has anyone's teachings and counsel been more impressive nor more sincerely remembered." Spencer thought the praise exaggerated, but gratifying.

The Indian Student Placement Program lay close to Elder Kimball's heart. But because it put Indian children in white homes for the school year, it was still widely distrusted on the Navajo reservation. To Elder Kimball it seemed the quickest, surest way to improve the Indian's lot. But to its opponents on the reservation it was a transparent device for proselyting, for providing white foster parents with cheap labor, and for breaking ties with Indian culture. The Church met these arguments by placing only children who had already been baptized and by insisting that generally the children should return to the reservation during the summer. The medical clinic through which children passed each fall had been upgraded; the case loads of supervising social workers had been cut; meetings for foster parents were held.

In 1960 Elder Kimball invited Mr. Jones, the Navajo tribal chairman, to come and see for himself the conditions in which the children lived. As they approached a foster home in Sandy, Utah, the chairman said, surprised, "Why, this is a *nice* home!" The little Navajo girl had come in from horseback riding, happy. He seemed to have expected to find her working in the field. Mr. Jones asked what work she did and she told him of her family chores — washing dishes in her turn, making her bed. He found that this little girl had been a Latter-day Saint before coming and that she would stay only until school was out, spending her summer on the reservation. He asked about her school and about how the white children treated her, then left, finally satisfied with the program.

Just months later, after much negotiating, Elder Kimball obtained permission to show a BYU-produced motion picture of the placement program, including footage of Mr. Jones, to the Tribal Council in Window Rock. He cancelled a speaking engagement and with Mark E. Petersen flew to Gallup, New Mexico, with the film. They were told that they could show the film in the evening, when the Council members had been invited to return to see it.

They arrived but the Council House was dark. They finally got someone to let them in. The chairman came by and excused himself; another leader came in and left. Finally, with heavy hearts, they rounded up a dozen women and children and a couple of men and showed the film. A wrestling match at the fair grounds had proved to be too much competition.

It appeared they had come on a futile mission and had wasted their efforts and expenses. They recalled the fifteen years of unsuccessful efforts to get recognition for the Church on the reservation and permission to acquire building sites for chapels. George Albert Smith, Matthew Cowley and Spencer Kimball had sat for days, waiting, without even being given a chance to present their case to the Tribal Council. This film seemed to them a critical effort to break through the resistance, but things had turned against them. They prayed with all their heart for help.

Things brightened when they received permission to show the film the next day to the Tribal Council just before their coffee break. They would have a captive audience of the whole Council!

As they drove to Window Rock again they pulled their car off the road for a moment of prayer. But at the Council House they were told they could not show the film until after the coffee break. They thought many of the Councilmen might not come back to watch. They set up their projector and had it working, when the power failed. They suspected sabotage. No one seemed concerned about remedying the situation. They telephoned for an extension cord to get power from another source, but the Council members started to return from their break and it looked as though the Council would go on with its business and the opportunity slip away.

The vice-chairman, a man they understood to be unfriendly to the Church, called for order, then to their delighted surprise invited them to say something about the picture while they waited. The extension cord came and they started the film. The sunlight through the windows and doors washed out the picture, but cloud cover moved in and provided semi-darkness during the showing. Elder Kimball sat where he could watch reactions and held his breath. He saw doubtful looks change to attention and interest, particularly when places and people they recognized came on the screen.

The picture ended; there was a general shuffle. Elder Kimball expected them to resume their work, but the vice-chairman made a long statement in Navajo expressing appreciation for the Church program. When another councilman proposed a standing vote of appreciation a number seemed obviously reluctant, but they did stand and the presiding officer called it unanimous.

The two apostles held a special prayer of thanksgiving. That night they arranged a public showing of the film in Window Rock and 350 people came to see it. The student placement program had turned a crucial corner.

In August, Elder Kimball went to Provo to meet the buses as they arrived from Arizona, loaded with Indian children for their winter schooling. He tried to do this each year. He followed them through their baths, shampoos, haircuts, medical and dental examinations. He sat at breakfast with some of them and played volleyball with a group of boys while they waited. The children seemed well-behaved and happy. He thanked the doctors and dentists and nurses who donated their services.

In September he toured the Southwest Indian Mission again. In an eight-hour testimony meeting with the 103 missionaries, he noted that

20 were full-blood or part-blood Indians. "I have seldom heard better testimonies." In meetings Indians often conducted, spoke, provided music.

In the 1960 October Conference Elder Kimball expressed his satisfaction at the gains. "Today the dark clouds are dissipating and great blessings are theirs." From a hundred members fifteen years earlier, the Church now counted 8400 Indians, better educated, less superstitious, more devoted to the Church.

Nearly ninety, President Clark also stood at the pulpit in that conference. People held their breath as he tottered forward, needing help to take the three or four steps from his chair. But as he raised his stentorian voice in greeting, a wave of relief and gratitude swept over the audience. Though President Clark's physical condition had deteriorated, "he was still himself above the knees," Spencer wrote in praise of the sermon.

J. Reuben Clark, Jr., was Spencer's first cousin. Like an older, more experienced brother, he had welcomed Spencer into the Quorum seventeen years earlier and had fussed at him about his health, had praised his conference addresses, had encouraged him in his special assignments. Spencer self-consciously felt himself the country cousin to this polished man with a long career in law and public office, ending in service as ambassador to Mexico. To Spencer it seemed that "he always says exactly the right word."

A few months later President Clark, who had once telephoned Spencer with the astounding news of a call to the Quorum of the Twelve, was dead.

17

A Worldwide Church

— "what will you be doing
when you are nineteen?"

Elder Kimball and Camilla had
been west as far as Hawaii before but not to the South Pacific or
Australia. Now, after October Conference 1960, they were assigned to
visit that area. President McKay, who "has the traits and qualities of the
Master in a large degree," gave Elder Kimball a special blessing. It
commended him for the faith and service of seventeen years as an
apostle and blessed him with the gift of wisdom and gave him authority
to make decisions as he felt moved without referring matters back to
the First Presidency and the Twelve. Elder Kimball warmed to this
expression of confidence.

The Kimballs and representatives of the Church auxiliary organizations flew to Sydney, where Elder Kimball presided at the conference
of Australia's only stake. He kept his sermons practical, as the stake was
only six months old, its members still inexperienced in their new
responsibilities. He urged them to worship and not merely attend at
sacrament meetings, to teach their boys to save money for missions, to
spread the gospel to their neighbors.

To Harold B. Lee, Acting President of the Council of the Twelve,
he reported:

I am bending and kneeling under the weight of the responsibility but feel strong and well and ready for the work. This program is lighter in hours and strain and tenseness than the office work at home has come to be. . . . The spring is dressing the lovely countryside with a new garment of fresh green. The roses are fragrant and everywhere giving color to the yards; the jacaranda trees, exquisitely beautiful, give a purplish haze to the vast area of red tile roof houses.

Immediately after the Sydney Stake conference he wrote the stake presidency. He complimented them on their great devotion and laid out some requests — to organize the high priests quorum fully; to add seventies from mission-minded elders; to complete elders quorum presidencies; to provide detailed reports on the work of stake missionaries; to organize a combined-wards choir for the next conference; to use some less-active men as ushers; to reach children of members who had not been baptized; to reach the many good people who had drifted into inactivity; to supply lists of marriages, youth activities, prospective missionaries, specific plans laid to increase sacrament meeting attendance; and on and on. He showed his interest in every detail and made every aspect of the work important.

In Brisbane, where he was to organize the first of two new stakes in Australia, he held some 250 interviews. In Melbourne he organized Australia's third stake. In New Zealand he organized the second and third stakes in the country.

In contrast to the hundreds of interviews with the faithful and honorable, both members and missionaries, the apostle spent black days in counseling and in participating in elders courts. Several missionaries who had become involved in sexual immorality were sent home. They showed deep remorse, except for one who seemed to be only superficially repentant. The situation made Elder Kimball heartsick. One of the elders, excommunicated the day before, sat with him for hours as the apostle took care of his correspondence, "just to be close. . . . I have much faith and confidence in him. He will leave in a couple of hours to meet his parents and his great embarrassments and to tread his deep waters. My heart goes out to him."

After Elder Kimball reported his actions, President Lee responded that he personally would phone one missionary's father, whom he knew well. "I am sure it will be a very severe sad blow. . . ." The father

With koala bear in Australia, 1960

had told Elder Lee that he "started out with the ambition to get high position in the business world and to make money, and now having achieved both, he had found that one letter from his missionary son in Australia was worth more to him than all the positions or money in the world." Elder Lee added, "I am hoping that he and his wife will rise above this great shock and hold on to their boy through the season of repentance to complete forgiveness."

Elder Kimball found in these problem missionaries a story of lax effort, much show-going, some dancing and dating, which had progressed to acts of fornication. As he interviewed many of the other missionaries,

> I did not tell them but they seemed to sense that excommunication was in the offing and some of them were beginning to realize that it was they who . . . were responsible for what should follow, for they with several others knew of the [beginnings of] conditions which were to become so serious that fellow missionaries would need to be handled. Any one of at least twenty Elders could have saved the terrible thing which was to happen had they been courageous enough to have reported it to the Mission President before the condition became acute. . . . every case was an evolutionary one

which started from what seemed innocent contacts, flirtations, dating, etc., and ended in misery for many souls including innocent parents and families at home.

"Why do they have to get into dark places?" he added. "Why do they have to forget their promises and covenants?"

And the next morning: "They were serving a light breakfast but I did not eat. With what is ahead I dared not eat, I need all the strength I can get from fasting." In the court "there were tears and sadness all around, the hearts were bleeding and prayers were soaring . . . ; it was a sad time altogether. . . . Surely we cannot tolerate immorality in the missions or even serious approaches to it. The gloomy day wore on. . . ."

In New Zealand, Elder Kimball found that the Church had such great identification with the Maoris that it was difficult to interest Europeans in it, though the future growth of the Church there would need to involve the dominant European group. In general, he did not want to interfere with the strong wish of many people to preserve the Maori culture. Yet sometimes the Maori language was used in meetings even though some present could not understand it, while everyone (including the Maoris) understood English. Elder Kimball wondered also whether the Maori Saints ought not to relegate the wild war dances and songs to an annual festival, held for the purpose of perpetuation, and substitute their peaceful, beautiful dances for more frequent use at Church entertainments.

> It has been like a whirlwind. . . . The stakes are now all organized. . . . I think that never before in our experience has one of the Twelve been entrusted with such responsibility and I have been very close to my Lord. I think never before has one member been given five stakes to organize, one after the other. Generally two of us go to organize one stake. I have shaken with awesome responsibility through these days and have prayed much and earnestly, and have felt the presence of my Lord and His guidance, and have relied so completely on Him I feel that the work has been done about as it should be. I do not think the Lord has made many errors. I realize with some concern that the small stakes . . . have some hard rowing ahead. . . .

Elder Kimball received a copy of a letter sent by a New Zealand Saint to friends:

> I marvel at the energy that drives this man. I suppose I could lift him up with one hand, there you are, size means nothing. . . . I

do not know, he was attracted to me like a magnet. He spoke to me and I could feel my many sins coming to the fore, I tried hard to get away from him, I did, but he caught me in the recreation hall as I had my back to him sitting down. He caught me and held me. Brother, he said, you are not a faithful Church member. I replied, from this time onward I will be. Thank you, he said, I know you can. He put his arms around my neck and hugged me. By Jove, it's hard to hold back the emotions surging within me. Those terrible sins, inactivity, breaking the commandments. I felt pretty bad.

I do not know then what attraction I had, but as I write I can only say, he saw me naked, a lost sheep as only a prophet can see. Two days later I was called in for an interview with him and I confessed everything. He prayed for me and blessed me. On Sunday the 20th he read my name out with a lot of others [for ordination and a leadership calling]. May I hold tight to the reins and never let go. I solemnly declare with all that's good within me, and through our Saviour Jesus Christ I will go forward from this day onward with the best that's in me doing the work.

Since they were already halfway around the world, Spencer and Camilla decided to complete the circle. They went from New Zealand to Australia to Singapore. "This is my first free breath nearly since October Conference," he wrote. It was December 22. The Kimballs tried to locate Church members in Singapore, but could not. On Christmas Day they travelled from Singapore to Saigon. This was the strangest Christmas day they had ever spent. The main celebration of Christmas, so far as they could see, was that restaurants and taxis doubled their prices for the day.

In Saigon there was an impression of reform — no beggars, open prostitution suppressed, strenuous efforts to reduce illiteracy. Communist threat hung over the country, however. They found two servicemen who were Church members and visited with them.

Bangkok; Rangoon; New Year's Day in Calcutta. The suffering of the millions in India hurt. "How I'd like to help them! But what help can be given? I could give some dollars to some and a million more would trample me under. . . . It seems so hopeless." Camilla broke down in tears at the poverty and filth and disease.

In each place the apostle noted the possibility of opening missionary work. Of Burma: "Yes, I'd proselyte in Burma, but not in our conventional style. I'd go back to Paul's program to some extent. Mission president who would go without his family and be prepared to rough it. No mission palace with a host of record keepers, typists, etc. . . . Establish the work by one of the 12. A mission president almost without portfolio. Start from small beginnings."

On to Benares, then Delhi. In Delhi Elder Kimball made inquiries about getting missionaries into India. The answer seemed to be that, while ostensibly there was complete religious freedom, in practice missionary visas would be so delayed as to greatly disrupt the work. His informant told him that a professor's visa had been held up for six months because his papers referred to a "sabbatical leave," which someone assumed was a religious matter.

In Delhi the apostle met with Mangal Dan Dipty, a twenty-seven-year-old Indian who had come by appointment to request baptism. At twenty-two he had been ordained to preach Pentecostal Christianity. Two years before Elder Kimball's visit he had read *The Articles of Faith* by James E. Talmage, and concluded that its teachings must be false. He also read the pamphlet *Joseph Smith Tells His Own Story.* Then as he lay on his bed, not yet asleep, he saw a great light and heard a voice saying that he should be careful, that he should read and understand, because what he had read was from God.

The Kimballs spent most of a day with him, teaching him the gospel and explaining to him the likely consequences of his baptism — that he would be cut off from his fifty-dollar-a-month income from preaching, from his friends, perhaps from his parents. "Let it come," he said determinedly. He might be the only member in all India and would not have the priesthood for a long time and might rarely be visited. "I am prepared to meet whatever problems arise," he said. He had come with a testimony, for baptism. But Elder Kimball still demurred, "I wonder if it would be better to let you wait and learn more about the gospel and the Church." The young man responded after a moment, tears in his eyes, "Whatever you say, I know is the will of God, but I came down here to be baptized, for that special purpose."

For three days the Indian pleaded for baptism, against the Church policy of protecting individuals from entering covenants hard to keep, so far from any branch of the Church. Finally Spencer agreed. He could not refuse baptism to one so sincere, so sure, so demanding of the blessing.

The three of them hired a taxi to take them to a river. No roads went to it directly, so they walked along a drain ditch. The water was filthy, but no better place could be found. With Elder Kimball wearing

In Egypt, 1960

his suit in the absence of the usual baptismal clothing, at a spot slightly less dirty than the rest he waded into the water, in mud to his calves and water to his waist. "Are you sure?" he asked again. And with the solemn prayer he baptized the eager convert.

As they left the water Spencer discovered that he had forgotten to take his papers from his pocket, and money and documents were soaked. The men dried them as best they could with newspaper, changed into dry clothes, and walked back to the waiting taxi. At the hotel Elder Kimball confirmed Dipty a member of The Church of Jesus Christ of Latter-day Saints and conferred upon him the gift of the Holy Ghost. And after lunch together in the hotel dining hall, the Kimballs took their leave of "this one young man, . . . a sheep among wolves."

At Karachi the Kimballs met a Baptist missionary couple who maintained a home for twelve orphans as well as carrying on their proselyting work. Elder Kimball saw in this "real Christian faith in action," and thought that the Church's first missionary efforts in Pakistan might well follow this pattern rather than the more conventional proselyting by young men.

At Teheran the two travelers found a branch of the Church among the Americans comprised of twenty-six families and totaling just over a hundred members. Two Iranian men were members, but they received so much criticism and persecution that they could not be more than marginally active and still continue to live in their country.

Here in Iran Spencer and Camilla first came into contact with biblical places and peoples, and the trip thereby took on additional interest. They landed at Beirut; Cairo; Luxor. Egyptian workers digging in crews reminded them of the children of Israel in Egypt. In Cairo they held Church services with a single American member family in the family's home.

Damascus; Jerusalem. After a lifetime of studying the scriptures, the trip from Damascus to Jerusalem by auto constituted for them a thrilling unfolding of wonder after wonder. It seemed that each hill and valley and plain had a name that gave it instant meaning and importance. Mount Hermon, Jericho, the River Jordan, Hebron, in Jerusalem all the spots associated with the Christ, Bethlehem, Qumran, Bethany, Meggido, Mount Tabor, the Sea of Galilee, Capernaum, Magdala, Cana, Nazareth.

Of all the places visited on their travels, the place said to have been the tomb where the body of Jesus was laid moved them the most. Unlike most other places for which an association with Christ's ministry was claimed, it had not been overbuilt by a chapel but was much as it might have been at the time of his death. The place was quiet. Only a few people came during all the morning Spencer and Camilla spent there, wrapped in scarves but warmed by the brilliant sun of January. They read to one another from the scriptures. "There was such a holy influence here that we stayed and stayed . . . , knelt together and each had a solemn prayer — a prayer of gratitude that we know the Lord and know Our Heavenly Father, and *know* that Jesus Christ lived and died and resurrected and rose and ascended and lives."

On to Greece; then to Rome. Here, for the first time, Spencer was on ground he had trodden before. "Points of interest were too near for a taxi and too far to walk, so we compromised by walking miles and miles. We still can't get over our long years of enforced economy when we were getting started in life. We save pennies to give away thousands. Can't seem to help it. Habit is a great force for good or evil, isn't it?" They stood with twenty-five thousand other people in St. Peter's

*Greeting from grandsons Stephen and Thomas Mack on
completion of trip around the world, 1961*

square as the Pope came to the window exactly at noon and spoke briefly to the crowd.

Madrid. They met with the group leader of Church members in Spain, where proselyting was forbidden despite a claim of religious liberty.

Lisbon; New York; Salt Lake City. They had been gone five months and had traveled around the world.

Elder Kimball returned to pick up the routine of visiting stake conferences every weekend. "This was a twenty-hour day, beginning at 5 a.m. and closing at 1 a.m.," he wrote of one such visit, "but it was glorious!"

Sometimes visits left no time between. From Idaho he once "flew home to Salt Lake. Camilla met me at the airport and brought my suitcase with clean clothes, and I gave her the soiled clothes and changed my suit in the restroom and I caught the plane for Oklahoma City."

The plane trips brought a mixture of interesting experiences and opportunities to help. On an airplane to Phoenix in bad weather the stewardess became ill, leaving only an inexperienced young man to substitute. As the plane bucked and twisted and passengers became airsick, Elder Kimball helped distribute sacks to those who needed them and got towels and tissues from the restroom to help people clean up.

Once because of airplane trouble it took him twelve hours to get home across the Great Plains. He wryly noted that he had new sympathy for the pioneers.

An airplane hostess asked, "Would you like something to drink?" Spencer asked, "What do you have?" She mentioned coffee, tea, Coca Cola. He shook his head, then rejoined, "Do you have any lemonade?" "No, but I could squeeze you some." Spencer quickly said, in mock horror, "Don't you squeeze me!"

On airplanes he found opportunity to make missionary contacts. He invited a bar owner from Glasgow, Montana, to call him up when he could say he had gone into some other business and had given up his own bad habits. He met three Basques; his little Spanish and their broken English added up to just enough for him to arrange a missionary referral. On a flight from Orlando to Atlanta he talked with a woman whom he persuaded to listen to missionaries; continuing on from Atlanta to Chicago he interested the stewardess in the gospel; between Chicago and Omaha he talked religion with a lady across the aisle (later he sent her literature); from Omaha to Salt Lake City he slept.

He cared for the strangers about him. A young mother on an overnight flight with a two-year-old daughter was stranded by bad weather in Chicago airport without food or clean clothing for the child and without money. She was two months pregnant and threatened with miscarriage, so she was under doctor's instructions not to carry the child unless it was essential. Hour after hour she stood in one line after another, trying to get a flight to Michigan. The terminal was noisy, full of tired, frustrated, grumpy passengers, and she heard critical references to her crying child and to her sliding her child along the floor with her foot as the line moved forward. No one offered to help with the soaked, hungry, exhausted child. Then, the woman later reported,

> someone came towards us and with a kindly smile said, "Is there something I could do to help you?" With a grateful sigh I accepted his offer. He lifted my sobbing little daughter from the cold floor and lovingly held her to him while he patted her gently on the back. He asked if she could chew a piece of gum. When she was settled down, he carried her with him and said something kindly to the others in the line ahead of me, about how I needed their help. They seemed to agree and then he went up to the ticket counter [at the front of the line] and made arrangements with the clerk for me to be put on a flight leaving shortly. He walked with us to a bench, where we chatted a moment, until he was assured that I would be fine. He went on his way. About a week later I saw a picture of Apostle Spencer W. Kimball and recognized him as the stranger in the airport.

As with the other apostles, on some weekends Elder Kimball simply presided at a conference, but on many others he was assigned to reorganize the stake presidency, which involved many additional hours of interviewing and instructing. Often he would not hesitate in selecting a new stake president. The choice would be clear, the impression certain. Other times there would be a disturbing confusion about the reorganization, an absence of any clear inspiration until a certain man would walk into the room for his interview. Then, suddenly, the apostle would feel "like light had penetrated the darkness."

Once as he and Elder Hugh B. Brown were reorganizing a stake in Utah they interviewed twenty-five or more stake leaders but received no impression that they had found the man the Lord wanted. Two men who had been mentioned as possibilities were out of town, but during the evening they returned and came in for interview. When the second man came in, who was just thirty-three years old and had been resident in the community for only a few months, both General Authorities felt assured immediately that this was the man.

On another occasion, as soon as a certain high councilor came in, Elder Kimball felt deeply impressed that he was to be the new stake president. The man accepted the call most graciously but without surprise. When asked why, he explained: "Six years ago when I was in the temple one day . . . I received the assurance that I would be the successor to the stake president when he was finally released. Since that day, I have been secretly and quietly doing my utmost to be prepared for it." The apostle asked how he would have felt if another had been called instead, and he replied: "I would have wondered how I had failed. I would have held to my inspirational experience but would have realized that it was I who had not measured up."

Another time, after many men had been interviewed, Elder Kimball asked the other General Authority assisting him, "How do you feel about the matter?" expecting him to comment on the various men. Instead his colleague responded with his definite view that one man was undoubtedly the right one. Elder Kimball then realized his error in stating the question as he had. He had a strong feeling toward a different man and now stood faced with the firm contrary expression of his colleague. But as the presiding official he felt both responsible for the decision and entitled to the inspiration in the matter. He moved on to other concerns, interviews, other business.

Time passed. Elder Kimball wrestled with his feelings. He did not wish to offend. Finally they interviewed again the man his companion had endorsed. Aware that he might be considered for the position, the man gave reasons of health and business problems which might interfere. When he left, the other General Authority said he knew that Elder Kimball had been struggling with the matter all afternoon and that his judgment and inspiration were right. They called the man Elder Kimball had been moved to call.

After April Conference 1961, Elder Kimball undertook an assignment of covering the whole United States, holding meetings with

stake presidents and working out relationships between full-time and
stake missionaries, to upgrade missionary work pursuant to President
McKay's slogan "Every Member a Missionary." He covered thirteen
thousand miles, zigzagging from coast to coast and from Canada to
Mexico, holding meetings in twenty-six cities, as well as presiding at
stake conferences along his path.

The trip around the world had whetted Spencer and Camilla's
appetite for travel. That December they mailed their 750
Christmas cards and went with Elder Howard W. Hunter and his
wife to the Near East during the Christmas break in stake conference
assignments.

In Egypt they visited Karnak and other places they had missed the
first time. They went to Iraq, to the ziggurat of Ur on the Euphrates
flood plain, and to the ruins of Babylon. The world of Abraham came
to life for Spencer. He read and dreamed and wrote about the patriarch.

On Christmas Eve 1961, the group reached Bethlehem. They
found crowds of people, estimated at twenty thousand, milling around
the Church of the Nativity. Inside, their disappointment compounded.
All was confusion. Two rival places, side by side, each with an attendant
competing for the tourists, claimed to be the actual birthplace. People
bowed and kissed the stones. Loudspeakers blared carols.

They left the town and went to the Shepherds' Field, perhaps the
place where the shepherds had heard the angelic message. Darkness
offered privacy, no attendants guarded its sanctity, few people were
about. The four felt a calmness here. They sang "Far, Far Away on
Judea's Plain" and then prayed, satisfied with the feeling they experienced of nearness to holy events.

For a week they walked through Jerusalem and other parts of
Palestine, first on the Arab side of the line and then on the Israeli side.

Before leaving Salt Lake City, the two apostles had volunteered to
handle stake conferences and other work in Europe. Now, as their visit
to Palestine ended, Elder Kimball conducted missionary meetings in
Vienna. He found that the rubble he had seen in Frankfurt six years
before was now cleaned up and the city was bustling. He presided at the
Stuttgart Stake conference and then at the Berlin Stake meetings.
From there he and Camilla went into East Berlin, the Communist zone,

beyond the Berlin Wall, which had gone up just a few months earlier to stem the flood of able-bodied, skilled workers leaving the Communist-controlled area of Germany.

East German soldiers stopped Spencer and Camilla, examined their passports, and searched their car. To appearances they were merely American tourists.

They drove about, watching to see if they were being followed, winding around until they came to the vicinity of the meetingplace, then parked the car and walked the last two blocks. The streets were poorly lit. A man walking down the block as they got out of the car turned and followed them for a short distance. As they came to the meetingplace no one was in sight; they ducked in quickly.

Inside the building a group of about eighty awaited them in the light and warmth, filling the small hall. The meeting had not been much publicized. There was no telephone service, and mail could not be considered private. In their loneliness, "in prison" as one sister put it, the sight of Elder Kimball, an apostle, "was like an angel from heaven."

The one boy attending was well below deacon's age, so three older men passed the sacrament. Through tears, behind heavily curtained windows, the congregation sang "I Need Thee Every Hour." The visiting apostle spoke on the sufferings of the Lord and on Joseph Smith's experiences in Liberty Jail. Both his emotions and the congregation's lay near the surface.

Elder Kimball marveled at the steadfastness of the members in their trials and difficulties. Missionary work had to be done quietly, only by referrals. The youth stood exposed to heavy pressure and indoctrination. One girl, preparing to take the college entrance examination was asked, "Whom do you hate?" Her professed belief in God and her denial that she hated America or capitalists precluded her from taking the examination. Attendance and activity of elders ran from 80 percent to 90 percent.

After the general meeting, Elder Kimball and the mission president met with the seven district leaders present. He wrote their names in capital letters in his journal, "for I think the Lord will do that. . . . I felt I was in the presence of great and good and noble men."

The leaders were hungry for news of the Church. Elder Kimball told them of changes in Church leadership; of the surge of missionary work in the world; of new stakes in Europe, the South Seas, Alaska and

Mexico City; of a new temple to be built in Oakland, California; of progress in the Indian missions.

The meetings over, the group said farewell. Some embraced the visitors as they left, some shed tears. On the dark street all seemed quiet, but as the two Americans came to the car, which one of the mission leaders had moved during the meeting for further safety, a woman watched from a third-story window. For a while they thought perhaps they were being followed by a car. At the checkpoint Elder Kimball folded up his notes from the meeting with the district leaders and tucked them into a fold in the seat. He did not want the names of the leaders to come into Communist hands. Search of the car did not turn up the notes, and they breathed easier as they zigzagged back into West Berlin. But they carried with them a sadness at the lonely, difficult situation of the Saints in East Germany.

From Berlin, Spencer and Camilla went to Denmark for missionary meetings, to the Hamburg Stake conference, to England on Church business, and back to the Holland Stake conference. On the first of February they returned home.

When later that year a physical examination revealed nothing unusual for a sixty-seven-year-old man, Spencer wrote: "Generally I feel so good I can hardly believe the years. I feel like a young man and work like one. It is always good to be reassured. I am older than my father and mother were when they died and older than many of my ancestors and I do not seem to have come from a long-lived family. I am glad I am as well as I am. I am grateful to the Lord for my health and hope I may serve to justify my health."

By 1963, Church membership had grown to over 1½ million in the United States alone and was rising at the rate of roughly one hundred thousand members a year in the world. An enormous building fund was budgeted yearly for new chapels and stake centers. A high-rise Church office building had been planned for downtown Salt Lake City, while Church organization and administrative procedure were being modified to contain the pressures of immense growth.

April Conference 1962 was the first conference to be broadcast coast-to-coast and by shortwave to South America. It created inhibitions, making the Brethren aware they spoke not only to members but to a more general audience which might be looking on out of curiosity. The format became more structured, with assigned subjects on occasion and stricter time limits. But it also meant the welcome end of what the General Authorities called "the anxious seat," as they now for the first time received advance notice of when they would speak. The loss of spontaneity seemed to Elder Kimball a small enough price to pay for the chance to reach millions.

With the increased complexity of administering the Church, Elder Kimball, now a senior member of the Council of the Twelve, took on increasingly heavy responsibilities. Several years before, with Elders Lee and Petersen, he had finished a new handbook for stake and ward leaders. Some of the General Authorities had resisted the idea of a handbook, feeling that there should be more reliance on inspiration in one's calling; others, including Elder Kimball, felt that the handbook provided a base on which inspired variation to suit local needs could be built.

For some years he had been chairman of the Budget Committee. Routinely the budget requests by Church departments outran expected income by millions of dollars, partly because a new push in missionary work led many mission presidents to request funds for buildings and equipment as though there were no limitation. Elder Kimball took the question of a balanced budget to the First Presidency and obtained their support for it. With that support he insisted that the departments, particularly those dealing with education and buildings, pare down their requests.

Other General Authorities saw things in expansionist terms and were willing to build and spend beyond current needs in expectation that growth in the Church would soon make up the difference, but Elder Kimball worked vigorously for a balanced budget each year.

The new Church Office Building, a twenty-six-story skyscraper, begun late in 1962, represented the one viewpoint. Elder Kimball on the other hand, felt somewhat apprehensive about the timing of the project. Three years later, after the building had reached ground level, with the construction of underground parking terraces completed, the project was delayed for several years in the interest of financial caution.

What Elder Kimball felt of millions of dollars, he also felt of a few. When he discovered that he had been provided a first-class plane ticket he changed it to tourist class, saving the Church forty dollars on his round trip to Chicago. In Phoenix he asked for a less expensive hotel room and saved three dollars. He tried to save the Church's money whenever he would have saved his own. He believed that the Church should build reserves, "at least a year's supply."

He had problems keeping the expanding building programs within their budget. When the Church Building Committee sometimes bypassed the budget process and went directly to the First Presidency for approval of deficit spending on new buildings, Elder Kimball, though standing ready to support the Presidency's decisions, insisted they should have been given all the facts in the matter, including the effect on the overall financial picture of the Church.

At year's end in 1963 Spencer wrote in his journal about the mounting pressure.

> I had a bad night last night . . . worrying so much about the budget which is to be presented on Thursday and the missionary work which is still new and so many other problems in connection with the Indian Program and otherwise. I could not seem to let my mind go to sleep. My responsibility is tremendous and the greatest it has ever been. It is a big Church now with 73 missions and 12,000 missionaries and nearly 400 stake missions and regional missions; what with the stake conferences and all of the interviews, I work early and late. I rolled and tumbled until into the night and then walked the floor awhile, and then slept on the couch. The wind howled and eerie voices came down the chimney. I was glad when the daylight came.

In 1963 Elder Kimball made a swing through Utah to see how the work with the Indians was going. He found in nearly every case that the white people called to train the Indians in branch work had succumbed to the temptation to do everything themselves. When the Indians proved undependable by white standards the workers lacked the patience to let them learn from mistakes.

Elder Kimball's advice was usually practical. When he had inspected an Indian village in Sevier Stake, "which we found still rather scrappy but much improved over our last visit, I urged the president to have them paint their houses and to clean up their front yards and to plant. Along the ditch bank we found a drunk Indian. We thought he had been hit by a car but he was just dead drunk." In Las Vegas he discussed a plan to build a bath and washrooms for the Indians at a settlement nearby.

New roads into the reservation, where fifteen years earlier only

nearly impassable rock and dirt roads had existed, made the missionary work more efficient. One Indian missionary had returned to drinking and had left his mission, but overall the progress was remarkable.
Whereas three years before, after rapid growth, there had been 8,400
Indian members, now there were 12,000. The backward, frightened
people, who had hid their faces or stood like a post, now shook hands
with warmth. Whereas they had once had to be cajoled to attend
meetings, now they came from distances voluntarily.

In Gallup the Indian leader conducting a meeting called on an
elderly man to offer the opening prayer. He did not respond until his
grandson, a returned missionary, whispered loudly across the benches,
"He wants you to pray." The man arose slowly and walked up the aisle
to the side of the pulpit and stood, unmoving. The grandson spoke up,
"He doesn't know how." At suggestion from the leader, the grandson
helped his grandfather up the steps to the pulpit, where the man stood
embarrassed. Then the boy, with folded arms, gave the invocation in
short Navajo phrases, which his grandfather repeated. They then
moved quietly back to their seats.

In Hopi country permission to build a chapel could not be obtained from the chiefs, but in Cibeque a new chapel had been built with
substantial contributions from the Apaches in cash and labor, nearly
half of it from nonmembers. In one meeting a male chorus of ten
Indian men sang, the first such group Elder Kimball had heard. He
lined up nine boys and gave each a dollar for his missionary fund.

In Lukachukai, on the Navajo reservation, in 1964, the apostle met
with a group of recently baptized Indians in an upper room of the
trading post. The Navajos asked through the translator, "Is this *The
Church* or is it just another church?" Elder Kimball answered and
seemed to satisfy them. They said they would like a building. He
answered that he would try to get them a building if they could get a lot
on which to build it. They said they did not want to wait for a big
building, but wanted to build a chapel tomorrow. They were so insistent that he ordered the few hundred dollars of building materials it
would cost to build a little structure.

They wanted an organization, and the twenty-one Indians there
unanimously voted to organize a branch. Without waiting they said
they wanted Brother Jack, a trader who was fair with them, to be
branch president. On the spot Elder Kimball and the mission president
called Brother Jack to serve and he accepted and then chose for his

counselors Thomas Little Ben and Joe Dick. Neither could speak English. The counselors were presented to the congregation to be made deacons, and after approval by the congregation Elder Kimball set the three apart. "It is the first time in my experience I have seen Navajos or Indians of any kind so boldly request the blessings of the Gospel and the Church. It is most thrilling and exhilarating."

In November Elder Kimball toured the Indian reservations of Montana, North Dakota, and South Dakota, meeting with missionaries, members, and investigators. He found some discouragement among the missionaries, who faced superstition, physical hardship, and strong opposition by other churches. His diagnosis was that more work and less mooning about their problems would help. To buoy up their spirits, he wrote new words to the song "Happy Days Are Here Again" and taught it to the missionaries.

In this new Northern Indian Mission "one little branch paid $19 fast offerings for the month, which is excellent and shows a gradual move toward assuming their responsibilities. The Indian women furnished much of the meals in each case, which is another indication of their taking their place. . . . Some are beginning to pay their tithing. It was remarkable, too, that the Indians were there pretty well on time."

A white girl was considering marriage to an Indian college student. Her parents came to Elder Kimball, objecting. He agreed with them that such a marriage carried with it greater risks than marriage between people of similar racial and cultural backgrounds, but he told them there was no wrong in it. He would not encourage it, but neither would he try to block it. A year later the young couple were married in the temple; Elder Kimball performed the ceremony. The bride's parents refused to attend.

In a meeting with stake presidents on the Indian program, Elder Harold B. Lee praised Elder Kimball's work and said that he would perhaps go down in Church history as the great Indian defender. President McKay said in response to Elder Kimball's request for greater support and cooperation from the Church auxiliary organizations, "There are no limits."

In November 1963, Elder Kimball was appointed chairman of the Missionary Committee, which oversaw the missionary program of the

Church. The group met every week to make recommendations to the President where each new missionary should be assigned among the missions of the world.

For some years Elder Kimball's concern for missionary work had found expression in dozens of stake and mission meetings, where he would call up to the stand the boys who were twelve. Having asked each boy his name, he would ask: "Are you a deacon? What will you be doing when you are nineteen?" If the twelve-year-olds did not respond, the apostle would sometimes say: "You'll be on missions, won't you! Haven't your bishops interviewed you for missions? Haven't your parents started mission funds?" He would then give each a dollar for his mission fund. He was hoping to impress the boys, but he was directing his message also at parents and leaders, emphasizing that they should start early to encourage and prepare boys for missionary service. (He sometimes called up girls, too, and gave them each a dollar to start a savings fund toward the expenses of traveling to be married in the temple.)

He had given an Indian boy in Duckwater, Nevada, a dollar to start his missionary fund and had written to the boy occasionally. Two years after the first contact they had met again at the boy's stake conference, when Elder Kimball had given him another dollar; and later the apostle sent the boy some books and then eight dollars. The boy had asked him to put the money in the bank for him. Now in a letter the boy sent two dollars of his own money to be added to the account, money he earned at the rate of ten dollars a month doing janitorial work.

In Virginia, one boy questioned about his mission plans answered that he could not go on a mission because he wanted to be a doctor. The apostle told him he would be a better doctor if he had been on a mission first, and he gave the boy a dollar. On the way back home a traveling companion handed him ten dollars from the boy's parents as an expression of their thanks. They sent the message, "If in your travels you can find ten more little boys on such an occasion, it would please us."

Elder Kimball distributed the ten dollars in Buckeye, Arizona. Three days later he received from a friend a package of silver dollars labelled "Seeds for the Spencer W. Kimball Missionary Garden." Another time a man gave him a specially made box containing forty silver dollars to be given out. Though others helped in this way, hundreds of dollars came out of his own pocket. He received many letters from missionaries who recalled the starter-dollar received years before, and from parents who said he had never spent a dollar to better purpose.

Dollars were handed out at other times, too. Once at dinner at a stake president's home Elder Kimball learned that a grandson present was named Spencer. He took out a dollar bill and said, "Do you know what I always do when I find a little boy by the name of Spencer?" The boy looked at him questioningly. When Elder Kimball handed him the dollar the boy was overjoyed. Another grandson of the stake president looked shyly out of the corner of his eye and said, "What do you do when you find a little boy named Faris?" Elder Kimball, realizing his mistake in tact, found he had only a twenty-dollar bill and promised to deliver the dollar to Faris the next day.

In October 1963, President McKay reorganized the First Presidency, calling Elders Hugh B. Brown and N. Eldon Tanner as his counselors. A vacancy in the Twelve he filled by calling Thomas S. Monson, one of the two men Elder Kimball had named when each apostle was asked for suggestions, as was sometimes done. It pleased Elder Kimball that he "seemed to be in line with the President's thinking and the Lord's thinking."

In charging Elder Monson as to his new responsibility, President McKay explained the principle of unity, wherein each member of the Council is to express his views without hesitation; but when the decision of the Council is made, its will is to be carried out wholeheartedly. "He is not true to his pledge," said the President, "if at any time he might say, 'The Council decided that way, but I thought differently.' He has no right to say that."

The day previously, Elder Kimball noted, there had been differences expressed between some of the Brethren — friendly but frank, and the exchange of views had cleared the atmosphere. With the kind of strong-minded men called as General Authorities, differences of opinion were inevitable. The President's words to Elder Monson served as a reminder to them all. On occasions when his brethren disagreed with his vigorously stated position, Elder Kimball was careful not to criticize.

A burning issue in the nation was civil rights, particularly the question of equal opportunity for blacks. The Church came under great criticism for its policy of withholding the priesthood from blacks.

In November 1962, someone had fastened a small bomb to the front door of the Salt Lake Temple. It had blown out the door and shattered some windows. No specific reason could be assigned to the act, but it seemed most likely related to the increasingly militant agitation for improved conditions for blacks.

In October Conference 1963, President Hugh B. Brown of the First Presidency commenced the proceedings with an official statement of the Church in support of full civil rights for all citizens. The statement came in response to black agitation. It did not refer at all to the question of conferring the priesthood, but it did affirm the Church's interest in secular equality for all. The statement gained substantial publicity across the country.

Elder Kimball had sympathy with blacks' feelings about their treatment generally, but he had no sympathy with the use of violence or coercive measures to achieve equality. When sixty blacks picketed the Church Office Building for three days, his advice was simply to ignore the demonstration. He felt that the Church practice in relation to holding the priesthood could not be changed just to respond to human wishes, but that such a change would require divine intervention.

He had great sympathy with individual blacks who were faithful members of the Church. When asked to make suggestions concerning the Church exhibit at the New York World's Fair in 1964 he thought that black faces could be included in the murals in recognition of the devout blacks who were members; he thought also that perhaps one or more blacks could serve as guides at the exhibit.

He felt sharply the double burden of Brother Monroe Fleming, a black friend who suffered persecution from other blacks because of his faithfulness to the Church which nevertheless did not give him the priesthood.

On November 22, 1963, as Elder Kimball sat in a committee meeting, Elder Howard W. Hunter came in white-faced, excited, carrying the news that President John F. Kennedy had been shot. He returned a few minutes later with word that the president had died at the hands of an assassin. The whole nation's attention turned to the shocking story. Elder Kimball participated in a memorial service in the Tabernacle honoring the dead president.

A few weeks later he attended another funeral when Richard R. Lyman died at ninety-three. Of the four General Authorities who attended the funeral only Elder Kimball had been in the Quorum when Brother Lyman had been excommunicated. It was he who, with Elder LeGrand Richards, had interviewed Brother Lyman several times and finally recommended in 1954 that he be rebaptized. "I kept hoping through the years that he would make another serious attempt to receive his [priesthood and temple] blessings back but apparently it did not seem important enough to him, or he didn't have the energy or the courage or something. At any rate, he died as a lay member of the Church without Priesthood, without endowments, without sealings, and it was sad indeed."

In the previous June he had felt the opposite emotion. Upon restoring by proxy the membership and temple blessings of a man who had died many years before, "there came an unusual feeling like someone was near me. There was no feeling of shock nor curiosity nor fear. I did not look around but there came over me a calm, sweet feeling of a presence. It was sweet and warming and I had the feeling that the man to whom I had just restored incomparable blessings was not far away. I felt warm."

That Christmas Spencer and Camilla spent in Salt Lake City with Olive Beth's family. Through the mail came a harvest of gratitude. Camilla one year wrote to her son: "People were most generous with us at Christmas. We have two fruit cakes, three boxes of citrus, a box of grapes, pecans, two boxes of dates, shelled walnuts, ten pounds of candy, three boxes of pears and about 600 Christmas cards, all because so many people love your Dad so much." And each year such gifts increased.

18

Supervision of the South American Missions

— "yes, President McKay, there are millions"

In May 1964 Elder Kimball was assigned to visit the seven missions in South America. In the five years since his earlier visit, there had been a marked increase in conversions, so that now the thousand missionaries on the continent baptized a thousand new members a month.

When the flight on which he and Camilla traveled arrived in Buenos Aires three hours late, they were met at the airport by A. Theodore Tuttle of the First Council of Seventy and all seven mission presidents. Greeting them, Elder Kimball jokingly asked whether the hundred or more people watching from the airport balcony were Church members; and as he asked the question, the crowd began singing a hymn and he realized that they had come and waited for hours to honor him. The people swarmed around the visitors in the airport with tears, smiles, embraces.

After meetings and interviews in the Buenos Aires area, the party crossed the broad Rio de la Plata into Uruguay. At Montevideo Spencer and Camilla were special guests of the American ambassador at a formal reception, the first time they had experienced such official honor. This improved standing of the Church made missionary work easier.

It annoyed Elder Kimball when a few missionaries in Uruguay grumbled that proselyting was hard work. He told a group of them: "Of course it is hard work. Missionary work is not supposed to be fun." For him a primary ground for doing something was duty. The rewards were not in the work itself but in its product. He told them that he had milked cows to raise money for his mission, had milked until his fingers were raw and throbbing, and on the mission itself had tramped the back country of Missouri hoping for a bed and a meal.

After the meeting there was a chicken dinner and then a missionary talent show. Disappointed that only the most talented missionaries had been given parts, Elder Kimball noted also in his journal a lack of missionary spirit in the show: "I did not mind a little of the slapstick, but when the whole evening of nearly three hours was occupied by it, it seemed to me a waste of time." In spite of these incidents he had high praise for the missionaries and for the mission president.

He pondered over the stark poverty of many South American members. Since runaway inflation made saving money almost impossible, their small income meant that travel to the United States for temple marriage would be a vain hope for nearly all of them. "I know we must have a temple in South America," he thought. He wondered about the luxuriousness of some of the mission headquarters when the people in the missions had to struggle so hard just to pay tithes on their little earnings. He noted with approval a group of missionaries in one area who had gone beyond ordinary proselyting to organize efforts to get street lighting installed.

At a city near Montevideo, where a chapel was under construction, Elder Kimball took off his coat and shoveled a few buckets of sand. Many of the converts were from a social class unaccustomed to manual labor, but he found them catching the spirit of cooperation. There were 147 of them on this holiday, passing cement blocks, shoveling sand, mixing cement. It was Monday, and they had plans to use the building for a conference on the following Sunday. This day they poured the floor and began building walls. After a week of intense work, on Sunday the conference did take place in the building, although plastic covered the window spaces, wires hung from the ceiling, and the dais consisted of rough planks. Elder Kimball arrived early and helped clean the floor and set up seats. Eleven hundred people crowded in, possibly the largest Church meeting in South American experience to that time. The man giving the closing prayer at the conference, in tears, kept repeating, "Gracias Padre, gracias, gracias por El Apostol."

The pace was intense. Elder Kimball drove himself long and hard through meetings and interviews. One mission president, trying to keep up, told a friend, "He's killing me."

The tour continued by plane up the coastline into Brazil. There were meetings in Porto Alegre, and then, later the same day, in Curitiba, almost halfway north to Rio de Janeiro.

In Curitiba two of the full-time church builders were black. "My heart bleeds for them. They bore fine, humble testimonies expressing sorrow for their deprivation, but no bitterness." One said he would give his life for the Lord's program: "I accept the Church and I am willing to wait for the millennium wherein there will be a change of my body and when I can trade this life for another. Please remember me in your prayers." He had served two of his three years in the Church in building chapels. The other man, who had been a member for five years, expressed gratitude for the love and brotherhood shown him.

Spencer embraced another black youth. "My heart went out to him. . . . I felt impressed to promise him blessings beyond his fondest imagination if he remained totally true to the Cause."

The group flew another two hundred miles northeast to Sao Paulo. At the airport banners of welcome appeared on three balconies. There were flashbulbs popping, a television camera, police lines. Elder Kimball wondered why the policemen were there. As the group left the plane a great crowd of about two thousand people surged forward in greeting and the police linked arms and pushed back, making room for the visitors to move ahead. People pressed forward, straining for a view or a touch. Flowers were thrust forward, signs of welcome waved. Elder Kimball shook hands with and spoke to as many as he could. In the crush he lost Camilla, the baggage, and other members of the group. Someone managed to push him into a car and the others finally joined him. He shook hands thrust through the window and the car moved slowly out, leaving him barely in control of his emotions, wishing to greet each individual but knowing he could not.

Spencer noted that as he entered meetings in many places the people sang "We Thank Thee, O God, for a Prophet." "This always humbles me to the dust. I try to feel that this is an honor for the

President of the Church and that I am just representing him. After the meeting, about ten children in white brought baskets full of flower petals and showered me with them. I was humbled again."

While based for several days in Rio de Janeiro the group stayed in a hotel by the sea. "The waves with their rhythmic and ceaseless frequency broke with music to my ears. I love the sea. I threw back the curtains, opened the window-door, stepped out on our little steel balcony and drank in the freshness of the Atlantic."

After trips from Rio de Janeiro to Brasilia and other cities in Brazil the group flew twelve hundred miles back to Cordoba, Argentina, for conferences, then to Mendoza and on to Santiago, Chile, across the Andes. The conferences continued in Chile, where there were a number of strong branches and three Church schools which, he was told, were among the best schools in South America. Then the group flew to the high Bolivian cities to investigate whether it would be desirable to send missionaries into that country. They met with several families of members who lived in Bolivia. In La Paz and Cochabamba the air was so thin that Spencer could not sleep at night except sitting up. They also visited branches in Peru and were able to meet briefly with the president of the country.

The party flew north to Quito, Ecuador, where they met with the only known Church member in the country, an English girl abandoned by her husband. They also checked with an attorney working on obtaining legal recognition for the Church in Ecuador.

A last meeting in Panama ended six weeks of intensive travel and meetings. After so long away, returning home felt good. "Of all the lovely places we have seen, nothing quite compares with our own view out of our own kitchen window."

"Today is my twenty-first birthday," Spencer wrote a few days later, on July 8, 1964. "Well do I remember that noon hour . . . when the call came over the telephone. What a glorious twenty-one years."

At October Conference 1964, the ninety-two-year-old President McKay spoke. A stroke and a heart attack during recent years had so crippled him that in the previous January he had "seemed to be somewhat discouraged . . . said he was going to get a little rest and if he was not improved he would probably ask the Lord to take him. This was a sad moment for us all." Then another stroke had struck him down. It had thickened his speech and sapped his strength but had not dulled his mind. Now, in October, he was given oxygen to breathe before being helped into the Tabernacle for conference. But the ailing President, loved and revered by the Latter-day Saints, continued to oversee the Church. The *Deseret News* gave a statistical picture of the burgeoning Church in 1964: 2,234,916 members, 410 stakes, 3749 wards and branches, 75 missions, 16,271 missionaries. The size of the Church had much more than doubled since Elder Kimball had received his call, but there were still just twelve apostles. The interviews, marriages, mission tours, stake conference assignments, and committee meetings increased with the size of the Church, but there were no more hours in the day.

One work week went in this way: On Monday he woke at 7:30, chagrined at having overslept by two hours. He worked at his desk all day. On Tuesday he was at the office at 6:30 in the morning. This was his heaviest day of committee work. At 7:00 A.M. the Missionary Committee met, assigning 170 missionaries to their mission areas. At 10:00 A.M. the Expenditure Committee approved requests for funds from the various units of the Church. He slipped away to perform a marriage in the temple. At 1:00 P.M. he spoke to the missionaries in the Mission Home, who were there for training before they went to their assigned fields. At 2:00 P.M. the Indian Affairs Committee considered the student placement program's progress. At 4:00 P.M. the Loan Committee of Beneficial Life Insurance Company, of which he was a member, considered loan applications. At 4:30 a BYU professor met with him. He worked on at the office until 6:30 in the evening, then worked at his desk at home after dinner until ten o'clock.

On Wednesday his first meeting started at 7:30 A.M. and he returned home at 6:00 P.M. without having had time for lunch. He worked at his desk through the evening. On Thursday, when the Twelve and then the Twelve with the First Presidency met for much of the day in the temple to conduct their business and to worship together, his first meeting started at 7:30 A.M. He spent the afternoon in interviews. Friday started with a wedding at 8:15 A.M. He worked late at his desk in the evening.

On Saturday he had a 6:15 A.M. airplane to catch and did not wake until 5:40. He bathed and threw on his clothes and was out of the door in five minutes and raced to the airport ten miles across town, through the airport on the run and up the plane stairs just as the door was closing. As soon as the seatbelt sign went off he rushed to the restroom to shave, comb, brush, and tie and button, then returned to greet the people he knew on the plane.

On Sunday night he went to bed fairly early. During the night he checked his watch and read 6:20; so he got up and bathed and shaved, only to realize then that his watch had been upside down and he had awakened at ten minutes before one.

In October Lyndon Johnson, President of the United States, appeared just before election day for a speech in the Tabernacle. President Hugh B. Brown was eager for the Twelve to attend, but to Elder Kimball it seemed a purely political meeting and an imposition. When President McKay sent word that he felt they should attend, the Twelve interrupted their meeting to go. Spencer was glad the speech was relatively mild, but he felt that candidates on both sides had imposed on President McKay by making a public display of calling on him shortly before the election and professing their great friendship.

Generally speaking, as an apostle Elder Kimball was nonpolitical in his approach. He always voted and tried to attend mass meetings in his neighborhood to select responsible representatives to party conventions, but he felt that General Authorities should avoid public positions on most political questions because of the potentially divisive effect. On a few occasions he spoke out on referenda, such as on sale of liquor by the drink in Utah and on Sunday closing, but these he considered to be basically moral rather than political issues.

In 1964 the First Presidency had decided to accept $2 million in federal funds to aid in hospital construction. After further consideration, in 1965 the Presidency and the Twelve felt strongly that accepting the funds would subject the Church hospital operation to undue federal regulation, and the money therefore was not accepted. The growing impact of federal government regulation concerned Elder Kimball.

> With numerous others, I am greatly disturbed at the rapid move of our government to socialism and what seems to be an approach toward dictatorship; with a controlled Supreme Court, the administration continues to impose more and more demands upon the people.... Taxes are becoming back-breaking; expenditures and waste are alarming. The Church must remain independent and furnish its own funds for all its own adventures and projects. The government seems too anxious to give, give, give to the poor, to the aged, to the schools, to everyone, and blinded

people feel they are getting something, whereas they pay it to the government so that the government can after great overhead expense return a part of it to the people. And every time a gift returns to the people — a so-called gift — it comes with fetters binding and tying and enslaving. For every block of funds given to the people, they lose a bigger block of liberty.

He noted with alarm a growing disrespect for authority. In Salt Lake City a group of "hoodlums" had appropriated Liberty Park as their own. When police tried to control the situation a thousand gathered in demonstration and twenty-two persons, including two policemen, suffered injuries in the battle.

In a riot in the Watts area of Los Angeles, burning, looting, and shooting cost a number of lives and millions of dollars in property damage. Spencer included news clippings of this in his journal.

By 1965 the Americanization of the Vietnamese war had begun. President Johnson ordered bombing of North Vietnam and the number of United States combat troops in the country rose above seventy-five thousand. As chairman of the Missionary Committee, Elder Kimball worried about the war's effect on the Church. "We are in a rather desperate situation. They are calling so many young men into the military and, in fact, the local draft boards are shorter of young men now than they were in the Korean War . . . ; many of our fine young men may have to go to war instead of in the mission field. It grieves us."

The Missionary Committee met with Selective Service officials. Since local draft boards had to produce a certain number of servicemen, every boy who obtained a ministerial deferment depleted the pool from which they could draw. Though the Church stood on sound legal ground, as had been previously established, the public relations problem posed by what others saw as evasion of military service by the Mormon boys would not go away. The Committee worked out a policy, implemented by the First Presidency, whereby each stake had a quota of one missionary each six months for each of its wards and branches. Young men otherwise exempt from the draft did not apply against the stake quota. Though the Committee hoped the policy would reduce the missionary force only a little, experience showed that the flow of missionaries diminished substantially.

In March 1965 Spencer celebrated his birthday. "I am seventy years old. I cannot believe it. I have had a few little touches of arthritis in my legs and hips of recent weeks. Today, it is gone. I put in long hard hours. I do work very hard. It seems to me I get little accomplished." Occasional heart pains worried him, but his doctor had no advice but to slow down. Spencer summarized the previous year: "Never have I had so many assignments and committee appointments. Never have I been so tied. Camilla and I spent two weeks in California in the summer, but otherwise, practically every day of the year I was 'hitting the ball.' "

In May the First Presidency and the Twelve divided the missions of the world into twelve areas. One of the twelve apostles was to supervise each area. Elder Kimball was assigned, with the assistance of Franklin D. Richards, to supervise the seven missions of South America which he had visited just the year before.

In October 1965 Elders Kimball and Richards flew to Quito, Ecuador, where they were met by the Andes Mission president, James Jesperson, and four missionaries. The next day this group, fasting, took a taxi to the top of a high hill in the center of Quito to dedicate the country for missionary work. They thought they would be alone, but they found on the hill a family who had also come by taxi, as sightseers. Elder Kimball sent the missionaries to invite the family and their driver to join in the service. They did so. Then he offered a dedicatory prayer.

In his journal Elder Kimball quoted from Elder Ballard's dedication of the whole of South America forty years before: "The work will go slowly for a time, just as an oak grows slowly from an acorn . . . but thousands will join the Church here. . . . The day will come when the Lamanites here will get their chance. The South American Mission is to be a power in the Church."

Elder Kimball exulted in the importance of this new beginning in Ecuador. And he worked to make the dedicatory prayer come true. As the group sat down to a hotel meal, he commented to the others that their waiter was a fine-looking young man and would make a good missionary for the Church. Elder Kimball ordered bread and milk, then asked the waiter if he had any children at home. "One son," the waiter answered. "Bread and milk will make him healthy," Elder Kimball said, "but he will be even healthier if you will feed him the food these young men have to give." The waiter looked puzzled. Then Elder Kimball explained that the young men were missionaries who had the gospel of Jesus Christ to teach. The waiter expressed interest in having the missionaries teach him.

Franklin D. Richards and Spencer W. Kimball with shoeshine boys, Otavalo, Ecuador, 1965

A. Theodore Tuttle and Spencer W. Kimball with president of Peru, 1964

From Quito the group drove to Otavalo where, in a little plaza, they sat in the shade while the driver repaired a flat tire. A clean-cut, businesslike boy asked to shine their shoes for a few cents and they agreed. Elder Kimball asked him his name, where he lived, whether he went to school. Then he told the boy, Cornelio, that there were things of more importance than money and that the missionaries would come to Otavalo with the message of the restored gospel of Christ. Elder Kimball promised to write him and gave him an Articles of Faith card with his name on, saying he would be back in Otavalo some day and would be eager to learn how Cornelio was getting along.

A few days later some Americans getting a shine from Cornelio were shown the card and were asked whether they knew this man from the United States. They excitedly wanted to know all about the matter; of course they knew him. Cornelio told them the man was staying in Quito. By this time Elder Kimball had moved on, but the family located the four elders who had been left there to begin the missionary work. The family was going to be in Quito for some months and they made their home available to the elders, providing a nucleus for the first Church activity in the country. When he learned this, Elder Kimball expressed the feeling that the Lord had scattered strong Latter-day Saint families to places where they could be useful to the work.

Laying the groundwork for new missionary efforts, Elder Kimball continued southward into Peru. In the Quillabamba area, where they planned to go, peasant guerrillas were fighting ranchers and government troops. "We do not want to be foolhardy and run into trouble," wrote Elder Kimball, "but I feel a great 'burden' upon me to expedite the work among the Indians. . . . I have felt impressed to go."

They found the city full of soldiers, an eight o'clock curfew, highways often chained closed. They slept in a primitive hotel, but Spencer was so exhausted that he slept well in spite of everything. The next morning he sat in the small town square, talking with the shoeshine boys. He played jacks with some little girls and one asked him to help her with a drawing. In assessing the prospects for missionary work, the visitors talked with business people, drove around the valley, visited with some peasants, but they had no difficulty with the fighting.

From Cuzco they flew into Bolivia, where Elder Kimball was delighted at the progress of the Church in cities he had visited before. At Cochabamba he met with 4 missionaries and 112 local people. Sixteen months earlier there had been no missionary in the city, no member, no contact. In La Paz, in place of the seven local people with whom he had met in a hotel room on his last visit, Elder Kimball met now with two hundred in a rented chapel.

The rest of the tour involved visiting established branches in Chile. Then Elders Kimball and Richards conducted a seminar in Montevideo with just the seven mission presidents and their wives.

On his return to Salt Lake City, Elder Kimball felt so confident of the strength and vigor of the Church in South America that he urged in the Council's Thursday temple meeting that Sao Paulo be organized as a stake. About twenty overseas stakes already existed, but this would be the first in South America. One of the General Authorities expressed strong reservations about the organization of more stakes outside North America. In response Marion G. Romney recalled the organization of the first stake outside North America and Hawaii: "In 1958 President David O. McKay invited me to go with him and Elder Stapley to dedicate the New Zealand Temple. When we were down there . . . I was sitting by him and we were having a luncheon and he turned to me and said, 'Brother Romney, I feel that the Lord wants us to organize a stake here.' He told me who was to be the stake president, George Beisinger, and he left the rest of the organization to me." And Elder Kimball cited President McKay's conclusion in 1960 regarding additional stakes in New Zealand and Australia: "Brethren, that is right. That is what the Lord wants." After discussion the proposal to establish a stake in Sao Paulo was put to the First Presidency and approved by them.

Elder Kimball resumed his other responsibilities, visiting stakes, conducting interviews and so on, the routine of a General Authority. The year ended quietly, he and Camilla taking a few days' vacation in Los Angeles. There Spencer worked each day on the book he was writing about repentance. Each afternoon he and Camilla went to a movie (one a triple feature). Much of the time it rained, producing some bad flooding in Southern California. They had no umbrellas and in hurrying through the rain Camilla slipped and knocked Spencer's feet out from under him. They both sprawled wide and flat on the pavement. A man helped Spencer get Camilla to her feet. As soon as they had ascertained that they had suffered only bruises, they laughed all the way to the hotel at the thought of the picture they must have offered of drunks too besotted to keep their feet.

They spent New Year's Eve on the train returning home, sitting in the dome car, holding hands, reminiscing.

In the spring of 1966 Elder Kimball arrived in Sao Paulo to organize the first South American stake. He did not notify the mission president exactly when he would arrive, so this time no crowd met him at the airport, "and this is the way I wanted it." After meetings and interviews he called as stake president a German-born Brazilian, who selected as his counselors two native Brazilians. Only one of the three spoke English. It seemed to Elder Kimball that this stake organization was a major step toward the realization of Elder Ballard's dedicatory prayer long before, that the Saints in South America would be "a power in the Church."

His vision for these people expanded. When half the congregation at one meeting in Sao Paulo proved to be of Italian descent, he thought that from here might come missionaries for Italy. With sacrifice, he felt, temples could be built in South America.

He had asked the American missionaries in Cuzco, Peru, one Thursday night to do nothing in the branch that a member could learn to do. And by that Sunday a young Peruvian had learned to play one hymn on the piano for the congregation. Elder Kimball knew that the people would rise to a challenge.

Back in Salt Lake City for most of the year, he continued his familiar work. Most weeks he performed a number of temple marriages, spending time talking with each couple and their families about the blessings of marriage and its obligations. "I had six marriages this morning and it is quite a debilitating experience," he wrote. "One gives about all he has to each person and it amounted to about three and a half hours, equal to a three and a half hour sermon."

On one occasion while Elder Kimball performed a marriage ceremony the grandfather of the groom suffered heart pains. A young doctor, there to witness the next wedding, came to the rescue. After the elderly gentleman revived, the ceremony continued. The second marriage was halfway through when the bride fainted and slumped over the altar. The doctor assisted again and revived her. Afterwards the apostle put his arm around the doctor and said, "I hope you won't leave me until I am finished today." The doctor laughingly agreed to stay, though the third wedding went smoothly.

In the fall Elder Kimball and Camilla returned to tour more South American missions. In Newark Airport their plane was cancelled with a simple "Sorry." As they had scheduled conferences to meet, he asked the airline for help in making alternate arrangements, but the agent seemed little interested. Elder Kimball said, in exasperation: "Sir, I seldom mention it, but I am one of the leaders of the Mormon Church. It might not be so sad for me if I missed this flight to Chile, but I have a tight schedule and several congregations would be disappointed if I should not arrive. I must get through if it is possible." With this identification, and with the awareness of the very substantial business the Church did with the airlines, the agent got to work and soon arranged for Elder Kimball and Camilla to fly on another airline. "I was embarrassed to use my rank," Spencer wrote, "but I felt I had to in this case."

They arrived in time to keep their commitments. For four days they drove from city to city on a tight-packed schedule, the apostle interviewing and exhorting, organizing and teaching, administering to the sick, working early and late, pushing hard. For three nights straight they slept sitting up in the car as the mission staff drove them long distances from one conference to another. When a mechanic looked at the engine of the mission car as the tour ended, he declared it was impossible that the car could have been running in that condition, with the generator brushes completely worn off.

From Chile they went to Montevideo, where they met with the seven mission presidents, then went to visit missionaries in Brazil and the new stake in Sao Paulo. Elders Kimball and Richards then organized the second South American stake in Buenos Aires. They interviewed seventy-five men and found seventy-three worthy to hold whatever positions they might be called to. Many wept with emotion when called to positions of responsibility. The building bulged with the 1440 in attendance. It was an exhilarating experience to participate in the birth of the new stake.

On the way back home, Spencer wrote:

> Oh how we slept! I slept like a log. How weary my body was, and yet it was not too obvious, for I carried on to the end of the most grueling and strenuous three weeks I can remember. How my near 72-year-old body could stand it is a mystery to everybody, apparently, and now even to me, for the strain has been long and almost continuous since leaving home. I am sure part of the strength has come from "purpose." This is the work of the Lord and He has been so tolerant, so kind, so considerate, and this

reminds me of the scripture: "But they that wait upon the Lord shall renew their strength; they shall mount up with wings as eagles; they shall run, and not be weary; and they shall walk, and not faint."

He had held more than fifty meetings, organized an overseas stake from the ground up, been in and out of airports thirty times, missed many meals. He wondered if his stamina had come from good food and hard work as a boy, from a father who gave him responsibility and insisted he finish the task — this and the blessings of the Lord.

Over the space of about four years Elder Kimball made two or three trips a year to South America. One in 1967 took him and Camilla to the new South Andes Mission. In La Paz, as they were on their way to the airport they found the two roads passing through a narrow place blockaded by political demonstrators with boulders, furniture and bonfires. Cars were backed up for blocks. But Elder Kimball had an assignment to be in Trujillo, Peru, that evening, where Church members would be waiting for him. To get to the airport he had to pass the roadblock. He stubbornly refused to be dissuaded.

Elder and Sister Kimball, with some missionaries helping, carried their suitcases through the crowd and past the barrier. Their eyes smarted from the tear gas the police had used and they nearly fainted from their exertions at an altitude of twelve thousand feet. They finally reached the airport an hour and a half late, caught the delayed flight, reached Lima and then drove for six and a half hours to Trujillo. The congregation of 350 was still enthusiastically waiting for them, though it was now after 9:00 P.M. It seemed to President Jesperson, who had met the visitors in Lima, that "I never felt the Spirit of the Lord stronger than I did that night."

On another trip the Kimballs and Jespersons had to spend a night in the cold airport lounge at Bogota, Colombia. Although the Jespersons' overcoats had gone ahead with their luggage, Sister Jesperson refused to take Elder Kimball's coat. So he waited until she slept, then walked over and covered her with it. The two men, now too cold to sleep comfortably, walked about the lounge through the night, discussing the missionary work.

As they traveled by car the next day Spencer napped with his head in Camilla's lap. When the question arose what the wives should do during a priesthood meeting, he suggested they might attend the meeting. "I don't hold the priesthood," Camilla said. Spencer replied, "You have been holding the priesthood all morning."

For twenty years Elder Kimball had identified with the Indians of North America. As he labored in South America he saw opportunities for other Indian peoples also to rise to their "full height" through education and faithfulness to the Church program.

On his first trip to South America in 1959 he had visited major cities on the eastern coast, dealing only with members of European descent. On his second mission tour he had visited also cities west of the Andes and had insisted on including in his itinerary a number of small villages in the mountains to evaluate the possibilities of bringing the gospel to the native Indians.

Just before he came to South America in October 1965 with the special responsibility to supervise all the missions in that continent, he had called on President McKay by appointment to discuss his vision for the Indians of South America.

He was ready and very gracious. His smile is captivating. He makes one feel that his greatest pleasure is to meet one, and that each one is very special. I took my large map of South America and laid it out on the table. . . . I pointed out to him Quito in Ecuador and told him of the millions of Indians [on] the Altiplano of the Andes range. He asked me, "Millions?" And I said, "Yes, President McKay, there are millions and they are pure-blood Indians who speak different Indian tongues and dialects." I told him of some of the valleys of the mountains which we intended to explore to see if proselyting would be possible there. I explained to him that we now have linguists in the Church [who can teach the missionaries the Indian languages so] that they could hear the Gospel, every man in his own tongue. . . . I said to him, "President McKay, . . . I think the time of the Lamanite has come for them to hear the Gospel." And he said, "Yes, it is time and they must hear it and you are the one of the Twelve who has the vision of it. . . . You have my blessing."

I thanked him kindly and arose to go, and when he attempted to get up, I urged that he remain seated and he said, "Why should I not get up?" And when I shook hands goodbye, he drew me to him and embraced me and said, "You go with my blessing." This was a glorious experience — to be in his presence; to have his undivided attention; to have him consider with me our program for the Indian.

As he made mission tours Elder Kimball was alert to the possibilities of expanding into Indian areas and having missionaries learn their languages. Finally, on a trip in 1967, he plunged directly into the work himself.

In Ecuador the elders brought him to Peguchi, a cluster of houses in the fields of corn and other crops. Some of the Indians who lived there spoke Spanish, but most spoke only Quechua. On the streets they smiled at the elders. At a junction of paths there was a little natural amphitheater, where obviously animals had pastured; here the meeting was to be held. A bus emptied of people returning from the city. The elders urged them to stop for the meeting and fifteen or twenty gathered.

One elder offered prayer and explained the meeting, then he introduced the mission president. While the president spoke, the elders ran up the road and down the road to find more Indians. Soon they came in twos and threes, shyly and fearfully, joining the group. As the president talked powerfully about the Indian heritage and the blessings promised in the Book of Mormon, the number grew to forty, sixty, eighty, and finally more than a hundred. They sat silently, wistfully, in their white pantaloons and blue ponchos, their little hats turned up.

The spirit warmed them. Elder Kimball began to speak. He wanted to weep for joy as he talked of the life and resurrection of Jesus Christ and His return to their ancestors in America. He pointed to the sky and told the story of the still small voice that came from heaven. Every eye followed his gesture to the sky as though the Savior were actually descending through the thin clouds that obscured the setting sun. Spencer bore his testimony that he brought the same message Christ had brought their forefathers, and he endorsed the four elders as teachers of truth. He offered to shake their hands, and after the meeting closed they rushed forward almost as a mob, thanked him, smiled, shook his hand. Their openness and enthusiasm seemed to him a precursor of great things. "Of all the meetings I have ever held or attended, I think this was the most inspired and stimulating and promising."

Elsewhere, in the cities, he saw dozens of drunk Indians staggering or lying in the gutters, and he wrote in his journal what a curse liquor was to the unsophisticated, often exploited Indians.

In the high mountain country of Peru, Ecuador and Bolivia there was much to see that was picturesque — the village markets, the colorful clothing, llamas and alpacas, roads so high that the visitors gasped for breath upon the slightest exertion, guineapigs scuttling underfoot in the huts awaiting their turn as dinner — but most of the Indians subsisted in wretched poverty. The few Indian members had new interest and new hope to lift them up.

From Argentina the group passed over the border back into Bolivia, up primitive, almost impassable roads to Quiriza, where six missionaries worked in this village well above ten thousand feet. The missionaries dressed in levis, boots and dark shirts, drank water dipped from the river (purified with tablets). One of the missionaries was a native of Quiriza who, after his conversion, had asked for the opportunity to go back with his wife to his birthplace to bring the gospel to his people.

There were no converts yet, but many friends and a huge Primary. Five hundred people attended the meeting. The missionaries, though living in the most primitive conditions, expressed a desire to remain there for the rest of their mission, weeping from deep feeling as they bore their testimony. While there, Elder Kimball broke ground for a small chapel at the mission president's request, even though no money had been appropriated for the building.

During the missionary meeting in Quiriza, Spencer noted two men standing ten feet from the door, waiting. When the meeting ended they cautiously and humbly approached him and handed him a little basket in which were a dozen small eggs. Of all the gifts he had ever received, none touched him more. It reminded him of the woman in the New Testament who brought her pence to the temple.

After all their journeying, arriving home in Salt Lake City Spencer said to Camilla, "I am satisfied with traveling and I'd be happy to just sit home and never leave — until Saturday morning when I go to Washington."

By 1967 the Church had a worldwide membership of more than 2½ million. To relieve some of the strain on the organization caused by the increase in numbers of stakes and missions without substantial increase in the number of General Authorities, a major administrative innovation was announced during the 1967 October Conference. Sixty-nine men were called as Regional Representatives of the Twelve to help supervise the 443 stakes. These men were not to be General Authorities but high level advisors who would serve as liaison between the stakes and the Quorum of the Twelve.

With Church growth came greater visibility. Critics charged that the Church practice of withholding priesthood from blacks was racist. Pressure for change intensified as the growing militancy of blacks and anti-war demonstrators communicated a feeling of disquiet and vulnerability to the whole country. Then, with general conference approaching, just two months after federal troops had been called into Detroit to quell a major riot by blacks, threatening letters were received by the Church suggesting possible disruption of the conference by persons in the "civil rights movement."

In the Saturday afternoon session a mentally disturbed man came down one of the balcony aisles while Thomas S. Monson was speaking. He shouted, "That's enough, Elder; turn it off." The people present, all keyed up for trouble, stiffened. The ushers grabbed the resisting heckler and took him out. The next day he tried to get into the Tabernacle again but the police prevented him from entering. No other trouble developed.

Shortly after conference a plane with Elder Kimball aboard, having set off for Los Angeles, had to return to the Salt Lake City airport and be searched because of a telephone call saying there was a bomb aboard. In his journal Spencer added that there was no reason to assume the threat was aimed at the Church through him.

By April Conference 1968, six months later, Martin Luther King had died by an assassin's bullet and the cities of the land had erupted in destructive riots. The National Guard stood sentry in many places. Within a few weeks Robert Kennedy died in Los Angeles, also struck down by an assassin. The peace and order of the nation seemed fragile indeed for it to be at the mercy of a few individuals.

Brigham Young University, on whose governing board Elder Kimball served, came under sharp criticism. The school's athletic teams, usually all white, symbolized to many the Church's practice with respect to blacks and the priesthood. When BYU teams played away from home, black members of other teams sometimes refused to com-

Delivering gift of sweater from Indians to President David O. McKay

With Indian team from Richfield, Utah, that participated in All-Church Basketball Tournament, 1967

pete, pickets demonstrated, flaming gasoline once was thrown on a basketball floor, and later Stanford University announced it would no longer schedule games with BYU. "The problems affecting the Church inspired by the war and the negro uprisings become ominous indeed. They remind me of the clouds of Elijah . . . 'And it came to pass in the meanwhile that the heaven was black with clouds and wind, and there was a great rain.' There are many problems that face us, and every effort seems to be against us to force us to change the Lord's program concerning the Negro. I am sure the future is black as the black clouds that Elijah saw."

The missionary system, still hampered by the military draft, seemed under a black cloud, too. When a boy drafted by the military filed a lawsuit, claiming among other things collusion between the Selective Service System and the Church in the matter of missionary deferments, his attorney indicated informally that President Tanner, Thomas S. Monson and Spencer W. Kimball would be subpoenaed for the taking of a sworn statement. This appeared a deliberate imposition, since Gordon B. Hinckley was more knowledgeable in the matter than any of them. The attorney for the plaintiff finally agreed to put his questions to Elder Hinckley. The lawsuit failed.

The Indian work, too, had its problems. In a Thursday temple meeting Elder Kimball presented to the Twelve the matter of the Quiriza meetinghouse as an experiment in building a very inexpensive structure for a group of Indians in a primitive village. The proposal was turned down on the ground that the Indians in the Bolivian settlement who would use the chapel were not yet members of the Church. Elder Kimball understood that reason, but he reacted with shock to statements by some that the Indians had no priority in proselyting efforts. He had operated for more than twenty years on the premise that the Indians did indeed have special claim upon the missionary efforts of the Church.

This concern was added to a feeling Elder Kimball had that the Indian work was slipping. A stake president came in, discouraged, prepared to let the Indian program go. He asked whether the results were worth the great effort. Elder Kimball told him of Bahee Billie and his wife Florence, he nearing his Ph.D. in soil chemistry, she a returned missionary. They had married in the temple. To Elder Kimball such successes were answer enough.

It distressed him when an Indian imposing on Church members with fraudulent claims of miracles had to be excommunicated for that and immorality, and another in Salt Lake City had to be dis-fellowshipped for causing dissension in the Indian community there and taking others away with him into a dance program competing with the Church. "It has hurt us to need to do this for an Indian, but they must learn discipline as well as the whites."

In Oklahoma, work with the Indians stalled because mission and stake each left it to the other. In the Box Elder area of Utah the work lagged. The Indian branch had been dissolved. The four hundred Indian youth who belonged to the Church among the two thousand at the Intermountain Indian School had been left with little organiza-tional support, little activity, little advancement in the priesthood. Elder Kimball scurried around shoring up the sagging supports for a program that demanded great devotion.

Late in 1967 Elder Kimball made his last visit to South America as area supervisor, touring missions and organizing a stake in Mon-tevideo. He was soon to receive another assignment, but he always retained a special feeling for the people of South America and con-tinued to be an ardent supporter of the missionary work among Indians of the Altiplano.

The year 1967 marked another important milestone in Spencer's life. On November 16 he and Camilla had been married for fifty years. A year ahead they had contacted their four children to arrange a family summer trip to Mexico. It had been twenty years since all four had been together with their parents at one time.

The five couples explored the ruins at Chichen Itza and Uxmal, in Yucatan, and the pyramids at Teotihuacan, near Mexico City. They rode the canal boats at Xochimilco and swam in the Pacific. Spencer surprised his family by going up in a parachute which was towed along the beach by a motorboat.

Although the ten-day trip was vacation, Spencer looked up the Church wherever he went. He attended meetings and spoke in Merida, attended to business with the mission president in Mexico City, and sought out the branch and missionaries in Acapulco.

Six months later at Christmastime the family gathered again from

*At golden wedding celebration of Spencer and Camilla
Kimball, 1967, with Edward, Andrew, Olive Beth, and
Spencer LeVan*

New Jersey, Michigan, Wisconsin, and Utah for a celebration of the
fiftieth wedding anniversary, with a total of thirty-six, all but three of
the clan, there to honor their parents and grandparents. Spencer
wrote: "Today we spent with the family. I have done little even at my
desk and nothing at the office but have pretty well devoted this week to
my family. They appreciated it very much since they stated that
throughout my church life I have given too little time to my family. . . .
It has been a glorious week. . . ."

At times when he tried to evaluate his performance he saw in his
wife and children his most difficult audience. He wrote: "Spoke at the
East Stratford Ward to a very large crowd — guess I did not do so well
— my family said nothing." Though they loved him, the family parceled out praise sparingly. When they responded enthusiastically he
knew he had done really well. At other times he could not tell. He
valued their approval highly.

Spencer's journal frequently noted his children's accomplishments. When he could, he attended the meetings at which his
grandsons received their Eagle Scout awards. He attended high school
wrestling matches. He once watched six different basketball games in

the All-Church tournament in which two grandsons played. He gave substantial gifts to each of the children, thinking it better to help them while they had financial struggles in getting established and their children educated and sent on missions than to leave a larger estate to be divided at his death. Camilla participated in all these expressions of love and concern, too.

The children always felt welcome to drop in unannounced, visit, and raid the refrigerator. Camilla loved to feed the family, however much work it might entail. They could not visit for more than a few minutes without her bringing out food. And whether the visitors were family or guests, Spencer always worried that they might not get enough to eat. There always proved to be plenty, but he could not refrain from asking, "Mama, are you sure you have enough?"

He noted in his journal that his children "seem to like to come home. We are getting paid well now for any sacrifice we made."

Their twenty-fifth wedding anniversary had seemed to mark a placid passage into middle age. Spencer and Camilla then had a grandchild, a fine new home, a well-established insurance and realty business, position in the community, a circle of lifetime friends. There was no hint of the drastic change which was soon to come.

The celebration of their second twenty-five years, spent in full-time Church service, appeared to mark a rapidly shortening span of life, a transition into old age with no reason to expect anything other than a continuation of that same Church service to the end. Of another sudden turning of the road in five years' time he had no inkling.

19

Teaching the Miracle of Forgiveness

— "Elder Kimball,
do you remember me?"

The problem of changing people, of raising their sights, preoccupied Elder Kimball. He felt it as he talked in a sophisticated ward in a university town, as he met with a group of disheartened missionaries, as he stood before a cluster of ragged Indians in the mountains of Bolivia. He also felt it as he faced a man or woman alone and used all his powers to build up faith and determination, to convince of the possibility of change.

In the New England Mission a discouraged elder, out just a month, told his mission president, "I'm going home tomorrow and there is nothing you can do to stop me." The mission president asked Elder Kimball to help. In an upper room of the mission home the apostle and the young man knelt and prayed together. Then Elder Kimball told the boy that he loved him and honored him for the sacrifices he had made to come on a mission, that he was of course free to leave, but that if he would stay he could be a great missionary. After they had talked for a while the apostle handed the elder paper and pen and said, "I want you to write a letter to your parents and tell them what you really feel right now, right now." The elder wrote: "Dear folks, I have decided I'm going to stay on my mission. I'm going to do the job."

Elder Kimball spoke to motivate people even more than to teach.

Sometimes he felt he had succeeded: "My talk was well received; the Lord was good to me." At other times, despite his very best efforts, it seemed to him he had failed to inspire the people he had come to help: "I floundered miserably"; "I rambled and made a failure."

He tried to suit his presentations to the occasion. When he spoke to uneducated groups through an interpreter, he used simple expression and practical advice. In other situations he could speak with eloquence, in the best of his sermons developing a rhythm and imagery which made his words memorable. Despite his many years as an apostle, after each sermon he still looked for some indication he had been helpful. He joked to Camilla once, reporting by letter: "My talk passed. I was not openly criticized."

After his four years of working with the South American missions Elder Kimball was reassigned by the First Presidency to supervise the Church in Great Britain. He shifted his attention and by September 1968 he was on his way to visit some of the missions and all of the stakes in the British Isles.

This assignment had special meaning to him. In 1837 his grandfather Heber had opened the first mission in Great Britain. In eight months Heber baptized fifteen hundred converts in England. Heber wrote, "I pulled off my coat and rolled up my sleeves and went at my duty with my whole soul, like a man reaping and binding wheat." Elder Kimball approached his task in the same way.

He felt that in Britain new enthusiasm was needed. It seemed to him that there was a fairly lax attitude toward missionary work. The British themselves sent very few missionaries out, explaining that economic conditions there were much less favorable than in the United States. Spencer felt sure the British Saints could send out missionaries if he could sufficiently motivate them to make the necessary sacrifices. At conferences he handed out ten-shilling notes from the podium to twelve-year-olds. Only five boys of fifty he asked had already started saving for a mission. After two weeks one boy reported back that he had already doubled his ten bob by doing odd jobs. Elder Kimball hoped these sparks would blaze.

Presiding at stake conferences in England and Scotland, he found nearly everywhere that though the statistics were low — sacrament meeting attendance often between 10 and 20 percent, home teaching nil to 20 percent, and so on — members seemed fairly well satisfied with what they were doing, resisting his push for more on the ground that they operated under difficult conditions of widely scattered membership and settled traditions. Elder Kimball consumed enormous energy in meeting after meeting, pressing them to raise their standards. Camilla wrote in her journal: "Spencer spoke again. How he holds up is a miracle!"

The low statistics resulted partly from the "baseball baptisms" of the early 1960s, when large numbers of young people were converted superficially through athletics and other youth activities. Aggressive missionary efforts had persuaded them to join the Church even without their families and without adequate understanding of the gospel or of the commitment they were making. The local leaders, long frustrated by the depressing effect of the large number of inactive members this had produced, now committed themselves to make individual contacts. Elder Kimball felt there would be substantial salvage if they carried through. Ultimately the Church would remove from its records the names of those "baseball" converts who proved belligerent or who could not be found.

Sometimes a whole lethargic stake needed a transfusion of vitality. Elder Kimball strained to give it. Other times a single Latter-day Saint needed his help. A bishop who had personality conflicts with ward members had asked to be released and declared his intention to become inactive. Spencer pleaded with him but could not dissuade him. When released in the conference he and his wife got up and left.

Elder Kimball met with a girl who felt she had a divine calling to convert one of the Beatles to the gospel. Unable to reach the musician by letter and refused an appointment, she planned to tie gospel tracts to a rock and throw it over the wall into his yard. Elder Kimball felt she was acting from immature infatuation rather than divine instruction.

Three days later she contacted Elder Kimball again. Still disturbed and frustrated, she wavered. Spencer spoke to her straight and urged her to return home. She seemed to want to follow his advice, yet could not give up the obsession of several years.

The next day he received a letter. "Dear Brother Kimball: I thank you and Sister Kimball for showing that sincere interest in me. Such a blessing to me. Actually, now that I am on my way back, the wheels in my brain are turning and making new plans and looking for new ambitions. . . . My patriarchal blessing cautions me to associate with those who will aid me in my desire for good. . . . I do realize now that I was really being led astray with the throttle wide open. There would be no telling where I would have ended up. . . . I am afraid that in the state I was in, that no one except an apostle of the Lord could have changed it."

The trip to Britain occupied more than three weeks, much of it in bad weather, on narrow roads, the drives long, the meals irregular, the stress almost continual. Elder Kimball toured three missions, interviewing two or three hundred missionaries individually, held four stake conferences including one reorganization, and conducted a three-day seminar for the seven missions in the British Isles. When he left he felt he had raised their sights somewhat.

A few months later he was back on another strenuous trip through England, Scotland, and Ireland, visiting missions and stakes in this land for which he had special responsibility. In some areas he could see little progress since his last visit; those leaders evinced almost a defeatist attitude. The whole process of evaluation proved difficult in some places because of inadequate record-keeping. In other areas a new enthusiasm had taken hold.

The missions were generally progressive and innovative, but Elder Kimball visited two missionaries who sat obdurate and lazy waiting for the remaining days of their mission to pass. "I was terribly disgusted with them."

In London he spent six hours on his feet in one day, urging, pleading, teaching, pressing for upgrading of expectations and work.

Camilla accompanied Spencer to the British missions and shared in the work. While he met with the men, she and the mission presidents' wives would hold meetings for the women.

As the fall, hectic with travel, passed into winter, she underwent surgery in Salt Lake City for removal of several small malignant growths on her face. There had been a similar operation the winter before, also. The doctor used only local anaesthetic and, though there was no pain, she could feel the cutting and sewing. Spencer now returned in kind a little of the faithful nursing Camilla had always provided him in his illnesses.

Spencer wrote in his journal in November: "Today is our 51st wedding anniversary . . . both of us forgot — 51 years of glorious married life, and how grateful I am for a companion of such stature and strength and kindness and affection."

*Greeting at Tokyo airport, 1968, with Mission President
Adney Komatsu at left*

That year, too, they had gone together to Camilla's birthplace. On assignment to Juarez Stake Spencer had taken her and her sister Mary and their daughter Olive Beth along. They drove from El Paso south to Colonia Juarez, a Mormon colony in the state of Chihuahua. Camilla wrote that "floods of memories came rushing back" as she saw the church and the schoolhouse, the swinging footbridge over the Piedras Verdes River, the small red brick house where she and Mary had been born, the house under whose porch the family, in hope of returning, had hidden a hundred quarts of freshly bottled blackberries before their flight, the bedroom where she had left her treasured doll and toys and letters and school papers behind. They drove over the dirt road to Pearson, from where the refugees had taken a jam-packed train to El Paso, afraid all the time that the rebels might waylay the train. "A train passed through while we were there in Pearson," she wrote, "making the memories even more vivid."

As 1968 ended, Spencer wrote:

For some 52 years Camilla and I have been together on New Year's Eve. We have spent some of them in foreign lands, but we have always been together and we have always had a good time.

Tonight after we had been to the gymnasium for a swim, we had a quiet little supper and spent the evening home alone, me at my desk, though I did sit through a one hour show at the television.

In Arizona for a stake conference Spencer visited with many friends from Gila Valley. "It seems to me," he wrote, "that friends of my own age are very old and are getting feeble. I cannot think of myself as being in their age class. I still feel so vigorous and strong and Camilla seems to be much younger and more sprightly than almost any of our contemporaries." On rare occasions he had a chest pang, but his heart seemed completely serviceable. For a few days he suffered misery from back pains, but this passed.

What began to concern him was renewed tenderness in his throat. When Dr. Cowan examined the throat he found a small spot that appeared granulated, a bad sign. Over the next two months the voice gradually deteriorated.

> Tonight, as I retire, I feel very discouraged. I begin to see what will happen to me and to my work. I asked Dr. Cowan not to take the biopsy until I get back from Britain. . . . there is a constant tenderness in my throat. . . . I told Dr. Cowan that I felt I would not try surgery again at this late date and I surely would not [have] a total laryngectomy. The deterioration of the voice seems to be moving at a rapid pace.

During several months Elder Kimball also suffered a bad infection. In one typical day he visited a specialist, trying to treat the debilitating infection; he performed a wedding ceremony; he preached a funeral sermon in Provo; and he rushed back to his office to deal with a series of problems which commanded his attention — a telegram that a young man had committed suicide, a visit with a young man with whom he had been working since his excommunication, a visit from a woman estranged from her husband who had been excommunicated for apostasy, a visit with a young man repentant for serious sins who wanted to go on a mission, a conference with a young boy and his pregnant girlfriend and her mother, another conference with a pair of foster parents who suspected their boy was involved in homosexuality. After six o'clock Elder Kimball stopped at the hospital to see a close friend who was dying of cancer. He got home at seven, had dinner, and spent the rest of the evening at his desk.

The next week, while waiting for an airplane, he felt physically uncomfortable and exhausted, but a young man clung to him for two hours asking a thousand questions and Spencer could not bring himself to ask for relief. Arriving in Nebraska, he wrote, "I started out very miserable and found myself wondering if I could get through the day, but after I got into the work in Omaha I seemed to become intoxicated with my work and forgot myself and it was a good day."

In the spring of 1969 Mangal Dan Dipty arrived in Salt Lake City. "He has considerably developed and polished since that day" when Elder Kimball had baptized him in a muddy river in India, "and is quite an attractive, personable young man of 32. . . . I took him home to dinner." Elder Kimball and a friend had helped finance him through college. Now that he was in Salt Lake City, Spencer invited him to some family activities — a picnic, Thanksgiving dinner, Christmas dinner. Brother Dipty began graduate study in social work at BYU and Spencer began a long process of seeking immigrant status for him through special legislation.

Elder Kimball went to Brigham Young University commencement exercises that spring, where he received an honorary doctor of laws degree. The citation emphasized his long and devoted service to his fellowmen. He noted in his journal: "I felt greatly honored, in fact, far beyond my deserts. I never could feel that they should have given it to me."

He had never felt completely satisfied about ending his college education after just one semester, though his anticipated call into the army and then his need to support a family had made it almost impossible to go on. Still, because he could never forget that other General Authorities were better educated, he felt flattered to receive this recognition and he felt a bit hurt that none of his family but Camilla were present. He would have liked them to be there.

Summer of 1969 brought another trip to Great Britain, starting this time in Belfast, Ireland. As they traveled to their meetingplace Elder Kimball noted trees cut down across the road, ripped-up paving blocks, burned-out cars and buses, gutted factory buildings, shops with shattered glass boarded up, streets barricaded with rolls of barbed wire. The city had been torn by civil strife between Catholics and Protestants. British soldiers stood by with guns at the ready. The scene reminded him strongly of Berlin in 1955.

For some time Spencer's left shoulder had pained him so much that he had difficulty in driving or in dressing himself. The pain flared now so that he spent most of a day in bed, getting up in the evening for his meetings. For several days he felt miserable but tried not to show it. On Sunday he attended a meeting in London, where the program had already been arranged, and he was called on to speak without warning. He took the occasion of President McKay's impending ninety-sixth birthday to tell of his experiences with the Brethren of the Council of the Twelve and particularly of his appreciation for the prophet, President McKay. Words flowed, "and I am sure the Lord blessed me, to make up for my deficiencies and illness. Some of the mission presidents said later that in all their lives they had never been so inspired. . . . I knew I was so weary and ill I could not have done it, so I was grateful to my Heavenly Father for coming to my rescue in such a magnificent way."

Elder Kimball organized a stake in Birmingham. "It was an exciting day." He urged that since now there were temples, stakes, patriarchs, visits from the General Authorities, and all the other blessings which could be obtained in the United States, faithful Saints should not feel they needed to emigrate but should build up the kingdom of God in Britain. In 1960 a single mission had covered the British Isles. In 1969 there were seven missions and seven stakes. A new era had dawned. Elder Kimball tried to communicate to the British Saints the excitement of participation in this growing, living thing.

Toward the end he began to feel the five weeks' accumulation of fatigue and neared exhaustion.

He arranged to be back in Salt Lake City in time for his regular Thursday meetings in the temple. In the meeting President Brown singled him out for praise of his devotion and service. Elder Kimball decided later the compliments were intended to soften the impact of the decision which had been reached while he was away to combine all the Church social services. This meant the end of the separate existence of the Indian Student Placement Program, which had been under his wing since its beginning.

"Undoubtedly it is right, but it did come as a pretty heavy jolt," he wrote. It was as though a beloved child had left home after growing from a single cell — one Indian girl, Helen John — to a program involving some four thousand children. High school and college graduates, missionaries, and happily married couples and leaders had come from the program. He now turned prime responsibility for it to someone else. The Church Indian Affairs Committee still had some responsibilities, but the heart of its activities had been cut out and transferred.

In 1969, just before October Conference, Spencer W. Kimball's book *The Miracle of Forgiveness* was published. The author meant it as a call to repentance and a guide on the road back from sin.

For years he had said he intended to write no book, that there were books enough by others who had more talent. And for fifteen years he stuck by that resolve, despite the urgings of many who wanted him to write. Numerous addresses at general conference and at BYU had been reprinted, sometimes in thousands of copies, but they had been written as speeches and not as books.

The experience which impelled him finally to write a book was the day-by-day counseling of people in trouble, the week-by-week interviewing of members being considered for responsible Church positions, the interviewing of missionaries as he toured the missions.

He often carried home more weight than he could shoulder and tossed sleepless with what he had heard. It seemed that no sin or human weakness existed which had not affected some or many of those he consoled or challenged. A man faithful in the Church had before his baptism killed a friend in a drunken stupor. Elder Kimball visited an arsonist in one prison, a rapist in another. Alcoholics who had beaten their wives and abandoned their families wanted help. Others struggled with adultery and fornication and incest and homosexual acts and heavy petting and masturbation, a range of sins from those most grievous to those requiring simply a change of direction.

People varied greatly in their reactions. One boy came all the way from Idaho to confess, and the apostle learned that what troubled him was masturbation he had indulged in a year prior to his baptism. On the other hand, an older man expressed surprise that he might be excommunicated for having committed nearly every sin in the book many times over.

A couple from Phoenix came about their seventeen-year-old son, who had gotten a sixteen-year-old girl pregnant. The stake president had insisted that the boy should marry the girl, but his parents had pressured him to reject this because he did not love her and his schooling would be interrupted. Elder Kimball pointed out that for the girl there were these same factors as well as her having the child. If she were willing, the boy should marry her. The father seemed to understand; the mother went out bitter and weeping and castigating Elder Kimball, having come for different advice.

The repentant came for help, the unrepentant for justification. Elder Kimball telephoned a young bishop one day and explained that a couple with him in his office were complaining that because they had slept together just once before their wedding their bishop had refused them a temple recommend. They wanted to be sealed in the temple before the child they had conceived was born, so that it would be "born under the covenant." They were incensed at the bishop and appealed to Elder Kimball to set him straight.

Over the phone the bishop confirmed the facts, uncertain what would follow. Elder Kimball then went on, speaking to the bishop in the hearing of the couple, to say he thought that excommunication proceedings should be commenced against the two because they were in a state of rebellion, being angered at their bishop instead of contrite at their sin. The startled couple were shaken by what they heard and quickly began to reconsider their position.

Elder Kimball repeatedly noted in his journal the load of counseling he bore:

> A brother came in to see me in the morning and spent about two hours with me. His wife had filed for divorce . . . because of continued conflict arising out of his immorality. . . . [At 8:30 P.M.] the distressed man of the morning returned, and his wife also, and spent the evening until 1:30 in the morning. I was trying to help him to find his way to repentance so that eventually he might possibly receive his family back.

> The entire day was spent with unpleasant interviews: A missionary who was in dishonor; a woman whose husband had deserted her and was in sin; another woman who with her five children had left her husband because of his confessed iniquities; and many other problems. I went home late in the evening greatly distressed and almost ill because of the many problems. I had dinner at noon with _____ who seemed so appreciative of a little moral support, he is going through serious times.

> I think I have not for years had so many cases of immorality come to me as in the past few days — broken homes because of infidelity of husbands and wives. I have struggled for hours and hours for the past few days trying to get people to see their situation and to repent. I have come to realize how powerful and subtle

is that evil one who makes them think that "black is white" and helps them to rationalize away all their errors and call them virtues when they are base vices.

Moral problems were revealed in other places besides his office. Ordaining and setting apart a long series of men called to positions in a stake, Elder Kimball assumed that all had been interviewed. But when he came to a bishop's counselor he set his hands upon his head and then quickly asked, "Did I interview you for this position?" When the man said no, the apostle interrupted the procedures and took the bishopric members aside for interview. The bishop, whom he had already ordained, was worthy and delightful. The counselor who had given him pause proved to have been guilty of repeated and gross adultery.

Missionaries in the missionary home, prepared to leave for their assignments, sometimes came to Elder Kimball to confess things they had not had the courage to tell their bishop or stake president. Sometimes they had already changed their lives and needed primarily to make confession and clear their conscience; sometimes they still had to make adjustment. In any event their having lied to those who interviewed them constituted a black mark. Elder Kimball often volunteered to fast with those who needed to humble themselves.

Though he had no patience with sin, he had almost infinite patience with sinners. At one time a new, tougher standard for interviewing missionaries had been proposed for consideration by the First Presidency and the Twelve. Elder Kimball noted, "I made a very desperate effort to try to keep some latitude in our interviews and not let the door be shut too tightly upon repentant young men and women."

A few times he went into flophouses and bars and gambling casinos in order to help those who wanted him, uneasy though he was at the possibility that people seeing him there might misunderstand.

A woman came up to him in the temple and grasped his hand. She asked, "Elder Kimball, do you remember me?" He was abashed. He could not make any connection. Embarrassed, he admitted, "I'm sorry, I do not remember." Instead of disappointment, relief lighted her face. "You worked and prayed with my husband and me until three o'clock in the morning. If after these nineteen years of repentance you do not remember me or my sins, perhaps the Lord will also remember them no more." She pressed his hand again and said, "Thank you. Goodbye."

A man from the Midwest came to visit, having just been sealed in the temple to his wife and their sons. Spencer recalled the early days of the man's membership in the Church. His wife had been so bitter, as had both sets of parents, that he had asked several times whether it would be permissible to divorce his wife and move away to escape the intolerable situation. Elder Kimball's advice was for him to remain and do all in his power to be conciliatory and to convert his wife by being the perfect father. Eventually she had been converted and had become active in the Church, her husband had been named branch president, and now they had come to the Salt Lake Temple to seal their bond.

Although heterosexual sex offenses provided a constant stream of distressing interviews over the years, a changing pattern emerged from homosexuality. In the early years of Elder Kimball's ministry these problems rarely surfaced, if they existed. But in the 1960s a growing number of cases came to his attention, partly because he, along with Mark E. Petersen, had received special assignment in 1959 to counsel homosexuals.

Despite the frequent claim by homosexuals that they had no control over their sexual orientation, Spencer believed that this problem, like all others, would yield to consistent prayerful exercise of self-restraint. He pointed out that homosexuals rarely were excommunicated for their past acts but usually only for their unwillingness to make the effort to change.

Young men with this problem who had been attending BYU had to meet with Elder Kimball for clearance before they could reregister. Some he admitted on probation; others he excluded.

On one occasion Elder Kimball spent four hours with two homosexual boys who left determined to stop their homosexual practices. He interviewed three repentant boys; the one who was not a Church member seemed ready for baptism. One boy to whom he refused readmission to BYU reacted angrily and his father threatened to sue the university for defamation. Several years later the boy wrote Elder Kimball a letter of gratitude from the mission field, expressing appreciation for the apostle's firmness coupled with love.

At 10:30 came a young man deep in sin who had resisted my helping him. He had ignored two of my letters. I finally called him and he was very curt and almost insulting. He said he had nothing to talk to me about. I told him positively that he had a great deal we had to talk about and that he had better be coming, and so this morning, I had the interview.

He began in a long explanation, stating that I was not qualified to handle his case or to understand it or to help him, and that it was his problem and that he did not wish to be pressed or hurried or pressured. I told him as long as he was a returned missionary and held the priesthood and was a member of the Church that we did have jurisdiction and that we did not intend to let him continue on with his sin; unless he was willing to cooperate, he would need to be immediately excommunicated from the Church. He finally began to yield and was willing to cooperate to some degree.

Elder Kimball met with four Church members in the Northwest, three of them returned missionaries and two of them college teachers. He put his best efforts into the interviews. After two hours "they claim they see no sin in the matter, but that it is merely a new way of life. . . . I was weary. I had worked so hard and put so much of myself into it trying to persuade them in the very few moments they gave me." But three months later he noted with delight that two of the men showed "tremendous progress."

A boy he had helped, and who expressed determination to straighten out his life, sent to Elder Kimball each month a crystal tumbler as a message that he had remained clean. For a number of months the tumblers came, but they finally stopped.

In Los Angeles Spencer met with an engineer who had been excommunicated for homosexual conduct. "I was happy when he was willing to come to see me. When I phoned him, it was dubious, but when he came, I made a soft approach, told him that he was excommunicated and therefore I had no jurisdiction but I had come to be helpful to him — that we loved him, the Lord loved him; we knew that basically he was a good man; and his eyes dimmed with tears and he said, 'This is the first time anyone from the Church has ever been kind to me in connection with this.' " He was not happy out of the Church. He bore his testimony. After an hour Elder Kimball had real hopes for his recovery.

Even though the total number of such cases was small in comparison to the thousands of devout and faithful people Spencer dealt with, it worried him. In 1968 he personally reported on the situation to President McKay, who agreed to an enlarged committee.

"We have lost some who did not cooperate and were belligerent and went to the large cities to hide," wrote Spencer, "but I feel there are many happy people today because of the work that Brother Petersen and I have done through the years."

While his special assignment from the Quorum channeled into his office many people with sexual sins, he continued to face the whole field of human weaknesses in his interviews. There was intolerance or vindictiveness. He dealt with white parents who railed against their daughter's engagement to a Mexican boy and refused to be present when the apostle married the young couple in the temple anyway. He worked with a husband embittered because the man who had committed adultery with his wife had been only disfellowshipped, ignoring the fact that the wife, whom he had forgiven, was not excommunicated either.

Over the years certain interviews seemed cumulatively a storm of "ignorance, superstition, skepticism, apostasy, immorality." He spent two hours with a man angrily insistent that the Church should allow prospective missionaries to be examined by chiropractors instead of doctors. He talked in seeming circles with a nonmember boy intent on distributing anti-Mormon literature among college students. He had a long interview with a returned missionary whose fragile faith had shattered over the withholding of priesthood from blacks; Elder Kimball felt "disturbed greatly for his future" and depressed, "feeling that I had done him little good." With a bishop who was asking to be released because he could not reconcile science and his understanding of the gospel Elder Kimball struggled and pleaded for hours; at the end he "had a feeling that perhaps we had helped to bolster his courage." One of the apostle's cousins delivered to him "revelations" which she had received for him, which indicated that upon fasting and praying for three days his voice would be restored and by great manifestations he would bring millions into the Church through her movement, called the Mission of Holiness. He spent much time trying to persuade her that the revelations she received were not from God.

All these experiences with people in great need of repentance and forgiveness led ultimately to a book. He had started with jotting down scriptures for people to study, then he developed some lists for recurring problems. By 1959 he had finally decided that there was need in the Church for "an extensive treatise on repentance." He spent untold hours over the next ten years, primarily during the time in the summer and at Christmas when the General Authorities had no regular assignments and were expected to rest. He never stinted his regular work to write; writing was an extra.

He soon found he had too much material, enough for two volumes. He liked to vacation where he could spread out his papers over several tables. After seven years he had all the chapters roughed out, but the manuscript was still unwieldy.

Finally, by the fall of 1967, the book had been set in type and Elder Kimball had galley proofs to read. But in conference with Marvin Wallin of Bookcraft, the publisher, and Bookcraft's editor George Bickerstaff it was decided that the book would have to be reduced in size. The author insisted that the price be low enough for the people to afford it for whom it had been written, and the editor felt that the book would be more readable if compressed somewhat. With the advice of the editor, Elder Kimball struggled for another two years to convey the original message in fewer words.

Elder Kimball passed the manuscript to Harold B. Lee, who pleased and embarrassed him by praising it in a meeting of the Twelve. Elder Lee said that on the basis of the half he had read "it was factual and heavily documented and adequate and covered the field beautifully." Delbert L. Stapley, who had read the manuscript, echoed those sentiments.

Finally, in 1969, the book came from the press. Spencer gave copies to all the Church leaders, to relatives and friends by the hundreds, and to troubled people he counseled — something like twelve hundred copies. He had no expectation of selling a great number. But to his amazement the book quickly sold out the first printing. Less than a year after publication twenty-eight thousand copies had nearly been exhausted and the publisher arranged for a fifth printing. The book became a best-seller. By 1977 more than 250,000 copies had been distributed.

In the thousands of letters from readers a few were negative; one couple who had found a copy in their apartment when they moved in denounced as sick the "sin-fixated, anti-sex author." But the response was overwhelmingly positive. As a result of the book the stream of people coming to see Elder Kimball about their moral transgressions grew greater still. A woman, repentant for forty-five years of a single adulterous act, came now and cleared her conscience by confessing. A sixty-five-year-old man had been carrying his sins, heavy on his conscience, for twenty-three years. He had read the book three times when he came in to ask Elder Kimball to guide him on the way to repentance. A man who had been excommunicated seven years earlier pointed to the book and said: "That's what brought me in. You called me a culprit and a sinner and transgressor and that brought me to my senses and I began to really repent and prepare myself for the restoration of my blessings. That book did it!"

For years a mail delivery rarely came without bringing letters of appreciation for the inspiration of *The Miracle of Forgiveness*.

20

Paying the Price for a Few Extra Years

— "we just all move over
and go forward"

President McKay was absent from the October Conference in 1969 and at ninety-six he lay in a near comatose state. At a meeting of the Twelve and the First Presidency the question came up: While President McKay continued so ill, should his counselors transact the business of the Church or should the Twelve? No final answer came from the discussion, but they determined that Harold B. Lee, representing the Twelve, should meet regularly with the President's counselors.

Finally on Sunday, January 18, 1970, President McKay died. Elder Kimball found out about it when he received a call from a neighbor in the morning asking if it were true. He hurriedly confirmed the information, then changed clothes and rushed to the Church Office Building. He could not locate Joseph Fielding Smith or Harold B. Lee, the two apostles senior to him, so he began to contact the General Authorities away on conference assignments. By ten o'clock Monday morning all but Elder Stapley had returned for a meeting to plan the funeral services. A committee, which included Elder Kimball, met with McKay family members to learn their wishes.

The committee wrestled with protocol. Aside from the three members of the Quorum of the Twelve who served as counselors in the

First Presidency, Alvin R. Dyer was a counselor and an apostle but not a member of the Quorum, and Thorpe B. Isaacson was a counselor but not an apostle. Elder Kimball proposed that it was important both to acknowledge the service of the counselors and to demonstrate the established order of responsibility upon the President's death. Accordingly he suggested that the cortege proceed with the fourteen members of the Quorum, then Elder Dyer, then the Patriarch, then Elder Isaacson, then the Assistants to the Twelve, the First Council of the Seventy, and the Presiding Bishopric. In the Tabernacle during the funeral service all the counselors would sit on the upper level, as at general conference. His proposal met with agreement.

The body of President McKay lay in state in the Church Office Building. As Spencer left his office on Tuesday evening, lines four or five abreast stretched more than two blocks in the rain. David O. McKay had been a member of the First Presidency since 1934, thirty-six of his ninety-six years. He had been President of the Church for nineteen years. Under his leadership the Church had grown from approximately one million to three million members. Two-thirds of the Church membership had never known any other President. When he became President the Church had 180 stakes. The five hundredth stake was organized at Reno on the day of his death. The number of missions doubled, the missionary force increased from two thousand to nearly twelve thousand. BYU studentbody grew from five thousand to twenty-five thousand.

Though his loss had been expected at any time for several years, people still had difficulty in conceiving the change. President McKay's graceful, witty manner, his imposing physical appearance, his deep warmth, all made people see him as THE prophet, to be classed with Joseph Smith and Brigham Young.

For the funeral service on Wednesday the Tabernacle was packed with dignitaries and Church members. After the Church leaders spoke their message of honor and faith, the cortege proceeded under clearing skies to the burial in the Salt Lake City Cemetery.

The next day the fourteen members of the Quorum met to consider the succession. Previously there had been discussion whether the Twelve should reorganize the First Presidency immediately, with Joseph Fielding Smith so elderly, but now each of the Twelve had opportunity to speak and they all agreed it was right to proceed with the reorganization promptly.

As the second apostle, Harold B. Lee made the formal motion to sustain Joseph Fielding Smith as President of the Church, which the Quorum approved. Then President Smith named Elder Lee and N. Eldon Tanner as his counselors. Spencer W. Kimball became Acting President of the Council of the Twelve. The four men were then ordained or set apart to their new responsibilities.

In setting Elder Kimball apart, President Lee said:

> The hearts of the people in this Church have been drawn towards you, perhaps as to few other men in our day, because of the kindly solicitude, the anxious concern, and your never-ceasing zeal in reaching out to the high, the low, the rich, the poor, the young, the old, and many are those who will call your name blessed. Particularly among the Lamanite people your name will go down in history as one of the greatest missionaries with the Lamanite people of this whole dispensation. But we admonish you, our beloved brother, to husband your strength, and to exercise the right you have to delegate responsibility, and divest yourself of the many details that otherwise would not give you the overview one should have of the whole work. . . .

Elder Kimball felt honored by his new responsibility to administer the affairs of the Quorum but his first nights were near sleepless and his days filled with tension. He was moved to a larger office, with additional secretaries, and was relieved of some of his committee assignments. Finally he graduated to organist for the Quorum. For twenty-seven years he had accompanied the singing only when Elder Lee was absent.

As acting head of the Quorum, Elder Kimball no longer had direct responsibility for the missions in Great Britain, but instead for missionary work in the whole world. Though his new position meant a significant shift to administrative duties, he continued most weeks to assign himself to visit stake conferences as he had for over twenty-six years.

After organizing a stake in Iowa, he wrote: "I was a bit apprehensive since some of the brethren are a bit opposed to making small stakes. I have never felt quite so strongly, since I feel whereas they lack some in numbers they generally pick up a good deal in activity and it gives more people an opportunity to serve."

Elder Kimball felt sad about the dissolution of a Spanish-speaking ward in Fresno, putting the people back into English-speaking wards. He thought there was inadequate understanding of the need for transitional arrangements for persons with no English language facility, who tended to be lost when put into regular wards. He raised this problem with the First Presidency when they met with the Quorum, and Elder Packer received assignment to make a study of it.

In Corpus Christi Elder Kimball found that the Spanish-speaking people constituted nearly half of the stake population, yet few served as leaders. They had been integrated into the Anglo wards and because of their different cultural pattern took a back seat to the more aggressive whites. Spencer urged that training courses and tolerance and going the second or third mile should be used as means to equalize things with the Spanish-speaking people.

For some time Spencer had felt his voice deteriorating. Finally Dr. Cowan had taken three samples of tissue from his throat, inserting a pipe an inch and a half wide for access with direct vision.

Five pathologists at the hospital could not agree on evaluation of the specimens. Two thought there was malignancy and three thought not. The specimens were sent off to two other cancer centers for diagnosis. Ultimately their answer came back just as equivocal — borderline, they called it. Dr. Cowan scheduled a further biopsy.

Coming so soon after the earlier operation, this one seemed a much greater ordeal. The lips, mouth and tongue were numbed, then a needle stuck through the neck into the throat to deaden it. The pipe was again forced down his throat and three samples of tissue taken. It was most disagreeable and he bled freely. After he recovered he attended temple meetings that same day, but nearly fainted there.

Dr. Cowan felt that the spot definitely was cancerous. Other opinion remained uncertain but leaned in the direction of treating the condition as malignant. The best advice obtainable was that surgery and radiation offered about the same percentage chance of cure, while radiation was less likely to destroy the remaining voice.

Spencer confided in President Tanner, who suggested a special prayer circle. On the next temple day the General Authorities met and pleaded with the Lord for Spencer. The invocation and the prayer at the altar touched him with their feeling. As Elder Hinckley anointed him "there was a tremble through my whole body, and it continued and there was a holy refining sweet influence through the whole meeting, and then President Tanner sealed the anointing and gave a marvelous blessing to me." Spencer wrote later: "As I was administered to by all the brethren I tingled all over — a very special feeling of nearness to my Heavenly Father and my brethren. . . . Never have I felt the spirit of unity among the brethren as today. . . . It was a day of days!!" At the conclusion of the administration Elder Lee took him in his arms and embraced him, as did several of the others.

Their further discussions of Church business and their lunch together, and even the series of interviews Spencer had afterward — with an adulterer and his paramour, with a returned missionary in sin — carried forward the same spirit. He felt it "a pleasing, holy day." "I felt surrounded in a spiritual atmosphere," he wrote. "I am so grateful for the brethren who went so much out of their way to bless me and to pray for me and to be with me, and to counsel with me."

Despite his doctor's urging that he should submit to treatment for his throat, Spencer now put it off. His voice seemed to have improved since the blessing.

In February 1970, on his way to a stake conference in Maine, Spencer stopped in New York to consult with Dr. Martin, who had operated on his throat in 1957. The doctor urged surgery as the right solution. He thought another biopsy unnecessary and said it would probably destroy what voice remained. Partial laryngectomy might be enough, but he insisted he must have consent to remove the whole larynx if during the operation his judgment so dictated. Spencer had set his mind pretty much against an operation, so he asked about radiation treatments. Dr. Martin thought radiation not a practicable solution and considered resistance to an operation ridiculous. Spencer tried to explain that he had no fear of death and that since he needed a voice in his work his voice was almost of the same importance as his life.

They set another appointment for the next day. As Spencer arrived that day Dr. Martin was on the telephone talking with Dr. Cowan: " . . . A man that has a growth in his larynx should have it out regardless of biopsies. . . . I am opposed to cobalt. . . . A biopsy would not settle it. . . . If he were an ordinary patient we could probably settle for another partial laryngectomy, but in his case it would probably take away the voice he has. . . ."

The doctor's best professional judgment was surgery or nothing. Spencer preferred, then, to do nothing for the time being, giving faith its chance to work. The fact that there had been no further growth since the last biopsy he attributed to the faith and prayers already exercised. The two men parted with the decision simply to keep close watch on the situation.

Spencer's seventy-fifth birthday passed. He enjoyed the challenge of his leadership of the Quorum. And he felt well. But as his voice turned hoarser, he felt inadequate, fearing that people merely tolerated it. The thought depressed him.

Elder Kimball offered to forego speaking in April Conference if the First Presidency thought his voice would prove an embarrassment to the Church. He was called on to speak first, however, immediately after the sustaining of President Joseph Fielding Smith in the solemn assembly. Elder Kimball spoke on the succession to the Presidency, answering those who questioned whether at his age Joseph Fielding Smith should become President: The Lord determined the succession. The qualifications for a prophet were to know the Lord and be able to speak his will to the people, and these vital qualifications Joseph Fielding Smith had.

Before the conference there had been threats of violence and mob action and bombs. (Elder Kimball had obtained an unlisted telephone number because of crank calls and threats.) Strict security measures had been taken at Temple Square. During the Sunday afternoon session a telephone message came that a bomb would go off in the Tabernacle. While Elder Tuttle continued speaking on the theme "If ye are prepared, ye shall not fear," the counselors deliberated and decided to depend on their faith and the precautions they had taken, the Brethren having participated in solemn prayer for protection. The call proved a hoax. When conference ended, Elder Kimball felt the Church settle back, confident that the Lord was at the helm and had called this new President.

Through the spring and summer, anti-war protests closed campuses throughout the country and riots and demonstrations disrupted many cities.

At the time of October Conference in 1970, Elder Kimball conducted the seminar for Regional Representatives. He had trouble with his voice and he went home downhearted. That night as he sat alone at home he wrote a letter to the First Presidency advising them that, as they had left the matter to his judgment, he would not try to speak in conference this time. His voice had worsened and he feared to damage the image of the Church for those millions watching on television who would not understand his situation.

Through the night he battled. Should he deliver the letter? Was he showing faith? If he gave in now, would he then begin to refuse whenever he had a chance to speak? He carried the letter with him all through Friday and Saturday morning. He asked Elder Lee's advice, who told him he need not be so sensitive and that his voice was acceptable. He spoke in conference and after the first few sentences felt secure again.

In February Spencer and Camilla visited Fiji and found that about half of the Church members there seemed to be descended from people in India. Elder Kimball had thoughts of using some of them when missionary work in India became feasible. He and Camilla visited the stakes in Tonga, then Samoa. They found the food, the singing, the dress exotic. The stake president in Tonga conducted stake conference in a white shirt, tie, coat, and lavalava, with bare feet and with a woven mat tied around his waist. After a chapel dedication the feast included eighty-seven small roast pigs, lobsters, chickens, salads, vegetables, and fruits.

Soon after this trip, Elder Kimball visited Mexico City, meeting with missionaries and stake and ward leaders as well as holding a public meeting. He emphasized the missionary work by borrowing a little boy from the audience. He held the baby in his arms, kissed him, and put a ten-peso note in his chubby fist as a start for his missionary fund. After the meeting all the mothers brought their babies forward to be kissed. He kissed about a hundred babies.

On returning from Tonga and Fiji and Mexico, he wrote a report on missionary work which established the direction of his thinking. He urged that all but the newer areas of the Church should largely provide their own missionaries, and that the excess missionaries from the United States could then be sent into newly developing areas. He posited that if the Church had done all it could, the Lord would provide means for opening countries now closed to proselyting. He thought that too often aid was given families in sending their children on missions when they had not yet sacrificed much, but that for those families with real need a good many affluent people in the Church would be willing to offer aid. He thought that the more affluent missionaries from the United States and Canada set standards of extravagance which made it difficult for native missionaries to keep up.

On his seventy-sixth birthday Elder Kimball was presiding at a stake conference in Kansas City. "I feel rather young and sprightly and with a great deal of vigor, though sometimes I have to rest a little oftener than I used to when I was younger. My voice is not very good and I am having much difficulty in getting sufficient voice to put over my program."

He tried to respond to nearly all the birthday cards which came in. He himself remembered birthdays assiduously and tried conscientiously to express his thanks for favors done him.

That summer he and Camilla spent a short vacation in California. "We have had a strenuous seven months since the little relaxation of last Christmas. I have worked about 14 or 15 hours average every day, Sunday with its conferences, etc., being no exception, and I am tired. I am exhausted and have had to push myself to get going." But, remembered Camilla of their stay at Aptos Beach: "Spencer insisted that we take long vigorous walks, down the beach and over the hills every day. He really pushed us both past what old folks should endure."

Elder Kimball wrote a letter of instructions to his office staff with suggestions. He outlined his usual work hours, running from early morning to late afternoon, and asked that they not say, "No, he is not here; he does not come on Mondays," or "He is not coming in today." Concerned that people might get the impression he was idle, he suggested the staff merely say that he was not available and take a message or make an appointment.

On examination, Dr. Cowan thought he observed some increase in the size of Spencer's cancerous spot. Spencer had noted increased soreness on the one side of his throat for weeks. It had been a year and a half since Dr. Martin had urged that he have a total laryngectomy.

Spencer scheduled further tests for early September and then with Camilla flew to England to participate in the Church's first area general conference, to be held at Manchester in late August. They flew on the airliner in the first-class section, contrary to their usual pattern, because the First Presidency had urged them to do so. As they got older the additional comfort on the long flight made a bigger difference than it had before.

As Spencer arrived at the hotel he saw one of his brethren of the Quorum and hurried to embrace him in a bear hug. He loved these men whose faith and responsibilities so nearly paralleled his own. After a long day of meetings with them he had once written, "My heart is singing!"

At the conference President Smith spoke. Ninety-five years old now and alone since the recent death of his wife Jessie, he had not felt up to attending the conference, but now he spoke with reassuring firmness: "We are and shall be a world Church. This is our destiny."

Elder Kimball, when called on without warning, spoke extemporaneously on the theme he had often used, that the British Saints could, with sacrifice, provide many missionaries to help build the world Church.

On his return home Spencer underwent further medical testing. "Today came the great bombshell," he wrote. "Today came the end of the world, or at least the beginning of the end. It has been going on a long time perhaps, but only today came the diagnosis and the shock."

Medical evaluation of his labored breathing and his sleeplessness despite excessive fatigue, which had troubled Spencer for some time, were interpreted for him as symptoms of a new, serious, progressive heart problem. The aorta had calcification which narrowed the opening and interfered with blood circulation. That made the heart pump harder but less efficiently and allowed the lungs to retain too much fluid.

In a younger man open-heart surgery would have offered the best solution, but at Spencer's age the doctor thought there would be no more than a fifty-fifty chance of surviving the operation, and a recovery period of many months would follow. Without surgery he might go on for a year or two but could simply drop dead at any time and without warning.

Spencer had thought some exercise good for him, but the doctor now told him to avoid any vigorous activities. For the time being he was to take digitalis to stimulate the heart and diuretics to reduce the lung fluid. Nothing more would be done until the question of a new malignancy in his throat was settled.

The next day Elder Kimball returned to his usual work. "Back in the usual swim, it seemed that the dream of yesterday had faded and everything seemed much the same. . . . I was so busy I had little time to move into a shortening world into which I had been introduced yesterday." Occasionally his thoughts reverted to the new threat of sudden death. "I kept praying that I might measure up TODAY and do a creditable service as presiding authority so long as I remained."

Thoughts of death flitted; he saw his brethren walking as his pallbearers. He felt no panic, only wonder and expectancy.

> Maybe I can overcome the weakness. Maybe I can be healed. I know I can if the Lord wants me here and needs me here, but that seems so far-fetched when there are so many brethren better qualified. I do not expect more than a momentary stir when the news is released, and as we have jokingly said many times, my leaving would make about as much stir as withdrawing my finger out of a glass of water or like blowing out one of many candles. The ranks fill up so soon. We just all move over and go forward. . . .

> I am surprised with myself. Somehow I had walked steadily and somewhat blindly toward the 96 of President McKay and the 95 of President Smith. . . . somehow I couldn't think of myself terminating. . . . I had hardly really envisioned myself walking into the twilight so soon. Yet I have come a long way. My father died of hardening of the arteries at 66 and my grandfather Heber C. Kimball was 67 and here I am nearly 77. . . . I hope I shall not be kept breathing after I am really dead. . . . Please ask them to let me die when the time comes and when my life is ended.

Camilla remembered the weeks that followed as "perhaps the most difficult of my life." A new specialist examining Spencer's throat suggested strongly the taking of a new biopsy and possible high voltage radiation treatment with cobalt.

Spencer tried to keep his heart condition secret, but with the weight loss and the impossible fatigue President Lee insisted on knowing the truth, and Spencer loosed his feelings and told him the extent of his heart and throat problems. President Tanner became party to the conversation and they arranged a special prayer circle in the temple for his benefit, at which administration to Spencer soothed him and gave him peace. Some of the Brethren stood aghast at the revelation that he was ill again, since he had given so little indication of it.

As general conference approached, Spencer sank into almost complete exhaustion, "so unlike his usual self," it seemed to Camilla, "I could hardly adjust my feelings." He worried about his conference sermon, having little energy for preparation. He decided to use an unconventional sermon he had given on other occasions, "Yes, I've Been to Heaven." With Camilla he agreed that after his past "hell fire and damnation" talks he might do well to indicate also the sweetness, kindness, love and godliness of righteous living. His talk told of the time when he posed for a portrait by Lee Greene Richards, to be hung in the temple, and the artist called him back from daydreaming with the strange question, "Brother Kimball, have you ever been to heaven?" Spencer's answer was that he had indeed had glimpses of heaven — in visiting with a German missionary who sold his blood regularly to stay on his mission, in a Navajo hogan where a childless couple sheltered eighteen orphans, in his own home when children and grandchildren gathered around for family home evening. To Camilla his was "the highlight of the conference talks and will be remembered for many years."

Immediately after conference Spencer submitted to a heart probe. Under partial anaesthesia he was aware they slit a place in his groin, then threaded tiny instruments into his heart through the artery. The doctors confirmed that he had a faulty valve, but also discovered a nearly blocked coronary artery. "A stunning discovery," fretted Camilla. It "sounded like the trump of doom." Spencer stayed in the hospital a day, then at home several days more. At the invitation of President Smith he flew with Camilla to Laguna Beach to stay for a few days. He rested, for once not working.

Lying in bed, relaxing, he said to Camilla that there were three whims he wanted to satisfy. The first was a pink shirt just like the local stake president had. They laughed and she agreed. The second was pajamas that exactly fit — not too large nor small, too long nor short. She agreed it was about time he had pajamas that fit. The third, an extravagant gown for her. Too sensible, she demurred.

A little while later, after Camilla asked him where he had bought the shirt, the stake president came bringing Spencer a birthday gift for his last seventy-six birthdays, a pink shirt. Spencer enjoyed wearing it while at home, but he could not bring himself to wear it in public.

On his return to Salt Lake City he underwent still another biopsy, with the tube in his throat so gagging him that it seemed a worse ordeal than ever before. The answer came in two days that the tissue specimens definitely were malignant. The doctors agreed that before the heart should be operated on, the throat cancer would have to be cleared up.

The next week Elder Kimball presided at a stake conference. He allowed himself to be driven directly to the airplane so that he would not have the long walks in the air terminals. He managed to control his schedule so that he did the necessary work but saved his strength. "It proved to me that I could control myself and limit my efforts. It proved to me that I could still carry forward a stake conference." He would not give in. Nor would Camilla. Trying hard to stay cheerful, she struggled to see that Spencer rested. "He is not an easy patient and I have a fight on my hands all the time to keep him from lifting or exerting himself."

Spencer took his first cobalt treatment. For about four minutes focused rays shot at the cancer, causing no pain. Regularly four times a week for about six weeks, he returned for this treatment. The target had been marked on his neck in red, so he wore a silk scarf around his neck to hide it.

He had some side effects as the radiation cumulated — some nausea, some swelling in the throat, fitful sleeping. He could not tell what came from the treatments, what from his heart conditions, what from the seven daily doses of medicine. His voice reduced to a whisper. The radiation affected his neck like a sunburn. And it seemed to dry his throat, so he coughed a lot, especially at night, which interfered with his sleep.

Each time he went to the hospital for his treatment he made the rounds of people he knew there. Others also recognized him and asked for his blessing.

With his voice reduced to almost nothing by the swelling, he turned over to Elder Benson the conducting of the Quorum business.

Spencer took only one assignment during this period. He went back to Arizona to dedicate a stake center in the Mount Graham Stake, where he had been president long years before. He could only whisper, but with a good-quality amplifier he could be heard — and he could rely on a high level of tolerance among his Gila Valley friends.

Spencer and Camilla drove up and down the valley, thinking this might be their last visit. They drove to Duncan, where the flood had occurred, past the ranch where Spencer and his stepbrother Wallace Jones had dug for water. They visited friends both well and ailing.

After Christmas, under instructions from the First Presidency, Spencer and Camilla went again to California for rest and recuperation. The series of treatments had ended and they were to return in about two weeks for further evaluation. Spencer's voice began to return as the swelling in his throat reduced.

Back in Salt Lake City again, Spencer was examined by his doctors who were pleased at the apparent cure of the cancer. Now that his throat had improved, something would have to be done about his heart. "I am definitely losing," he wrote one day, "— my heart causes my weakness. I am carrying on with difficulty." But then the next day he felt much better; the day after that, miserable.

The doctor recommended open-heart surgery, suggesting now that he had perhaps a 75 percent chance of survival and five or six good years thereafter; without surgery he faced further rapid deterioration.

Elder Kimball consulted with President Lee and President Tanner, because he considered that his life belonged to the Church. They discussed the question with him but would not make the decision for him. He wondered why he should "fight so hard to extend my life when perhaps my time had come and I knew there were other brethren who could carry on my work better than I could." But he finally decided to undergo the surgery with its risks, and Camilla agreed.

The surgeon scheduled the operation for immediately after 1972 April Conference and urged his patient to cancel all his conferences and other obligations until at least the end of June, when he might hope to start regaining strength.

This left only a limited time — a month — to clean up all his affairs, so they could be put in the hands of others for a time, or permanently. He and Camilla established trust funds with some hundreds of dollars for a mission for each of their many grandchildren, with another amount for schooling. Money not used would revert to the Church for missionary work, particularly among the Indians.

It came to seem almost a race between the calendar and his heart. He could feel his strength slipping away. To minimize the strain of waiting, he spoke in the first session of conference. He cleared his desk as much as he could. President Lee mentioned in the conference that Elder Kimball faced an operation, and people crowded around afterwards to wish him well. His brother Del came from California and his sister Alice and brother Gordon came from Arizona to see him before the operation. Only these four of Andrew Kimball's children survived. Andrew, Spencer's son, came from New Jersey to visit.

People gathered, not wishing to seem to say goodbye, but reluctant to miss what could be the last chance on earth to share his affection.

When Spencer Brinkerhoff, the son of his dead sister Clare, stopped by Elder Kimball's home the apostle drew his nephew down and embraced him tightly as he said, "If I don't make it through this operation, what would you like me to tell your mother?"

After the last session of conference the First Presidency and the

Council of the Twelve gathered in the temple to give Elder Kimball a special administration. Because President Smith was now too feeble to take active charge, President Tanner anointed Elder Kimball and President Lee sealed the anointing. Each of the Brethren warmly shook hands with or embraced Elder Kimball and wished him well. For her peace of mind Camilla also received a blessing. They were finally ready.

"Wednesday, April 12," Camilla noted in her journal. "This was the fateful day. Ed, Olive Beth and I were all at the hospital shortly after 6:00 A.M. to be with Spencer before they took him into surgery. I was surprised that I took it as calmly as I did, only a few tears. Somehow after the blessing at the temple I have felt all will be well."

The operation took four and a half hours, during which time the heart was bypassed for two hours. To gain access to the heart the surgeon, Dr. Russell Nelson, had to split the sternum and spread the ribs. He replaced one of the heart valves with a steel and plastic ball and cage and patched in a piece of artery, borrowed from inside the chest, to bypass the nearly obstructed coronary artery.

The family waited in the hospital. Their friend Dr. Homer Ellsworth entered the operating room periodically and brought out bulletins on the progress. The critical point was when the repair had been finished and the heart attempted to resume its functioning. Dr. Nelson would later tell Spencer and Camilla that he felt the Lord had guided his hand. The operation went perfectly in the smallest detail, a rare occurrence.

For days afterward Spencer suffered nausea, cold sweat, weakness, and excruciating pain, especially from his ribs. The hours seemed interminable, the days stretched endlessly. He needed blood transfusions and intravenous feeding. In the small hospital room he had a feeling of claustrophobia and bouts of depression and frustration. So many visitors thronged in — relatives and Church leaders — that resting proved difficult. "No matter how much I love people, visiting with them takes all my strength," he said.

Outside the hospital, in mid-April, it snowed. Camilla scraped the ice off the windshield to rush home in the car for an hour or two and then return. She slept in the room with Spencer, on a cot, where she was available constantly.

As Spencer lay, often groggy under the drugs, he liked to have Camilla hold his hand. He mumbled, often incoherently, apparently

Recovering from open-heart surgery, 1972

trying to solve Church problems. Once she heard him say, "It seems to me if they have been faithful and active for some time they should receive their blessings."

However slow it seemed, Spencer did improve over the course of two weeks. But just as he was about to be released to go home, his heart began fibrillating badly. He looked ill, his breathing became difficult, his feet and hands turned cold, he felt nauseated. He stayed on another day or two, then when his condition normalized he went home. He had an insistent urge to cough, but the pain when he did was excruciating.

The days ran together, some better, some pure misery. He received a number of blessings by the priesthood, and when Harold B. Lee visited him Spencer asked about the propriety of that. President Lee replied that he had said to the General Authorities, "Spencer lives from blessing to blessing." He gave him another blessing, reassuring him of the love of his Heavenly Father and of the Brethren and that the Lord had work for him to fulfill.

Hundreds of cards and letters came from concerned friends and from Church members Spencer and Camilla did not know. Camilla personally answered those from people she knew. Others received form acknowledgments from Spencer, which Camilla signed. He would not leave any unanswered.

A month after the operation Spencer felt well enough to resume his journal briefly. After nine weeks he began daily entries again. His first daily entry indicates he performed the wedding ceremony for Randy Mack, their oldest grandson. The next day he traveled to Laguna Beach. Even there, pain and sleeplessness dogged him. For three days the Lees stayed with them. Camilla noted, "This was a great honor."

A week later Spencer discovered that he could not close his eye and the left side of his face became paralyzed. Almost in a panic he and Camilla consulted a doctor, who said, after examining him: "Well, I might just as well tell you the truth and not hide it from you. You have had a stroke." What tragedy it seemed, to have gone through cancer and heart surgery, only to fall prey to a wholly different ailment! The world seemed to crash about them. They cut short their plans in California and hurried to Salt Lake City on the first plane. President Lee and his wife met them at the airport.

Further examination showed that there had been no stroke at all, but only an attack of Bell's palsy. As great a nuisance and embarrassment as the palsy could be, it was as nothing beside a stroke, and would probably disappear spontaneously in a matter of weeks. The discovery came as a great relief after the terrible anxieties of dealing with a supposed stroke.

On July 2, 1972, while still recuperating, Elder Kimball received a phone call that President Joseph Fielding Smith had passed away suddenly and quietly, his heart simply stopping. He would have been ninety-six two weeks later.

President Lee, shocked at the news, went out to the home. Upon seeing the lifeless body, he dropped to his knees beside the couch and held President Smith's hands, as though it were hard to let him go.

The day after the funeral the Quorum of the Twelve met to consider reorganization of the First Presidency. After each had spoken, on Elder Kimball's motion as second in seniority the discussion ended with designation of Harold B. Lee to succeed to the position of President of the Church. Elder Kimball then felt an awesome responsibility as he spoke for the assembled apostles in ordaining President Lee.

President Lee selected as his counselors N. Eldon Tanner and Marion G. Romney. He set them apart to their offices and then set Spencer W. Kimball apart as President of the Council of the Twelve.

The palsy gradually disappeared and Spencer gained strength through the rest of the summer. He first worked part days, then full days, then took on a stake conference with help. When he overdid he paid in discomfort and swelling.

From the day Harold B. Lee became Church President, Spencer and Camilla Kimball "prayed earnestly night and morning and in between" for his welfare. "We have been terrified at the thought," wrote Camilla, that "Spencer would become the President of the Church." That possibility, though, seemed remote. Spencer was four years older than the President and had continual health problems. The radiation treatments seemed to have stopped the throat cancer and his heart had improved, yet ever since the Bell's palsy he had suffered a nerve-racking rumbling in his head, somewhat as if he had water in his ear. Some voices he could barely hear. But the doctor knew neither cause nor cure. He had his eardrum punctured in a vain effort to improve the condition.

On top of this Camilla had an emergency appendectomy. One afternoon in November 1972, unwilling to disturb Spencer in his meetings, she drove from her doctor's office to the hospital and checked herself in for an emergency operation. Spencer was called out of his meeting only as Camilla was wheeled to the operating room.

A week later, still in much pain from an infection in her wound, she made all the arrangements herself to be released from the hospital, because "Spencer had a very full schedule." He drove her home from the hospital and spent much time all week nursing her; he was "most kind and thoughtful," Camilla felt. After almost three weeks her fever broke and the wound healed.

A few weeks later she underwent another operation to remove a mildly cancerous growth, spending four days in the hospital. Spencer would later have a small skin cancer removed from his nose, where his glasses rubbed. Sometimes the couple felt as if they were beginning to fall apart.

But Elder Kimball continued to work at a terrific pace. One weekend he flew to Hilo, Hawaii, for a stake conference, returning to the mainland on Monday. Because of fog the plane could not land in Los Angeles and finally went on to Denver. Elder Kimball could not get to Salt Lake City until Tuesday morning. On Thursday afternoon he returned to Hawaii for another stake conference. Leaving Salt Lake at 4:30 in the afternoon, he slept that night in Laie. He spoke to the students at the Church College on Friday, visited the Polynesian Cultural Center, went to the temple, and met with the missionaries. On Saturday he met with other missionaries, then with seminary students, then with top stake leaders, then with other stake leaders, then in a more general leadership meeting. On Sunday morning he met with the bishops at eight. At ten he spoke first to the children and then to the general session of stake conference. In the afternoon he conducted interviews. Near midnight he left for home. The plane landed in Salt Lake at 10:30 in the morning and he spent the afternoon and evening at work.

As *The Miracle of Forgiveness* moved into its tenth printing at conference time in October 1971 and was scheduled for translation into four other languages, Elder Kimball continued to spend time working on the same sorts of morals cases that had first led him to write the book. He took his counseling personally and mourned when two boys wrote refusing any further help, intending to go their own way.

At Munich for area general conference, 1973

Though others repented and seemed likely to succeed, each failure hurt.

The warm reception of the book made him willing to allow publication of another containing some of his sermons, selected and edited by his son Ed. He went over them carefully himself, hoping they too might do people some good, and they were published as *Faith Precedes the Miracle*. Again he contributed most of his royalties to missionary work, especially among the Indians.

That October he dedicated a chapel on the Hopi Reservation, between Polacca and Keames Canyon. For nearly fifteen years he and others had been trying to get permission to build there but had been opposed by some influential Hopis. This victory was a tangible sign of progress.

Though much of the Indian work had been taken over by others, he continued to care deeply about it. He felt annoyed when the American Indian Movement, which had been embattled at Wounded Knee, South Dakota, demanded a million dollars from the Church to help rehabilitate the Indians. The Church, with its own program to help Indians, ignored the demand. A group of Indians marched up

Main Street in Salt Lake City on a "peace mission" to Temple Square, but in view of recent experience in Washington, where AIM members had occupied government offices and caused much damage, the Church security people simply closed the gates of Temple Square to the marchers.

Elder Kimball's work of teaching, counseling and administration went on as before, whether he was sick or well. But in health or weakness he kept up his massive correspondence, including faithful replies to letters from his grandchildren:

Dear Grandpaw
    How are you? in the somer we will move to Prolvall.
Dear Grandmo
    i hop you are not in pain
Love,
                        Joseph

Dear Joseph:
    Thank you for that very excellent letter you wrote to "Grandpa." I think you do very well in your letter writing.
    Neither Grandma nor myself is suffering any pain, and we thank you for your interest.
    We have just crossed the big Pacific Ocean and visited Korea and Japan and we met about 800 or 900 missionaries like you will be when you get to be about 19. Maybe you can go to Japan or Korea or to Russia or to India or some such place when you go on your mission.
    We returned a week ago and have been very busy. We are going into General Conference, and I will be speaking on the Sunday morning session, about the last speaker, so it might be possible that you could see me and hear me.
    Please give our love to all of the family
    With great affection,
                        Grandpa

April Conference in 1973 was the sixtieth general conference since Elder Kimball had become a General Authority — thirty years. In a meeting with the Mission Representatives of the Twelve and the First Council of the Seventy, he set out his dream of the future. First there would be organization of pioneering stakes in such areas as Japan,

Addressing general conference, 1973

Korea, the Philippines, and other countries. Then those areas would develop so they could send missionaries out to their own people, enough to free excess missionaries from the United States and Canada to open up new countries. Finally those now-developing areas would provide a surplus which, joined with those from America, would move outward to the great nations still empty on the map of missionary work — India, China, Russia, Poland, Iraq, Pakistan — and ultimately every nation and people. "I believe that the Lord is not wholly pleased with our limited efforts to teach the world. I firmly believe in my simple faith that when we are ready to reach the countries of the world with missionaries, the Lord will find a way to open the political doors of the nations."

Spencer and Camilla flew to South Africa on Church assignment that fall; they arrived a few days early so they could visit Krueger Park. They saw the exotic wildlife — baboons, impalas, buffalos, wart hogs, wildebeests, dik-diks, zebras, jackals, elephants, a giraffe which lions had killed and around which the lions gathered, feeding — "a thrilling day" Spencer wrote, "a dream come true. For many, many years I have hoped to see the animals in the wild."

He plunged into Church work in South Africa, meeting with missionaries and members. When someone expressed surprise at his strong handshake, he replied, "I milked cows the first half of my life so I could shake hands the other half." His memory for people was still remarkable, too, which made it only an isolated lapse when, in South Africa, he asked one of the missionaries about himself, only to discover that the young man lived two houses away from his own in Salt Lake City and was the son of very good friends. He jokingly told him never to reveal their secret, but he himself told the story to the parents when he got home.

As 1973 ended, Spencer wrote:

> Today is Christmas and a joyous occasion for most people. We had breakfast and opened our gifts. . . . Camilla began getting things ready for the Christmas dinner and in due time there came all the Macks who were home — Olive Beth and Grant and Stephen and Spencer from Ricks College and Tommy and little Camilla and the Indian girl Arlene, then Ed and his family totaling nine came in, and Andrew's son Andrew and his wife and baby and Andrew's daughter Susan and Terry and their baby, and Dan Dipty whom I had baptized in a tributary of the Ganges River in India some years

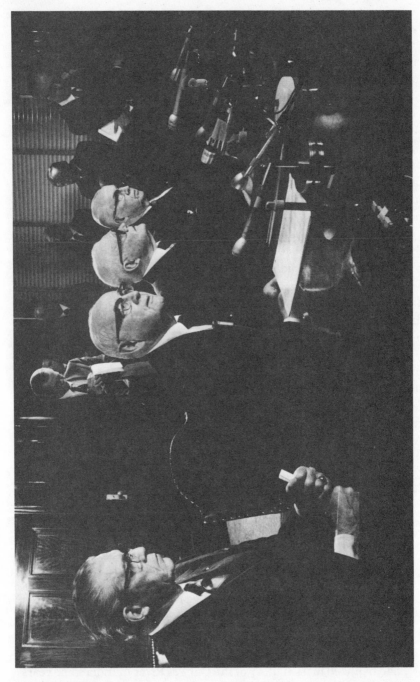

First Presidency and President of the Quorum of the Twelve Apostles at press conference, December 31, 1973: N. Eldon Tanner, Spencer W. Kimball, Marion G. Romney, Ezra Taft Benson

ago. We had a fine dinner, then we continued to visit and sing songs. We had a very pleasant day.

The next evening, after a quiet day at his desk, Elder Kimball received a phone call from Arthur Haycock, President Lee's secretary, asking him to come quickly to the hospital because the President was very ill. He grabbed his coat and rushed to the hospital but found that there was nothing he could do except pray. President Lee's room was filled with doctors and nurses and equipment. The doctors worked frantically to revive the President but could not. President Lee died at about nine o'clock.

Others now turned to Elder Kimball, as President of the Quorum of the Twelve, for leadership. He suppressed his own feelings of grief and shock to see to the arrangements for funeral services to honor this close friend and leader of thirty years. The telephone rang incessantly with messages of good wishes and support. He felt the nearly overwhelming weight of new responsibility on his shoulders. He asked himself if he had the strength to carry it, but knew that God would give him strength as He always had in the past.

After the funeral tribute to President Lee on Saturday, December 29, the apostles met in the Salt Lake Temple on Sunday to reorganize the First Presidency. As had happened each time before, the Quorum named the senior apostle the President of the Church, to be God's principal spokesman to men. Elder Kimball became the twelfth in the succession begun by Joseph Smith and Brigham Young. He had been forty-eight when called to the apostleship in 1943. Now he was nearly seventy-nine, with thirty years' experience as an apostle.

Ezra Taft Benson, now the second apostle in seniority, spoke for the members of the Quorum as they laid their hands upon the head of Spencer Woolley Kimball and ordained him President of The Church of Jesus Christ of Latter-day Saints. The new President then set apart N. Eldon Tanner and Marion G. Romney as his first and second counselors.

On the next day, New Year's Eve, the reorganization which had just taken place was announced at a major press conference. Scores of cameras from newspapers, magazines and television recorded the event. People would be wanting to know what this change in leadership meant for the Church, what changes in emphasis might be expected. Addressing that question, President Kimball noted that, along with other Church leaders, he had had a chance to help shape existing programs and would expect to carry them forward without any radical redirection. But he did speak of several matters he would personally stress: home and family and the training of youth; missionary service to spread the gospel; teaching and encouragement to the Indians of North and South America; loyalty of Church members to their countries; and temple work.

In answering questions, President Kimball covered a number of additional subjects: He indicated that since his heart surgery he was in relatively good health. He thought that women who are able to concentrate on child-rearing should do so. The Church policy with respect to blacks and the priesthood could change, but the matter was in the hands of the Lord. And he felt optimistic about the future of the United States. The press conference closed.

The old year closed. A new year waited its turn.

21

The Prophet of the Lord

— "lengthen your stride"

With the new year Camilla Kimball tried to ease the crushing burden of responsibility on her husband. "He's the last resort of authority on earth now," she softly told an interviewer, "and it sets him apart so. He has the final responsibility for so many decisions; there's no place for him to go except to the Lord."

At least when he came home, Camilla promised herself, he would find a haven of peace. She had long handled the business of house and yard, seeing to repairs, arranging for the lawn to be mowed, cultivating the flowers and vegetables growing in their yard. Mealtimes already were juggled to fit his hard-pressed schedule. Some things, like keeping their financial records, he continued to insist were his responsibility. "I try to shelter him," she said, but there was not much more she could do. "It's hard for me to see him under such pressure. This responsibility to be Prophet, Seer, Revelator, and President of the Church is almost overwhelming."

President Kimball, too, was surprised at the extra stress. It was not that his new work occupied any more of his time than before; that would have been impossible. But the weight of added decision-making was worse than he had ever imagined it would be. He had thought he understood what being President would entail, but he now realized that he had underestimated the strain. One day, dragging with fatigue from this calling which had come unbidden, he joked wryly with his family, "If I had known it was going to be like this, I would never have run for the office." And asked by a reporter what kind of entertainment he most enjoyed, he now replied, "Sleep."

Much of the strain was a result of President Kimball's sense of aloneness among men. Each word he spoke and each act he did took on unique meaning to many Church members who seemed to expect his every movement to be inspired. Camilla once said, "It puts us on a pedestal where everything we say or do is watched and reported." For thirty years he had taken his major problems to the Brethren who presided over him for their counsel or decision. He had asked their advice in life-and-death matters, such as whether to undertake open-heart surgery or treatment for cancer. But now there was no one on earth to whom he could turn over his problems. At President Lee's funeral he had said, "A giant redwood has fallen and left a great space in the forest." It had been left for Spencer Kimball to fill that space — alone.

Yet he was not wholly alone. One night in his bed at home he woke with a sudden strong impression that President Lee, though unseen, was present there right in front of him. It was not a frightening but a reassuring experience. There was no express message, just a sense that President Lee was there to evidence a warm, continuing interest in the work of the Church.

On another occasion, again in his bedroom at home, President Kimball had a similar experience. "During the night ... while half asleep trying to work out my problems, ... I looked up and my father, Andrew Kimball, came toward me. He was tall and well built, and I recognized him and rushed to him and embraced him. That was all, but it left a warm, good feeling with me."

And he had no doubt that the Lord often guided him as he dealt with the myriad questions relating to Church governance. On most weekdays he and his counselors met in a decision-making session, reviewing a wide range of matters. For example, one Friday as they met at 8:00 A.M. they heard a report on an anti-abortion rally in which a stake president had participated; decided on a nominee to the National Council on the Humanities; authorized one of the General Authorities to accept an appointment to a state advisory committee; sent a letter of condolence to the family of a deceased relative of one of the General

Authorities; designated someone to represent the Church at an anti-abortion program in California; discussed and referred to the Missionary Executive Committee a request by a mission president that his assistant be allowed to conduct interviews for temple recommends; concluded that a divorced person, without having her endowments and upon establishing that she would be worthy to receive a temple recommend, could enter the temple for the sole purpose of being sealed to her living parents. They referred to the Department of Public Communications an inquiry about the Church's possible participation in a forthcoming film on Joseph Smith; reviewed a report of the Investment Advisory Committee; talked about a man to help the Education Department in fund-raising efforts; reviewed and denied an appeal from a doctor who had been excommunicated for performing extensive nontherapeutic abortions; discussed the proper relationship between the Nauvoo Mission and Nauvoo Restoration, Inc., and assigned a counselor to report back. The counselors urged the President to rest a few days in Laguna Beach while on a forthcoming appointment in California.

After an hour alone dealing with these problems, the First Presidency had the Presiding Bishopric and presidencies of the Aaronic Priesthood MIA join them. Together they discussed the experience in transition of the organization from an auxiliary to a priesthood activity and heard reports from the AP-MIA leaders, who were then excused.

With the Presiding Bishopric they discussed the appropriate procedure for raising funds for expansion of the Utah Valley LDS Hospital; decided to ask the Missionary Committee to be sure proper Church court procedures were followed in the case of missionaries excommunicated for misconduct; discussed sending a letter to bishops warning of the risks in some popular courses on human sexuality; approved the wearing of pant suits as part of nurses' uniforms in Church hospitals; concluded that making public announcement of the termination of disfellowshipment further publicized the original transgression unnecessarily; discussed the problem of the failure of some units to submit timely reports; considered a management consultant's study of the Presiding Bishopric's Office.

After the Presiding Bishopric had left, the First Presidency turned to consideration of still additional items. They referred to the Committee on Expenditures a request for reimbursement of the increased expenses arising from extensions of missionary passports in Mexico.

They approved the cover design for a priesthood manual. They authorized a letter of explanation concerning dropping a student from BYU for refusal to adhere to his promise to conform to the grooming standards there; approved a recommendation that mileage allowances be increased to reflect increased costs; received a report on the building of a greenhouse at the St. George Temple; and referred to the Presiding Bishopric the question whether the Salt Lake Stake Home should be brought under the Social Services Department.

The meeting adjourned at 11:10. The remainder of the day was filled with many other appointments. President Kimball managed to nap for a few minutes to refresh himself, then signed letters extending formal missionary calls (there were sometimes three hundred such letters in a week).

As President, he found himself elected chairman of the boards of various enterprises which the Church owned or in which it had large interest: Z.C.M.I. department store; Zions First National Bank; Beneficial Life Insurance Company; Utah Home Fire Insurance Company; KSL radio and television; Utah Hotel Corporation; Zions Securities Corporation; Utah-Idaho Sugar Company.

Another of his necessary concerns was public relations. The acute hostility toward the Church of the nineteenth century had passed, but the Church still looked for friends. And there were many countries in which Church missionary activity was forbidden or hindered. Partly to increase good will and partly out of traditional courtesy, President Kimball received in his office ambassadors, political leaders, and other distinguished guests; he represented the Church on public occasions, provided appropriate messages for holidays, and so on. As he traveled in the United States and abroad he gave interviews to newsmen and met with government representatives to build friendships for the Church.

To his office came the devout and the curious. Though the thirty-year flow of troubled Latter-day Saints in need of counsel had been greatly reduced in deference to the overriding importance of his new work of overseeing all the Church, he still tried to greet visitors when he could. One little boy, brought into his office to shake his hand, stated frankly, "I wanted to see you before you died." A great many others came with the same thought in mind. President Kimball squeezed them into cracks of time between other appointments. He maintained the

President Gerald Ford and President Spencer W. Kimball with
Primary children on White House lawn, 1976

First Presidency, N. Eldon Tanner, Spencer W. Kimball, and
Marion G. Romney, with President Jimmy Carter, 1977

perspective that people came to see him as the holder of the office more than to see him as an individual.

As President Kimball and Spencer Kinard left an elevator on their way to a luncheon they hesitated. A friend of Kinard's said, "Turn to your left, Spence." President Kimball responded with a smile, "Anything you say." Chuckling, he added, "It's been a long time since anyone called me Spencer, but I can't remember when anyone called me Spence."

From Church units all over the world President Kimball received many more invitations to speak than he could possibly accept, but he responded as far as he felt able. When he could arrange to speak, large crowds often assembled. In Mesa, Arizona, fifteen thousand attended; in Mexico, sixteen thousand; at BYU, twenty-three thousand; in Landover, Maryland, twenty-three thousand; and so on.

As April Conference of 1974 approached, President Kimball nervously worked on five major addresses, anxious about this new responsibility to preside over the general conference. When his son Ed visited him briefly in his office, he seemed a bit preoccupied. A moment after Ed had left, President Kimball, sensing that he had been less attentive than usual, followed his son out to the entrance to wave goodbye. Still not satisfied, he telephoned the next day to apologize for having been somewhat distracted during their conversation.

At the beginning of the conference in a seminar for Regional Representatives, President Kimball talked about missionary work. Though the theme was not new, Elder Gordon B. Hinckley wrote in response: "That was the greatest talk ever given in these seminars. . . . None of us can ever be quite the same after that." President Kimball had outlined his conception of an expanded missionary program. He urged that countries now absorbing missionaries from the United States should develop their own corps and ultimately provide a surplus to join those from the United States in teaching the populous nations not yet open to missionary work. The Lord would open those doors when the Church had done all it could. The emphasis was the same as he had made a year earlier, but this time he spoke as President of the Church, and with special urgency. He asked his listeners and all the Church, "Are we prepared to lengthen our stride?"

And on another occasion he reiterated: "So much depends upon our willingness to make up our minds. . . . I am not calling for flashy, temporary differences in our performance levels, but a quiet resolve . . . to do a better job, to lengthen our stride."

Speaking to capacity crowd at BYU Marriott Center, 1974

The phrase "Lengthen your stride" caught people's imagination and became an important slogan in spurring Church members to greater efforts. President Kimball taught repeatedly the duty of missionary service for every able young man in the Church and he specifically requested Church members to join their prayers for the removal of restrictions in countries closed to missionary work. The number of full-time missionaries serving had increased from fourteen thousand to seventeen thousand in the four years júst before he became President; it increased to twenty-six thousand in the first three and a half years of his Presidency.

April 6, two days after the seminar for Regional Representatives, was the day of the solemn assembly, at which the members of the Church, each priesthood group in turn and then the general membership, voted for the first time to sustain Spencer W. Kimball as President of the Church. On that occasion nearly all the immediate family and a great number of other relatives attended the conference as a group, then went to the Kimball home afterwards, about 150 in all, for a buffet meal Camilla had prepared. Because there had been threats against the President of the Church, a city policeman in addition to the Church security staff had been posted to watch the house. President Kimball shook the officer's hand and invited him in, but he declined. Later the President filled a plate with food and slipped out unobtrusively to take it to the officer on duty. He might have asked one of his children or grandchildren to take the plate, or might have rationalized that the man was simply performing the job he was paid for, but he did not. Later still, after passing a box of peanut brittle among the late stayers, he took the box also out to the officer.

At ten o'clock that night President Kimball telephoned from the Church offices to tell Camilla that Church security officials, nervous about the threats, wanted them to spend the night at the Hotel Utah. Camilla packed a suitcase, then a security man drove her to the hotel, taking her in through a back service door and up the freight elevator. All night a guard sat in the hall outside their room. To enter their room identification was established by four knocks and the password "Cumorah." "A very disconcerting experience," it seemed to Camilla. "Arthur Haycock brought us some milk and hard rolls since Spencer had had little to eat all day."

For a week security remained extra tight. On Monday a guard drove Camilla home to do her washing. On Tuesday they returned so she could clean house, and when President Kimball later arrived along with his security man all four sat down to a supper of hot stew. "Who would ever have thought," wrote Camilla in frustration, "that we who love our independence and our privacy so much would be so surrounded by guards?"

President Kimball left strict instructions with his counselors that in the event of kidnaping, then or at any future time, no ransom was to be paid. To pay ransom would merely expose all Church representatives to increased risk.

In the summer President Kimball gave evidence, if it were necessary, that he intended to "lengthen his stride," too. Whereas during the previous years the pattern had been for one area conference to be conducted each year — Manchester in 1971, Mexico City in 1972, Munich in 1973 and Stockholm in 1974 — President Kimball scheduled seven area conferences for the next year in various cities of South America and the Far East.

As the new temple being built in Washington, D.C., came to completion, President Kimball went to Washington to participate in ceremonies marking that event. The public, including United States President Gerald Ford, many governmental officials, and 750,000 other people toured the building and learned of its purposes before it was dedicated and then open only to holders of temple recommends.

While he was in Washington President Kimball accepted an invitation to offer the daily prayer at the beginning of the United States Senate. As he arrived at the Senate and was about to be introduced, however, there were only six senators on the floor of the chamber. Someone apologized for the small number present to hear him, but he answered: "That's all right. I was not going to pray to them, anyway."

In November, after the hundreds of thousands of visitors had toured the Washington Temple, President Kimball formally dedicated the building in the ten dedicatory services which were necessary to accommodate the numbers who wished to participate.

As Christmas time approached Camilla noted that this "marks the first year of Spencer's Presidency." When a busload of seminary students caroling at various homes in the neighborhood stopped at the Kimball home, they were asked inside by President Kimball, who would not listen to their refusals. "It's cold and snowy outside," he argued, "and besides, you can't go without something to eat." And he passed around Christmas cookies and candy. A delivery man who brought a package to the house during the holidays was touched at being invited in by the President of the Church to visit.

"It has been an extremely busy, eventful year," concluded Camilla. "I feel he has been greatly blessed with health and strength and the inspiration which we have both prayed so earnestly he might have."

In February 1975 the first of the year's area conferences took President Kimball to South America, where he had for several years supervised the Church's interests. He received the warmest kind of welcome from the thousands who gathered in Sao Paulo for the Brazilian conference. Before the opening of the first conference session, President Kimball stood and announced that a temple would be built there, as he displayed an architect's drawing of the building. Many of the surprised Saints wept openly. The temple ordinances, which had been available to them only at great distance and often-impossible expense, would now be within their reach.

During the following weekend another area conference was held in Buenos Aires for Saints from Argentina, Uruguay, Paraguay and Chile. The remainder of the area conferences that year would be held in the summer.

In the spring President Kimball spoke at a Lamanite youth conference for Southern California. While he was in San Diego he took opportunity to travel to Camp Pendleton, forty miles away, to meet with Vietnamese members of the Church who were among the refugees evacuated at the collapse of the Saigon government. Some had hymn books which they had included in the pitiful handful of belongings they had been able to bring with them. Camilla told them of her own experience as a refugee from the Mexican revolution in 1912, though at least she had come to a country where she had relatives and where she spoke the language.

In May President Kimball returned to Thatcher to speak at the baccalaureate exercises of Eastern Arizona State College, which was the successor both to the LDS Academy where he had gone to high school, and to Gila Junior College, which his older two children had attended.

He and Camilla were met with an outpouring of affection from Church members and old friends. When his sister Alice came to visit with him in Thatcher, she entered the room and gave him a kiss, then greeted others present. Finally she kissed him again, saying, "Did I kiss you already?" Her brother Spencer quipped, "The first time must not have impressed you much."

On this trip back to Arizona, where he had spent more than half his life, he noted how many of the people he had known had died, how few of the places he remembered as a boy remained the same. With a sense of the humor in it, he pointed and said, "Is that direction south?" When someone answered yes, he went on, "I knew it used to be south, but so many other things have changed since we lived here that I thought they might have changed that, too."

He had left Gila Valley thirty-two years before, universally liked and admired. Because he represented the Church now, that too had changed in the minds of a few people. The baccalaureate service had originally been scheduled for Thursday, but since President Kimball would not have been able to come on that day the college had changed the service to Friday. Some students protested the change, and during the service a bomb threat was received by the police, requiring that the building be cleared. The call came as the meeting was nearly at an end, so the threat did not disrupt the service itself, but it hurt President Kimball that he was apparently the object of such anger.

The next day at the graduation, President Kimball was invited to stand in line and greet the graduates as they received their diplomas. Since some students might resent his participation, however, he preferred simply to sit on the stand. But as the students passed across the stage, nearly all of them veered to where he sat in order to shake his hand.

After about a year of service as chairman of the board of many of the corporations controlled by the Church, President Kimball concluded that too much time, which he could better spend in other ways, was being eaten up by board meetings. As a consequence, he resigned most of the positions, retaining only those which seemed most important to his calling, such as Deseret Management Corporation, a holding company for other Church business enterprises; Bonneville International, controlling unit for Church radio and television outlets; and the Church Board of Education, the controlling body for BYU, Ricks

College, seminaries and institutes, and other Church schools in many countries.

In August 1975 more area conferences were held in Tokyo, Hong Kong, Taipei, Manila, and Seoul. President Kimball announced in Tokyo the construction of a temple there, the first in the Far East. The numerous area conferences and the new temples fostered his objectives of extending all the benefits of the Church to members throughout the world.

As part of his insistence on "taking the Church to the people" President Kimball scheduled seventeen area conferences for the next year, in the Pacific and Europe. He also arranged for a series of fifty-eight solemn assemblies between 1975 and 1977 throughout North America to which priesthood leaders, area by area, were gathered for instructions by the President and other General Authorities. Where possible these were held in temples, but otherwise in chapels.

One day, for example, President Kimball conducted a solemn assembly for several thousand priesthood leaders in the Logan Temple from 7:00 A.M. to 10:30 A.M. He then traveled to Salt Lake City, where a similar meeting began at 2:00 P.M. in the Salt Lake Temple for leaders from the Salt Lake Valley. In the evening he conducted a third such session for leaders from the Utah Valley.

As the last of these three solemn assemblies ended, President Kimball spotted one of his sons singing in the chorus. In an unembarrassed, unaffected manner, as he left the meeting and all the men stood to show respect, he went over and embraced and kissed his son.

In November President Kimball announced a new temple, this one in Seattle, Washington. The same month the five stakes in Mexico City were divided so as to make fifteen stakes at one time, the largest organizational task in Church history. And just a few months later President Kimball announced a temple to be built in Mexico City. Still other temples were soon in the planning stages. And some of the existing temples were remodeled for use of film and sound presentation, then rededicated by the President after nonmembers in the communities where they were located had been invited to examine the buildings and learn about their function before the temples were closed again to all but recommend holders.

On Christmas Day 1975 the Kimballs had dinner with their son Ed's family. Some neighbors asked whether missionaries they were entertaining might come over and meet President Kimball. Ed responded that he hoped his father could enjoy the holiday undisturbed. But when President Kimball learned of the request he insisted on walking to the neighbor's home to meet the elders.

A week later, after New Year's dinner at the Kimball home, family members were enjoying the chance to visit. Four teenage boys came to the door asking to meet President Kimball. He invited them in, had them take off their coats and sit down, visited at length, then posed with them for pictures they wanted to take. When he learned that they had not eaten, he had Camilla prepare a meal for them and chatted with them while they ate. After they had left, someone asked whether all that was necessary. President Kimball responded, "I belong to all the people, not just to my family."

Early in 1976 President Kimball undertook a strenuous series of nine area conferences in three weeks in American Samoa, Western Samoa, New Zealand, Fiji, Tonga, Australia, and Tahiti. In these places he and the other Church leaders who traveled with him met with an enthusiastic, colorful reception, with native dances and elaborate ceremonials. They were showered with gifts of flowers, shells, and handicrafts.

During most of the tour President Kimball suffered from influenza, yet he simply would not give in to illness. He managed to attend nearly all the meetings, ceremonials, receptions, visits to government leaders, and press conferences which filled the crowded schedule. He gave forty speeches, attended thirty-seven conference sessions plus cultural programs in each place, held sixteen press conferences or interviews, and met individually with many priesthood leaders and members.

In American Samoa the stake president and his wife had just had a son, whom they named Spencer Eldon in honor of the two members of the First Presidency who presided at the conference. When President Kimball learned of this he took his hat off and said, "I am honored." He then made his way through the crowd to President Tanner to inform him, "This good man named his son after you."

President Kimball explained at conferences that he recognized it was impossible for most members to attend conferences in Salt Lake

City. "This Church belongs to the people, so we bring the conference to you. We want people to stay where they are and build Zion."

As Zion grew, administrative changes to accommodate the growing Church occurred under President Kimball's energetic leadership. In October Conference 1975 he had activated the full First Quorum of the Seventy, and among those he called to join that quorum was George D. Lee, a Navajo. In April 1976 the diversity of the increasingly international Church became even more evident when a Japanese-American, a Belgian and a Dutchman were called to the First Quorum of the Seventy. At that same conference President Kimball presented for addition to the Pearl of Great Price revelations to Joseph Smith and to Joseph F. Smith on the state of the dead. The next year he was to move all the Assistants to the Twelve to membership in the new First Quorum of the Seventy. There were many other minor changes in Church organization and procedure, and they came in breathtaking sequence.

One of the General Authorities said to friends that he had thought, when Spencer W. Kimball succeeded to the Presidency, that the Church could anticipate a period of consolidation. President Lee, known as a strong, innovative administrator, had been influential, both as counselor in the First Presidency and as President, in a number of major changes in the Church program. President Kimball, older and with a history of ill health, might be expected to provide a time of calm. The General Authority admitted he had seldom in his life been more wrong.

In June President Kimball went to Rexburg, Idaho, to meet with many of the nearly forty thousand people, 90 percent of them members of the Church, who had been driven from their homes by the failure of the Teton Dam. A wall of water had completely destroyed Sugar City and heavily damaged other cities in the path of the flood. The welfare needs were vastly greater than those of the Duncan flood with which he had dealt as stake president forty years earlier through the fledgling Church Welfare Program, but the organization and resources of the Church were enough greater now to provide truckload after truckload of food, blankets, and the myriad things needed by people who had evacuated their houses without time to pack their belongings. And the manpower of the Church even from surrounding states was available to help with the massive cleanup operation.

That summer President Kimball held area conferences in London, Glasgow and Manchester, just five years after the first area conference of all had been held in Manchester, thus completing a cycle. While in England he organized a stake in Preston, where his grandfather Heber had performed the first nine baptisms in England in the River Ribble in 1837. And on his return from Britain President Kimball journeyed to Sheldon, Vermont, to dedicate a monument to the memory of Heber C. Kimball, erected by Heber's descendants near the place he was born 175 years before.

Continual threats against President Kimball by apostates eventually threatened to displace the Kimballs from their home. To the President it was unimportant where he lived; an apartment in the Hotel Utah would be closer to his work and would save him travel time each day. But he knew that for Camilla it would amount to giving up any semblance of independence and privacy. Her beloved flowers and garden, life on a quiet residential street among neighbors of thirty years — all would be forfeit to the threats made against her husband. They decided to remain where they were as long as they could.

Though the repair of President Kimball's heart had given him new vitality, he kept suffering minor breakdowns. He still had the minor hearing problem, too, dating from the Bell's palsy, which made it seem always as though he had water in his ear. He had tried a hearing aid but cast it aside in distaste as not yet really necessary.

Despite his aversion to taking any kinds of drugs, because of the heart repair he took various medications to avoid blood clots and fluid accumulations. He had some small skin cancers removed. He also had some pains in the muscles of his legs. When Ed suggested that he take aspirin for the leg pains he said he did not want to take any more pills because he was already "the piller" of the Church.

President Kimball's eyesight gradually dimmed as the lenses of his eyes clouded. The doctor said that at some point he would need to have the cataracts removed and artificial lenses implanted, though that could be put off for a while.

But one morning in March 1977 he awoke and found everything blurred; reading proved difficult. He wondered at the suddenness of the change. At Utah Technical College in Provo, where he went to give a dedicatory address for the new facilities, he stumbled embarrassingly over his text. He did not know how apparent it might be to the audience, but he felt depressed about it. General conference was only a short while away and he wondered how he would manage with the many talks he was scheduled to give.

The doctors examined and tested but could not find the problem, except that it lay in the retina, not in the lenses after all. President Kimball began to have his talks typed in large print so that he could read them more easily.

He and Camilla joked about the old machine wearing out, about their hillside cemetery plots waiting with a marvelous view of the valley. They both had a horror of dwindling usefulness, preferring the sudden stop to the cumulating disabilities. They remembered the last years of other Presidents, when physical strength and clear memory had faded, and they hoped they would be spared that. Camilla wept at the thought of their dragging on and on, in the glare of lights to the end. The President dreaded, too, the time when he could not pull his full share of the load and more. He could do no other than push on, as long as strength would last, but he did not have to like what was happening.

Elder Kimball had once written of President McKay: "He was always composed. He was not frightened [just] because he could not do everything. He accepted [the physical limitation of his last years] as it came." President Kimball himself could not decline in health so gracefully. He felt frustrated at each new limitation on his ability to carry on as vigorously as he had when younger. But, he said, "I just keep going on and on, like a calendar." With all his physical problems, he remained firmly committed to doing his utmost as long as the Lord would preserve him.

As modest as he was about his personal accomplishments, President Kimball did not hesitate boldly to proclaim his prophetic mission. In April Conference 1977 he testified:

> In our day, as in times past, many people expect that if there be revelation it will come with awe-inspiring, earth-shaking display. For many it is hard to accept as revelations those numerous ones in Moses' time, in Joseph's time, and in our own year — those revelations which come to prophets as deep, unassailable impressions settling down on the prophet's mind and heart as dew from heaven or as the dawn dissipates the darkness of night.

Expecting the spectacular, one may not be fully alerted to the constant flow of revealed communication. I say, in the deepest of humility, but also by the power and force of a burning testimony in my soul, that from the prophet of the Restoration to the prophet of our own year, the communication line is unbroken, the authority is continuous, and light, brilliant and penetrating, continues to shine. The sound of the voice of the Lord is a continuous melody and a thunderous appeal. For nearly a century and a half there has been no interruption.

Believing himself preserved by God for the specific purpose of leading the Latter-day Saints, Spencer W. Kimball brought to the Church Presidency a combination of humility and certitude, physical weakness and indomitable will, intelligence and spirituality. He responded to every call, however questioning of his own abilities, determined to make himself fit to serve. And as he asked others to lengthen their stride and quicken their step, he led the way.

Index

Attributes or Conditions

Student Placement Program, 320-321; shows student-placement film to Navajo Tribal Council, 321-322; tours Southwest Indian Mission, 322-323; gives practical advice for helping Indians, 340; notes personal growth of Indians through the gospel, 341-342; organizes Navajo branch at request of Indians, 341-342; tours northern Indian reservations, 342; counsels with parents of white girl desiring to marry Indian, 342; sees opportunities for teaching Indians in South America, 361; meets with Indians in Ecuador, 362; mission tour in South America, 362-363; proposal for meetinghouse in Bolivia turned down, 366; concern for Indian work, 366-367; dedicates chapel on Hopi Reservation, 404; continuing interest in Indian work, 404

President and Prophet: becomes twelfth Church President, 8, 409; meets with press, 409-410; receives letter from Dr. Russell Nelson concerning his physical condition, 8; notes increased stress of calling, 411-412; experiences sense of aloneness as President, 412; spiritual experiences of reassurance, 412; decision-making sessions with counselors, 412-414; chairman of the boards of various enterprises, 414; streams of visitors to office, 414-416; concern with public relations, 414; speaking invitations, 416; prepares for general conference, 416; outlines concept of expanded missionary program, 416-418; sustained in solemn assembly as President of the Church, 418; security measures, 418-419; increase in number of area conferences, 419, 422; dedicates Washington Temple, 419; receives carolers at Christmas, 419-420; travels to South America for area conferences, 420; announces Sao Paulo Temple, 420; addresses Lamanite youth conference, 420; visits Vietnamese members at Camp Pendleton, 420; speaks at baccalaureate exercises of Eastern Arizona College, 420, 421; resigns corporate positions, 421; presides at area conferences in the Far East, 422; conducts series of solemn assemblies, 422; announces temples for Tokyo, Seattle, and Mexico City, 422; presides at nine area conferences in South Pacific, 423; activates the full First Quorum of the Seventy, 424; presents revelations for addition to scripture, 424; meets with flood-devastated Saints in Rexburg, Idaho, 424; presides at area conferences in Britain, 425; proclaims prophetic role, 426-427

Reactions and Experiences
(the latter in parentheses)

Administrations and healings, 229-230, 250, 256, 261, 263, 270, 298, 307, 389-390, 399, 401, (32, 143, 214, 229-230, 264, 397); animals, (33, 36-37, 39, 103, 407); apostates, 217, 279, 425; argument, 150, 272; arson, (182-183); authority, respect for, 353; banking, (98, 103, 105-107, 116-117, 123-125, 127); baptism, (33, 329-330); basketball, 64-65, 103; blacks, 29, 173, 231, 316-317, 345, 349, 364-366, 410; books, 404; business, (116-130, 141, 179, 184, 187); Camilla, 71, 83-96, 141, 175, 191, 202, 275, 290, 309, 310, 317, 373; cancer, 262, 301, (309); carving, (252-253, 271); children, 137, 144-153, 165, 176, 201, 212, 223, 253-254, 279, 306, 309, 367-369, 398, (100, 102, 103); Church attendance, 149, (32, 38, 81); Church service, 108, 111, 117, 156, 169-173, 175, 188-195, 204-205, 284, 310, 337, 398, 409, 411, (101-102, 111-112, 130, 169-179, 181, 412-414); correspondence, 278, 309, 405; courtship, (84-96); cultures, preservation of native, 318, 327; dancing, 132; danger, (213, 215, 299-300); death, 213, 219, 264, 301-302, 304, 390, 394-395, 398, 426, (29, 43, 46, 54, 77, 108, 110, 113, 167, 219, 263); debt, 128, dignity, 233; disagreement, 172-173, 228, 344, 357; discipline, 128, 150; discouragement, (75-76, 126, 210, 241, 261, 262, 263, 292, 296, 303, 310, 375); dishonesty, 124, 142; divorce, 316; dreams, 87, 229, 237, 259, 302, 304, 412; drouth, (25, 30); duty, 348, (41, 348); education, 59, 68, 81, 83, 88, 135-136, 149, 152, 153, 181, 243, 245, 274, 376; embarrassment, (33); evil spirit, (237-238, 265); example, 131; excommunication, (207, 217, 325); faith, (25); family, approval of, 194, 202, 368; family loyalty, 52, 166-169, 175-176, 201-202, 222-223, 376; fasting, (30, 45, 192, 195, 196, 273, 327); father, 24, 25-26, 107, 110-111, 194, 221, 276, 302, 412; fear, 285, (21, 28, 35, 56, 139, 145, 237, 251, 263, 273, 291, 301); fighting, (34); flood, (176, 424); foreign language groups, 388-389; forgiveness and reconciliation, 171-172, 189, 197-198, 234, 257; friends, 153, 156, 202, 255, (131-134, 165, 184-186, 198, 216, 260); gambling, 179; General Authorities, feelings toward, 196, 204, 207-208, 220, 226-227, 250, 255-256, 267-270, 286-287, 293, 304, 306, 312, 323, 361, 377, 387, 390, 393-394; gospel, importance of, 253-254; government regulation, 127, 352; growth from experience, 340, 358; habit, 331; hail, (30); hardships, 143, 201, 278; history, personal, 271, 284-285, 308; history, world, (255); home, 184, 190; homosexuality, 271, 381-383; honors, 159, 170, 202, 225, 231, 304, 349-350, 376; hunting, 132, (81); idleness, 393; illness, (40, 42, 99, 100, 102, 103, 104-105, 110, 137-143, 166-167, 173, 182, 214, 225, 226,